BEST CHEFS AMERICA

2013

FOREWORD BY MICHAEL RUHLMAN

Published and distributed by Best Chefs in America, LLC
218 King Street, Suite 200, Charleston, SC 29401

PLEASE NOTE
Best Chefs America has used its best efforts in assembling material for inclusion in Best Chefs America® 2013 but does not warrant that the information contained in the book is complete or accurate, and does not assume, and hereby disclaims, any liability to any person for any loss or damage caused by errors or omissions in Best Chefs America® 2013 whether such errors or omissions result from negligence, accident, or any other cause.

ISBN 978-0-9889774-0-2

First Edition of 2,500

Designed by Braxton Crim
Creative Consulting by Carlye Jane Dougherty
Photography by Andrew Cebulka

PRINTED IN THE UNITED STATES OF AMERICA

TO THE CHEFS

BC|A TABLE OF CONTENTS

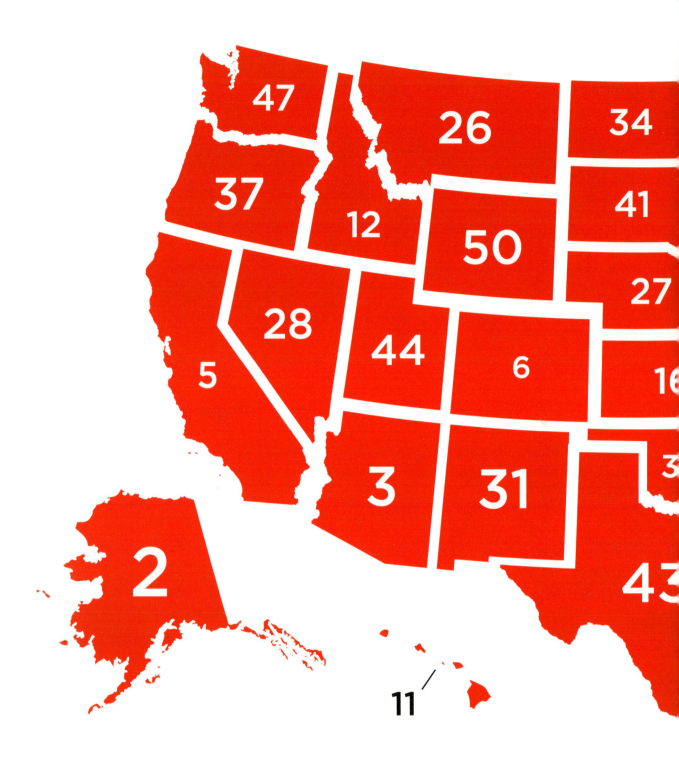

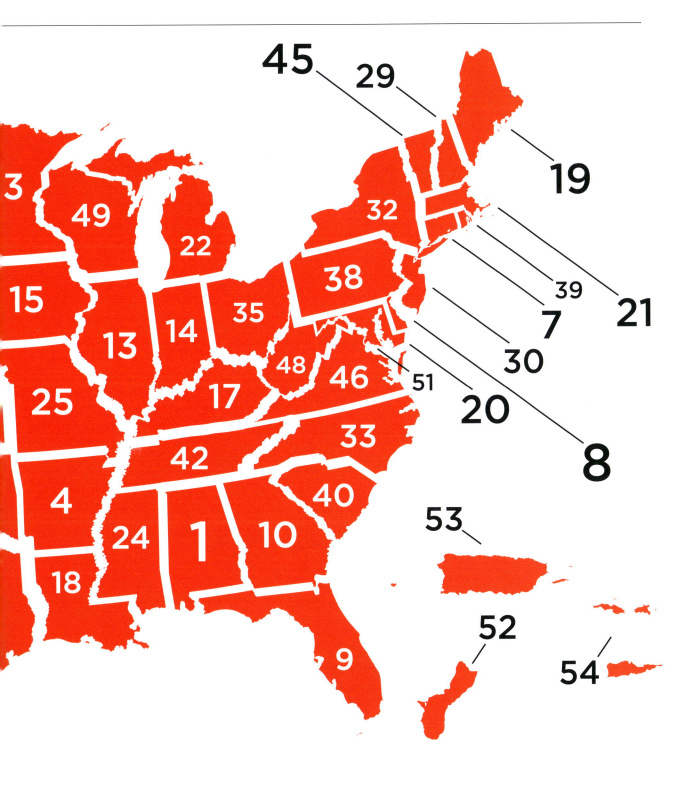

FOREWORD

BY MICHAEL RUHLMAN

I N MY YOUNGER AND MORE VULNERABLE YEARS, A DEAR FRIEND GAVE ME SOME ADVICE I've been turning over in my mind ever since. We were aspiring novelists, enamored of Scott Fitzgerald and his generation, and probably would have been astonished to glimpse the respected food writer and literary biographer we became as adults. And yet, happily, here we are and it is now, in writing this foreword to a book devoted to chefs, that his words come back to me so meaningfully.

"Michael," he said, as we toddled tipsily up First Avenue to an apartment we shared in Manhattan, "Don't want to become famous. I can't imagine anything more awful. What I want most is to be respected by my peers."

Pretty wise for a 23-year-old ne'er-do-well (Blake Bailey would go on to write numerous award-winning books of international acclaim). He was absolutely right. He enjoys great respect among authors, though he's not likely to be known by anyone buying books at an airport. Likewise, I am not apt to be recognized by most restaurant goers, though I'm well known in the chef world. Lack of major celebrity is a blessing that allows us to carry on with work that we happen to be good at.

Such, I daresay, is my advice to young chefs. What every talented chef-restaurateur should aspire to is to be happy in their work and have a happy and thriving customer base, and respect from one's colleagues, not celebrity. For what does big fame bring a chef? Rocco DiSpirito became famous, even infamous, to the point that we can no longer taste the efforts of his extraordinary craftsmanship in the kitchen. Gordon Ramsay was once a great cook—and still is, no doubt—but how would anyone know?

Indeed, I'd wager that the majority of the "25 Most Influential Chefs" listed here no longer or rarely cook *because* of their success at cooking. This is not a judgment in any way, only an acknowledgment of the irony of the profession. I hope that they and the many like them are

happy, and have made good choices with the opportunities they earned through the very hard work of restaurant cooking.

I bring up these former restaurant cooks only to draw a distinction between celebrity at large and the respect among one's peers in the chef-restaurateur world, which is what *Best Chefs America* is about.

I learned in culinary school that there is no true honor in the term "chef." Anyone can be trained to run a kitchen. But to be a great *cook,* that's another thing entirely. If a chef points to a line cook and whispers to a companion, "That guy can cook like nobody's business," well, there's no higher compliment in a professional kitchen.

But what about the rest of us? How are we to know who can *really* cook? That's where this book comes in. Yes, it's a compendium of talented "chefs," but they are respected among their peers for being amazing *cooks* as well as for running great kitchens and devising killer menus served in rooms you feel excited to be in. That's what we really want to know, in our hometown or in a city we happen to be visiting: *Where do the best chefs like to eat? Who are their favorite cooks?*

This is what *Best Chefs America* comprises. It is the first exhaustively researched, anonymously attributed list of nearly 4,700 chefs throughout America considered by their peers to be among the best. This book is meant to guide the consumer to those restaurants chosen by chefs in each city, rather than by food critics or Yelpers. Enormous pains were taken to make this an unbiased list. For instance, chefs couldn't nominate themselves, and one couldn't simply nominate a buddy without numerous others also naming him or her. Nor did any chef pay, or receive pay, to be in this book—it's not that kind of publication.

Instead, nearly seventy thousand phone calls were made by a staff of 23 callers and data crunchers. That many more were involved with other facets of this book. Read Gabe Joseph's introduction about the work involved—it's astonishing what the Best Chefs America team accomplished in under a year. I toured the offices last summer and saw all the cold callers trying to reach busy chefs—and believe me, chefs are hard to reach even if they *want* to talk to you.

The book opens with what the staff gleaned from these tens of thousands of phone calls: the twenty-five most influential chefs in the country. "What?" I hear people crying. "Jacques Pépin? He's no restaurant chef." Or "Where's Grant Achatz?" and "Thomas Keller? How did that shoemaker get on the list?!" I say let the conversations and debates begin. I expect that many gourmands, proud of their city's restaurant scene, will tut-tut certain choices and be angered by the inevitable omissions. This book is the first of its kind and will only get better as more chefs contribute their opinions.

There has never been a greater time in America to be a cook and chef, and for that reason there has also never been a better time to head out to local restaurants as they blossom in big cities and small towns as never before. This book makes it a helluva lot more easy and exciting to do so.

PUBLISHER'S NOTE

BY BILL BLALOCK

CHEFS KNOW BEST. BETTER THAN FOOD CRITICS OR ANY TYPE OF INTERNET survey, chefs know who the "best chefs" are in their hardworking, demanding and creative profession. With this in mind, we set out to call chefs across the United States, and conduct thousands of one-on-one confidential interviews to find out who chefs considered to be the "best" among their peers. To be considered the "best" is the highest honor any professional, including chefs, can receive and those included in this book should be very proud to have their work acknowledged by their fellow chefs. *Less than 1% of all chefs and professional cooks in America made it into our book!*

The magnitude of this undertaking was staggering – to personally conduct thousands of detailed chef interviews, each taking upwards of 30 minutes each, with busy chefs who had never heard of our new organization. But we achieved it. Our dedicated staff worked day and night to interview over 5,000 chefs in all U.S. States and Territories.

Our approach required a sophisticated telephone system to handle the sheer call volume and to record calls for accuracy. Proprietary software helped us aggregate and sort through the enormous amount of data we collected throughout the course of our interviews, and aided us in determining who should be included as a "Best Chef in America."

Predictably, the responses we got from chefs ranged from skepticism to whole-hearted enthusiasm for what we were attempting to do. Fortunately, most chefs were excited to speak with us, embracing ours as a forum where they could give a true appraisal of their peers, confidentially and with no strings attached. It became even clearer as we got further along in our interviews that the chef world has been ready for us for a long time.

My sincere thanks go out to each and every chef, all 5,114 of them, who took valuable time out of their busy day or night to be interviewed by our callers. We are gratified not only by the sheer number of chefs who agreed to be interviewed, but also by their enthusiasm for our undertaking. Many of the chefs inside this year's volume work incredibly hard and in relative obscurity practicing and perfecting their craft. It is with great pleasure we publically and formally recognize all of these accomplished chefs who were selected by their peers to be included in this inaugural edition of *Best Chefs America*.

BILL BLALOCK
President and CEO, Best Chefs America

INTRODUCTION

BY GABE JOSEPH

C HEFS ARE INCREDIBLY HARD TO REACH. THIS IS SOMETHING WE LEARNED EARLY on in pursuit of our interviews. Not that we were altogether naïve going into this project—everyone who conducted interviews for *Best Chefs America* had been involved with food and bev in one way or another and had a good idea of just how busy chefs are. Early on, however, we were fighting more than just chef availability. We were up against the skepticism everyone has when a stranger calls on the phone and asks for something. Still, we knew there was no better way to find out the answer to the question we were asking: *Who are the best and most influential chefs in America according to the chefs themselves?*

So we called, left voice messages, emailed, scheduled and rescheduled with countless hostesses, managers, restaurant owners and chefs to obtain our phone interviews. Over a period of ten months we made more than 70,000 calls to get the 5,114 chef interviews that went into making this book. And when asked recently if there was anything particularly surprising about the process, my response was simple: "Chefs are incredibly hard to reach." We are still stunned we were able to speak with so many.

To get the ball rolling, our team did extensive research across the U.S. to figure out the core group of chefs we should interview in each city. Chefs were also chosen to take our interview by other chefs and food enthusiasts through online nominations. Once we established this "seed" group of chefs to interview, their replies populated our database with more prospective interviewees. As chefs were interviewed, we recorded their replies, counted those among their peers whom they acknowledged as Best Chefs, and asked them to nominate other chefs we should interview. We then set out to interview those nominated as well as those acknowledged as Best Chefs. Chefs were not told who nominated them to be interviewed or whether they were mentioned as a Best Chef.

In addition to the confidentiality of nominations and mentions, we built in other safeguards to ensure the integrity of our process. For example, chefs were asked not to mention themselves—but if they did, they received no points for the mention. Our scoring software allowed us to reduce the value of replies that were potentially biased in instances where the interviewee mentioned the chef who nominated them, a chef within their own restaurant, or a single chef as a reply to multiple questions.

In each of these fifteen- to thirty-minute interviews, we asked several questions that could advance a chef if they were acknowledged including: *Thinking about chefs nationally, which three chefs do you respect the most? Which three local chefs do you respect the most? If you were to ask any one chef in your area to prepare a meal for you, your family, and/or close friends, who would it be?*

In the end, the more than 50,000 total acknowledgements yielded 4,650 chefs fit to be called Best Chefs.

Our process also enabled us to identify the most influential chefs in the United States. An *influential* chef is one who has the power to affect the way chefs cook and think about cooking. The twenty-five listed in the opening section represent some of the most authoritative and respected chefs in the industry. As teachers, innovators, preservationists and philanthropists, their influence is broad and varied. Some have made important contributions by introducing new techniques and ways of thinking about cooking. Others have made their mark by reviving heritage methods and ingredients, thereby preserving endangered traditional foodways. We are pleased to be able to honor these talents and highlight some of their contributions.

The beautiful photographs by photographer Andrew Cebulka illustrate the emerging trends and ingredients we discovered through our chef interviews. When discussing these trends with the chefs we often heard terms such as "local," "fresh," "seasonal" and "simple." These buzzwords point to an undeniably clear theme: *hyperlocalization*. Self-sufficiency, rather than dependence on far-away sources for ingredients is something many cooks aspire to by pursuing such undertakings as restaurant farms, rooftop gardens, beekeeping and fermentation. Through these methods they gain greater control over the ingredients with which they work. Cultivating their own vegetables, grains, herbs, spices, honeys and all sorts of fermented items ultimately allows cooks to express their individual flavor like never before.

One thing that excites me about this book is that I feel we have remedied the scourge of the Internet age: too much data and not enough wisdom. Type something into Google and you get thousands of search results, but it's hard to know which ones to trust. Inside *Best Chefs America* you will find the collective wisdom of thousands who can be trusted on the subject of cooking, the cooks themselves. The names are not there because of PR campaigns or paid placement. The only way to become a Best Chef is to earn the respect of your peers through the hard work it takes to be great at the craft of cooking.

Growing up, when I would disapprove of someone else's choices, my dad would remind me, *"De gustibus non est disputandum"* ("There must not be debate concerning tastes"). We at *Best Chefs America* are not the arbiters of taste; we have left that up to the chefs, as they are far more qualified. Instead of disputing and discrediting, they have given accolades to those they most admire.

We now take great pleasure in allowing the chefs to speak.

GABE JOSEPH
Chief Operating Officer, Best Chefs America

THE CHEFS

MOST
INFLUENTIAL
CHEFS

JOSÉ ANDRÉS

José Andrés is an internationally recognized culinary innovator, passionate advocate for food and hunger issues, author, educator, television personality, and chef and owner of ThinkFoodGroup. His flagship restaurant Jaleo, located in Washington, DC, serves avant-garde and traditional Spanish cuisine.

Chef Andrés has published several cookbooks and is the founder of World Central Kitchen, which aims to find sustainable solutions to ending food insecurity and malnutrition. He teaches at Harvard University as part of the course "Science and Cooking" and also teaches a food course at George Washington University.

DAN BARBER

In May 2000, Dan Barber opened Blue Hill in New York with family members David and Laureen Barber. It was soon followed by Blue Hill at Stone Barns. Both restaurants focus on locally sourced food with respect for artisanal techniques.

Dan was appointed by President Obama to serve on the President's Council on Physical Fitness, Sports and Nutrition. He continues the work that he began as a member of Stone Barns Center's board of directors: to blur the line between the dining experience and the educational, bringing the principles of good farming directly to the table.

MARIO BATALI

With twenty-two restaurants, nine cookbooks and a host of television shows, Mario Batali is one of the most respected and recognizable chefs working today. Chef Batali opened his flagship Manhattan restaurant Babbo in 1998. An exuberant celebration of the best of Italian food, wine and lifestyle, Babbo's menu incorporates the finest and freshest seasonal ingredients.

Mario and his business partner, Joe Bastianich, own seventeen restaurants across the country. Since September 2011, Mario has starred in *The Chew*, a daytime talk show on ABC that celebrates and explores life through food.

RICK BAYLESS

Rick Bayless is chef and owner of Topolobampo in Chicago. Topolobampo features authentic Mexican cuisine, and Chef Bayless' work has earned him the Mexican Order of the Aztec Eagle—the highest form of decoration that can be given to a foreigner whose work has benefitted Mexico.

Rick has published seven cookbooks, and his PBS show *Mexico - One Plate at a Time* is beginning its ninth season. He heads the Frontera Farmer Foundation, which attracts support for small Midwestern farms, and the Frontera Scholarship, which provides a full-tuition culinary scholarship to a Mexican-American student every year.

JOHN BESH

John Besh is a chef and native son dedicated to the culinary riches of southern Louisiana. His flagship restaurant, August, located in New Orleans, celebrates the ingredients, techniques and heritage of the region.

Chef Besh's successes include the creation of Besh Restaurant Group Catering with its nine acclaimed restaurants, The John Besh Foundation, and the publication of his two cookbooks: *My New Orleans and My Family Table.*

Through his foundation, John works to protect and preserve the culinary heritage and foodways of New Orleans and the Gulf Coast area.

DANIEL BOULUD

Daniel Boulud is chef and owner of several award-winning restaurants, including his flagship DANIEL in New York. Considered one of America's leading culinary authorities, Chef Boulud is inspired by the rhythm of the seasons and is renowned for the contemporary appeal he adds to soulful cooking rooted in French tradition.

In 2006, Daniel was named a Chevalier de la Legion d'Honneur by the French government for his contribution to the advancement of French culinary culture. He has published six books and produced three seasons of the television series *After Hours with Daniel.*

SEAN BROCK

Sean Brock, one of the South's most renowned chefs, is Executive Chef at McCrady's and Husk in Charleston, South Carolina. His cuisine is a celebration of Southern ingredients and techniques. Chef Brock is an advocate for seed preservation and grows a number of heirloom crops on his farm on Wadmalaw Island, just outside of Charleston.

In 2013, Sean is set to release a cookbook and open up Husk Nashville. He still refers to his collection of 19th century Southern cookbooks to educate himself on Southern food history and to discover new ways to resurrect antebellum cuisine.

DAVID BURKE

David Burke is Executive Chef at Townhouse, the flagship restaurant of the David Burke Group. Blurring the lines between chef, artist, entrepreneur and inventor, Chef Burke is one of the leading pioneers in American cooking today. His fascination with ingredients and the art of the meal has fueled a thirty-year career marked by creativity, critical acclaim and the introduction of revolutionary products and cooking techniques.

David's talents have been showcased recently on television, including *Top Chef Masters*, and he is actively involved with culinology—blending culinary arts and food technology.

DAVID CHANG

David Chang is the chef and founder of Momofuku, with restaurants in New York City, Sydney and Toronto. Chef Chang's first cookbook, *Momofuku*, came out in the fall of 2009, and his quarterly print journal *Lucky Peach*, produced with Peter Meehan and McSweeney's, launched in the summer of 2011.

David is also collaborating to create new equipment for use in the food sciences, and in the fall of 2012—along with executive producer Anthony Bourdain—he launched a sixteen episode series on PBS called *The Mind of a Chef*.

TOM COLICCHIO

Tom Colicchio is chef and owner of Craft Restaurants, which began with the opening of Craft in New York in 2001. He has been consistently recognized for his simple, elegant style of cooking. In addition to overseeing his restaurant group, Chef Colicchio has published three cookbooks and serves as head judge on Bravo's hit reality cooking series *Top Chef*.

This spring, Tom will appear in *A Place at the Table*, a documentary about poverty and hunger in America. He and his restaurants give back to the community by supporting various local and national charities.

BOBBY FLAY

Bobby Flay's flagship restaurant Mesa Grill opened in New York in 1991 and has come to represent his signature style of American cookery: marrying flavors of the Southwest with his love of grilling. Chef Flay has successfully opened dozens of restaurants across the country to great acclaim, including Bolo, Bar Americain, Bobby Flay Steak and Bobby's Burger Palace.

Bobby shares his knowledge and enthusiasm for food through his cookbooks and cooking programs, and he continues to work tirelessly to challenge the way Americans view and taste food—making it bold, zesty and always fun.

JOSE GARCES

Since opening his first restaurant in 2005, Jose Garces has emerged as one of the nation's most gifted chefs and restaurateurs. Chef Garces owns fifteen restaurants in five cities, and his award-winning concepts include authentic Andalusian tapas and Peruvian small plates, modern Mexican street food and European bistro fare.

Jose owns Luna Farm in Bucks County, Pennsylvania, where he and his team grow produce used in his East Coast restaurants. His second cookbook, *The Latin Road Home*, takes readers on a culinary and cultural tour of Ecuador, Spain, Mexico, Cuba and Peru.

DANIEL HUMM

Daniel Humm is Executive Chef and co-owner of Eleven Madison Park in New York, where he creates modern, sophisticated French cuisine that emphasizes purity, simplicity and seasonal ingredients. Chef Humm is a native of Switzerland and knew from an early age that his true passion was cooking. A classicist who embraces contemporary gastronomy, his delicate and precise cooking style is experienced through constantly evolving menus.

In 2012, Daniel opened the NoMad Hotel in New York, where he continues to garner attention for his innovative interpretation of contemporary French cuisine.

PAUL KAHAN

Paul Kahan is Executive Chef and partner of Blackbird in Chicago. Chef Kahan is a nationally recognized face among Chicago chefs, with an ever-growing list of accolades for Blackbird as well as his other restaurants: The Publican, avec, Big Star and Publican Quality Meats.

Paul's focus is passionately seasonal and unconventionally creative, and he is dedicated to the inspiration of classical cuisine. He is celebrated for his highly individual approach to cooking and has earned praise as one of America's most influential working chefs.

THOMAS KELLER

Thomas Keller is world-renowned for his culinary skills and exceptionally high standards. He is the Executive Chef/Owner of The French Laundry in Yountville, California, recognized the world over as one of the most significant restaurants in the US.

Chef Keller was instrumental in establishing the Bocuse d'Or USA Foundation and currently serves as President. In the spring of 2011, French President Nicolas Sarkozy designated Chef Keller a Chevalier of The French Legion of Honor in recognition of his commitment to the traditions of French cuisine and his role in elevating cooking in America. He is only the third American culinary figure to be so honored.

EMERIL LAGASSE

Emeril Lagasse is chef and owner of thirteen restaurants across the United States. Emeril's, his flagship, is a cornerstone of dining in New Orleans. As a national TV personality, Chef Lagasse has hosted more than 2,000 shows on the Food Network and is the food correspondent for ABC's *Good Morning America*. He is also the best-selling author of seventeen cookbooks.

In 2002, Emeril established the Emeril Lagasse Foundation to support children's educational programs that inspire and mentor young people through the culinary arts, nutrition, healthy eating and important life skills.

MASAHARU MORIMOTO

Masaharu Morimoto—known to millions as the star of *Iron Chef and Iron Chef America*—has garnered critical and popular acclaim for his seamless integration of Western and Japanese ingredients. Chef Morimoto received practical training in sushi and traditional Kaiseki cuisine in Hiroshima before moving to the United States.

In 2001, Morimoto opened his first restaurant, Morimoto, in Philadelphia. The success of Morimoto Philadelphia led to several new concepts across the country and around the world. Chef Morimoto published his first cookbook, *Morimoto: The New Art of Japanese Cooking*, in 2007.

JACQUES PÉPIN

Known as one of the best culinary teachers in the world, Jacques Pépin serves as the Dean of Special Programs at The International Culinary Center in New York. His warmth, humor and extraordinary knowledge have made him a powerful presenter and priceless resource in the culinary world. He is also an adjunct faculty member at Boston University and a founder of the American Institute of Wine and Food.

Jacques has published dozens of books and launched twelve public television shows, including one he co-hosted with the late Julia Child.

WOLFGANG PUCK

Wolfgang Puck has changed the way many Americans cook and eat by mixing classic French techniques with Asian and California-influenced aesthetics using the highest quality ingredients. His flagship restaurant, Spago, opened in 1982 and was an instant success.

In addition to maintaining a culinary empire, Chef Puck is actively involved in many philanthropic endeavors and charitable organizations. Central to all he undertakes is Wolfgang's Eat, Love, Live philosophy, which encompasses a commitment to use the freshest and most natural ingredients available, to celebrate local farmers, and to use humanely raised animal products.

MICHEL RICHARD

Michel Richard is Executive Chef at Central Michel Richard in Washington, DC, and at restaurants of the same name in Las Vegas and Atlantic City. Chef Richard was a pioneer of French-California cooking before moving to DC, where he has come to exemplify the art of cuisine and a love for his profession.

Michel has published three books: Home Cooking with a French Accent, *Happy in the Kitchen* and *Sweet Magic*. He regularly appears at charitable events and culinary festivals across the country and designs menus for the National Gallery of Art.

ERIC RIPERT

Eric Ripert is chef and co-owner of New York's Le Bernardin. Since his start at the famed restaurant in 1991, he has established himself as one of the world's most respected chefs. Chef Ripert is grateful for his early exposure to the cuisine of Antibes, France and to that of Andorra—a small country next to Spain.

Eric hosts the Reserve Channel show *On the Table*, and he is Chair of City Harvest's Food Council, which works to raise funds and increase the quality and quantity of food donations to New York's neediest.

FRANK STITT

Frank Stitt's fondness for humble southern ingredients comes directly from his roots in rural Alabama. The menu at his flagship restaurant, Highlands Bar and Grill, which opened in 1982, combines simple Southern ingredients with French sauces and braises.

Chef Stitt is involved with Slow Food and is a standing board member of the Jones Valley Urban Farm and Pepper Place Farmer's Market, both in Birmingham. Frank was one of the first Alabama chefs to champion sustainable agriculture, an effort in which he has had far-reaching influence.

MICHAEL SYMON

Michael Symon is chef and owner of Lola Bistro in Cleveland, Ohio. Since its opening in 1997, Lola has become a cornerstone of the city's dining scene. Chef Symon, a Cleveland native, creates boldly flavored, deeply satisfying dishes with influences from his Greek and Sicilian background. His other restaurants include Lolita, Roast and B Spot.

Michael shares his exuberant, approachable cooking style and infectious laugh with viewers on the Food Network and Cooking Channel. His second cookbook, *Carnivore*, was dedicated to meat lovers and published in October 2012.

MARC VETRI

Trained in Bergamo, Italy, Marc Vetri brings a bold, contemporary sensibility to classic Italian cooking. His intimate, fine-dining restaurant, Vetri, opened in the heart of Philadelphia in 1998. Chef Vetri's outstanding pastas, innovative flavor combinations and artful presentations capture diners' imaginations and have propelled him to the forefront of culinary trends. His style is simple, yet pronounced, utilizing only the freshest seasonal and local ingredients.

Marc is actively involved in many philanthropic causes, most notably the Vetri Foundation for Children, which has a mission to promote healthy living habits among at-risk youth.

JEAN-GEORGES VONGERICHTEN

Jean-Georges Vongerichten is responsible for the operation and success of a constellation of restaurants worldwide. After extensive travels, he developed a love for the exotic and aromatic flavors of the East. His signature cuisine abandons the traditional use of meat stocks and creams. Instead, he features the intense flavors and textures from vegetable juices, fruit essences, light broths and herbal vinaigrettes.

Chef Vongerichten's flagship restaurant, Jean-Georges, opened in 1997, showcasing his culinary vision, redefining industry standards and revolutionizing the way we eat. Jean-Georges has authored several cookbooks and appeared in numerous television shows.

SIMPLE AS SALT
Chefs are cutting back on the spices and allowing the food to speak for itself.

AUBURN

DAVID BANCROFT
Acre

210 E Glenn Ave
Auburn, AL 80218

ERON BASS
Café 123

123 S 8th St
Opelika, AL 36801
334.737.0069
cafeonetwentythree.com

BIRMINGHAM

NEVILLE BAAY
El Barrio

2211 2nd Ave N
Birmingham, AL 35203
205.868.3737
elbarriobirmingham.com

RANDALL BALDWIN
Dyron's Lowcountry

121 Oak St
Mountain Brook, AL 35213
205.834.8257
dyronslowcountry.com

BRANDON CAIN
Saw's Soul Kitchen

215 41st St S
Birmingham, AL 35222
205.591.1409
facebook.com/sawskitchen

JEFFREY HANSELL
Veranda on Highland

2220 Highland Ave S
Birmingham, AL 35205
205.939.5551
verandaonhighland.com

CHRIS HASTINGS
Hot and Hot Fish Club

2180 11th Ct S
Birmingham, AL 35205
205.933.5474
hotandhotfishclub.com

JAMES LEWIS
Bettola

2901 2nd Ave S
Birmingham, AL 35233
205.731.6499
bettolarestaurant.com

HALLER MAGEE
Satterfield's

3161 Cahaba Heights Rd
Birmingham, AL 35243
205.969.9690
satterfieldsrestaurant.com

CHRIS NEWSOME
Ollie Irene

2713 Culver Rd
Mountain Brook, AL 35223
205.769.6034
ollieirene.com

MAURICIO PAPAPIETRO
Brick and Tin

214 20th St N
Birmingham, AL 35205
205.297.8636
brickandtin.com

NICK PIHAKIS
Jim 'N Nick's

1908 11th Ave S
Birmingham, AL 35205
205.320.1060
jimnnicks.com

GEORGE REIS
Ocean

1218 20th St S
Birmingham, AL 35205
205.933.0999
oceanbirmingham.com

JOHN ROLEN
Bottega Restaurant and Café

2240 Highland Ave S
Birmingham, AL 35205
205.939.1000
bottegarestaurant.com

BRIAN SOMERSHIELD
Trattoria Centrale

207 20th St N
Birmingham, AL 35203
205.202.5612
trattoriacentrale.com

FRANK STITT
Highlands Bar and Grill

2011 11th Ave S
Birmingham, AL 35205
205.939.1400
highlandsbarandgrill.com

DAPHNE

RYAN GLASS
Camellia Café

61 Section St
Fairhope , AL 36521
251.928.4321
camelliacafe.com

HUNTSVILLE

JAMES BOYCE
Cotton Row

100 Southside Square
Hunstville, AL 35801
256.382.9500
cottonrowrestaurant.com

LUKE HAWKE
Cotton Row

100 Southside Square
Huntsville, AL 35801
256.382.9500
cottonrowrestaurant.com

MATTHEW MARTIN
Huntsville, AL

MOBILE

PETE BLOHME
Panini Pete's

19 S Conception St
Mobile, AL 36602
251.405.0031
paninipetes.com

ALEX PERRY
NoJa

6 N Jackson St
Mobile, AL 36602
251.433.0377
nojamobile.com

MONTGOMERY

ROB MCDANIEL
SpringHouse

12 Benson Mill Rd
Alexander City, AL 35010
256.215.7080
springhouseatcrossroads.com

WESLEY TRUE
TRUE

503 Cloverdale Rd
Montgomery, AL 36106
334.356.3814
truemontgomery.com

ANCHORAGE

JAMES ADKISON
Sacks Café

328 G St
Anchorage, AK 99501
907.276.3546
sackscafe.com

JACK AMON
Marx Bros. Café

627 W 3rd Ave
Anchorage, AK 99501
907.278.2133
marxcafe.com

GUY CONLEY
Ginger

425 W 5th Ave
Anchorage, AK 99501
907.929.3680
gingeralaska.com

REUBEN GERBER
Crow's Nest

939 W 5th Ave
Girdwood, AK 99501
907.343.2217
captaincook.com

PATRICK HOOGERHYDE
Bridge Catering

221 W Ship Creek Ave
Anchorage, AK 99501
907.644.8300
bridgeseafood.com

AARON KELLER
Seward's Folly

1811 Abbott Rd
Anchorage, AK 99507
907.222.1218

BRETT KNIPMEYER
Kinley's Restaurant and Bar

3230 Seward Hwy
Anchorage, AK 99503
907.644.8953
kinleyrestaurant.com

LENA MORISATH
Pho Lena

2904 Spenard Rd
Anchorage, AK 99503
907.277.9777
pholena.com

ALEX PEREZ
Table 6

3210 Denali St #8
Anchorage, AK 99503
907.562.6000
table6.net

JASON PORTER
Seven Glaciers

1000 Arlberg Ave
Girdwood, AK 99587
907.754.2237
alyeskaresort.com

CHRIS RATTARO
Jack Sprat

165 Olympic Mountain Lp
Girdwood, AK 99587
907.783.5225
jacksprat.net

CHRISTOPHER VANE
Crush

343 W 6th Ave
Anchorage, AK 99501
907.865.9198
crushak.com

SEWARD

ERIK SLATER
Seward Windsong Lodge

31772 Herman Leirer Rd
Seward, AK 99664
907.224.7116
sewardwindsong.com

ARIZONA

CHANDLER

PATRICK BRAY
Roy's

7151 W Ray Rd
Chandler, AZ 85226
480.705.7697
roysrestaurant.com

CONOR FAVRE
Sheraton Wild Horse Pass

5594 Wild Horse Pass Blvd
Chandler, AZ 85226
602.225.0100
wildhorsepassresort.com

BRIAN PETERSON
Cork

4991 S Alma School Rd #101
Chandler, AZ 85248
480.883.3773
corkrestaurant.net

FLAGSTAFF

FRANK BRANHAM
Cottage Place

126 W Cottage Ave
Flagstaff, AZ 86001
928.774.8431
cottageplace.com

JAMIE THOUSAND
Satchmo's

2320 N 4th St
Flagstaff, AZ 86004
928.774.7292
satchmosaz.com

PARADISE VALLEY

BEAU MACMILLAN
Elements

5700 E McDonald Dr
Paradise Valley, AZ 85253
480.948.2100
sanctuaryoncamelback.com

JEREMY PACHECO
LON's

5532 N Palo Cristi Rd
Paradise Valley, AZ 85253
602.955.7878
hermosainn.com

PHOENIX

JUSTIN BECKETT
Beckett's Table

3717 E Indian School Rd
Phoenix, AZ 85018
602.954.1700
beckettstable.com

CHRIS BIANCO
Pizzeria Bianco

623 E Adams St
Phoenix, AZ 85004
602.258.8300
pizzeriabianco.com

KEVIN BINKLEY
Binkley's Restaurant

6920 E Cave Creek Rd
Cave Creek, AZ 85331
480.437.1072
binkleysrestaurant.com

MICHAEL BUND
Ruth's Chris

2201 E Camelback Rd
Phoenix, AZ 85016
602.957.9600
ruthschris.com

MATT CARTER
Zinc Bistro

15034 N Scottsdale Rd #140
Phoenix, AZ 85254
480.603.0922
zincbistroaz.com

MICHAEL DEMARIA
M Culinary Concepts

20645 N 28th St
Phoenix, AZ 85050
602.200.5757
mculinary.com

SILVANA ESPARZA
Barrio Café

2814 N 16th St
Phoenix, AZ 85006
602.636.0240
barriocafe.com

NOBUO FUKUDA
Nobuo at Teeter House

622 E Adams St
Phoenix, AZ 85004
602.254.0600
nobuofukuda.com

KENNETH GIORDANO
Durant's

2611 N Central Ave
Phoenix, AZ 85004
602.264.5967
durantsaz.com

JAGGER GRIFFIN
Ocean Prime

5455 E High St
Phoenix, AZ 85054
480.347.1313
oceanprimephoenix.com

CHRISTOPHER GROSS
Christopher's Crush

2502 E Camelback Rd
Phoenix, AZ 85016
602.522.2344
christophersaz.com

VINCENT GUERITHAULT
Vincent

3930 E Camelback Rd
Phoenix, AZ 85018
602.224.0225
vincentsoncamelback.com

AARON MAY
Over Easy

4730 E Indian School Rd
Phoenix, AZ 85018
602.468.3447
eatatovereasy.com

JARED PORTER
The Parlor Pizzeria

1916 E Camelback Rd
Phoenix, AZ 85016
602.248.2480
theparlor.us

MAKO SEGAWA
Roy's

5350 E Marriott Dr
Phoenix, AZ 85054
480.419.7697
roysrestaurant.com

MARK TARBELL
Tarbell's

3213 E Camelback Rd
Phoenix, AZ 85018
602.955.8100
tarbells.com

SCOTTSDALE

JASON ALFORD
Roka Akor

7299 N Scottsdale Rd
Scottsdale, AZ 85253
480.306.8800
rokaakor.com

CHARLEEN BADMAN
FnB

7125 E 5th Ave #31
Scottsdale, AZ 85251
480.284.4777
fnbrestaurant.com

CE BIAN
Roka Akor

7299 N Scottsdale Rd
Scottsdale, AZ 85253
480.306.8800
rokaakor.com

MICHAEL CAIRNS
Montelucia Resort & Spa

4949 E Lincoln Dr
Scottsdale, AZ 85253
480.627.3200
montelucia.com

PAYTON CURRY
Brat Haus

3622 N Scottsdale Rd
Scottsdale, AZ 85251
480.947.4006
brathausaz.com

LESTER GONZALES
Cowboy Ciao

7133 E Stetson Dr
Scottsdale, AZ 85251
480.946.3111
cowboyciao.com

JOSHUA HEBERT
Posh

7167 E Rancho Vista Dr #111
Scottsdale, AZ 85251
480.663.7674
poshscottsdale.com

LEE HILLSON
The Phoenician

6000 E Camelback Rd
Scottsdale, AZ 85251
480.941.8200
thephoenician.com

JON-PAUL HUTCHINS
Le Cordon Bleu

8100 E Camelback Rd #1001
Scottsdale, AZ 85251
480.990.3773
chefs.edu

SHINJI KURITA
ShinBay

7001 N Scottsdale Rd
Scottsdale, AZ 85253
480.664.0180
shinbay.com

EDDIE MATNEY
Eddie's House

7042 E Indian School Rd
Scottsdale, AZ 85251
480.946.1622
eddieshouseaz.com

MEL MECINAS
Talavera

10600 E Crescent Moon Dr
Scottsdale, AZ 85263
480.513.5085
talaverarestaurant.com

ANDREW NAM
Stingray

4302 N Scottsdale Rd
Scottsdale, AZ 85251
480.941.4460
stingraysushi.com

JACQUES QUALIN
J&G Steakhouse

6000 E Camelback Rd
Scottsdale, AZ 85251
480.214.8000
jgsteakhousescottsdale.com

LOGAN STEPHENSON
Isabella's Kitchen

8623 E Thompson Peak Pkwy
Scottsdale, AZ 85255
480.502.3100
grayhawkgolf.com

MATT ZDEB
Sushi Roku

7277 E Camelback Rd
Scottsdale, AZ 85251
480.970.2121
innovativedining.com

SEDONA

LISA DAHL
Cucina Rustica

7000 State Route 179 #126A
Sedona, AZ 86351
928.284.3010
cucinarustica.com

FRANCOIS DE MELOGUE
L'Auberge de Sedona

301 L'Auberge Ln
Sedona, AZ 86336
800.905.5745
lauberge.com

JEFF SMEDSTAD
Elote Café

771 Hwy 179
Sedona, AZ 86336
928.203.0105
elotecafe.com

TEMPE

YUPHA DEQUENNE
Yupha's Thai Kitchen

1805 E Elliot Rd
Tempe, AZ 85284
480.839.0576
yuphasthaikitchen.com

KELLY FLETCHER
House of Tricks

114 E 7th St
Tempe, AZ 85281
480.968.1114
houseoftricks.com

TUCSON

ADDAM BUZZALINI
Maynard's Market & Kitchen

400 N Toole Ave
Tucson, AZ 85701
520.545.0577
maynardsmarket.com

JANOS WILDER
Downtown Kitchen

135 S 6th Ave
Tucson, AZ 85701
520.623.7700
downtownkitchen.com

FAYETTEVILLE

DARWIN BEYER
Meiji

3878 N Crossover Rd #8
Fayetteville, AR 72703
479.521.5919
meijinwa.com

DARIN BOLES
Bordinos

310 W Dickson St
Fayetteville, AR 72701
479.527.6795
bordinos.com

NICK GIBBS
Theo's

318 N Campbell Ave
Fayetteville, AR 72701
479.527.0086
theosfayetteville.com

WILLIAM LYLE
Ella's Restaurant

465 Arkansas Ave
Fayetteville, AR 72701
479.582.1400
ellasrestaurant.com

HOT SPRINGS

DIANA BRATTON
Café 1217

1217 Malvern Ave
Hot Springs, AR 71901
501.318.1094
cafe1217.net

LITTLE ROCK

DONNIE FERNEAU
Rocket Twenty One

2601 Kavanaugh Blvd
Little Rock, AR 72205
501.603.9208
twentyonerestaurant.com

ALEX GUZMAN
Sushi Café

5823 Kavanaugh Blvd
Little Rock, AR 72207
501.663.9888
sushicaferocks.com

CAPI PECK
Trio's

8201 Cantrell Rd
Little Rock, AR 72227
501.221.3330
triosrestaurant.com

SPRINGDALE

MILES JAMES
James at the Mill

3906 Greathouse Springs Rd
Springdale, AR 72762
479.443.1400
jamesatthemill.com

INGREDIENT: GEODUCKS

AGOURA HILLS

GERALDO LUCIDI
Grissini

30125 Agoura Rd
Agoura Hills, CA 91301
818.735.9711
grissiniristoranteitaliano.com

ALAMEDA

JOHN THIEL
Pappo

2320 Central Ave
Alameda, CA 94501
510.337.9100
papporestaurant.com

ANAHEIM

YVES MASQUEFA
Yves' Restaurant & Wine Bar

5753 E Santa Ana Canyon Rd
Anaheim Hills, CA 92807
714.637.3733
yvesbistro.com

RON PLATA
Roy's

321 W Katella Ave
Anaheim, CA 92802
714.776.7697
roysrestaurant.com

MICHAEL ROSSI
The Ranch

1025 E Ball Rd
Anaheim, CA 92805
714.817.4200
theranch.com

DAVID SLAY
Park Ave

11200 Beach Blvd
Stanton, CA 90680
714.901.4400
parkavedining.com

ANDREW SUTTON
Napa Rose

1600 Disneyland Dr
Anaheim, CA 92802
714.300.7170
disneyland.disney.go.com

NICK WEBER
Catal Restaurant & Uva Bar

1580 Disneyland Dr
Anaheim, CA 92802
714.774.4442
patinagroup.com

BAKERSFIELD

BRAD WISE
The Padre Hotel

1702 18th St
Bakersfield, CA 93301
661.427.4900
thepadrehotel.com

BERKELEY

KYLE ANDERSON
Slow

1966 University Ave
Berkeley, CA 94704
510.647.3663
slowberkeley.com

SEAN BAKER
Gather

2200 Oxford St
Berkeley, CA 94704
510.809.0400
gatherrestaurant.com

PAUL BERTOLLI
Fra' Mani Handcrafted Foods

1311 8th St
Berkeley, CA 94710
510.526.7000
framani.com

WENDY BRUCKER
Trattoria Corso

1788 Shattuck Ave
Berkeley, CA 94709
510.704.8004
trattoriacorso.com

VANESSA DANG
Vanessa's Bistro

1715 Solano Ave
Berkeley, CA 94707
510.525.8300
vanessasbistro.com

BRANDON DUBEA
Angeline's Louisiana Kitchen

2261 Shattuck Ave
Berkeley, CA 94704
510.548.6900
angelineskitchen.com

ROGER FOYER
Caffe Venezia

1799 University Ave
Berkeley, CA 94703
510.849.4681
caffevenezia.com

CHRISTIAN GEIDEMAN
Ippuku

2130 Center St
Berkeley, CA 94704
510.665.1969
ippukuberkeley.com

GREGOIRE JACQUET
Gregoire

2109 Cedar St
Berkeley, CA 94709
510.883.1893
gregoirerestaurant.com

TODD KNIESS
Bistro Liaison

1849 Shattuck Ave
Berkeley, CA 94709
510.849.2155
liaisonbistro.com

AMY MURRAY
Revival Bar + Kitchen

2102 Shattuck Ave
Berkeley, CA 94704
510.549.9950
revivalbarandkitchen.com

ROSCOE SKIPPER
Rivoli

1539 Solano Ave
Berkeley, CA 94707
510.526.2542
rivolirestaurant.com

DAVID TANIS
Berkeley, CA

DAVID VARDY
O Chame

1830 4th St
Berkeley, CA 94710
510.841.8783
ochame.com

JEROME WAAG
Chez Panisse

1517 Shattuck Ave
Berkeley, CA 94709
510.548.5525
chezpanisse.com

ALICE WATERS
Chez Panisse

1517 Shattuck Ave
Berkeley, CA 94709
510.548.5525
chezpanisse.com

BEVERLY HILLS

KALEO ADAMS
Polo Lounge

9641 Sunset Blvd
Beverly Hills, CA 90210
310.887.2777
beverlyhillshotel.com

ALEJANDRO ARRIETA
208 Rodeo

208 Via Rodeo Dr
Beverly Hills, CA 90210
310.275.2428
208rodeo.com

MASSIMO DENARO
Sfixio

9737 Santa Monica Blvd
Beverly Hills, CA 90210
310.385.1800
sfixio.net

CODY DIEGEL
Caulfield's

9360 Wilshire Blvd
Beverly Hills, CA 90212
310.388.6860
caulfieldsbeverlyhills.com

FRANCIS DIMITRIUS
Villa Blanca

9601 Brighton Way
Beverly Hills, CA 90210
310.859.7600
villablancarestaurant.com

JOSEPH ELEVADO
Livello

9291 Burton Way
Beverly Hills, CA 90210
310.385.5302
viceroyhotelsandresorts.com

DAVID HANDS
Bouchon Bistro

235 N Canon Dr
Beverly Hills, CA 90210
310.271.9910
bouchonbistro.com

LEE HEFTER
CUT

9500 Wilshire Blvd
Beverly Hills, CA 90212
310.276.8500
wolfgangpuck.com

CA

JORDAN KAHN
Red Medicine

8400 Wilshire Blvd
Beverly Hills, CA 90211
323.651.5500
redmedicinela.com

BERNHARD MAIRINGER
BierBeisl

9669 Santa Monica Blvd
Beverly Hills, CA 90210
310.271.7274
bierbeisl-la.com

WALTER MAYEN
Mastro's Steakhouse

246 N Canon Dr
Beverly Hills, CA 90210
310.888.8782
mastrosrestaurants.com

LARRY NICOLA
Nic's Beverly Hills

453 N Canon Dr
Beverly Hills, CA 90210
310.550.5707
nicsbeverlyhills.com

JAMES OVERBAUGH
The Belvedere

9882 S Santa Monica Blvd
Beverly Hills, CA 90212
310.551.2888
peninsula.com

JOSE PRADO
Cocina Primavera

9111 W Olympic Blvd
Beverly Hills, CA 90212
310.550.7834
primaverala.com

WOLFGANG PUCK
Spago

176 N Canon Dr
Beverly Hills, CA 90210
310.385.0880
wolfgangpuck.com

ALEX STRATTA
Scarpetta Beverly Hills

225 N Canon Dr
Beverly Hills, CA 90210
310.499.4199
montagebeverlyhills.com

YOJI TAJIMA
Yojisan Sushi

260 N Beverly Dr
Beverly Hills, CA 90210
424.245.3799
yojisan.com

HIROYUKI URASAWA
Urasawa

218 N Rodeo Dr
Beverly Hills, CA 90210
310.247.8939

CORONA DEL MAR

TRAVIS FLOOD
Landmark

3520 E Coast Hwy
Corona Del Mar, CA 92625
949.675.5556
landmarknewport.com

ALFONSO VANGE
The Bungalow

2441 E Coast Hwy
Corona Del Mar, CA 92625
949.673.6585
thebungalowrestaurant.com

CORTE MADERA

MAURIZIO MAZZON
Il Fornaio

223 Corte Madera Ave
Corte Madera, CA 94925
415.927.4400
ilfornaio.com

COSTA MESA

CAT CORA
CCQ

3333 Bear St
Costa Mesa, CA 92626
714.708.3333
catcora.com

ALAN GREELEY
The Golden Truffle

1767 Newport Blvd
Costa Mesa, CA 92627
949.645.9858
goldentruffle.com

FLORENT MARNEAU
Marche Moderne

3333 Bristol St #3001
Costa Mesa, CA 92626
714.434.7900
marchemoderne.net

ROSS PANGILINAN
Leatherby's Cafe Rouge

615 Town Center Dr
Costa Mesa, CA 92626
714.429.7640
patinagroup.com

COTO DE CAZA

JOHN MILLER
Coto de Caza Golf & Racquet Club

25291 Vista Del Verde
Coto De Caza, CA 92679
949.207.9897
clubcorp.com

CULVER CITY

SEBASTIEN CORNIC
Meet in Paris

9727 Culver Blvd
Culver City, CA 90232
310.815.8222
meetrestaurantla.com

BENJAMIN FORD
Ford's Filling Station

9531 Culver Blvd
Culver City, CA 90232
310.202.1470
fordsfillingstation.net

EVAN FUNKE
Bucato

3280 Helms Ave
Culver City, CA 90232

KEIZO ISHIBA
K-ZO

9240 Culver Blvd
Culver City, CA 90232
310.202.8890
k-zo.com

AKASHA RICHMOND
Akasha

9543 Culver Blvd
Culver City, CA 90232
310.845.1700
akasharestaurant.com

LAURENT TRIQUENEAUX
Bistro Laurent

3936 Sepulveda Blvd
Culver City, CA 90230
310.398.6863
bistrolaurentla.com

DANA POINT

RAJ DIXIT
Stonehill Tavern

1 Monarch Beach Resort N
Dana Point, CA 92629
949.234.3318
michaelmina.net

ANGEL FABIAN
The Harbor Grill

34499 Golden Lantern St
Dana Point, CA 92629
949.240.1416
harborgrill.com

MARISSA GERLACH
Raya

1 Ritz Carlton Dr
Dana Point, CA 92629
949.240.2000
ritzcarlton.com

ANTONIO GUERRERO
Wind & Sea

34699 Golden Lantern St
Dana Point, CA 92629
949.496.6500
windandsearestaurants.com

DANVILLE

ESIN DECARION
Esin

750 Camino Ramon
Danville, CA 94526
925.314.0974
esinrestaurant.com

EL SEGUNDO

SCOTT REED
Second City Bistro

223 Richmond St
El Segundo, CA 90245
310.322.6085
secondcitybistro.com

BEN WRIGHT
Jackson's Food + Drink

2041 Rosecrans Ave #190
El Segundo, CA 90245
310.606.5500
jacksonsfoodanddrink.com

EUREKA

BRYAN HOPPER
The Benbow Inn

445 Lake Benbow Dr
Garberville, CA 95542
707.923.2124
benbowinn.com

JIM HUGHES
Brick & Fire Bistro

1630 F St
Eureka, CA 95501
707.268.8959
brickandfirebistro.com

CORY SMITH
Restaurant 301

301 L St
Eureka, CA 95501
800.404.1390
carterhouse.com

FRESNO

FLORO BUGNOSEN
Campagnia Restaurant

1185 E Champlain Dr
Fresno, CA 93720
559.433.3300
campagnia.net

TONY GOMEZ
Fleming's

639 E Shaw Ave #149
Fresno, CA 93710
559.222.5823
flemingssteakhouse.com

RYAN JACKSON
School House
Restaurant & Tavern

1018 S Frankwood Ave
Sanger, CA 93657
559.787.3271
schoolhousesanger.com

VATCHE MOUKHTARIAN
Cracked Pepper Bistro

389 E Shaw Ave
Fresno, CA 93710
559.222.9119
crackedpepperbistro.com

SCOTT SAUER
Max's Bistro & Bar

1784 W Bullard Ave
Fresno, CA 93711
559.439.6900
maxsbistro.com

MIKE SHACKELFORD
Trelio Restaurant

438 Clovis Ave
Clovis, CA 93612
559.297.0783
treliorestaurant.com

JUSTIN SHANNON
Pismo's Coastal Grill

7937 N Blackstone Ave
Fresno, CA 93711
559.439.9463
pismos.com

LUZ TRIGOSO
Limon

9455 N Fort Washington Rd
Fresno, CA 93730
559.435.1015
limonfresno.com

FULLERTON

TIMOTHY PLUMB
The Summit House

2000 E Bastanchury Rd
Fullerton, CA 92835
714.671.4111
summithouse.com

GARDEN GROVE

LISA VO
Brodard Chateau

9100 Trask Ave
Garden Grove, CA 92844
714.899.8273
brodard.net

GLENDALE

NADAV BASHAN
Bashan Restaurant

3459 N Verdugo Rd
Glendale, CA 91208
818.541.1532
bashanrestaurant.com

PIERO TOPPUTO
Trattoria Amici

783 Americana Way
Glendale, CA 91210
818.502.1220
amicila.com

HALF MOON BAY

DOUGLAS DEGEETER
Cetrella

845 Main St
Half Moon Bay, CA 94019
650.726.4090
cetrella.com

JOHN KARBOWSKI
Cetrella

845 Main St
Half Moon Bay, CA 94019
650.726.4090
cetrella.com

HERMOSA BEACH

TIN VUONG
Abigaile

1301 Manhattan Ave
Hermosa Beach, CA 90254
310.798.8227
abigailerestaurant.com

HOLLYWOOD

CHRISTINE BANTA
Cafe La Boheme

8400 Santa Monica Blvd
West Hollywood, CA 90069
323.848.2360
cafelaboheme.us

BRANDON BOUDET
Dominick's

8715 Beverly Blvd
West Hollywood, CA 90048
310.652.2335
dominicksrestaurant.com

LAUREN CARTMEL
Comme Ça

8479 Melrose Ave
West Hollywood, CA 90069
323.782.1104
commecarestaurant.com

DANIEL CSOTAI
Tula's

4222 Vineland Ave
North Hollywood, CA 91602
818.980.8000
beverlygarland.com

CELESTINO DRAGO
Osteria Drago

8741 W Sunset Blvd
West Hollywood, CA 90069
310.657.1182
osteriadrago.com

CHRIS FELDMEIER
Osteria Mozza

6602 Melrose Ave
Hollywood, CA 90038
323.297.0100
osteriamozza.com

EVAN GOTANDA
Osteria Drago

8741 W Sunset Blvd
West Hollywood, CA 90069
310.657.1182
osteriadrago.com

DANIEL JOLY
Mirabelle

8768 W Sunset Blvd
West Hollywood, CA 90069
310.659.6022
mirabelleonsunset.com

ANTHONY KEENE
Gordon Ramsay at the London

1020 N San Vicente Blvd
West Hollywood, CA 90069
310.358.7788
gordonramsay.com

DAVID LENTZ
Hungry Cat

1535 N Vine St
Hollywood, CA 90028
323.462.2919
thehungrycat.com

JOE MARTINEZ
SUR

606 N Robertson Blvd
West Hollywood, CA 90069
310.289.2824
surrestaurantandbar.com

NENO MLADENOVIC
Dan Tana's

9071 Santa Monica Blvd
West Hollywood, CA 90069
310.275.9444
dantanasrestaurant.com

DAVID MYERS
Comme Ça

8479 Melrose Ave
West Hollywood, CA 90069
323.782.1104
commecarestaurant.com

JONATHAN PETERS
Palihouse Courtyard Brasserie

8465 Holloway Dr
West Hollywood, CA 90069
323.656.4100
palihouse.com

CHRIS PHELPS
Salt's Cure

7494 Santa Monica Blvd
West Hollywood, CA 90046
323.850.7258
saltscure.com

MARIA SANTI
Fabiolus Cucina Italiana

6270 Sunset Blvd
Hollywood, CA 90028
323.467.2882
fabiolus.info

NANCY SILVERTON
Osteria Mozza

6602 Melrose Ave
Hollywood, CA 90038
323.297.0100
osteriamozza.com

ZAK WALTERS
Salt's Cure

7494 Santa Monica Blvd
West Hollywood, CA 90046
323.850.7258
saltscure.com

GISELLE WELLMAN
Petrossian Paris

321 N Robertson Blvd
West Hollywood, CA 90048
310.271.0576
petrossian.com

NORIO YAMAMOTO
Robata JINYA

8050 W 3rd St
West Hollywood, CA 90048
323.653.8877
jinya-la.com

HUNTINGTON BEACH

ROY HENDRICKSON
Zimzala

500 Pacific Coast Hwy
Huntington Beach, CA 92648
714.960.5050
restaurantzimzala.com

ANGELO JULIANO
Baci Italian Restaurant

18748 Beach Blvd
Huntington Beach, CA 92648
714.965.1194
bacirestaurant.com

IRVINE

GEETA BANSAL
Clay Oven

15435 Jeffrey Rd
Irvine, CA 92618
949.552.2851
clayovenirvine.com

YVES FOURNIER
Andrei's Conscious Cuisine

2607 Main St
Irvine, CA 92614
949.387.8887
andreisrestaurant.com

TED HILL
6ix Park Grill

17900 Jamboree Rd
Irvine, CA 92614
949.225.6666
hyatt.com

CATHY PAVLOS
Lucca Café

6507 Quail Hill Pkwy
Irvine, CA 92603
949.725.1773
luccacafe.com

SUSIE PHAN
Phans55

6000 Scholarship
Irvine, CA 92612
949.724.1236
phans55.com

LAFAYETTE

PHILIPPE CHEVALIER
Chevalier

960 Moraga Rd
Lafayette, CA 94549
925.385.0793
chevalierrestaurant.com

LAGUNA BEACH

RYAN ADAMS
Three Seventy Common

370 Glenneyre St
Laguna Beach, CA 92651
949.494.8686
370common.com

MARC COHEN
Watermarc Restaurant

448 S Coast Hwy
Laguna Beach, CA 92651
949.376.6272
watermarcrestaurant.com

THOMAS CRIJNS
Brussels Bistro

222 Forest Ave
Laguna Beach, CA 92651
949.376.7955
brusselsbistro.com

AZMIN GHAHREMAN
Sapphire Laguna

1200 S Coast Hwy #101
Laguna Beach, CA 92651
949.715.9888
sapphirellc.com

KEVIN JERROLD-JONES
Tabu Grill

2892 S Coast Hwy
Laguna Beach, CA 92651
949.494.7743
tabugrill.com

CASEY OVERTON
The Loft

30801 S Coast Hwy
Laguna Beach, CA 92651
949.715.6420
montagelagunabeach.com

AMAR SANTANA
Broadway

328 Glenneyre St
Laguna Beach, CA 92651
949.715.8234
broadwaybyamarsantana.com

LINDSAY SMITH-ROSALES
Nirvana Grille

303 Broadway St #101
Laguna Beach, CA 92651
949.497.0027
nirvanagrille.com

CRAIG STRONG
Studio

30801 S Coast Hwy
Laguna Beach, CA 92651
949.715.6420
studiolagunabeach.com

ROB WILSON
Montage Laguna Beach

30801 S Coast Hwy
Laguna Beach, CA 92651
949.715.6000
montagelagunabeach.com

LARKSPUR

FABRICE MARCON
Left Bank Brasserie

507 Magnolia Ave
Larkspur, CA 94939
415.927.3331
leftbank.com

JARED ROGERS
Picco

320 Magnolia Ave
Larkspur, CA 94939
415.924.0300
restaurantpicco.com

LIVERMORE

MATT GRECO
Wente Vineyards

5050 Arroyo Rd
Livermore, CA 94550
925.456.2450
wentevineyards.com

LONG BEACH

JOB AGUILAR
Naples Rib Company

5800 E 2nd St
Long Beach, CA 90803
562.439.7427
ribcompany.com

PAUL BUCHANAN
Primal Alchemy

3819 E 7th St
Long Beach, CA 90804
562.400.5659
primalalchemy.com

DAVID COLEMAN
Michael's on Naples

5620 E 2nd St
Long Beach, CA 90803
562.439.7080
michaelsonnaples.com

WALTER COTTA
L'Opera

101 Pine Ave
Long Beach, CA 90802
562.491.0066
lopera.com

VICTOR JUAREZ
Fuego

700 Queensway Dr
Long Beach, CA 90802
562.435.7676
fuegolongbeach.com

LOS ANGELES

JOSE ACEVEDO
Yxta Cocina Mexicana

601 S Central Ave
Los Angeles, CA 90021
213.596.5579
yxta.net

KAJSA ALGER
STREET

742 N Highland Ave
Los Angeles, CA 90038
323.203.0500
eatatstreet.com

GINO ANGELINI
Angelini Osteria

7313 Beverly Blvd
Los Angeles, CA 90036
323.297.0070
angeliniosteria.com

GOVIND ARMSTRONG
Post & Beam

3767 Santa Rosalia Dr
Los Angeles, CA 90008
323.299.5599
postandbeamla.com

RAMIRO ARVIZU
La Casita Mexicana

4030 Gage Ave
Bell, CA 90210
323.773.1898
casitamex.com

BENJAMIN BAILLY
Los Angeles, CA

TODD BARRIE
Upstairs 2

2311 Cotner Ave
Los Angeles, CA 90064
310.231.0316
upstairs2.com

JEREMY BERLIN
Church & State Bistro

1850 Industrial St
Los Angeles, CA 90021
213.405.1434
churchandstatebistro.com

JEAN PIERRE BOSC
Kendall's Brasserie

135 N Grand Ave
Los Angeles, CA 90012
213.972.7322
patinagroup.com

AZNIV BOZOGHLIAN
Carlitos Gardel

7963 Melrose Ave
Los Angeles, CA 90046
323.655.0891
carlitosgardel.com

SOSSI BRADY
Marouch

4905 Santa Monica Blvd
Los Angeles, CA 90029
323.662.9325
marouchrestaurant.com

VICTOR CASANOVA
Gusto

8432 W 3rd St
Los Angeles, CA 90048
323.782.1778
gusto-la.com

JOSEF CENTENO
Baco Mercat

408 S Main St
Los Angeles, CA 90013
213.687.8808
bacomercat.com

GILBERTO CETINA
Chichen Itza

3655 S Grand Ave
Los Angeles, CA 90007
213.741.1075
chichenitzarestaurant.com

ROY CHOI
Kogi BBQ Trucks

Los Angeles, CA
323.315.0253
kogibbq.com

MICHAEL CIMARUSTI
Providence

5955 Melrose Ave
Los Angeles, CA 90038
323.460.4170
providencela.com

BEN COHN
Westside Tavern

10850 W Pico Blvd
Los Angeles, CA 90064
310.470.1539
westsidetavernla.com

BRENDAN COLLINS
Waterloo & City

12517 Washington Blvd
Los Angeles, CA 90066
310.391.4222
waterlooandcity.com

CARMINE COMPETELLI JR.
Carmines II

10463 Santa Monica Blvd
Los Angeles, CA 90025
310.441.4706
carminesla.com

MAYET CRISTOBAL
The Getty Center

1200 Getty Center Dr
Los Angeles, CA 90049
310.440.6810
getty.edu

MAUREEN D'ATH
Artisan House

600 S Main St
Los Angeles, CA 90014
213.622.6333
artisanhouse.net

JAIME MARTIN DEL CAMPO
La Casita Mexicana

4030 Gage Ave
Bell, CA 90210
323.773.1898
casitamex.com

COLE DICKINSON
Ink.

8360 Melrose Ave
Los Angeles, CA 90069
323.651.5866
mvink.com

VINNY DOTOLO
Animal

435 N Fairfax Ave
Los Angeles, CA 90048
323.782.9225
animalrestaurant.com

PAUL DOWNER
Edendale

2838 Rowena Ave
Los Angeles, CA 90039
323.666.2000
theedendale.com

ERIN EASTLAND
Cube Café

615 N La Brea Ave
Los Angeles, CA 90036
323.939.1148
eatatcube.com

CHRISTOPHE EME
Los Angeles, CA

NICK ERVEN
MessHall

4500 Hillhurst Ave
Los Angeles, CA 90027
323.660.6377
messhallkitchen.com

SUSAN FENIGER
STREET

742 N Highland Ave
Los Angeles, CA 90038
323.203.0500
eatatstreet.com

MICAH FIELDS
The Restaurant at The Standard

550 S Flower St
Los Angeles, CA 90071
213.892.8080
standardhotels.com

ADAM FLEISCHMAN
Umami Burger

850 S La Brea Ave
Los Angeles, CA 90036
323.931.3000
umami.com

NEAL FRASER
bld
7450 Beverly Blvd
Los Angeles, CA 90036
323.930.9744
bldrestaurant.com

SANDY GENDEL
Pace
2100 Laurel Canyon Blvd
Los Angeles, CA 90046
323.654.8583
peaceinthecanyon.com

ANDRE GINEKIS SR.
Locanda Veneta
8638 W 3rd St
Los Angeles, CA 90048
310.274.1893
locandaveneta.net

SUZANNE GOIN
Lucques
8474 Melrose Ave
Los Angeles, CA 90048
323.655.6277
lucques.com

MARK GOLD
Eva
7458 Beverly Blvd
Los Angeles, CA 90036
323.634.0700
evarestaurantla.com

MANUEL GONZALEZ
TAPS Fish House & Brewery
101 E Imperial Hwy
Brea, CA 92821
714.257.0101
tapsfishhouse.com

JAMES GRAHAM
Ba Restaurant
5100 York Blvd
Los Angeles, CA 90042
323.739.6243
restaurantba.com

ERIC GREENSPAN
The Foundry On Melrose
7465 Melrose Ave
Los Angeles, CA 90036
323.651.0915
thefoundryonmelrose.com

IAN GRESIK
Drago Centro
525 S Flower St
Los Angeles, CA 90071
213.228.8998
dragocentro.com

DAVID GUSSIN
STK
755 N La Cienega Blvd
Los Angeles, CA 90069
310.659.3535
stkhouse.com

ILAN HALL
The Gorbals
501 S Spring St
Los Angeles, CA 90013
213.488.3408
thegorbalsla.com

QUINN HATFIELD
Hatfield's
6703 Melrose Ave
Los Angeles, CA 90038
323.935.2977
hatfieldsrestaurant.com

TONY HERNANDEZ
Off Vine
6263 Leland Way
Los Angeles, CA 90028
323.962.1900
offvine.com

RICHARD HODGE
BLVD 16
10740 Wilshire Blvd
Los Angeles, CA 90024
310.474.7765
blvd16.com

CHRISTOPHER HORA
Los Angeles, CA
christopherhora.com

SYDNEY HUNTER
Café Pinot
700 W 5th St
Los Angeles, CA 90071
213.239.6500
patinagroup.com

BRIAN HUSKEY
Eva
7458 Beverly Blvd
Los Angeles, CA 90036
323.634.0700
evarestaurantla.com

GLENN ISHII
Noe
251 S Olive St
Los Angeles, CA 90012
213.356.4100
noerestaurant.com

JOHN KEENAN
Craft
10100 Constellation Blvd
Los Angeles, CA 90067
310.279.4180
craftrestaurantsinc.com

SHIGE KUDO
Shibucho
3114 Beverly Blvd
Los Angeles, CA 90057
213.387.8498
shibucho.com

JOHN LECHLEIDNER
WP24
900 W Olympic Blvd
Los Angeles, CA 90015
213.743.8824
wolfgangpuck.com

WONNY LEE
Hamasaku
11043 Santa Monica Blvd
Los Angeles, CA 90025
310.479.7636
hamasakula.com

LUDO LEFEBVRE
LudoBites
Los Angeles, CA
ludolefebvre.com

SCOTT LINQUIST
Border Grill
445 S Figueroa St
Los Angeles, CA 90071
213.486.5171
bordergrill.com

MEGAN LOGAN
Nick & Stef's Steakhouse
330 Hope St
Los Angeles, CA 90071
213.680.0330
patinagroup.com

ROBERT LUNA
Malo
4326 W Sunset Blvd
Los Angeles, CA 90029
323.664.1011
malorestaurant.com

SALVATORE MARINO
Il Grano
11359 Santa Monica Blvd
Los Angeles, CA 90025
310.477.7886
ilgrano.com

ARMANDO MARTINEZ
Los Angeles, CA

SHACHI MEHRA
Los Angeles, CA
shachimehra.com

ORI MENASHE
Bestia
2121 E 7th Pl
Los Angeles, CA 90021
213.514.5724
bestiala.com

JASON MICHAUD
Red Hill
1325 Echo Park Ave
Los Angeles, CA 90026
213.482.0886
redhillrestaurant.com

GORAN MILIC
Divino
11714 Barrington Ct
Los Angeles, CA 90049
310.472.0886
divinobrentwood.com

GAVIN MILLS
Wood & Vine
6280 Hollywood Blvd
Los Angeles, CA 90028
323.334.3360
woodandvine.com

MATT MOLINA
Pizzeria Mozza
641 N Highland Ave
Los Angeles, CA 90036
323.297.0101
pizzeriamozza.com

KRIS MORNINGSTAR
Ray's and Stark Bar
5905 Wilshire Blvd
Los Angeles, CA 90036
323.857.6180
patinagroup.com

NIKI NAKAYAMA
n/naka
3455 Overland Ave
Los Angeles, CA 90034
310.836.6252
n-naka.com

BRYANT NG
The Spice Table

114 S Central Ave
Los Angeles, CA 90012
213.620.1840
thespicetable.com

KAZUNORI NOZAWA
Sugarfish

600 W 7th St #150
Los Angeles, CA 90017
213.627.3000
sugarfishsushi.com

ERIC ONG
Humble Potato

8321 Lincoln Blvd
Los Angeles, CA 90045
323.989.2242
humblepotato.com

ANTONIO ORLANDO
Matteo's

2321 Westwood Blvd
Los Angeles, CA 90064
310.475.4521
matteosla.com

OTTAVIO PALMERI
Palmeri Ristorante

11650 San Vicente Blvd
Los Angeles, CA 90049
310.442.8446
palmeriristorante.com

ERIC PARK
Black Hogg

2852 W Sunset Blvd
Los Angeles, CA 90026
323.953.2820
blackhogg.com

ANGELO PELONI
La Bruschetta

1621 Westwood Blvd
Los Angeles, CA 90024
310.477.1052
lbwestwood.com

T. NICHOLAS PETER
The Little Door

8164 W 3rd St
Los Angeles, CA 90048
323.951.1210
thelittledoor.com

ALFONSO RAMIREZ
Montebello, CA

310.707.6361
chefalfonsoramirez.com

RAFFAELE SABATINO
Pecorino

11604 San Vicente Blvd
Los Angeles, CA 90049
310.571.3800
pecorinorestaurant.com

RUSSELL SAITO
The Edison

108 W 2nd St #101
Los Angeles, CA 90012
213.613.0000
edisondowntown.com

STEVE SAMSON
Sotto

9575 W Pico Blvd
Los Angeles, CA 90035
310.277.0210
sottorestaurant.com

SIMONE SANTOPIETRO
Obika Mozzarella Bar

10250 Santa Monica Blvd
Los Angeles, CA 90067
310.556.2452
obikala.com

JOHN RIVERA SEDLAR
Rivera Restaurant

1050 S Flower St #102
Los Angeles, CA 90015
213.749.1460
riverarestaurant.com

PAUL SHOEMAKER
Juicy Lucy

735 S Figueroa St
Los Angeles, CA 90017
213.683.1030

JON SHOOK
Animal

435 N Fairfax Ave
Los Angeles, CA 90048
323.782.9225
animalrestaurant.com

JARED SIMONS
Escuela Taqueria

7615 Beverly Blvd
Los Angeles, CA 90036
323.932.6178

JOSHUA SMITH
Los Angeles, CA

JOACHIM SPLICHAL
Patina

141 S Grand Ave
Los Angeles, CA 90012
213.972.3331
patinarestaurant.com

JEREMY STRUBEL
Sirena

8265 Beverly Blvd
Los Angeles, CA 90048
323.852.7000
sirenarestaurant.com

LUIS SULAT
Pips on La Brea

1356 S La Brea Ave
Los Angeles, CA 90019
323.954.7477
pizzapastasalads.com

ARI TAYMOR
Alma

952 S Broadway
Los Angeles, CA 90015
213.444.0984
alma-la.com

TARA THOMAS
Traxx

800 N Alameda St #122
Los Angeles, CA 90012
213.625.1999
traxxrestaurant.com

VAHAN TOKMADJIAN
O Bar & Kitchen

819 S Flower St
Los Angeles, CA 90017
213.784.3048
barandkitchenla.com

SUZANNE TRACHT
Jar

8225 Beverly Blvd
Los Angeles, CA 90048
323.655.6566
thejar.com

KATSUYA UECHI
Katsuya

800 W Olympic Blvd
Los Angeles, CA 90015
213.747.9797
sbe.com

MICHAEL VOLTAGGIO
Ink.

8360 Melrose Ave
Los Angeles, CA 90069
323.651.5866
mvink.com

DAKOTA WEISS
NINETHIRTY at the W

930 Hilgard Ave
Los Angeles, CA 90024
310.443.8211
ninethirtyw.com

JOSHUA WHIGHAM
The Bazaar Beverly Hills

465 S La Cienega Blvd
Los Angeles, CA 90048
310.246.5555
thebazaar.com

HIRAOKI YAMADA
Itacho

7311 Beverly Blvd
Los Angeles, CA 90036
323.938.9009
itachorestaurant.com

SANG YOON
Father's Office

3229 Helms Ave
Los Angeles, CA 90034
310.736.2224
fathersoffice.com

MICHAEL YOUNG
Ombra

3737 Cahuenga Blvd
Los Angeles, CA 90068
818.985.7337
ombrala.com

RICARDO ZARATE
Mo-Chica

514 W 7th St
Los Angeles, CA 90014
213.622.3744
mo-chica.com

LOS GATOS

MARTY CATTANEO
Dio Deka

210 E Main St
Los Gatos, CA 95030
408.354.7700
diodeka.com

ROSS HANSON
Restaurant James Randall

303 N Santa Cruz Ave
Los Gatos, CA 95030
408.395.4441
restaurantjamesrandall.com

DAVID KINCH
Manresa

320 Village Ln
Los Gatos, CA 95030
408.354.4330
manresarestaurant.com

CHRISTOPHER SCHLOSS
Cin-Cin Wine Bar

368 Village Ln
Los Gatos, CA 95030
408.354.8006
cincinwinebar.com

JIM STUMP
Los Gatos Brewing Company

130-G N Santa Cruz Ave
Los Gatos, CA 95030
408.395.9929
lgbrewingco.com

BRIAN WESELBY
Forbes Mill Steakhouse

206 N Santa Cruz Ave
Los Gatos, CA 95030
408.395.6434
forbesmillsteakhouse.com

MALIBU

GENO BAHENA
La Costa Mission

21337 Pacific Coast Hwy
Malibu, CA 90265
310.317.0110
genobahena.com

CAROLINE BERTSCH
The Sunset

6800 Westward Beach Rd
Malibu, CA 90265
310.589.1007
thesunsetrestaurant.com

VICTOR MORALES
Carbon Beach Club

22878 Pacific Coast Hwy
Malibu, CA 90265
310.456.6444
malibubeachinn.com

BIJAN SHOKATFARD
Geoffrey's Malibu

27400 Pacific Coast Hwy
Malibu, CA 90265
310.457.1519
geoffreysmalibu.com

FRANCESCO VELASCO
Tra di Noi

3835 Cross Creek Rd
Malibu, CA 90265
310.456.0169
francescovelasco.com

MANHATTAN BEACH

ANN CONNESS
Tin Roof Bistro

3500 N Sepulveda Blvd #100
Manhattan Beach, CA 90266
310.939.0900
tinroofbistro.com

BRYON FREEZE
Circa

903 Manhattan Ave
Manhattan Beach, CA 90266
310.374.4422
circamb.com

GUY GABRIELE
Café Pierre

317 Manhattan Beach Blvd
Manhattan Beach, CA 90266
310.545.5252
cafepierre.com

DAVID LEFEVRE
M.B. Post

1142 Manhattan Ave
Manhattan Beach, CA 90266
310.545.5405
eatmbpost.com

ORLANDO NOVOA
American Farmhouse Tavern

924 N Sepulveda Blvd
Manhattan Beach, CA 90266
310.376.8044
americanfarmhousetavern.com

DARREN WEISS
Darren's Restaurant

1141 Manhattan Ave
Manhattan Beach, CA 90266
310.802.1973
darrensrestaurant.com

MARINA DEL REY

DANIEL ROBERTS
Café del Rey

4451 Admiralty Way
Marina del Rey, CA 90292
310.823.6395
cafedelreymarina.com

MENDOCINO

JAMIE GRIFFITH
955 Ukiah Street Restaurant

955 Ukiah St
Mendocino, CA 95460
707.937.1955
955restaurant.com

ALAN KANTOR
MacCallum House

45020 Albion St
Mendocino, CA 95460
707.937.5763
maccallumhouse.com

DAVID LAMONICA
Café Beaujolais

961 Ukiah St
Mendocino, CA 95460
707.937.5614
cafebeaujolais.com

MENLO PARK

STEVE CATALANO
LB Steak

334 Santana Row
Menlo Park, CA 95128
408.244.1180
lbsteak.com

DMITRY ELPERIN
The Village Pub

2967 Woodside Rd
Woodside, CA 94062
650.851.9888
thevillagepub.net

BRENDY MONSADA
LB Steak

898 Santa Cruz Ave
Menlo Park, CA 94025
650.321.8980
lbsteak.com

PETER RUDOLPH
Madera

2825 Sand Hill Rd
Menlo Park, CA 94025
650.561.1540
maderasandhill.com

MILL VALLEY

TYLER FLORENCE
El Paseo

17 Throckmorton Ave
Mill Valley, CA 94941
415.388.0741
elpaseomillvalley.com

ROBERT PRICE
Bungalow 44

44 E Blithedale Ave
Mill Valley, CA 94941
415.381.2500
bungalow44.com

MISSION VIEJO

SALVATORE FASO
Piccolino

28731 Los Alisos Blvd
Mission Viejo, CA 92692
949.380.7261
piccolinomv.com

MODESTO

VINCENT ALVARADO
Dewz Restaurant

1505 J St
Modesto, CA 95354
209.549.1101
dothedewz.com

MICHAEL GOULARTE
Galletto Ristorante

1101 J St
Modesto, CA 95354
209.523.4500
galletto.biz

MONROVIA

JASON PATELA
Caffe Opera

402 S Myrtle Ave
Monrovia, CA 91016
626.305.0094
operamonrovia.com

MONTEREY

JAMES ANDERSON
La Bicyclette

Dolores St & 7th Ave
Carmel, CA 93923
831.622.9899
labicycletterestaurant.com

TONY BAKER
Montrio Bistro

414 Calle Principal
Monterey, CA 93940
831.648.8880
montrio.com

JASON BALESTRIERI
Cantinetta Luca

Dolores St & 7th Ave
Carmel, CA 93921
831.625.6500
cantinettaluca.com

JULIEN BELLIARD
Cafe Rustica

10 Delfino Pl
Carmel Valley, CA 93924
831.659.4444
caferusticavillage.com

MATT BOLTON
Pacific's Edge

120 Highlands Dr
Carmel, CA 93923
831.622.5445
pacificsedge.com

CHRISTOPHE BONY
Casanova

Mission St & 5th Ave
Carmel, CA 93923
831.625.2727
casanovarestaurant.com

JUSTIN COGLEY
Aubergine

Monte Verde St & 7th Ave
Carmel, CA 93921
831.624.8578
laubergecarmel.com

JOHN COX
Sierra Mar

47900 State Hwy 1
Big Sur, CA 93920
831.667.2200
postranchinn.com

BERT CUTINO
Sardine Factory

701 Wave St
Monterey, CA 93940
831.373.3775
sardinefactory.com

PEDRO DE LA ORUZ
Fandango

223 17th St
Pacific Grove, CA 93950
831.372.3456
fandangorestaurant.com

DIDIER DUTERTRE
Bistro Moulin

867 Wave S
Monterey, CA 93940
831.333.1200
bistromoulin.com

CHRIS FUKUSHIMA
Ocean Sushi Deli

2701 David Ave
Pacific Grove, CA 93950
831.649.1320
oceansushi.com

BILL KARAKI
Taste Café & Bistro

1199 Forest Ave
Pacific Grove, CA 93950
831.655.0324
tastecafebistro.com

LEVI MEZICK
Restaurant 1833

500 Hartnell St
Monterey, CA 93940
831.643.1833
restaurant1833.com

BRANDON MILLER
Mundaka

San Carlos St & 7th Ave
Carmel, CA 93921
831.624.7400
mundakacarmel.com

CAL STAMENOV
Marinus at Bernardus Lodge

415 W Carmel Valley Rd
Carmel Valley, CA 93924
831.658.3595
bernardus.com

TED WALTER
Passionfish

701 Lighthouse Ave
Pacific Grove, CA 93950
831.655.3311
passionfish.net

CY YONTZ
Rio Grill

101 Crossroads Blvd
Carmel, CA 93923
831.625.5436
riogrill.com

MORGAN HILL

SALVATORE CALISI
Sicilia in Bocca

25 W Main Ave
Morgan Hill, CA 95037
408.778.0399

MOUNTAIN VIEW

DAVID HILL
Scratch

401 Castro St
Mountain View, CA 94041
650.237.3132
scratchmtnview.com

ANTONIO LOPEZ
CasCal

400 Castro St
Mountain View, CA 94041
650.940.9500
cascalrestaurant.com

ALEX XALXO
Sakoon

357 Castro St
Mountain View, CA 94041
650.965.2000
sakoonrestaurant.com

NAPA

STEPHEN BARBER
Farmstead

738 Main St
St. Helena, CA 94574
707.963.9181
longmeadowranch.com

JOSE BRAVO-GUZMAN
Pearl

1339 Pearl St #104
Napa, CA 94559
707.224.9161
therestaurantpearl.com

DAVID BREEDEN
The French Laundry

6640 Washington St
Yountville, CA 94599
707.944.2380
frenchlaundry.com

MICHAEL CHIARELLO
Bottega

6525 Washington St
Yountville, CA 94559
707.945.1050
botteganapavalley.com

NASH COGNETTI
Tra Vigne

1050 Charter Oak Ave
St. Helena, CA 94574
707.963.4444
travignerestaurant.com

GREG COLE
Cole's Chop House

1122 Main St
Napa, CA 94559
707.224.6328
coleschophouse.com

DAVE CRUZ
ad hoc

6476 Washington St
Yountville, CA 94599
707.944.2487
adhocrestaurant.com

ROBERT CURRY
Auberge du Soleil

180 Rutherford Hill Rd
Rutherford, CA 94573
707.963.1211
aubergedusoleil.com

CURTIS DIFEDE
Oenotri

1425 1st St
Napa, CA 94559
707.252.1022
oenotri.com

SCOTT EKSTROM
Angele

540 Main St
Napa, CA 94559
707.252.8115
angelerestaurant.com

KEN FRANK
La Toque

1314 McKinstry St
Napa, CA 94559
707.257.5157
latoque.com

PERRY HOFFMAN
Etoile

1 California Dr
Yountville, CA 94599
888.242.6366
chandon.com

TODD HUMPHRIES
Kitchen Door

610 1st St
Napa, CA 94559
707.226.1560
kitchendoornapa.com

BOB HURLEY
Hurley's

6518 Washington St
Yountville, CA 94599
707.944.2345
hurleysrestaurant.com

PHILIPPE JEANTY
Bistro Jeanty

6510 Washington St
Yountville, CA 94599
707.944.0103
bistrojeanty.com

THOMAS KELLER
The French Laundry

6640 Washington St
Yountville, CA 94599
707.944.2380
frenchlaundry.com

SCOTT KENDALL
Carpe Diem

1001 2nd St
Napa, CA 94559
707.224.0800
carpediemwinebar.com

NAI KANG KUAN
Morimoto

610 Main St
Napa, CA 94559
707.252.1600
morimotonapa.com

TERRY LETSON
Fume

4050 Byway E
Napa, CA 94558
707.257.1999
fumebistro.com

JORDAN MACKEY
Restaurant Cuvee

1650 Soscol Ave
Napa, CA 94559
707.224.2330
cuveenapa.com

CINDY PAWLCYN
Cindy's Backstreet Kitchen

1327 Railroad Ave
St. Helena, CA 94574
707.963.1200
cindysbackstreetkitchen.com

RICHARD REDDINGTON
Redd

6480 Washington St
Yountville, CA 94599
707.944.2222
reddnapavalley.com

NICK RITCHIE
Alex Italian

1140 Rutherford Rd
Rutherford, CA 94573
707.967.5500
alexitalianrestaurant.com

TYLER RODDE
Oenotri

1425 1st St
Napa, CA 94559
707.252.1022
oenotri.com

STEPHEN ROGERS
PRESS St. Helena

587 St. Helena Hwy
St. Helena, CA 94574
707.967.0550
presssthelena.com

MICHAEL SANDOVAL
Bouchon

6534 Washington St
Yountville, CA 94599
707.944.8037
bouchonbistro.com

DONNA SCALA
Bistro Don Giovanni

4110 Howard Ln
Napa, CA 94558
707.224.3300
bistrodongiovanni.com

SUMMER SEBASTIANI
All Seasons Bistro

1400 Lincoln St
Calistoga, CA 94515
707.942.9111
allseasonsnapavalley.net

BRANDON SHARP
Solbar

755 Silverado Trail
Calistoga, CA 94515
707.226.0850
solagecalistoga.com

HIRO SONE
Terra

1345 Railroad Ave
St. Helena, CA 94574
707.963.8931
terrarestaurant.com

MATT SPECTOR
JoLé Restaurant and Bar

1457 Lincoln Ave
Calistoga, CA 94515
707.942.5938
jolerestaurant.com

MICHAEL TUOHY
Napa, CA

MARCOS URIBE
Celadon

500 Main St
Napa, CA 94559
707.254.9690
celadonnapa.com

WILL WRIGHT
Bounty Hunter

975 1st St
Napa, CA 94559
707.226.3976
bountyhunterwinebar.com

NEWPORT BEACH

TAKASHI ABE
Bluefin

7952 E Pacific Coast Hwy
Newport Beach, CA 92657
949.715.7373
bluefinbyabe.com

MATT BRIGGS
Mastro's Ocean Club

8112 E Coast Hwy
Newport Beach, CA 92657
949.376.6990
mastrosrestaurants.com

LUIGI FINEO
Andrea Ristorante

22701 S Pelican Hill Rd
Newport Coast, CA 92657
949.467.6800
pelicanhill.com

SAL MANIACI
Sapori Ristorante

1080 Bayside Dr
Newport Beach, CA 92660
949.644.4220
saporinb.com

RICH MEAD
Sage Restaurant

2531 Eastbluff Dr
Newport Beach, CA 92660
949.718.9650
sagerestaurant.com

PASCAL OLHATS
Brasserie Pascal

327 Newport Center Dr
Newport Beach, CA 92660
949.640.2700
pascalnpb.com

PABLO QUIROZ
The Dock

2816 LaFayette Ave
Newport Beach, CA 92663
949.673.3625
eatatthedock.com

CHANG SIVILAY
Newport Coast, CA

KEITH STICH
Wildfish Seafood Grille

1370 Bison Ave
Newport Beach, CA 92660
949.720.9925
wildfishseafoodgrille.com

OAKHURST

GUNNAR THOMPSON
Erna's Elderberry House

48688 Victoria Ln
Oakhurst, CA 93644
559.683.6800
chateausureau.com

OAKLAND

KIM ALTER
Haven

44 Webster St
Oakland, CA 94607
510.663.4440
havenoakland.com

CHRISTOPHER CHEUNG
Marica

5301 College Ave
Oakland, CA 94618
510.985.8388
maricafood.wordpress.com

RICK HACKETT
Bocanova

55 Webster St
Oakland, CA 94607
510.444.1233
bocanova.com

CHARLIE HALLOWELL
Pizzaiolo

5008 Telegraph Ave
Oakland, CA 94609
510.652.4888
pizzaiolooakland.com

ROBERT HOLT
Marzano

4214 Park Blvd
Oakland, CA 94602
510.531.4500
marzanorestaurant.com

JONATHAN LUCE
Bellanico

4238 Park Blvd
Oakland, CA 94602
510.336.1180
bellanico.net

RUSSELL MOORE
Camino

3917 Grand Ave
Oakland, CA 94610
510.547.5035
caminorestaurant.com

JONAH RHODEHAMEL
Oliveto

5655 College Ave
Oakland, CA 94618
510.547.5356
oliveto.com

CHRIS SHEPHERD
Bellanico

4238 Park Blvd
Oakland, CA 94602
510.336.1180
bellanico.net

JULYA SHIN
Pizzaiolo

5008 Telegraph Ave
Oakland, CA 94609
510.652.4888
pizzaiolooakland.com

JAMES SYHABOUT
Commis

3859 Piedmont Ave
Oakland, CA 94611
510.653.3902
commisrestaurant.com

MICHAEL WILD
BayWolf

3853 Piedmont Ave
Oakland, CA 94611
510.655.6004
baywolf.com

MANFRED WREMBEL
Plum

2214 Broadway
Oakland, CA 94612
510.444.7586
plumoakland.com

ORANGE

GREG DANIELS
Haven Gastropub

190 S Glassell St
Orange, CA 92866
714.221.0680
havengastropub.com

SANDRO ONTIVEROS
Citrus City Grille

122 N Glassell St
Orange, CA 92866
714.639.9600
citruscitygrille.com

GABBI PATRICK
Gabbi's Mexican Kitchen

141 S Glassell St
Orange, CA 92866
714.633.3038
gabbipatrick.com

MICHAEL PHILIPPI
The Hobbit

2932 E Chapman Ave
Orange, CA 92869
714.997.1972
hobbitrestaurant.com

OXNARD

TODD AARONS
Tierra Sur

3201 Camino Del Sol
Oxnard, CA 93030
805.983.1560
tierrasuratherzog.com

YASERT CAN
Simi Valley, CA

GABE GARCIA
Tierra Sur

3201 Camino Del Sol
Oxnard, CA 93030
805.983.1560
tierrasuratherzog.com

KARL HOLST
Spanish Hills Country Club

999 Crestview Ave
Camarillo, CA 93010
805.388.5000
spanishhillscc.com

TIM KILCOYNE
SideCar

3029 E Main St
Ventura, CA 93003
805.653.7433
thesidecarrestaurant.com

CHAD MANDEL
Rhumb Line

1510 Anchors Way Dr
Ventura, CA 93001
805.642.1200
rhumblineventura.com

CHAD MINTON
Oak Grill at Ojai Valley Inn

905 Country Club Rd
Ojai, CA 93023
805.646.1111
ojairesort.com

TATIANA MOQUECA
Moqueca Brazilian Cuisine

3550 S Harbor Blvd
Oxnard, CA 93035
805.204.0970
moquecarestaurant.com

DIDIER POIRIER
71 Palm

71 N Palm St
Ventura, CA 93001
805.653.7222
71palm.com

DENIS RION
Cigale Café

704 Lindero Canyon Rd
Oak Park, CA 91377
818.991.2442
cigalecafe.com

JOSE SANDOVAL
Aloha Steakhouse

364 S California St
Ventura, CA 93001
805.652.1799
alohasteakhouse.com

PANAGIOTIS SKOURTIS
The Greek at the Harbor

1583 Spinnaker Dr #101
Ventura, CA 93001
805.650.5350
greekattheharbor.com

FABIO VIVIANI
Café Firenze

563 W Los Angeles Ave
Moorpark, CA 93021
805.532.0048
cafefirenze.net

DAVID WEISS
Café Fiore

66 S California St
Ventura, CA 93001
805.653.1266
cafefiore.net

PACIFIC PALISADES

PETER EDWARDS
Bel-Air Bay Club

16801 Pacific Coast Hwy
Pacific Palisades, CA 90272
310.454.1391
belairbayclub.com

ALAIN GIRAUD
Maison Giraud

1032 Swarthmore Ave
Pacific Palisades, CA 90272
310.459.7562
maison-giraud.com

PALO ALTO

CHARLIE AYERS
Calafia Cafe

855 El Camino Real
Palo Alto, CA 94301
650.322.9200
calafiapaloalto.com

NICOLE BAVERSO
Pampas

529 Alma St
Palo Alto, CA 94301
650.327.1323
pampaspaloalto.com

BRUNO CHEMEL
Baume

201 S California Ave
Palo Alto, CA 94306
650.328.8899
baumerestaurant.com

MARCO FOSSATI
Quattro

2050 University Ave
East Palo Alto, CA 94303
650.470.2889
fourseasons.com

C.J. HAMMER
Saint Michael's Alley

806 Emerson St
Palo Alto, CA 94301
650.326.2530
stmikes.com

ARNULFO HERNANDEZ
Reposado

236 Hamilton Ave
Palo Alto, CA 94301
650.833.3151
reposadorestaurant.com

AMBJORN LINDSKOG
Bistro Elan on Birch St

2363A Birch St
Palo Alto, CA 94306
650.327.0284
bistroelan.com

LUIGI MAVICA
Il Fornaio

520 Cowper St
Palo Alto, CA 94301
650.853.3888
ilfornaio.com

MARIO ORTEGA
Evvia

420 Emerson St
Palo Alto, CA 94301
650.326.0983
evvia.net

ANDY PHILLIPS
Gravity

544 Emerson St
Palo Alto, CA 94301
650.327.3161
gravitywinebar.com

FABRICE ROUX
Joya

339 University Ave
Palo Alto, CA 94301
650.853.9800
joyarestaurant.com

PASADENA

JORGE AVILA
Arroyo Chop House

536 S Arroyo Pkwy
Pasadena, CA 91105
626.577.7463
arroyochophouse.com

CLAUD BELTRAN
Noir Food & Wine

40 N Mentor Ave
Pasadena, CA 91106
626.795.7199
noirfoodandwine.com

DAVID FEAU
The Royce

1401 S Oak Knoll Ave
Pasadena, CA 91106
626.585.6410
roycela.com

TIM GUILTINAN
The Raymond Restaurant

1250 S Fair Oaks Ave
Pasadena, CA 91105
626.441.3136
theraymond.com

MONIQUE KING
Firefly Bistro

1009 El Centro St
South Pasadena, CA 91030
626.441.2443
eatatfirefly.com

PHIL LEE
Vol. 94

239 E Colorado Blvd
Pasadena, CA 91101
626.356.9494
vol94.com

LAURENT QUENIOUX
Vertical Wine Bistro

70 N Raymond Ave
Pasadena, CA 91103
626.795.3999
verticalwinebistro.com

GRANT ROWE
Green Street

146 Shoppers Ln
Pasadena, CA 91101
626.577.7170
greenstreetrestaurant.com

JONATHAN WIENER
Pasadena, CA

RYAN WILSON
Lawry's Restaurants, Inc.

234 E Colorado Blvd #500
Pasadena, CA 91101
888.552.9797
lawrysonline.com

PEBBLE BEACH

BENJAMIN BROWN
The Lodge at Pebble Beach

1700 17-Mile Dr
Pebble Beach, CA 93953
831.647.7500
pebblebeach.com

PABLO MELLIN
Roy's

270 17-Mile Dr
Pebble Beach, CA 93953
831.647.7500
pebblebeach.com

PICO RIVERA

HENRY CHRISTENSEN
Dal Rae

9023 E Washington Blvd
Pico Rivera, CA 90660
562.949.2444
dalrae.com

POINT REYES STATION

CHRISTIAN CAIAZZO
Osteria Stellina

11285 California 1
Point Reyes Station, CA 94956
415.663.9988
osteriastellina.com

RANCHO PALOS VERDES

RUDIE YOUNG
Admiral Risty

31250 Palos Verdes Dr W
Rancho Palos Verdes, CA 90275
310.377.0050
admiral-risty.com

RANCHO SANTA MARGARITA

SEAN REYNOLDS
Hanna's

22195 El Paseo
Rancho Santa Margarita, CA 92688
949.709.2300
hannasprimesteak.com

REDONDO BEACH

BERT AGOR JR.
Kincaid's

500 Fishermans Wharf
Redondo Beach, CA 90277
310.318.6080
kincaids.com

ROBERT BELL
Chez Melange

1611 S Catalina Ave
Redondo Beach, CA 90277
310.540.1222
chezmelange.com

THOMAS ORTEGA
Ortega 120

1814 S Pacific Coast Hwy
Redondo Beach, CA 90277
310.792.4120
ortega120.com

DOMINIQUE THEVAL
Dominique's Kitchen

522 S Pacific Coast Hwy
Redondo Beach, CA 90277
424.247.9054
dominieskitchen.com

REDWOOD CITY

JOHN BENTLEY
John Bentley's

2915 El Camino Real
Redwood City, CA 94061
650.365.7777
johnbentleys.com

MICHAEL DOTSON
Martins West

831 Main St
Redwood City, CA 94063
650.366.4366
martinswestgp.com

DONATO SCOTTI
Donato Enoteca

1041 Middlefield Rd
Redwood City, CA 94063
650.701.1000
donatoenoteca.com

RIVERSIDE

ROBERTO ARGENTINA
Farm Artisan Foods

22 E State St
Redlands, CA 92373
909.792.1162
farmartisanfoods.com

JOHANNES BACHER
Johannes

196 S Indian Canyon Dr
Palm Springs, CA 92262
760.778.0017
johannesrestaurants.com

ALEN BADZAK
Europa

1620 S Indian Trail
Palm Springs, CA 92264
760.327.2314
villaroyale.com

DIOS BAGUYO
Duane's Prime Steaks
and Seafood

3649 Mission Inn Ave
Riverside, CA 92501
888.326.4448
missioninn.com

RUDY CAMPUZANO
Indian Wells Country Club

46000 Club Dr
Indian Wells, CA 92210
760.345.2561
indianwellscountryclub.com

DAVE CONN
Tinto

1800 E Palm Canyon Dr
Palm Springs, CA 92264
760.323.1711
garcesgroup.com

MARIO CURCI
Jake's Palm Springs

664 N Palm Canyon Dr
Palm Springs, CA 92262
760.327.4400
jakesreadytoeat.com

BERNARD DERVIEUX
Cuistot

72595 El Paseo
Palm Desert, CA 92260
760.340.1000
cuistotrestaurant.com

HERVE GLIN
Cork Tree

74950 Country Club Dr
Palm Desert, CA 92260
760.779.0123
thecorktree.com

HENRY GONZALEZ
Spaggi's

1651 W Foothill Blvd
Upland, CA 91786
909.579.0497
spaggis.com

JIN HEO
Okura Robata

78370 California 111 #150
La Quinta, CA 92253
760.564.5820
okurasushi.com

EMMANUEL JANIN
La Brasserie Bistro and Bar

78477 California 111
La Quinta, CA 92253
760.771.4400
labrasserielaquinta.com

BRIAN KIEPLER
Ace Hotel & Swim Club

701 E Palm Canyon Dr
Palm Springs, CA 92264
760.325.9900
acehotel.com

JEAN-PAUL LAIR
Le Vallauris

385 W Tahquitz Canyon Way
Palm Springs, CA 92262
760.325.5059
levallauris.com

PIERRE PELECH
Chez Pierre

44250 Town Center Way
Palm Desert, CA 92260
760.346.1818
chezpierrebistro.com

ALESSANDRO PRESTIFILIPPO
Gourmet Italia

27499 Ynez Rd
Temecula, CA 92951
951.676.9194
gourmetitaliarestaurants.com

OSCAR ROJAS
Trilussa

68718 E Palm Canyon Dr
Cathedral City, CA 92234
760.328.2300
trilussarestaurant.com

JIMMY SCHMIDT
Morgan's in the Desert

49-499 Eisenhower Dr
La Quinta, CA 92253
760.564.7600
morgansinthedesert.com

FRANCISCO SOLANO
Solano's Bistro

78075 Main St
La Quinta, CA 92253
760.771.6655
solanosbistro.com

JESSE SOUZA
Circa 59

1600 N Indian Canyon Dr
Palm Springs, CA 92262
760.778.6659
psriviera.com

MOE TELLO
LG's Prime Steakhouse

78525 California 111 #100
La Quinta , CA 92253
760.771.9911
lgsprimesteakhouse.com

STEFAN WECK
The Grand Oak Steakhouse

10600 Highland Springs Ave
Cherry Valley, CA 92223
951.845.1151
hsresort.com

ROSS

DAN BAKER
Marche aux Fleurs

23 Ross Common
Ross, CA 94957
415.925.9200
marcheauxfleursrestaurant.com

SACRAMENTO

BRUNO AMATO
Il Fornaio

400 Capitol Mall
Sacramento, CA 95814
916.446.4100
ilfornaio.com

TARO ARAI
Mikuni

1565 Eureka Rd
Roseville, CA 95661
916.797.2112
mikunisushi.com

ROBYN BERGMAN
Mustard Seed

222 D St #11
Davis, CA 95616
530.758.5750
mustardseeddavis.com

PAUL BERGMAN
Mustard Seed

222 D St #11
Davis, CA 95616
530.758.5750
mustardseeddavis.com

MARK BERKNER
Taste

9402 Main St
Plymouth, CA 95669
209.245.3463
restauranttaste.com

BRET BOHLMANN
Boulevard Bistro

8941 Elk Grove Blvd
Elk Grove, CA 95624
916.685.2220
frontiernet.net /~boulevardbistro

PAJO BRUICH
Enotria

1431 Del Paso Blvd
Sacramento, CA 95815
916.922.6792
enotria.com

BIBA CAGGIANO
Biba

2801 Capitol Ave
Sacramento, CA 95816
916.455.2422
biba-restaurant.com

JONATHON CLEMMONS
The Porch Restaurant and Bar

1815 K St
Sacramento, CA 95811
916.444.2423
theporchsacramento.com

MITCHELL DAVIS
Il Fornaio

1179 Galleria Blvd #P-118
Roseville, CA 95678
916.788.1200
ilfornaio.com

JORDAN DAVIS
Selland's Market Café

5340 H St
Sacramento, CA 95819
916.736.3333
sellands.com

GREG DUNN
Scott's Seafood Grill & Bar

9711 Greenback Ln
Folsom, CA 95630
916.989.6711
scottsseafood.net

MICHAEL FAGNONI
Hawks

5530 Douglas Blvd
Granite Bay, CA 95746
916.791.6200
hawksrestaurant.com

GUY FIERI
Johnny Garlic's

10505 Fairway Dr
Roseville, CA 95678
916.789.2000
johnnygarlics.com

TERRY GLODREY
Monkey Cat

805 Lincoln Way
Auburn, CA 95603
530.888.8492
monkeycat.com

BRIAN HAWKINS
Sienna Restaurant

3909 Park Dr
El Dorado Hills, CA 95762
916.941.9694
siennarestaurants.com

MOLLY HAWKS
Hawks

5530 Douglas Blvd
Granite Bay, CA 95746
916.791.6200
hawksrestaurant.com

CERILO HERNANDEZ
Zinfandel Grille

2384 Fair Oaks Blvd
Sacramento, CA 95825
916.485.7100
zinfandelgrille.com

DAVID HILL
Chef's Table

6843 Lonetree Blvd
Rocklin, CA 95677
916.771.5656
chefdavidstable.com

BILL JOHN
Scott's Seafood Grill & Bar

4800 Riverside Blvd
Sacramento, CA 95822
916.379.5959
scottsseafood.net

MICHAEL JORDAN
Back Wine Bar & Bistro

25075 Blue Ravine Rd
Folsom, CA 95630
916.986.9100
backwinebar.com

ROBERTO LAINEZ
Ravenous Café

7600 Greenhaven Dr
Sacramento, CA 95831
916.399.9309
ravenouscafe.com

DARRELL MADEIRA
Crush 29

1480 Eureka Rd
Roseville, CA 95661
916.773.2929
crush29.com

RICK MAHAN
The Waterboy

2000 Capitol Ave
Sacramento, CA 95811
916.498.9891
waterboyrestaurant.com

EDWARD MARTINEZ
Hawks

5530 Douglas Blvd
Granite Bay, CA 95746
916.791.6200
hawksrestaurant.com

CARLOS MARTINEZ
Paul Martin's American Bistro

1455 Eureka Rd
Roseville, CA 95661
916.783.3600
paulmartinsamericanbistro.com

JOSE MARTINEZ
Ruth's Chris

501 Pavilions Ln
Sacramento, CA 95825
916.286.2702
ruthschris.com

SHANE MCMAHON
La Provence

110 Diamond Creek Pl
Roseville, CA 95747
916.789.2002
laprovenceroseville.com

WENDI MENTINK
Bidwell Street Bistro

1004 E Bidwell St
Folsom, CA 95630
916.984.7500
bidwellstreetbistro.com

PATRICK MULVANEY
Mulvaney's B&L

1215 19th St
Sacramento, CA 95811
916.441.6022
mulvaneysbl.com

BILLY NGO
Kru

2516 J St
Sacramento, CA 95816
916.551.1559
krurestaurant.com

CHRISTIAN PALMOS
Cafeteria 15L

1116 15th St
Sacramento, CA 95814
916.492.1960
cafeteria15l.com

ADAM PECHAL
Thir13en

1300 H St
Sacramento, CA 95814
916.594.7669
thir13en.com

FRED REYES
Buckhorn Steakhouse

2 Main St
Winters, CA 95694
530.795.4503
buckhornsteakhouse.com

OLIVER RIDGEWAY
Grange

926 J St
Sacramento, CA 95814
916.492.4450
grangesacramento.com

RANDALL SELLAND
The Kitchen

2225 Hurley Way
Sacramento, CA 95825
916.568.7171
thekitchenrestaurant.com

MORGAN SONG
Ambience

6440 Fair Oaks Blvd
Sacramento, CA 95608
916.489.8464
ambiencerestaurantsac.com

MICHAEL THIEMANN
Ella

1131 K St
Sacramento, CA 95814
916.443.3772
elladiningroomandbar.com

JAY VEREGGE
Ten22

1022 2nd St
Sacramento, CA 95814
916.441.2211
ten22oldsac.com

ADAM WALSWORTH
Osteria Fasulo

2657 Portage Bay E #8
Davis, CA 95616
530.758.1324
osteriafasulo.com

DENEB WILLIAMS
Firehouse

1112 2nd St
Sacramento, CA 95814
916.442.4772
firehouseoldsac.com

CHRIS WOO
Magpie Café

1409 R St #102
Sacramento, CA 95811
916.452.7594
magpiecaterers.com

NOAH ZONCA
Sacramento, CA

SAN CLEMENTE

CHRIS STARR
Iva Lee's

555 N El Camino Real
San Clemente, CA 92672
949.361.2855
ivalees.com

SAN DIEGO

DOMENICO ALIOTO
Baci Ristorante

1955 Morena Blvd
San Diego, CA 92110
619.275.2094
sandiegobaci.com

PAUL ARIAS
The Fishery

5040 Cass St
San Diego, CA 92109
858.272.9985
thefishery.com

PETE BALISTRERI
Tender Greens

2400 Historic Decatur Rd
San Diego, CA 92106
619.226.6254
tendergreensfood.com

DANIEL BARRON
Blue Point

565 5th Ave
San Diego, CA 92101
619.233.6623
bluepointsd.com

ERIC BAUER
Veladora

5921 Valencia Cir
Rancho Santa Fe, CA 92067
858.759.6216
ranchovalencia.com

AMANDA BAUMGARTEN
Herringbone

7837 Herschel Ave
La Jolla, CA 92037
858.459.0221
herringboneeats.com

OLIVIER BIOTEAU
Farmhouse Café

2121 Adams Ave
San Diego, CA 92116
619.269.9662
farmhousecafesd.com

MAX BONACCI
El Take It Easy

3926 30th St
San Diego, CA 92104
619.291.1859
eltakeiteasy.com

WILLIAM BRADLEY
Addison

5200 Grand Del Mar Way
San Diego, CA 92130
858.314.1900
addisondelmar.com

JAISON BURKE
The Pearl

1410 Rosecrans St
San Diego, CA 92106
619.226.6100
thepearlsd.com

JON BURWELL
Crab Catcher

1298 Prospect St
La Jolla, CA 92037
858.454.9587
crabcatcher.com

MARIO CASSINERI
BICE

425 Island Ave
San Diego, CA 92101
619.239.2423
bicesandiego.com

SERGIO CASTILLO
Brigantine Seafood

2725 Shelter Island Dr
San Diego, CA 92106
619.224.2871
brigantine.com

FABRIZIO CAVALLINI
Bencotto

750 W Fir St
San Diego, CA 92101
619.450.4786
lovebencotto.com

HANIS CAVIN
Carnitas' Snack Shack

2632 University Ave
San Diego, CA 92104
619.294.7675
carnitassnackshack.com

PEPE CCAPATINTA
Piatti

2182 Avenida De La Playa
La Jolla , CA 92037
858.454.1589
piatti.com

STEFANO CERESOLI
Caffe Bella Italia

1525 Garnet Ave
San Diego, CA 92109
858.273.1224
caffebellaitalia.com

KAI CHALATHORN
Amarin Thai

3843 Richmond St
San Diego, CA 92103
619.296.6056
amarinthaisandiego.com

GREGORY CHAVEZ
Leroy's Kitchen + Lounge

1015 Orange Ave
Coronado, CA 92118
619.437.6087
leroyskitchenandlounge.com

TONY CHU JUNG SU
Del Mar Rendezvous

1555 Camino Del Mar #102
Del Mar, CA 92014
858.755.2669
delmarrendezvous.com

JAMES CLARK
Croce's

802 5th Ave
San Diego, CA 92101
619.233.4355
croces.com

BARRY COALSON
La Bastide Bistro

10006 Scripps Ranch Blvd #104
San Diego, CA 92131
858.577.0033
labastidebistro.com

JC COLÓN
Kensington Grill

4055 Adams Ave
San Diego, CA 92116
619.281.4014
kensingtongrill.com

LAURA DE MARTIN
Sally's Seafood on the Water

1 Market Pl
San Diego, CA 92101
619.358.6740
sallyssandiego.com

AMY DIBIASE
Shores

8110 Camino Del Oro
La Jolla, CA 92037
858.456.0600
theshoresrestaurant.com

TREY FOSHEE
George's at the Cove

1250 Prospect St
La Jolla, CA 92037
858.454.4244
georgesatthecove.com

KATIE GREBOW
Café Chloe

721 9th Ave
San Diego, CA 92101
619.232.3242
cafechloe.com

JEAN MICHEL DIOT
Tapenade

7612 Fay Ave
La Jolla , CA 92037
858.551.7500
tapenaderestaurant.com

TOMMY FRAIOLI
Sea Rocket Bistro

3382 30th St
San Diego, CA 92104
619.255.7049
searocketbistro.com

VINCENT GRUMEL
Vincent's

113 W Grand Ave
Escondido, CA 92025
760.745.3835
vincentsongrand.com

SCOTT THOMAS DOLBEE
Kitchen 1540

1540 Camino Del Mar
Del Mar, CA 92014
858.793.6460
laubergedelmar.com

ANTONIO FRISCIA
Gaijin Noodle + Sake House

627 4th Ave
San Diego, CA 92101
619.238.0567
gaijinsd.com

BERNARD GUILLAS
Marine Room

2000 Spindrift Dr
San Diego, CA 92037
858.459.7222
marineroom.com

SIMON DOLINKY
Saltbox

1047 5th Ave
San Diego, CA 92101
619.515.3003
saltboxrestaurant.com

CHRIS GARDNER
Eddie V's

1270 Prospect St
La Jolla, CA 92037
858.459.5500
eddiev.com

JONATHAN HALE
The Prado

1549 El Prado
San Diego, CA 92101
619.557.9441
balboaparkweddings.com

JOHNNY DURAN
Top of the Market

750 N Harbor Dr
San Diego, CA 92132
619.234.4867
thefishmarket.com

MATT GORDON
Urban Solace

3823 30th St
San Diego, CA 92104
619.295.6464
urbansolace.net

FABRICE HARDEL
Westgate Room
at Westgate Hotel

1055 2nd Ave
San Diego, CA 92101
619.238.1818
westgatehotel.com

STEVE FERGUSON
Waters Fine Foods

1105 W Morena Blvd
San Diego, CA 92110
619.276.8803
waterscatering.com

CHRISTIAN GRAVES
Jsix Restaurant

616 J St
San Diego, CA 92101
619.531.8744
jsixrestaurant.com

RICARDO HEREDIA
Alchemy

1503 30th St
San Diego, CA 92102
619.255.0616
alchemysandiego.com

KEN IRVINE
Bleu Boheme

4090 Adams Ave
San Diego, CA 92116
619.255.4167
bleuboheme.com

JEFF JACKSON
The Lodge at Torrey Pines

11480 N Torrey Pines Rd
La Jolla, CA 92037
858.453.4420
lodgetorreypines.com

VICTOR JIMENEZ
Cowboy Star Restaurant
and Butcher Shop

640 10th Ave
San Diego, CA 92101
619.450.5880
thecowboystar.com

LUKE JOHNSON
La Jolla, CA

BRIAN JOHNSON
San Diego, CA

RYAN JOHNSTON
Whisknladle

1044 Wall St
La Jolla , CA 92037
858.551.7575
whisknladle.com

SANDEEP KAMBO
Royal India

329 Market St
San Diego, CA 92101
619.269.9999
royalindia.com

JAGDEEP KAMBO
Royal India

3860 Valley Center Dr
San Diego, CA 92103
858.792.1111
royalindia.com

AL KELLENBERGER
The Range Kitchen & Cocktails

1263 University Ave
San Diego, CA 92103
619.269.1222
therangesd.com

JASON KNIBB
NINE-TEN

910 Prospect St
La Jolla, CA 92037
858.964.5400
nine-ten.com

CHRIS KURTH
Grant Grill

326 Broadway
San Diego, CA 92101
619.744.2077
grantgrill.com

SEAN LANGLAIS
The Oceanaire Seafood Room

400 J St
San Diego, CA 92101
619.858.2277
theoceanaire.com

HONG LUU
Siagon on Fifth

3900 5th Ave
San Diego, CA 92103
619.220.8828
saigononfifth.menutoeat.com

BRAD LYONS
Slater's 50/50

2750 Dewey Rd
San Diego, CA 92807
619.398.2600
slaters5050.com

P.J. MACALUSO
Manhattan

7766 Fay Ave
La Jolla, CA 92037
858.459.0700
manhattanoflajolla.com

COLIN MACLAGGAN
Ave 5

2760 5th Ave #100
San Diego, CA 92103
619.542.0394
avenue5restaurant.com

JOE MAGNANELLI
Cucina Urbana

505 Laurel St
San Diego, CA 92101
619.239.2222
cucinaurbana.com

JASON MAITLAND
Red Light District

409 F St
San Diego, CA 92101
619.255.2800
rldsd.com

BRIAN MALARKEY
Searsucker

611 5th Ave
San Diego, CA 92101
619.233.7327
searsucker.com

GEORGE MORRIS
Beaumont's Eatery

5662 La Jolla Blvd
La Jolla, CA 92037
858.459.0474
beaumontseatery.com

FRED PIEHL
The Smoking Goat

3408 30th St
San Diego, CA 92104
619.955.5295
thesmokinggoatrestaurant.com

MICHEL MALECOT
The French Gourmet

960 Turquoise St
San Diego, CA 92109
858.488.1725
thefrenchgourmet.com

CUC THI NGUYEN
Le Bambou

2634 Del Mar Heights Rd
Del Mar, CA 92014
858.259.8138
lebamboudelmar.com

PATRICK PONSATY
Coronado, CA

EUGENIO MARTIGNAGO
West Steak and Seafood

4980 Avenida Encinas
Carlsbad, CA 92008
760.930.9100
weststeakandseafood.com

PAUL NILES
Vagabond Kitchen

2310 30th St
San Diego, CA 92104
619.255.1035
vagabondkitchen.com

ASHLEY POPAT
Masala

314 5th Ave
San Diego, CA 92101
619.232.5050
masalarestaurant.com

PAUL MCCABE
La Valencia Hotel

1132 Prospect St
La Jolla, CA 92037
858.551.3765
lavalencia.com

MOUMEN NOURI
Kous Kous Moroccan Bistro

3940 4th Ave #110
San Diego, CA 92103
619.295.5560
kouskousrestaurant.com

BRIAN REDZIKOWSKI
Flavor Del Mar

1555 Camino Del Mar #322
Del Mar, CA 92014
858.755.3663
flavordelmar.com

JASON MCLEOD
Box Tree Restaurants Inc.

San Diego, CA
312.852.6308
chefjasonmcleod.com

YUKITO OTA
Sushi Ota

4529 Mission Bay Dr
San Diego, CA 92109
858.270.5047
sushiota.com

JOHN REYNOLDS
Palm

615 J St
San Diego, CA 92101
619.702.6500
thepalm.com

RAFFAELLA MORELLI
Salvatore's Cucina Italiana

750 Front St
San Diego, CA 92101
619.544.1865
salvatoresdowntown.com

JOHN PARKS
Fish 101

1468 N Coast Hwy 101
Encinitas, CA 92011
760.943.6221
fish101restaurant.com

SAL REYNOSO
Donovan's

4340 La Jolla Village Dr
La Jolla , CA 92122
858.450.6666
donovanssteakhouse.com

MATT RICHMAN
Table 926

926 Turquoise St
San Diego, CA 92109
858.539.0926
table926.com

JEFF ROSSMAN
Terra American Bistro

7091 El Cajon Blvd
San Diego, CA 92115
619.293.7088
terrasd.com

ROB RUIZ
Harney Sushi

3964 Harney St
San Diego, CA 92110
619.295.3272
harneysushi.com

CARL SCHROEDER
Market

3702 Via De La Valle
Del Mar, CA 92014
858.523.0007
marketdelmar.com

DEBORAH SCOTT
Vintana Wine + Dine

1205 Auto Park Way
Escondido, CA 92029
760.745.7777
cohnrestaurants.com

NICK SHINTON
Truluck's

8990 University Center Ln
San Diego, CA 92122
858.453.2583
trulucks.com

ANTHONY SINSAY
Burlap

12995 El Camino Real #21
Del Mar, CA 92130
858.369.5700
burlapeats.com

MAREYJA SISBARRO
Brockton Villa

1235 Coast Blvd
La Jolla , CA 92037
858.454.7393
brocktonvilla.com

JON SLOAN
Roy's

333 W Harbor Dr
San Diego, CA 92101
619.239.7697
roysrestaurant.com

JEFFREY STRAUSS
Pamplemousse Grille

514 Via De La Valle
Solana Beach, CA 92075
858.792.9090
pgrille.com

SUREE SUKSUDECHA
Siam Nara Thai Cuisine

8993 Mira Mesa Blvd
San Diego, CA 92126
858.566.1300
siamnara.com

RICH SWEENEY
R Gang Eatery

3683 5th Ave
San Diego, CA 92103
619.677.2845
rgangeatery.com

TYLER THRASHER
San Diego, CA

KATSUYA UECHI
Katsuya

600 F St
San Diego, CA 92101
619.814.2000
sbe.com

MANNY VARGAS
Café Bleu Bistro and Wine Bar

807 W Washington St
San Diego, CA 92103
619.291.1717
cafebleusd.com

VINCENT VIALE
Bernard'O

12457 Rancho Bernardo Rd
San Diego, CA 92128
858.487.7171
bernardorestaurant.com

STEPHANE VOITZWINKLER
Bertrand at Mister A's

2550 5th Ave #406
San Diego, CA 92103
619.239.1377
bertrandatmisteras.com

DAVID WARNER
JRDN

723 Felspar St
Pacific Beach, CA 92109
858.270.2323
t23hotel.com

CHAD WHITE
Sea Rocket Bistro

3382 30th St
San Diego, CA 92104
619.255.7049
searocketbistro.com

STEPHEN WINDOW
Roppongi

875 Prospect St
La Jolla, CA 92037
858.551.5252
roppongiusa.com

MARTIN WOESLE
Mille Fleurs

6009 Paseo Delicias
Rancho Santa Fe, CA 92067
858.756.3085
millefleurs.com

ABEL WOLDEMICHAEL
Muzita Abyssinian Bistro

4651 Park Blvd
San Diego, CA 92116
619.546.7900
muzita.com

SAN FRANCISCO

MATTHEW ACCARRINO
SPQR

1911 Fillmore St
San Francisco, CA 94115
415.771.7779
spqrsf.com

NICK ADAMS
Corner Store

5 Masonic Ave
San Francisco, CA 94118
415.359.1800
thecornerstore-sf.com

ALEXANDER ALIOTO
Seven Hills

1550 Hyde St
San Francisco, CA 94109
415.775.1550
sevenhillssf.com

CARLOS ALTAMIRANO
Piqueo's

830 Cortland Ave
San Francisco, CA 94110
415.282.8812
piqueos.com

SHARON ARDIANA
Gialina

2842 Diamond St
San Francisco, CA 94131
415.239.8500
gialina.com

MIKAEL AUDRY
Hyde Street Bistro

1521 Hyde St
San Francisco, CA 94109
415.292.4415
hydestreetbistrosf.com

NICOLAUS BALLA
Bar Tartine

561 Valencia St
San Francisco, CA 94110
415.487.1600
bartartine.com

BRIDGET BATSON
Gitane

6 Claude Ln
San Francisco, CA 94108
415.788.6686
gitanerestaurant.com

DAVID BAZIRGAN
Fifth Floor

12 4th St
San Francisco, CA 94103
415.348.1555
fifthfloorrestaurant.com

JONATHAN BEARD
Bistro Aix

3340 Steiner St
San Francisco, CA 94123
415.202.0100
bistroaix.com

EDGAR BEAS
Chez Papa Resto

4 Mint Plaza
San Francisco, CA 94103
415.546.4134
chezpaparesto.com

CHRIS BEERMAN
Citizen's Band

1198 Folsom St
San Francisco, CA 94103
415.556.4901
citizensbandsf.com

JASON BERTHOLD
RN74

301 Mission St
San Francisco, CA 94105
415.543.7474
rn74.com

NICOLAS BORZEE
Bouche

603 Bush St
San Francisco, CA 94108
415.956.0396
bouchesf.com

DANNY BOWIEN
Mission Chinese

2234 Mission St
San Francisco, CA 94110
415.863.2800
missionchinesefood.com

STUART BRIOZA
State Bird Provisions

1529 Fillmore St
San Francisco, CA 94115
415.795.1272
statebirdsf.com

MICHAEL BUHAGIAR
Harris'

2100 Van Ness Ave
San Francisco, CA 94109
415.673.1888
harrisrestaurant.com

JULIO CACERES
Le P'tit Laurent

699 Chenery St
San Francisco, CA 94131
415.334.3235
leptitlaurent.net

ALESSANDRO CAMPITELLI
Chiaroscuro

550 Washington St
San Francisco, CA 94111
415.362.6012
chiaroscurosf.com

ROGER CHONG
Zushi Puzzle

1910 Lombard St
San Francisco, CA 94123
415.931.9319
zushipuzzle.com

JOHN CLARK
Foreign Cinema

2534 Mission St
San Francisco, CA 94110
415.648.7600
foreigncinema.com

THIERRY CLEMENT
L'Ardoise

151 Noe St
San Francisco, CA 94114
415.437.2600
ardoisesf.com

MASSIMILIANO CONTI
La Ciccia

291 30th St
San Francisco, CA 94131
415.550.8114
laciccia.com

BRETT COOPER
Outerlands

4001 Judah St
San Francisco, CA 94122
415.661.6140
outerlandssf.com

CHRIS COSENTINO
Incanto

1550 Church St
San Francisco, CA 94131
415.641.4500
incanto.biz

ERIK COSSELMON
Kokkari

200 Jackson St
San Francisco, CA 94111
415.981.0983
kokkari.com

DOMINIQUE CRENN
Atelier Crenn

3127 Fillmore St
San Francisco, CA 94123
415.440.0460
ateliercrenn.com

GARY DANKO
Restaurant Gary Danko

800 N Point St
San Francisco, CA 94109
415.749.2060
garydanko.com

DANEL DE BETELU
Baker Street Bistro

2953 Baker St
San Francisco, CA 94123
415.931.1475
bakerstreetbistro.com

BEN DE VRIES
Luella

1896 Hyde St
San Francisco, CA 94109
415.674.4343
luellasf.com

GAINES DOBBIN
Chenery Park

683 Chenery St
San Francisco, CA 94131
415.337.8537
chenerypark.com

MARK DOMMEN
One Market

1 Market St
San Francisco, CA 94105
415.777.5577
onemarket.com

JOEY ELENTERIO
Aziza

5800 Geary Blvd
San Francisco, CA 94121
415.752.2222
aziza-sf.com

JASON FOX
Commonwealth

2224 Mission St
San Francisco, CA 94110
415.355.1500
commonwealthsf.com

RUGGERO GADALDI
Pesce

2227 Polk St
San Francisco, CA 94109
415.928.8025
pescebarsf.com

PHILIPPE GARDELLE
Chapeau!

126 Clement St
San Francisco, CA 94118
415.387.0408
chapeausf.com

GONZALO GONZALEZ
Nopalito

306 Broderick St
San Francisco, CA 94117
415.437.0303
nopalitosf.com

SRIJITH GOPINATHAN
Taj Campton Place

340 Stockton St
San Francisco, CA 94108
415.955.5555
tajhotels.com

MARK GORDON
Rose's Café

2298 Union St
San Francisco, CA 94123
415.775.2200
rosescafesf.com

SUZETTE GRESHAM
Acquerello

1722 Sacramento St
San Francisco, CA 94109
415.567.5432
acquerello.com

ANDY HENDERSON
Local: Mission Eatery

3111 24th St
San Francisco, CA 94110
415.655.3422
localmissioneatery.com

GERALD HIRIGOYEN
Piperade

1015 Battery St
San Francisco, CA 94111
415.391.2555
piperade.com

EDDIE HONG
Kiji

1009 Guerrero St
San Francisco, CA 94110
415.282.0400
kijirestaurant.com

BARRY HORTON
Local Love Catering

San Francisco, CA
510.917.0190
locallovecatering.com

BRANDON JEW
Bar Agricole

355 11th St
San Francisco, CA 94103
415.355.9400
baragricole.com

LAURENCE JOSSEL
Nopa

560 Divisadero St
San Francisco, CA 94117
415.864.8643
nopasf.com

RAVI KAPUR
Liholiho Yacht Club

San Francisco, CA
liholihoyachtclub.com

LAURENT KATGELY
Chez Spencer

82 14th St
San Francisco, CA 94103
415.864.2191
chezspencer.net

HUBERT KELLER
Fleur de Lys

777 Sutter St
San Francisco, CA 94109
415.673.7779
hubertkeller.com

NICOLE KRASINKI
State Bird Provisions

1529 Fillmore St
San Francisco, CA 94115
415.795.1272
statebirdsf.com

MOURAD LAHLOU
Aziza

5800 Geary Blvd
San Francisco, CA 94121
415.752.2222
aziza-sf.com

DENNIS LEARY
Canteen

817 Sutter St
San Francisco, CA 94109
415.928.8870
sfcanteen.com

COREY LEE
Benu

22 Hawthorne St
San Francisco, CA 94105
415.685.4860
benusf.com

MARK LIBERMAN
AQ

1085 Mission St
San Francisco, CA 94103
415.341.9000
aq-sf.com

JACQUES MANUERA
Bistro Central Parc

560 Central Ave
San Francisco, CA 94117
415.931.7272
bistrocentralparc.com

RAJKO MARIN
Tadich Grill

240 California St
San Francisco, CA 94111
415.391.1849
tadichgrill.com

YO MATSUZAKI
Ozumo

161 Steuart St
San Francisco, CA 94105
415.882.1333
ozumosanfrancisco.com

TRIPP MAULDIN
San Francisco, CA

PAMELA MAZZOLA
Prospect

300 Spear St
San Francisco, CA 94105
415.247.7770
prospectsf.com

MATT MCNAMARA
Sons & Daughters

708 Bush St
San Francisco, CA 94108
415.391.8311
sonsanddaughterssf.com

THOMAS MCNAUGHTON
Flour + Water

2401 Harrison St
San Francisco, CA 94110
415.826.7000
flourandwater.com

MICHAEL MINA
Michael Mina

252 California St
San Francisco, CA 94111
415.397.9222
michaelmina.net

TEAGUE MORIARTY
Sons & Daughters

708 Bush St
San Francisco, CA 94108
415.391.8311
sonsanddaughterssf.com

MORGAN MUELLER
Jardiniere

300 Grove St
San Francisco, CA 94102
415.861.5555
jardiniere.com

NANCY OAKES
Boulevard

1 Mission St
San Francisco, CA 94105
415.543.6084
boulevardrestaurant.com

BRADLEY OGDEN
One Market

1 Market St
San Francisco, CA 94105
415.777.5577
onemarket.com

ROLAND PASSOT
La Folie

2316 Polk St
San Francisco, CA 94109
415.776.5577
lafolie.com

DANIEL PATTERSON
Coi

373 Broadway
San Francisco, CA 94133
415.393.9000
coirestaurant.com

MATTHEW PAUL
Slow Club

2501 Mariposa St
San Francisco, CA 94110
415.241.9390
slowclub.com

CHARLES PHAN
Slanted Door

1 Ferry Building #3
San Francisco, CA 94111
415.861.8032
slanteddoor.com

GAYLE PIRIE
Foreign Cinema

2534 Mission St
San Francisco, CA 94110
415.648.7600
foreigncinema.com

GERALDO RAMIREZ
The House of Prime Rib

1906 Van Ness Ave
San Francisco, CA 94109
415.885.4605
houseofprimerib.net

JUDY RODGERS
Zuni Café

1658 Market St
San Francisco, CA 94102
415.552.2522
zunicafe.com

RICHARD ROSEN
Chenery Park

683 Chenery St
San Francisco, CA 94131
415.337.8537
chenerypark.com

MITCHELL ROSENTHAL
Town Hall

342 Howard St
San Francisco, CA 94105
415.908.3900
townhallsf.com

AUGUST SCHUCHMAN
Woodhouse Fish Co.

2073 Market St
San Francisco, CA 94114
415.437.2722
woodhousefish.com

AMARYLL SCHWERTNER
Boulette's Larder

1 Ferry Building #48
San Francisco, CA 94111
415.399.1155
bouletteslarder.com

GREGORY SHORT
Masa's Restaurant

648 Bush St
San Francisco, CA 94108
415.989.7154
masasrestaurant.com

RON SIEGEL
Michael Mina

252 California St
San Francisco, CA 94111
415.397.9222
michaelmina.net

JOSHUA SKENES
Saison

178 Townsend St
San Francisco, CA 94107
415.828.7990
saisonsf.com

CRAIG STOLL
Delfina

3621 18th St
San Francisco, CA 94110
415.552.4055
delfinasf.com

MATT STRAUS
Heirloom Café

2500 Folsom St
San Francisco, CA 94110
415.821.2500
heirloom-sf.com

KEIKO TAKAHASHI
Keiko a Nob Hill

1250 Jones St
San Francisco, CA 94109
415.829.7141
keikoanobhill.com

DAVID TAYLOR
San Francisco, CA

STAFFAN TERJE
Perbacco

230 California St
San Francisco, CA 94111
415.955.0663
perbaccosf.com

SEAN THOMAS
The Blue Plate

3218 Mission St
San Francisco, CA 94110
415.282.6777
blueplatesf.com

JEREMIAH TOWER
San Francisco, CA

jeremiahtower.com

SAN JOSE

JUN CHON
Bluefin

754 The Alameda #10
San Jose, CA 95126
408.931.6875
bluefinsj.com

CHIHO LEE
Daimo Chinese Restaurant

1456 E 14th St
San Leandro, CA 94577
510.351.8131
daimorestaurant.com

SAN LUIS OBISPO

MICHAEL TUSK
Quince

470 Pacific Ave
San Francisco, CA 94133
415.775.8500
quincerestaurant.com

SCOTT COOPER
Le Papillon

410 Saratoga Ave
San Jose, CA 95129
408.296.3730
lepapillon.com

SHAUN BEHRENS
Luna Red

1023 Chorro St
San Luis Obispo, CA 93401
805.540.5243
lunaredslo.com

PHIL WEST
Range

842 Valencia St
San Francisco, CA 94110
415.282.8283
rangesf.com

ANDY HATCHER
The Grill on the Alley

172 S Market St
San Jose, CA 95113
408.294.2244
thegrill.com

GIUSEPPE DIFRONZO
Giuseppe's

891 Price St
Pismo Beach, CA 93449
805.773.2870
giuseppesrestaurant.com

DENNIS WONG
Le Soleil

133 Clement St
San Francisco, CA 94118
415.668.4848
lesoleilsf.com

STEVE HAUGHIE
Arcadia

100 W San Carlos St
San Jose, CA 95113
408.278.4555
michaelmina.net

MIKE DUFFY
Novo

726 Higuera St
San Luis Obispo, CA 93401
805.543.3986
novorestaurant.com

HOWARD WONG
Tommy Toy's

655 Montgomery St
San Francisco, CA 94111
415.397.4888
tommytoys.com

ROBERT SAPIRMAN
Citrus

355 Santana Row
San Jose, CA 95128
408.551.0010
hotelvalencia-santanarow.com

TOM FUNDARO
Villa Creek

1144 Pine St
Paso Robles, CA 93446
805.238.3000
villacreek.com

SAN LEANDRO

MARC ZIMMERMAN
Alexander's

448 Brannan St
San Francisco, CA 94107
415.495.1111
alexanderssteakhouse.com

CHEHENG LEE
Daimo Chinese Restaurant

1456 E 14th St
San Leandro, CA 94577
510.351.8131
daimorestaurant.com

LAURENT GRANGIEN
Bistro Laurent

1202 Pine St
Paso Robles, CA 93446
805.226.8191
bistrolaurent.com

CHRIS KOBAYASHI
Artisan

839 12th St
Paso Robles, CA 93446
805.237.8084
artisanpasorobles.com

ERICH KOBERL
Koberl at Blue

998 Monterey St
San Luis Obispo, CA 93401
805.783.1135
epkoberl.com

JENSEN LORENZEN
The Cass House

222 N Ocean Ave
Cayucos, CA 93430
805.995.3669
casshouseinn.com

SANTOS MACDONAL
Il Cortile

608 12th St #101
Paso Robles, CA 93446
805.226.0300
ilcortileristorante.com

GENNARO ROSATO
Gennaro's Grill and Garden

450 Marsh St
San Luis Obispo, CA 93401
805.782.9999
gennarosgrillandgarden.com

NEIL SMITH
Windows on the Water

699 Embarcadero #7
Morro Bay, CA 93442
805.772.0677
windowsmb.com

WILL TORRES
Restaurant at JUSTIN Vineyards

11680 Chimney Rock Rd
Paso Robles, CA 93446
805.238.6932
justinwine.com

GREGG WANGARD
Marisol at the Cliffs

2757 Shell Beach Rd
Pismo Beach, CA 93449
805.773.2511
cliffsresort.com

CHARLES WEBER
Adelina's Bistro

1645 Trilogy Pkwy
Nipomo, CA 93444
805.343.7500
adelinasbistro.com

SAN MATEO

SACHIN CHOPRA
All Spice

1602 S El Camino Real
San Mateo, CA 94402
650.627.4303
allspicerestaurant.com

PRESTON DISHMAN
Viognier

222 E 4th Ave
San Mateo, CA 94401
650.685.3727
viognierrestaurant.com

SANTA ANA

SAL FERRARA
Antonello Ristorante

3800 S Plaza Dr
Santa Ana, CA 92704
714.751.7153
antonello.com

ARON HABIGER
The Crosby

400 N Broadway
Santa Ana, CA 92701
714.543.3543
thisisthecrosby.com

LUIS PEREZ
Lola Gaspar

211 W 2nd St
Santa Ana, CA 92701
714.972.1172
lolagaspar.com

JASON QUINN
Playground

220 E 4th St #102
Santa Ana, CA 92701
714.560.4444
playgrounddtsa.com

SANTA BARBARA

MOLLIE AHLSTRAND
Trattoria Mollie

1250 Coast Village Rd
Montecito, CA 93108
805.565.9381
trattoriamollie.com

ALEXIS BAYET
Arnoldi's Café

600 Olive St
Santa Barbara, CA 93101
805.962.5394
arnoldis.com

ARMANDO BENITEZ
Cava

1212 Coast Village Rd
Montecito, CA 93108
805.969.8500
cavarestaurant.com

ALESSANDRO CARTUMINI
Bella Vista

1260 Channel Dr
Santa Barbara, CA 93108
805.969.2261
fourseasons.com

JOHN DOWNEY
Downey's

1305 State St
Santa Barbara, CA 93101
805.966.5006
downeyssb.com

DARIO FURLATI
Ca' Dario

37 E Victoria St
Santa Barbara, CA 93101
805.884.9419
cadario.net

AVERY HARDEN
Arts & Letters Café

7 E Anapamu St
Santa Barbara, CA 93101
805.730.1463
artsandletterscafe.com

BRANDON HUGHES
Wine Cask

813 Anacapa St
Santa Barbara, CA 93101
805.966.9463
winecask.com

MATTHEW JOHNSON
Stonehouse

900 San Ysidro Ln
Santa Barbara, CA 93108
805.565.1724
sanysidroranch.com

GREG MURPHY
Bouchon Santa Barbara

9 W Victoria St
Santa Barbara, CA 93101
805.730.1160
bouchonsantabarbara.com

ROBERT PEREZ
Seagrass

30 E Ortega St
Santa Barbara, CA 93101
805.963.1012
seagrassrestaurant.com

DAVID REARDON
Miro

8301 Hollister Ave
Goleta, CA 93117
805.571.4204
bacararesort.com

LEONARD SCHWARTZ
Lucky's

1279 Coast Village Rd
Montecito, CA 93108
805.565.7540
luckys-steakhouse.com

JAMES SIAO
Coast

31 W Carrillo St
Santa Barbara, CA 93101
805.879.9100
canarysantabarbara.com

JAMES SLY
Sly's

686 Linden Ave
Carpinteria, CA 93013
805.684.6666
slysonline.com

RAMON VELAZQUEZ
Cielito

1114 State St
Santa Barbara, CA 93101
805.965.4770
cielitorestaurant.com

JUSTIN WEST
Julienne

138 E Canon Perdido St
Santa Barbara, CA 93101
805.845.6488
restaurantjulienne.com

SANTA CATALINA ISLAND

PAUL HANCOCK
Avalon Grille

423 Crescent Ave
Avalon, CA 90704
310.510.7494
visitcatalinaisland.com

SANTA CRUZ

BRANDON DIFIGILO
Soquel, CA

BRIAN DROSENOS
Aquarius

175 W Cliff Dr
Santa Cruz, CA 95060
831.460.5012
aquariussantacruz.com

JOSE ESPINOZA
El Palomar

1336 Pacific Ave
Santa Cruz, CA 95060
831.425.7575
elpalomarcilantros.com

GIOVANNI GUERISOLI
Ristorante Barolo

8041 Soquel Dr
Aptos, CA 95003
831.688.8495
baroloristorante.com

ASHLEY HOSMER
Shadowbrook

1750 Wharf Rd
Capitola, CA 95010
831.475.1511
shadowbrook-capitola.com

RYAN ISAAK
Santa Cruz , CA

MURIEL LOUBIERE
Au Midi

7960 Soquel Dr
Aptos, CA 95003
831.685.2600
aumidi.com

SANTOS MAJANO
Soif Wine Bar

105 Walnut Ave
Santa Cruz, CA 95060
831.423.2020
soifwine.com

RYAN SHELTON
Le Cigare Volant

328 Ingalls St
Santa Cruz, CA 95060
831.425.6771
lecigarevolant.com

KATHERINE STERN
La Posta

538 Seabright Ave
Santa Cruz, CA 95062
831.457.2782
lapostarestaurant.com

DAMANI THOMAS
Oswald

121 Soquel Ave
Santa Cruz, CA 95060
831.423.7427
oswaldrestaurant.com

AYOMA WILEN
Pearl of the Ocean

736 Water St
Santa Cruz, CA 95060
831.457.2350
pearloftheocean.net

SANTA MONICA

JASON BOWLIN
Catch

1910 Ocean Way
Santa Monica, CA 90405
310.581.7714
hotelcasadelmar.com

RIAN BRANDENBURG
Tender Greens

201 Arizona Ave
Santa Monica, CA 90401
310.587.2777
tendergreens.com

BRUCE CHOI
Enterprise Fish Co.

174 Kinney St
Santa Monica, CA 90405
310.392.8366
enterprisefishco.com

JOSIAH CITRIN
Melisse

1104 Wilshire Blvd
Santa Monica, CA 90401
310.395.0881
melisse.com

COLLIN CRANNELL
The Lobster

1602 Ocean Ave
Santa Monica, CA 90401
310.458.9294
thelobster.com

STEFANO DE LORENZO
La Botte

620 Santa Monica Blvd
Santa Monica, CA 90401
310.576.3072
labottesantamonica.com

TONY DISALVO
Whist

1819 Ocean Ave
Santa Monica, CA 90401
310.260.7511
viceroyhotelsandresorts.com

RAY GARCIA
Fig

101 Wilshire Blvd
Santa Monica, CA 90401
310.319.3111
figsantamonica.com

MASSIMO GASPARINI
Santa Monica, CA

SETH GREENBERG
The Penthouse

1111 2nd St
Santa Monica, CA 90403
310.393.8080
thehuntleyhotel.com

ANDREW KIRSCHNER
Tar and Roses

602 Santa Monica Blvd
Santa Monica, CA 90401
310.587.0700
tarandroses.com

JOHN-CARLOS KURAMOTO
Michael's

1147 3rd St
Santa Monica, CA 90403
310.451.0843
michaelssantamonica.com

JOSIE LE BALCH
Josie

2424 Pico Blvd
Santa Monica, CA 90405
310.581.9888
josierestaurant.com

RAPHAEL LUNETTA
JiRaffe

502 Santa Monica Blvd
Santa Monica, CA 90401
310.917.6671
jirafferestaurant.com

JEFF MAHIN
Stella Rossa Pizza Bar

2000 Main St
Santa Monica, CA 90405
310.396.9250
stellarossapizzabar.com

RENE MATA
Chinois on Main

2709 Main St
Santa Monica, CA 90405
310.392.9025
wolfgangpuck.com

SVEN MEDE
One Pico

1 Pico Blvd
Santa Monica, CA 90405
310.587.1717
shuttersonthebeach.com

MARK MOLLICA
La Vecchia Cucina

2654 Main St
Santa Monica, CA 90405
310.399.7979
lavecchiacucina.com

WASANA PISAIKUN
Bangkok West

606 Santa Monica Blvd
Santa Monica, CA 90401
310.395.9658
bangkokwestthaicuisine.com

MIGUEL RAMIREZ
Chez Jay

1657 Ocean Ave
Santa Monica, CA 90401
310.395.1741
chezjays.com

PERFECTO ROCHER
Santa Monica, CA

JONATHAN NEIL ROGERS
Bizou Grill

2450 Colorado Ave #1050W
Santa Monica, CA 90404
310.453.8500
cafebizou.com

DOMENICO SALVATORE
Il Forno

2901 Ocean Park Blvd
Santa Monica, CA 90405
310.450.1241
ilfornocaffe.com

HIROSHI SHIMA
Sushi Roku

1401 Ocean Ave
Santa Monica, CA 90401
310.458.4771
innovativedining.com

NICK SHIPP
Upper West

3321 Pico Blvd
Santa Monica, CA 90405
310.586.1111
theupperwest.com

SARATOGA

PETER ARMELLINO
Plumed Horse

14555 Big Basin Way
Saratoga, CA 95070
408.867.4711
plumedhorse.com

JOSIAH SLONE
Sent Sovi

14583 Big Basin Way
Saratoga, CA 95070
408.867.3110
sentsovi.com

SAUSALITO

CHAD CALLAHAN
Sausalito, CA

YOSHI DARRIN
Sushi Ran

107 Caledonia St
Sausalito, CA 94965
415.332.3620
sushiran.com

JUSTIN EVERETT
Murray's Circle

601 Murray Cir
Sausalito, CA 94965
415.339.4750
cavallopoint.com

A SAMANA
Scoma's

588 Bridgeway
Sausalito, CA 94965
415.332.9551
scomassausalito.com

OLIVIER SOUVESTRE
Le Garage

85 Liberty Ship Way #109
Sausalito, CA 94965
415.332.5625
legaragebistrosausalito.com

SEAL BEACH

VICTOR AVILA
Spaghettini

3005 Old Ranch Pkwy
Seal Beach, CA 90740
562.596.2199
spaghettini.com

SHERMAN OAKS

HENRI ABERGEL
Mistral

13422 Ventura Blvd
Sherman Oaks, CA 91423
818.981.6650
mistralrestaurant.com

ROGER FABROCINI
Fab's

4336 Van Nuys Blvd
Sherman Oaks, CA 91403
818.995.2933
fabscornercucina.com

AARON ROBINS
Boneyard Bistro

13539 Ventura Blvd
Sherman Oaks, CA 91423
818.906.7427
boneyardbistro.com

PAUL ROSENBLUH
Firefly Bistro

1009 El Centro St
South Pasadena, CA 91030
626.441.2443
eatatfirefly.com

SONOMA

BRIAN ANDERSON
Bistro 29

620 5th St
Santa Rosa, CA 95404
707.546.2929
bistro29.com

DINO BUGICA
Diavola

21021 Geyserville Ave
Geyserville, CA 95441
707.814.0111
diavolapizzeria.com

ANDREW CAIN
Sante

100 Boyes Blvd
Sonoma, CA 95476
707.938.9000
fairmont.com

CARLO CAVALLO
Meritage Martini
Oyster Bar & Grille

165 W Napa St
Sonoma, CA 95476
707.938.9430
sonomameritage.com

GARY CHU
Osake

2446 Patio Ct
Santa Rosa, CA 95405
707.542.8282
osake.garychus.com

NICK DEMEREST
Harvest Moon Café

487 1st St W
Sonoma, CA 95476
707.933.8160
harvestmooncafesonoma.com

DUSKIE ESTES
zazu kitchen + farm

3535 Guerneville Rd
Santa Rosa, CA 95401
707.523.4814
zazurestaurant.com

RYAN FANCHER
Barndiva

231 Center St
Healdsburg, CA 95448
707.431.0100
barndiva.com

ANTONIO GHILARDUCCI
Depot Hotel

241 1st St W
Sonoma, CA 95476
707.938.2980
depotsonoma.com

MATEO GRANADOS
Mateo's

214 Healdsburg Ave
Healdsburg, CA 95448
707.433.1520
mateoscocinalatina.com

CHAD HARRIS
Fremont Diner

2698 Fremont Dr
Sonoma, CA 95476
707.938.7370
thefremontdiner.com

DOUGLAS KEANE
Healdsburg Bar and Grill

245 Healdsburg Ave
Healdsburg, CA 95448
707.433.3333
healdsburgbarandgrill.com

JEFFERY LLOYD
Café La Haye

140 E Napa St
Sonoma, CA 95476
707.935.5994
cafelahaye.com

DANNY MAI
Tolay

745 Baywood Dr
Petaluma, CA 94954
707.283.2900
tolayrestaurant.com

LOUIS MALDONADO
Spoonbar

219 Healdsburg Ave
Healdsburg, CA 95448
707.433.7222
spoonbar.com

JESSE MALGREN
Madrona Manor

1001 Westside Rd
Healdsburg, CA 95448
800.258.4003
madronamanor.com

JEFF MALL
Zin

344 Center St
Healdsburg, CA 95448
707.473.0946
zinrestaurant.com

ED METCALFE
Shiso

19161 California 12
Sonoma, CA 95476
707.933.9331
shisorestaurant.com

ARMANDO NAVARRO
El Dorado Kitchen

405 1st St W
Sonoma, CA 95476
707.996.3030
eldoradosonoma.com

NORMAN OWENS
Hot Box Grill

18350 California 12
Sonoma, CA 95476
707.939.8383
hotboxgrill.com

ARI ROSEN
Campo Fina

330 Healdsburg Ave
Healdsburg, CA 95448
707.395.4640
campo-fina.com

JOSH SILVERS
Jackson's

135 4th St
Santa Rosa, CA 95401
707.545.4300
jacksonsbarandoven.com

MARK STARK
Willi's Wine Bar

4404 Old Redwood Hwy
Santa Rosa, CA 95403
707.526.3096
starkrestaurants.com

JOHN STEWART
zazu kitchen + farm

3535 Guerneville Rd
Santa Rosa, CA 95401
707.523.4814
zazurestaurant.com

KEN TOMINAGA
Hana

101 Golf Course Dr
Rohnert Park, CA 94928
707.586.0270
hanajapanese.com

JOHN TOULZE
the girl and the fig

110 W Spain St
Sonoma, CA 95476
707.938.3634
thegirlandthefig.com

ANN TUSSEY
Sweet T's Restaurant + Bar

2097 Stagecoach Rd #100
Santa Rosa, CA 95404
707.595.3935
sweettssr.com

DUSTIN VALETTE
Dry Creek Kitchen

317 Healdsburg Ave
Healdsburg, CA 95448
707.431.0330
charliepalmer.com

BRIAN WEST
Risibisi

154 Petaluma Blvd N
Petaluma, CA 94952
707.766.7600
risibisirestaurant.com

ANDREW WILSON
Carneros Bistro & Wine Bar

1325 Broadway
Sonoma, CA 95476
707.931.2042
thelodgeatsonoma.com

STOCKTON

DANIEL DURAND
Le Bistro

3121 W Benjamin Holt Dr
Stockton, CA 95219
209.951.0885
lebistrostockton.com

DIDIER GERBI
Towne House at Wine & Roses

2505 W Turner Rd
Lodi, CA 95242
209.371.6160
loditownehouse.com

RUBEN LARRAZOLO
Alebrijes Mexican Bistro

10 W Oak St
Lodi, CA 95240
209.368.1831
alebrijesbistro.com

JIM MURDACA
Pietro's

317 E Kettleman Ln
Lodi, CA 95240
209.368.0613
pietroslodi.com

STUDIO CITY

MARCOS ARANA
River Rock Lounge

12833 Ventura Blvd
Studio City, CA 91604
818.432.7500
riverloungela.com

GUSTAVO GONZALES
The Bistro Garden at Coldwater

12950 Ventura Blvd
Studio City, CA 91604
818.501.0202
bistrogarden.com

ADAM HORTON
Raphael

11616 Ventura Blvd
Studio City, CA 91604
818.505.3337
raphaelonventura.com

THE SEA RANCH

PHILLIP KAUFMAN
Black Point Grill

60 Sea Walk Dr
The Sea Ranch, CA 95497
707.785.2371
searanchlodge.com

TIBURON

JUAN SALAZAR
The Caprice

2000 Paradise Dr
Tiburon, CA 94920
415.435.3400
thecaprice.com

TOLUCA LAKE

DAVIDE GHIZZONI
Ca' Del Sole

4100 Cahuenga Blvd
Toluca Lake, CA 91602
818.985.4669
cadelsole.com

TRUCKEE

DOUGLAS DALE
Wolfdale's

640 N Lake Blvd
Tahoe City, CA 96145
530.583.5700
wolfdales.com

BEN DUFRESNE
PlumpJack Café Squaw Valley

1920 Squaw Valley Rd
Olympic Valley, CA 96146
530.583.1578
plumpjackcafe.com

YASUO KAMADA
Naked Fish

3940 Lake Tahoe Blvd #3
South Lake Tahoe, CA 96150
530.541.3474
thenakedfish.com

DAVID LUTZ
Tahoe City, CA

BILLY MCCOLLOUGH
Dragonfly

10118 Donner Pass Rd
Truckee, CA 96161
530.587.0557
dragonflycuisine.com

ANDREW SHIMER
Christy Hill

115 Grove St
Tahoe City, CA 96145
530.583.8551
christyhill.com

LEROY WALKER
Bistro 234

234 E Main St
Turlock, CA 95380
209.668.4234
bistro234.com

TUSTIN

YVON GOETZ
The Winery

2647 Park Ave
Tustin, CA 92782
714.258.7600
thewineryrestaurant.net

SEAN HWANG
RA Sushi Bar Restaurant

2401 Park Ave
Tustin, CA 92782
714.566.1700
rasushi.com

VAN NUYS

UELI HUEGLI
Swiss Chef

13727 Victory Blvd
Van Nuys, CA 91401
818.904.1500
swisschefusa.com

VENICE

EMMANUEL DOSSETTI
Zinque

600 Venice Blvd
Venice, CA 90291
310.437.0970
lezinque.com

CASEY LANE
The Tasting Kitchen

1633 Abbot Kinney Blvd
Venice, CA 90291
310.392.6644
thetastingkitchen.com

TRAVIS LETT
Gjelina

1429 Abbot Kinney Blvd
Venice, CA 90291
310.450.1429
gjelina.com

JOSEPH MILLER
Joe's Restaurant

1023 Abbot Kinney Blvd
Venice, CA 90291
310.399.5811
joesrestaurant.com

MARIN SANTOS
Centanni

1700 Lincoln Blvd
Venice, CA 90291
310.314.7275
centannivenice.com

VISALIA

DAVID VARTANIAN
Vintage Press

216 N Willis St
Visalia, CA 93291
559.733.3033
thevintagepress.com

GREG VARTANIAN
Vintage Press

216 N Willis St
Visalia, CA 93291
559.733.3033
thevintagepress.com

WALNUT CREEK

PETER CHASTAIN
Prima Ristorante

1522 N Main St
Walnut Creek, CA 94596
925.935.7780
primawine.com

SHANE MCANELLY
Va De Vi

1511 Mount Diablo Blvd
Walnut Creek, CA 94596
925.979.0100
vadevi.com

SCOTT WALL
Lark Creek

1360 Locust St
Walnut Creek, CA 94596
925.256.1234
larkcreek.com

PHILIP YANG
Sasa

1432 N Main St
Walnut Creek, CA 94596
925.210.0188
sasawc.com

WESTLAKE VILLAGE

TOMMASO BARLETTA
Tuscany il Ristorante

968 Westlake Blvd #4
Westlake Village, CA 91361
805.495.2768
tuscany-restaurant.com

MAURIZIO RONZONI
Rustico

1125 Lindero Canyon Rd
Westlake Village, CA 91362
818.889.0191
tuscany-restaurant.com

ALBERTO VAZQUEZ
Rock Chef Rolls

766 Lakefield Rd
Westlake Village, CA 91361
855.727.2011
rockchefrolls.com

WOODLAND HILLS

CHRISTOPHER KUFEK
Saddle Peak Lodge

419 Cold Canyon Rd
Calabasas, CA 91302
818.222.3888
saddlepeaklodge.com

ROBERT LIA
The Villa

22160 Ventura Blvd
Woodland Hills, CA 91364
818.704.1185
chefrobertlia.com

BRANDON POWELL
Fleming's

6373 Topanga Canyon Blvd
Woodland Hills, CA 91367
818.346.1005
flemingssteakhouse.com

YOSEMITE NATIONAL PARK

PERCY WHATLEY
The Ahwahnee Hotel

1 Ahwahnee Dr
Yosemite National Park, CA 95389
209.372.1435
yosemitepark.com

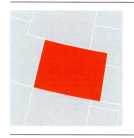

ASPEN

KATHLEEN CROOK
Steak House No. 316

316 E Hopkins Ave
Aspen, CO 81611
970.920.1893
steakhouse316.com

TODD SLOSSBERG
Plato's

845 Meadows Rd
Aspen, CO 81611
970.925.4240
platosaspen.com

JAMEY FADER
Big Red F Restaurant Group

1928 Pearl St
Boulder, CO 80302
303.448.9182
bigredf.com

BARCLAY DODGE
Pacifica

307 S Mill St
Aspen, CO 81611
970.920.9775
pacificaaspen.com

TICO STARR
Rustique Bistro

216 S Monarch St
Aspen, CO 81611
970.920.2555
rustiquebistro.com

BRADFORD HEAP
Colterra

210 Franklin St
Niwot, CO 80503
303.652.0777
colterra.com

CHRIS LANTER
Cache Cache Bistro

205 S Mill St
Aspen, CO 81611
970.925.3835
cachecache.com

KEITH THEODORE
Syzygy

308 E Hopkins Ave
Aspen, CO 81611
970.925.3700
syzygyrestaurant.com

ASHLEY HOOK
The Kitchen

1039 Pearl St
Boulder, CO 80302
303.544.5973
thekitchencommunity.com

BOULDER

ANDREA MENICHETTI
Casa Tua

403 S Galena St
Aspen, CO 81611
970.920.7277
casatualifestyle.com

COREY BUCK
John's Restaurant

Boulder, CO
303.444.5232
johnsrestaurantboulder.com

SAKIMA ISAAC
Laudisio Italian

1710 29th St #1076
Boulder, CO 80301
303.442.1300
thel.com

ALLISON RICHMAN
Rabbit's Garden

Aspen, CO
970.379.0440
rabbitsgarden.com

RADEK CERNY
L'Atelier

1739 Pearl St
Boulder, CO 80302
303.442.7233
latelierboulder.com

IAN KLEINMAN
Boulder, CO

LACHLAN MACKINNON-PATTERSON
Frasca Food and Wine

1738 Pearl St
Boulder, CO 80302
303.442.6966
frascafoodandwine.com

HUGO MATHESON
The Kitchen

1039 Pearl St
Boulder, CO 80302
303.544.5973
thekitchencommunity.com

JOHN PLATT
Riffs Urban Fare

1115 Pearl St
Boulder, CO 80302
303.440.6699
riffsboulder.com

STEVE REDZIKOWSKI
Oak at Fourteenth

1400 Pearl St
Boulder, CO 80302
303.444.3622
oakatfourteenth.com

JASON ROGERS
Oskar Blues

1555 S Hover Rd
Longmont, CO 80501
303.823.6685
oskarblues.com

ERIC SKOKAN
Black Cat Farm Table Bistro

1970 13th St
Boulder, CO 80302
303.444.9110
blackcatboulder.com

JORDAN WALLACE
Pizzeria Locale

1730 Pearl St
Boulder, CO 80302
303.442.3003
pizzerialocale.com

BRECKENRIDGE

MATTHEW FACKLER
Relish

137 S Main St
Breckenridge, CO 80424
970.453.0989
relishbreckenridge.com

KEVIN MCCOMBS
Ski Tip Lodge

764 Montezuma Rd
Dillon, CO 80435
970.496.4202
keystoneresort.com

MICHAEL O'BRIEN
Hearthstone

130 S Ridge St
Breckenridge, CO 80424
970.453.1148
hearthstonerestaurant.biz

DAVID WELCH
Food Hedz

842 Summit Blvd #19
Frisco, CO 80443
970.668.2000
foodhedzcafe.com

CARBONDALE

CLAUDE VAN HORTON
Russets

225 Main St
Carbondale, CO 81623
970.963.3036
russets.net

COLORADO SPRINGS

JOSH BEEMER
Rabbit Hole

101 N Tejon St
Colorado Springs, CO 80903
719.203.5072
rabbitholedinner.com

BERTRAND BOUQUIN
The Broadmoor

1 Lake Ave
Colorado Springs, CO 80906
719.577.5775
broadmoor.com

CARLOS ECHEANDIA
Carlos Bistro

1025 S 21st St
Colorado Springs, CO 80904
719.471.2905

JASON GUST
Tapateria

2607 W Colorado Ave
Colorado Springs, CO 80904
719.471.8272
tapateria.com

BON HEWLETT
Phantom Canyon Brewing Company

2 E Pikes Peak Ave
Colorado Springs, CO 80903
719.635.2800
phantomcanyon.com

BEN HOFFER
Manitou Springs, CO

LAWRENCE JOHNSON
Warehouse and Gallery

25 W Cimarron St
Colorado Springs, CO 80903
719.475.8880
thewarehouserestaurant.com

AARON JOHNSON
Warehouse and Gallery

25 W Cimarron St
Colorado Springs, CO 80903
719.475.8880
thewarehouserestaurant.com

JEFF KNIGHT
Manitou Springs, CO

KETIL LARSEN
Club at Flying Horse

1880 Weiskopf Pt
Colorado Springs, CO 80921
719.494.1222
flyinghorsecolorado.com

BROTHER LUCK
Craftwood Inn

404 El Paso Blvd
Colorado Springs, CO 80829
719.685.9000
craftwood.com

PHIL MEYER
Walter's Bistro

146 E Cheyenne Mountain Blvd
Colorado Springs, CO 80906
719.630.0201
waltersbistro.com

PETE MORENO
MacKenzie's Chop House

128 S Tejon St
Colorado Springs, CO 80903
719.635.3536
mackenzieschophouse.com

BRIAN SACK
Famous Steakhouse

31 N Tejon St
Colorado Springs, CO 80903
719.227.7333
thefamoussteakhouse.net

SCOTT SAVAGE
Cliff House

306 Canon Ave
Manitou Springs, CO 80829
719.785.2415
thecliffhouse.com

ANDREW SHERRILL
Blue Star

1645 S Tejon St
Colorado Springs, CO 80905
719.632.1086
thebluestar.net

ADAM STEPHENS
Colorado Springs, CO

ERIC VEIDT
The Margarita at Pine Creek

7350 Pine Creek Rd
Colorado Springs, CO 80919
719.598.8667
coloradoeats.com

BRIAN WALLACE
Madeleine's

1 Lake Ave
Colorado Springs, CO 80906
719.634.7711
broadmoor.com

STEVE WEBER
Garden of the Gods Club

3320 Mesa Rd
Colorado Springs, CO 80904
719.632.5541
gardenofthegodsclub.com

CRESTED BUTTE

JASON VERNON
Soupcon

127 Elk Ave
Crested Butte, CO 81224
970.349.5448
soupconcrestedbutte.com

DENVER

DANIEL ASHER
Root Down

1600 W 33rd Ave
Denver, CO 80211
303.993.4200
rootdowndenver.com

BOB BLAIR
Fuel Café

3455 Ringsby Ct
Denver, CO 80216
303.996.6988
fuelcafedenver.com

FRANK BONANNO
Mizuna

225 E 7th Ave
Denver, CO 80203
303.832.4778
frankbonanno.com

TOM BOWLES
Denver, CO

JOHN BROENING
Duo

2413 W 32nd Ave
Denver, CO 80211
303.477.4141
duodenver.com

JUSTIN BRUNSON
Masterpiece Delicatessen

1575 Central St
Denver, CO 80211
303.561.3354
masterpiecedeli.com

LUCAS CHANDLER
Il Posto

2011 E 17th Ave
Denver, CO 80206
303.394.0100
ilpostodenver.com

WAYNE CONWELL
Sushi Sasa

2401 15th St #80
Denver, CO 80202
303.433.7272
www.sushisasa.com

JUSTIN CUCCI
Linger

2030 W 30th Ave
Denver, CO 80211
303.993.3120
lingerdenver.com

JENSEN CUMMINGS
Slotted Spoon / Meatball Eatery

2730 S Colorado Blvd #19
Denver, CO 80222
303.756.3072
slotted-spoon.com

MARK DENITTIS
Il Mondo Vecchio

1174 S Cherokee St
Denver, CO 80223
303.744.6328
ilmondovecchio.net

PATRICK DUPAYS
Z Cuisine

2239 W 30th Ave
Denver, CO 80211
303.477.1111
zcuisineonline.com

JEAN-PHILIPPE FAILYAU
Park Burger

2643 W 32nd Ave
Denver, CO 80211
303.862.8461
parkburger.com

MARK FISCHER
Phat Thai

2900 E 2nd Ave
Denver, CO 80206
303.388.7428
phatthai.com

BRANDON FOSTER
Vesta Dipping Grill

1822 Blake St
Denver, CO 80202
303.296.1970
vestagrill.com

TROY GUARD
TAG RAW BAR

1423 Larimer St
Denver, CO 80202
303.996.2685
tagrawbar.com

ANDREW HARDIN
Lola

1575 Boulder St
Denver, CO 80211
720.570.8686
loladenver.com

LEO HARVEY
Jezebel's

3301 Tejon St
Denver, CO 80211
303.433.3060
jezebelslohi.com

CHUCK JAMES
1515 Restaurant

1515 Market St
Denver, CO 80202
303.571.0011
1515restaurant.com

JENNIFER JASINSKI
Rioja

1431 Larimer St
Denver, CO 80202
303.820.2282
riojadenver.com

SEAN KELLY
LoHi Steakbar

3200 Tejon St
Denver, CO 80211
303.927.6334
lohisteakbar.com

TOSHI KIZAKI
Sushi Den

1487 S Pearl St
Denver, CO 80210
303.777.0826
sushiden.net

BRIAN LAIRD
Deno's Mountain Bistro

78911 U.S. 40
Winter Park, CO 80482
970.726.5332
denoswp.com

MAX MACKISSOCK
Squeaky Bean

1500 Wynkoop St #101
Denver, CO 80202
303.623.2665
thesqueakybean.net

JEFF OSAKA
twelverestaurant

2233 Larimer St
Denver, CO 80205
303.293.0287
twelverestaurant.com

SCOTT PARKER
Table 6

609 Corona St
Denver, CO 80218
303.831.8800
table6denver.com

HA PHAM
New Saigon

630 S Federal Blvd
Denver, CO 80219
303.936.4954
newsaigon.com

JOREL PIERCE
Euclid Hall

1317 14th St
Denver, CO 80202
303.595.4255
euclidhall.com

HUNTER PRITCHETT
Luca D'Italia

711 Grant St
Denver, CO 80203
303.832.6600
lucadenver.com

DANA RODRIGUEZ
Bistro Vendome

1420 Larimer St
Denver, CO 80202
303.825.3232
bistrovendome.com

JAMES RUGILE
Mizuna

225 E 7th Ave
Denver, CO 80203
303.832.4778
mizunadenver.com

ALBERTO SABBADINI
Denver, CO

ALEX SEIDEL
Fruition

1313 E 6th Ave
Denver, CO 80218
303.831.1962
fruitionrestaurant.com

MATT SELBY
Vesta Dipping Grill

1822 Blake St
Denver, CO 80202
303.296.1970
vestagrill.com

MANGAL SIGNH
Azitra

535 Zang St
Broomfield, CO 80021
303.465.4444
azitra.us

TYLER SMITH
Café Terracotta

5649 S Curtice St
Littleton, CO 80120
303.794.6054
cafeterracottalittleton.com

MARTY STEINKE
Denver, CO

LON SYMENSMA
ChoLon

1555 Blake St
Denver, CO 80202
303.353.5223
cholon.com

KEVIN TAYLOR
Restaurant Kevin Taylor

1106 14th St
Denver, CO 80202
303.820.2600
ktrg.net

MATTHEW VAWTER
Fruition

1313 E 6th Ave
Denver, CO 80218
303.831.1992
fruitionrestaurant.com

CLINT WANGSNES
Zengo Denver

1610 Little Raven St
Denver, CO 80202
720.904.0965
richardsandoval.com

TYLER WIARD
Elway's

2500 E 1st Ave
Denver, CO 80206
303.399.5353
elways.com

ELISE WIGGINS
Panzano

909 17th St
Denver, CO 80202
303.296.3525
panzano-denver.com

DURANGO

DAVID STEWART
Seasons of Durango

764 Main Ave
Durango, CO 81301
970.382.9790
seasonsofdurango.com

SERGIO VERDUZCO
East by Southwest

160 E College Dr
Durango, CO 81301
970.247.5533
eastbysouthwest.com

EDWARDS

PAUL ANDERS
Sweet Basil

193 Gore Creek Dr #201
Vail, CO 81657
970.476.0125
sweetbasilvail.com

DAVID BIELECKI
Larkspur

458 Vail Valley Dr
Vail, CO 81657
970.754.8050
larkspurvail.com

TODD BULLIS
Juniper

97 Main St
Edwards, CO 81632
970.926.7001
juniperrestaurant.com

DAVID CLAWSON
Game Creek Restaurant

278 Hanson Ranch Rd
Vail, CO 81657
970.754.4280
gamecreekclub.com

PAUL FERZACCA
La Tour

122 E Meadow Dr
Vail, CO 81657
970.476.4403
latour-vail.com

BILL GREENWOOD
Beano's Cabin

550 E Lionshead Cir
Vail, CO 81657
970.754.3463
beanoscabinbeavercreek.com

DAVID GUTOWSKI
Grouse Mountain Grill

141 Scott Hill Rd
Avon, CO 81620
970.949.0600
grousemountaingrill.com

NICK HALEY
Zino Ristorante

27 Main St
Edwards, CO 81632
970.926.0777
zinoristorante.com

PETER HILLBACK
Vail, CO

970.390.2189

KELLY LIKEN
Restaurant Kelly Liken

12 Vail Rd #100
Vail, CO 81657
970.479.0175
kellyliken.com

ATSUSHI MINAMI
Yama Sushi

168 Gore Creek Dr
Vail, CO 81657
970.476.7332
yamasushivail.com

TAKESHI OSAKI
Osaki's

100 E Meadow Dr
Vail, CO 81657
970.476.0977

MIKE REGRUT
Vail, CO

THOMAS SALAMUNOVICH
Larkspur

458 Vail Valley Dr
Vail, CO 81657
970.754.8050
larkspurvail.com

STEVE TOPPLE
Ludwig's

20 Vail Rd
Vail, CO 81657
970.479.5481
sonnenalp.com

DAVID WALFORD
Splendido

17 Chateau Ln
Beaver Creek, CO 81620
970.845.8808
splendidobeavercreek.com

FORT COLLINS

JASON SHAEFFER
Chimney Park Restaurant

406 Main St
Windsor, CO 80550
970.686.1477
chimneypark.com

RICO

EAMONN O'HARA
The Argentine Grille

124 S Hwy 145
Rico, CO 81332
800.365.1971
ricohotel.com

STEAMBOAT SPRINGS

KATE RENCH
Café Diva

1855 Ski Time Square Dr
Steamboat Springs, CO 80487
970.871.0508
cafediva.com

BRIAN VAUGHN
Bistro CV

345 Lincoln Ave
Steamboat Springs, CO 80487
970.879.4197
bistrocv.com

TELLURIDE

ELIZA GAVIN
221 South Oak

221 S Oak St
Telluride, CO 81435
970.728.9507
221southoak.com

MARK REGGIANNINI
La Marmotte

150 W San Juan Ave
Telluride, CO 81435
970.728.6232
lamarmotte.com

STEPHEN ROTH
Telluride Ski Resort

565 Mountain Village Blvd
Telluride, CO 81435
970.728.6900
tellurideskiresort.com

CHAD SCOTHORN
Cosmopolitan Restaurant

300 W San Juan Ave
Telluride, CO 81435
970.728.1292
cosmotelluride.com

BUD THOMAS
Telluride, CO

970.708.1496
chefbud.com

DANBURY

BERNARD BOUISSOU
Bernard's

20 West Ln
Ridgefield, CT 06877
203.438.8282
bernardsridgefield.com

TRACEY KYDES
Cafe on the Green

100 Aunt Hack Rd
Danbury, CT 06811
203.791.0369
cafeonthegreenrestaurant.com

ESSEX

DAVID BORSELLE
Bar Bouchee

8 Scotland Ave
Madison, CT 06450
203.318.8004
barbouchee.com

JOHN BRESCIO
Liv's Oyster Bar

166 Main St
Old Saybrook, CT 06475
860.395.5577
livsoysterbar.com

JASON GROTEN
Gabrielle's

78 Main St
Centerbrook, CT 06409
860.767.2440
gabrielles.net

NOEL JONES
Pip's at the Copper Beech Inn

46 Main St
Ivoryton, CT 06442
860.767.5311
copperbeechinn.com

PRASHANT JOSSE
Brushmill by the Waterfall

129 W Main St
Chester, CT 06412
860.526.9898
thebrushmill.com

JONATHAN RAPP
River Tavern

23 Main St
Chester, CT 06412
860.526.9417
rivertavernrestaurant.com

KRISTOFER ROWE
Chestnut Grille

100 Lyme St
Old Lyme, CT 06371
860.434.1667
beeandthistleinn.com

GREENWICH

JEAN-LOUIS GERIN
Restaurant Jean-Louis

61 Lewis St
Greenwich, CT 06830
203.622.8450
restaurantjeanlouis.com

FORREST PASTERNACK
Morello

253 Greenwich Ave
Greenwich, CT 06830
203.661.3443
morellobistro.com

HARTFORD

JOSEF AIGNER
Brew Bakers

169 Main St
Middletown, CT 06457
860.852.0001
mybrewbakers.com

TYLER ANDERSON
Millwright's

77 West St
Simsbury, CT 06070
860.651.5500
millwrightsrestaurant.com

VINNIE CARBONE
Carbone's

588 Franklin Ave
Hartford, CT 06114
860.296.9646
carboneshartford.com

JOHN CHEN
Feng

93 Asylum St
Hartford, CT 06103
860.549.3364
fengrestaurant.com

CELESTINO CIALFI
Peppercorn's Grill

357 Main St
Hartford, CT 06106
860.547.1714
peppercornsgrill.com

CHRISTIANE GEHAMI
Arugula Bistro

953 Farmington Ave
West Hartford, CT 06107
860.561.4888
arugula-bistro.com

BILLY GRANT
Bricco Trattoria

124 Hebron Ave #1A
Glastonbury, CT 06033
860.659.0220
billygrant.com

RYAN JONES
The Mill at 2T

2 Tunxis Rd
Tariffville, CT 06081
860.658.7890
themillat2t.com

JEFFREY LIZOTTE
ON20

1 State St
Hartford, CT 06103
860.722.5161
ontwenty.com

SCOTT MILLER
Max's Oyster Bar

964 Farmington Ave
West Hartford, CT 06107
860.236.6299
maxrestaurantgroup.com

HUNTER MORTON
Max Downtown

185 Asylum St
Hartford, CT 06103
860.522.2530
maxrestaurantgroup.com

DAVID SELLERS
Max Fish

110 Glastonbury Blvd
Glastonbury, CT 06033
860.652.3474
maxrestaurantgroup.com

CHRIS TORLA
Trumbull Kitchen

150 Trumbull St
Hartford, CT 06103
860.493.7417
trumbullkitchen.com

STEVEN WOLF
Republic

39 Jerome Ave
Bloomfield, CT 06001
860.216.5852
republicct.com

LAKEVILLE

GEORGE COURGNAUD
Le Laurentis

227 Main St
Lakeville, CT 06039
860.596.4231
lelaurentis.com

NEW CANAAN

PRASAD CHIRNOMULA
Thali

87 Main St
New Canaan, CT 06840
203.972.8332
thali.com

TIM LABANT
Schoolhouse at Cannondale

34 Cannon Rd
Wilton, CT 06897
203.834.9816
schoolhouseatcannondale.com

BRIAN LEWIS
Elm

73 Elm St
New Canaan, CT 06840
203.920.4994
elmrestaurant.com

LUIS LOPEZ
Chef Luis

129 Elm St
New Canaan, CT 06840
203.972.5847
chefluis.net

NEW HAVEN

DENISE APPEL
Zinc

964 Chapel St
New Haven, CT 06510
203.624.0507
zincfood.com

JEFF CAPUTO
Mory's

306 York St
New Haven, CT 06511
203.562.3157
morys1849.org

MICHAEL FOX
Mikro

3000 Whitney Ave
Hamden, CT 06518
203.553.7676
mikrobeerbar.com

JOHN GERVASI
University of New Haven

300 Boston Post Rd
New Haven, CT 06516
203.932.7000
newhaven.edu

MANUEL ROMERO
Ibiza

39 High St
New Haven, CT 06510
203.865.1933
ibizarestaurantnewhaven.com

CLAUDIO SAN FRANCESCO
Jeffrey's Restaurant by Claudio

501 New Haven Ave
Milford, CT 06460
203.878.1910
jeffreysofmilford.com

JEAN PIERRE VUILLERMET
Union League Cafe

1032 Chapel St
New Haven, CT 06510
203.562.4299
unionleaguecafe.com

NEW LONDON

PAUL KRAWIC
Octagon

625 North Rd
Groton, CT 06340
860.326.0360
octagonsteakhouse.com

DANIEL MEISER
Oyster Club

13 Water St
Mystic, CT 06355
860.415.9266
oysterclubct.com

LUIGI SFERRAZZA
Recovery Room

445 Ocean Ave
New London, CT 06320
860.443.2619
recoveryroomrestaurant.com

JAMES WAYMAN
Oyster Club

13 Water St
Mystic, CT 06355
860.415.9266
oysterclubct.com

NORWALK

ARIK BENSIMON
The Spread

70 N Main St
Norwalk, CT 06854
203.939.1111
thespreadsono.com

ADAM HALBERG
Barcelona

63 N Main St
Norwalk, CT 06854
203.899.0088
barcelonawinebar.com

MICHEL NISCHAN
The Dressing Room

27 Powers Ct
Westport, CT 06880
203.226.1114
dressingroomhomegrown.com

DAVID RAYMER
Strada 18

122 Washington St
South Norwalk, CT 06854
203.853.4546
strada18.com

PIETRO SCOTTI
Da Pietro's

36 Riverside Ave
Westport, CT 06880
203.454.1213
dapietros.com

MATT STORCH
Match

98 Washington St
South Norwalk, CT 06854
203.852.1088
matchsono.com

BILL TAIBE
LeFarm

256 Post Rd E
Westport, CT 06880
203.557.3701
lefarmwestport.com

PUTNAM

KARA BROOKS
Still River Café

134 Union Rd
Eastford, CT 06242
860.974.9988
stillrivercafe.com

JAMES MARTIN
85 Main

85 Main St
Putnam, CT 06260
860.928.1660
85main.com

SHARON

BENNETT CHINN
When Pigs Fly Southern BBQ

29 W Main St
Sharon, CT 06069
860.492.0000
hudsonvalleybbq.com

STAMFORD

MATTHEW SCHMALLE
Capital Grille

230 Tresser Blvd
Stamford, CT 06901
203.967.0000
thecapitalgrille.com

WATERBURY

NICOLA MANCINI
La Tavola

702 Highland Ave
Waterbury, CT 06708
203.755.2211
latavolaristorante.com

CAROLE PECK
Good News Café

694 Main St S
Woodbury, CT 06798
203.266.4663
good-news-cafe.com

JOEL VIEHLAND
Community Table

223 Litchfield Turnpike
Washington, CT 06777
860.868.9354
communitytablect.com

MIDDLETOWN

BRIAN SCHROEDER
1861

423 N Broad St
Middletown, DE 19709
302.376.7956
1861restaurant.com

REHOBOTH BEACH

HARI CAMERON
a(MUSE.)

44 Baltimore Ave
Rehoboth Beach, DE 19971
302.227.7107
amuse-rehoboth.com

JAY CAPUTO
Espuma

28 Wilmington Ave
Rehoboth Beach, DE 19971
302.227.4199
espuma-restaurant.com

CHRISTIAN COLGAN
Hooked Seafood & Martini Bar

18585 Coastal Hwy #23
Rehoboth Beach, DE 19971
302.827.4944
hookedseafoodandmartinibar.com

ANDREW FEELEY
Eden

23 Baltimore Ave
Rehoboth Beach, DE 19971
302.227.3330
edenrestaurant.com

LION GARDNER
Blue Moon

35 Baltimore Ave
Rehoboth Beach, DE 19971
302.227.6515
bluemoonrehoboth.com

DRU TEVIS
Blue Moon

35 Baltimore Ave
Rehoboth Beach, DE 19971
302.227.6515
bluemoonrehoboth.com

ROBERT WOOD
Cultured Pearl

301 Rehoboth Ave
Rehoboth Beach, DE 19971
302.227.8493
culturedpearl.us

SHAWN XIONG
Confucius Chinese Cuisine

57 Wilmington Ave
Rehoboth Beach, DE 19971
302.227.3848
confuciusrehobothbeach.com

WILMINGTON

ANTHONY CARNEVALE II
Chelsea Tavern

821 N Market St
Wilmington, DE 19801
302.482.3333
chelseatavern.com

MERRY CATANUTO
House of William and Merry

1336 Old Lancaster Pike
Hockessin, DE 19707
302.234.2255
williamandmerry.com

AL CHU
Mikimotos

1212 N Washington St
Wilmington, DE 19801
302.656.8638
mikimotos.com

PATRICK D'AMICO
Harry's Savoy Grill

2020 Naamans Rd
Wilmington, DE 19810
302.475.3000
harrys-savoy.com

MICHAEL DIBIANCA
Moro

1307 N Scott St
Wilmington, DE 19806
302.777.1800
mororestaurant.net

JASON DIETTERICK
Stone Balloon Winehouse

115 E Main St
Newark, DE 19711
302.266.8111
stoneballoonwh.com

DE

DESMOND EDWARDS
Orillas Tapas Bar

902 N Market St
Wilmington, DE 19801
302.575.9244
orillastapasbar.com

WILLIAM HOFFMAN
House of William and Merry

1336 Old Lancaster Pike
Hockessin, DE 19707
302.234.2255
williamandmerry.com

ROBBIE JESTER
Piccolina Toscana

1412 N Dupont St
Wilmington, DE 19806
302.654.8001
piccolinatoscana.com

DAVID LATTOMUS
The Green Room

42 W 11th St
Wilmington, DE 19890
302.594.3154
hoteldupont.com

JULIO LAZZARINI
Vinoteca 902

902 N Market St
Wilmington, DE 19801
302.575.9244
vinoteca902.com

DAVID LEO BANKS
Harry's Savoy Grill

2020 Naamans Rd
Wilmington, DE 19810
302.475.3000
harrys-savoy.com

SEAN MCNEICE
Ulysses American Gastropub

1716 Marsh Rd
Wilmington, DE 19810
302.691.3456
ulyssesgastropub.com

DONNY MERRILL
Krazy Kat's

528 Montchanin Rd
Wilmington, DE 19710
302.888.4200
krazykatsrestaurant.com

KEITH MILLER
Green Room at the Hotel du Pont

42 W 11th St
Wilmington, DE 19801
302.594.3154
hoteldupont.com

ANTONIO RAMOS
Soffritto Italian Grill

1130 Capitol Trail
Newark, DE 19711
302.455.1101
soffritto.com

ROGER SURPIN
Domaine Hudson

1314 N Washington St
Wilmington, DE 19801
302.655.9463
domainehudson.com

BOCA RATON

ZACH BELL
Addison Reserve Country Club

7201 Addison Reserve Blvd
Delray Beach, FL 33446
561.455.1220
addisonreserve.cc

PATRICK BROADHEAD
Max's Harvest

169 NE 2nd Ave
Delray Beach, FL 33444
561.381.9970
maxsharvest.com

NITINUN CHUNSAWANG
Lemongrass Asian Bistro

101 Plaza Real SE
Boca Raton, FL 33432
561.544.8181
lemongrassasianbistro.com

ARTURO GISMONDI
Arturo's Ristorante

6750 N Federal Hwy
Boca Raton, FL 33487
561.997.7373
arturosrestaurant.com

NADER JAOUHAR
Cielo

501 E Camino Real
Boca Raton, FL 33432
561.447.3640
bocaresort.com

JOHN LENHARD
Darbster

6299 N Federal Hwy
Boca Raton, FL 33487
561.586.2622
darbster.com

CHRIS MIRACOLO
Max's Harvest

169 NE 2nd Ave
Delray Beach, FL 33444
561.381.9970
maxsharvest.com

NICK MORFOGEN
32 East

32 E Atlantic Ave
Delray Beach, FL 33444
561.276.7868
32east.com

ANDREW SWERSKY
Artizan Flatbread Company

141 Via Naranjas
Boca Raton, FL 33432
561.395.0380
artizanflatbreadcompany.com

BRADENTON

GREG CAMPBELL
Pier 22 Restaurant

1200 1st Ave W
Bradenton, FL 34205
941.748.8087
pier22dining.com

MATT DEASON
Beach Bistro

6600 Gulf Dr
Holmes Beach, FL 34217
941.778.6444
beachbistro.com

DANA JOHNSON
Savory Scenes Catering

Bradenton, FL
savoryscenes.com

CAPE CORAL

GREG SCARLATOS
Angelina's Ristorante

24041 S Tamiami Trail
Bonita Springs, FL 34134
239.390.3187
angelinasofbonitasprings.com

CLEARWATER

DOUG BEBELL
Mystic Fish

3253 Tampa Rd
Palm Harbor, FL 34684
727.771.1800
3bestchefs.com

JOHN HARRIS
Rusty's Bistro

1160 Gulf Blvd
Clearwater Beach, FL 33767
727.595.1611
sheratonsandkey.com

KYLE LATSHA
Carlouel Yacht Club

1091 Eldorado Ave
Clearwater Beach, FL 33767
727.446.9162
carlouel.net

DESTIN

TIM CREEHAN
Cuvee Bistro

36120 Emerald Coast Pkwy
Destin, FL 32541
850.650.8900
cuveebistrodestin.com

JASON DUGAN
Santiago's Bodega

207 Petronia St #101
Key West, FL 33040
305.296.7691
santiagosbodega.com

CHRISTOPHER PONTE
Café Ponte

13505 Icot Blvd
Clearwater, FL 33760
727.538.5768
cafeponte.com

GIOVANNI FILIPPONE
Vue on 30A

4801 W County Hwy 30A
Santa Rosa Beach, FL 32459
850.267.1240
vueon30a.com

BILLY MCCROSSIN
Green Turtle Inn

81219 Overseas Hwy
Islamorada, FL 33036
305.664.2006
greenturtlekeys.com

TOM PRITCHARD
Salt Rock Grill

19325 Gulf Blvd
Indian Shores, FL 33785
727.593.7625
saltrockgrill.com

CHRIS MONGOGNA
Fire Restaurant

7 Town Center Lp C-11
Santa Rosa Beach, FL 32459
850.231.9020
restaurantfire.com

BRENDAN MICA
Hot Tin Roof

0 Duval St
Key West, FL 33040
305.296.7701
oceankey.com

COCOA

EROL TUGRUL
Café Margaux

220 Brevard Ave
Cocoa, FL 32922
321.639.8343
margaux.com

BRIAN MURRAY
Fish Out of Water

34 Goldenrod Cir
Santa Rosa Beach, FL 32459
850.534.5050
watercolorresort.com

JUSTIN NORRIS
Key West Yacht Club

2315 N Roosevelt Blvd
Key West, FL 33040
305.296.5389
keywestyachtclub.com

DAYTONA BEACH

SAMUEL A. MOGGIO
The Cellar Restaurant

220 Magnolia Ave
Daytona Beach, FL 32114
386.258.0011
thecellarrestaurant.com

JOHN SALLMAN
Beach Walk Café
at Henderson Park Inn

2700 Scenic Hwy 98
Destin, FL 32541
850.650.7100
beachwalkhendersonpark.com

CHRIS OTTEN
Nine One Five

915 Duval St
Key West, FL 33040
305.296.0669
915duval.com

FLORIDA KEYS

HENRY SALGADO
Spanish River Grill

737 E 3rd Ave
New Smyrna Beach, FL 32169
386.424.6991
thespanishrivergrill.com

ANDREW BERMAN
Kojin Noodle Bar

601 Duval St
Key West, FL 33040
305.296.2077

LUIS POUS
Dining Room at Little Palm Island

28500 Overseas Hwy
Little Torch Key, FL 33042
305.872.2551
littlepalmisland.com

ALEX ROSADO
Dining Room at Little Palm Island

28500 Overseas Hwy
Little Torch Key, FL 33042
305.872.2551
littlepalmisland.com

CHRISTOPHER ROUNDS
Antonia's

615 Duval St
Key West, FL 33040
305.294.6565
antoniaskeywest.com

DOUG SHOOK
Louie's Backyard

700 Waddell Ave
Key West, FL 33040
305.294.1061
louiesbackyard.com

MICHAEL WILSON
Michaels Restaurant

532 Margaret St
Key West, FL 33040
305.295.1300
michaelskeywest.com

MASA YOSHIMOTO
Ambrosia

1401 Simonton St
Key West, FL 33040
305.293.0304
keywestambrosia.com

FT. LAUDERDALE

BOB AXENFELD
Ireland's Steakhouse

250 Racquet Club Rd
Weston, FL 33326
954.349.5656
bonaventureresortandspa.com

TIMOTHY BOYD
Mustard Seed Bistro

256 S University Dr
Plantation, FL 33324
954.533.9326
mustardseedbistro.com

BILL BRUENING
Sunfish Grill

2775 E Oakland Park Blvd
Ft. Lauderdale, FL 33306
954.561.2004
sunfishgrill.com

STANTON BUNDY
Royal Pig Pub

350 E Las Olas Blvd
Ft. Lauderdale, FL 33301
954.617.7447
royalpigpub.com

CHI CHAN
Ft. Lauderdale, FL

LAUREN DESHIELDS
Market 17

1850 SE 17th St #109
Ft. Lauderdale, FL 33316
954.835.5507
market17.com

ANGELO ELIA
Casa D'Angelo

1201 N Federal Hwy
Ft. Lauderdale, FL 33304
954.564.1234
casa-d-angelo.com

JEREMY FORD
3030 Ocean

3030 Holiday Dr
Ft. Lauderdale, FL 33316
954.765.3030
3030ocean.com

MARC GRUVERMAN
Capital Grille

2430 E Sunrise Blvd
Ft. Lauderdale, FL 33304
954.446.2000
thecapitalgrille.com

TETSU HAYAKAWA
Marumi Sushi

8271 W Sunrise Blvd
Plantation, FL 33322
954.318.4455
marumisushi.net

KHALED IBRAHIM
Via Luna

1 N Fort Lauderdale Beach Blvd
Ft. Lauderdale, FL 33304
954.302.6460
ritzcarlton.com

TOBY JOSEPH
Wild Sea Oyster Bar and Grille

620 E Las Olas Blvd
Ft. Lauderdale, FL 33301
954.467.0045
riversidehotel.com

JIN KAITA
Café Sharaku

2736 N Federal Hwy
Ft. Lauderdale, FL 33306
954.563.2888
cafesharaku.com

ABOUD KOBAITRI
La Brochette Bistro

2635 N Hiatus Rd
Cooper City, FL 33026
954.435.9090
labrochettebistro.com

DEAN JAMES MAX
3030 Ocean

3030 Holiday Dr
Ft. Lauderdale, FL 33316
954.765.3041
3030ocean.com

MARK MILITELLO
Hospitality Makers Consulting

Ft. Lauderdale, FL
310.691.2596
hospitalitymakers.com

JOSEPH QUINN
da Campo Osteria

3333 NE 32nd Ave
Ft. Lauderdale, FL 33308
954.226.5002
dacamporestaurant.com

GIOVANNI ROCCHIO
Valentino's Cucina Italiana

1145 S Federal Hwy
Ft. Lauderdale, FL 33316
954.523.5767
valentinoscucinaitaliana.com

BRIAN RUTHERFORD
Bistro Mezzaluna

1821 SE 10th Ave
Ft. Lauderdale, FL 33316
954.522.9191
bistromezzaluna.com

ALLEN SUSSER
Chef Allen's Consulting

3389 Sheridan St #557
Hollywood, Fl 33021
305.528.3700
chefallens.com

LAURENT TASIC
Sage French Café

2378 N Federal Hwy
Ft. Lauderdale, FL 33305
954.565.2299
sagecafe.net

JOHNNY VINCZENCZ
Johnny V

625 E Las Olas Blvd
Ft. Lauderdale, FL 33301
954.761.7920
johnnyvlasolas.com

MICHAEL WAGNER
Lola's on Harrison

2032 Harrison St
Hollywood, FL 33020
954.927.9851
lolasonharrison.com

FT. MYERS

ROGER CHASTAIN
Sunshine Grille

8700 Gladiolus Dr
Ft. Myers, FL 33908
239.489.2233
sunshinegrillefm.com

GAINESVILLE

RAY LEUNG
Dragonfly

201 SE 2nd Ave #104
Gainesville, FL 32601
352.371.3359
dragonflysushi.com

CLIF NELSON
Paramount Grill

12 SW 1st Ave
Gainesville, FL 32601
352.378.3398
paramountgrill.com

JACKSONVILLE

DENNIS CHAN
Blue Bamboo

3820 Southside Blvd
Jacksonville, FL 32216
904.646.1478
bluebamboojacksonville.com

DWIGHT DELUDE
Dwight's Bistro

1527 Penman Rd
Jacksonville Beach, FL 32250
904.241.4496
dwightsbistro.com

SAM EFRON
Taverna

1986 San Marco Blvd
Jacksonville, FL 32207
904.398.3005
tavernasanmarco.com

TOM GRAY
Moxie Kitchen + Cocktails

4972 Big Island Dr
Jacksonville, FL 32246
904.345.0594
moxiefl.com

BEN GROSHELL
Marker 32

14549 Beach Blvd
Jacksonville, FL 32250
904.223.1534
marker32.com

ENZA HUFF
Enza's

10601 San Jose Blvd
Jacksonville, FL 32257
904.268.4458
enzas.net

MIKE HUFF
Enza's

10601 San Jose Blvd
Jacksonville, FL 32257
904.268.4458
enzas.net

ADAM HYATT
Roy's

2400 3rd St S
Jacksonville Beach, FL 32250
904.241.7697
roysrestaurant.com

JEFF KEANE
The Raintree Restaurant

102 San Marco Ave
St. Augustine, FL 32084
904.824.7211
raintreerestaurant.com

KEVIN LANGTON
Jacksonville, FL

RICK LAUGHLIN
Salt

4750 Amelia Island Pkwy
Amelia Island, FL 32034
904.277.1100
ritzcarlton.com

CONRAD MARTIN
Conrad's Steakhouse

4010 U.S. 1 S #121
St. Augustine, FL 32086
904.794.9440
conradssteakhouse.com

MATTHEW MEDURE
Matthew's Restaurant

2107 Hendricks Ave
Jacksonville, FL 32207
904.396.9922
matthewsrestaurant.com

DAVID MEDURE
Restaurant Medure

818 A1A N
Ponte Vedra Beach, FL 32082
904.543.3797
restaurantmedure.us

TED PETERS
Azurea

1 Ocean Blvd
Atlantic Beach, FL 32233
904.249.7402
azurearestaurant.com

NICK ROBSON
Eleven South

216 11th Ave S
Jacksonville Beach, FL 32250
904.241.1112
elevensouth.com

SCOTT SCHWARTZ
29 South

29 S 3rd St
Fernandina Beach, FL 32034
904.277.7919
29southrestaurant.com

BRIAN SIEBENSCHUH
Restaurant Orsay

3630 Park St
Jacksonville, FL 32205
904.381.0909
restaurantorsay.com

POM SOUVANNASOTH
Poms Signature Restaurant

9822 Tapestry Park Cir # 107
Jacksonville, FL 32246
904.641.2450
pomsrestaurant.com

MIAMI

KAL ABDALLA
A Fish Called Avalon

700 Ocean Dr
Miami Beach, FL 33139
305.532.1727
afishcalledavalon.com

JACOB ANAYA
Azul

500 Brickell Key Dr
Miami, FL 33131
305.913.8358
mandarinoriental.com

MAURICIO ARANA
Pied a Terre

1701 James Ave
Miami Beach, FL 33139
305.531.4533
piedaterrerestaurant.com

TIMON BALLOO
Sugarcane Raw Bar Grill

3250 NE 1st Ave
Miami, FL 33137
786.369.0353
sugarcanerawbargrill.com

MICHELLE BERNSTEIN
Michy's

6927 Biscayne Blvd
Miami, FL 33138
305.759.2001
michysmiami.com

ARNAUD BERTHELIER
Coral Gables, FL

ANDRE BIENVENU
Joe's Stone Crab

11 Washington Ave
Miami Beach, FL 33139
305.673.0365
joesstonecrab.com

AARON BROOKS
EDGE Steak & Bar

1435 Brickell Ave
Miami, FL 33131
305.358.3535
fourseasons.com

LAURENT CANTINEAUX
Juvia

1111 Lincoln Rd
Miami Beach, FL 33139
305.763.8272
juviamiami.com

NINA COMPTON
Scarpetta

4441 Collins Ave
Miami Beach, FL 33140
305.674.4660
fontainebleau.com

THOMAS CONNELL
La Cote

4441 Collins Ave
Miami Beach, FL 33140
305.674.4710
fontainebleau.com

KEVIN CORY
Naoe

661 Brickell Key Dr
Miami, FL 33131
305.947.6263
naoemiami.com

PAULA DASILVA
1500 Degrees

4525 Collins Ave
Miami Beach, FL 33140
305.674.5594
1500degreesmiami.com

JULIE FRANS
Essensia Restaurant & Lounge

3025 Collins Ave
Miami Beach, FL 33140
305.908.5458
thepalmshotel.com

EZIO GAMBA
Cioppino

455 Grand Bay Dr
Key Biscayne, FL 33149
305.365.4500
ritzcarlton.com

MATTHIEU GODARD
db Bistro Moderne

255 Biscayne Blvd Way
Miami, FL 33131
305.421.8800
dbbistro.com

RICHARD HALES
Sakaya Kitchen

3401 N Miami Ave #125
Miami, FL 33127
305.576.8096
sakayakitchen.com

MICHAEL HAWK
Fontainebleau Miami Beach

4441 Collins Ave
Miami Beach, FL 33140
305.538.2000
fontainebleau.com

CINDY HUTSON
Ortanique

278 Miracle Mile
Coral Gables, FL 33134
305.446.7710
cindyhutsoncuisine.com

JAMES KING
Miami, FL

COREY LAMBERT
Swine Southern Table & Bar

2415 Ponce de Leon Blvd
Coral Gables, FL 33134
786.360.6433
facebook.com/swinesouthern

DEWEY LOSASSO
The Forge

432 41st St
Miami Beach, FL 33140
305.538.8533
theforge.com

ROMEO MAJANO
Romeo's Café

2257 SW 22nd St
Miami, FL 33145
305.859.2228
romeoscafe.com

JEFF MCINNIS
Yardbird Southern Table & Bar

1600 Lenox Ave
Miami Beach, FL 33139
305.538.5220
runchickenrun.com

GABRIEL MEDICI
Miami, FL

TED MENDEZ
Barton G

1427 West Ave
Miami Beach, FL 33139
305.672.8881
bartong.com

JOSE MENDIN
Pubbelly

1418 20th St
Miami Beach, FL 33139
305.532.7555
pubbelly.com

SERGIO NAVARRO
Pubbelly

1418 20th St
Miami Beach, FL 33139
305.532.7555
pubbelly.com

FERNANDO NAVAS
SUSHISAMBA

600 Lincoln Rd
Miami Beach, FL 33139
305.673.5337
sushisamba.com

TIM NICKEY
La Gorce Country Club

5685 Alton Rd
Miami Beach, FL 33140
305.866.4421
lagorcecc.com

PASCAL OUDIN
Pascal's on Ponce

2611 Ponce De Leon Blvd
Coral Gables, FL 33134
305.444.2024
pascalmiami.com

MICHAEL PIROLO
Macchialina Taverna Rustica

820 Alton Rd
Miami Beach, FL 33139
305.534.2124
macchialina.com

CHRISTIAN PLOTCZYK
Rosa Mexicano

900 S Miami Ave #161
Miami, FL 33130
786.425.1001
rosamexicano.com

CHRISTIAN POOLE
Thierry's Catering & Event Design

915 NW 72nd St
Miami, FL 33150
305.635.6626
thierrycatering.com

GIORGIO RAPICAVOLI
Eating House

804 Ponce de Leon Blvd
Coral Gables, FL 33134
305.448.6524
eatinghousemiami.com

MICHAEL REIDT
Area 31

270 Biscayne Blvd Way
Miami, FL 33131
305.424.5234
area31restaurant.com

DOUGLAS RODRIGUEZ
OLA Miami

1745 James Ave
Miami Beach, FL 33139
305.695.9125
olamiami.com

PHILIPPE RUIZ
Restaurant Du Cap

600 Brickell
Miami, FL 33131

MICHAEL SCHWARTZ
Michael's Genuine Food & Drink

130 NE 40th St
Miami, FL 33137
305.573.5550
michaelsgenuine.com

DANIEL SERFER
Blue Collar

6730 Biscayne Blvd
Miami, FL 33138
305.756.0366
bluecollarmiami.com

SERGIO SIGALA
Cecconi's

4385 Collins Ave
Miami Beach, FL 33140
786.507.7902
cecconismiamibeach.com

CHRISTOPHER SZYJKA
Provence Grill

1223 Lincoln Rd
Miami Beach, FL 33139
305.531.1600
provencegrill.com

CHRISTIAN TESTA
La Gloutonnerie Vintage Kitchen

81 Washington Ave
Miami Beach, FL 33139
305.503.3811
lagloutonnerie.com

GREG TRUE
Red Fish Grill

9610 Old Cutler Rd
Miami, FL 33156
305.668.8788
redfishgrill.net

PETER VAUTHY
Red, the Steakhouse

119 Washington Ave
Miami Beach, FL 33139
305.534.3688
redthesteakhouse.com

BJOERN WEISSGERBER
Miami, FL

KRIS WESSEL
Florida Cookery

1545 Collins Ave
Miami Beach, FL 33139
786.276.0333
florida-cookery.com

CESAR ZAPATA
The Federal

5132 Biscayne Blvd
Miami, FL 33137
305.758.9559
thefederalmiami.com

NAPLES

FABRIZIO AIELLI
Sea Salt

1186 3rd St S
Naples, FL 34102
239.434.7258
seasaltnaples.com

VINCENZO BETULIA
Osteria Tulia

466 5th Ave S
Naples, FL 34102
239.213.2073
tulianaples.com

KEITH CASEY
KC American Bistro

885 Vanderbilt Beach Rd
Naples, FL 34108
239.566.2371
kcamericanbistro.com

SEBASTIEN MAILLARD
Le Lafayette

375 13th Ave
Naples, FL 34102
239.403.7861
lelafayette.com

PETER MAREK
Marek's Collier House

1121 Bald Eagle Dr
Marco Island, FL 34145
239.642.9948
marekrestaurant.com

NICOLAS MERCIER
USS Nemo

3745 Tamiami Trail N
Naples, FL 34103
239.261.6366
ussnemorestaurant.com

ADAM NARDIS
M Waterfront Grille

4300 Gulf Shore Blvd N
Naples, FL 34103
239.263.4421
mwaterfrontgrille.com

GUILLAUME ROBIN
The Grill at the Ritz-Carlton

280 Vanderbilt Beach Rd
Naples, FL 34108
239.598.6644
ritzcarlton.com

ALBERTO VARETTO
Alberto's on Fifth

868 5th Ave S
Naples, FL 34102
239.430.1060
albertosonfifth.com

NORTH MIAMI BEACH

TIM ADRIOZOLA
Timo

17624 Collins Ave
Sunny Isles Beach, FL 33160
305.936.1008
timorestaurant.com

RICHARD GRAS
J&G Grill

9703 Collins Ave
Bal Harbour, FL 33154
305.993.3333
jggrillmiami.com

MAKOTO OKUWA
Makoto

9700 Collins Ave
Bal Harbour, FL 33154
305.864.8600
makoto-restaurant.com

JORDI VALLES
St. Regis Bal Harbour Resort

9703 Collins Ave
Bal Harbour, FL 33154
305.993.0688
stregisbalharbour.com

ANDY YEAGER
Mister Collins

10295 Collins Ave
Bal Harbour, FL 33154
305.455.5460
mistercollins.com

OCALA

CHAD KARP
La Cuisine

48 SW 1st Ave
Ocala, FL 34471
352.433.2570
lacuisineocala.com

JAMES SCHUMANN
Cuvee Wine & Bistro

2237 SW 19th Ave Rd
Ocala, FL 34471
352.351.1816
cuveewineocala.con

ORLANDO

KHALID BENGHALLEN
The Venetian Room

8101 World Center Dr
Orlando, FL 32821
407.238.8060
thevenetianroom.com

KATHLEEN BLAKE
The Rusty Spoon

55 W Church St #101
Orlando, FL 32801
407.401.8811
therustyspoon.com

MATTHEW AUSTIN CARGO
Prato

124 N Park Ave
Winter Park, FL 32789
407.262.0050
prato-wp.com

BERNARD CARMOUCHE
Emeril's Orlando

6000 Universal Blvd #702
Orlando, FL 32819
407.224.2424
emerilsrestaurants.com

MARCO CUDAZZO
Adriatico Trattoria Italiana

2417 Edgewater Dr
Orlando, FL 32804
407.428.0044
adriatico-trattoria.com

KEVIN FONZO
K Restaurant

1710 Edgewater Dr
Orlando, FL 32804
407.872.2332
krestaurant.net

SCOTT HUNNEL
Victoria & Albert's

4401 Grand Floridian Way
Lake Buena Vista, FL 32830
407.939.3862
victoria-alberts.com

MAC LYNCH
Roy's

7760 W Sand Lake Rd
Orlando, FL 32836
407.352.4844
roysrestaurant.com

JAMIE MCFADDEN
Cuisiniers Catering

5470 Lake Howell Rd
Winter Park, FL 32792
407.975.8763
jamiemcfadden.com

BRANDON MCGLAMERY
Luma on Park

290 S Park Ave
Winter Park, FL 32789
407.599.4111
lumaonpark.com

JAMES PETRAKIS
The Ravenous Pig

1234 N Orange Ave
Winter Park, FL 32789
407.628.2333
theravenouspig.com

JULIE PETRAKIS
The Ravenous Pig

1234 N Orange Ave
Winter Park, FL 32789
407.628.2333
theravenouspig.com

MATTHEW PRICE
Capital Grille
9101 International Dr #1000
Orlando, FL 32819
407.370.4392
thecapitalgrille.com

ANDREAS PROISL
Isleworth Country Club
6100 Payne Stewart Dr
Windermere, FL 34786
407.909.2000
isleworth.com

GREGORY RICHIE
Emeril's Tchoup Chop
6300 Hollywood Way
Orlando, FL 32819
407.503.2467
emerilsrestaurants.com

KEVIN SPENCER
Spencer's for Steaks and Chops
6001 Destination Pkwy
Orlando, FL 32819
407.313.8625
thehiltonorlando.com

KEVIN TARTER
Chef's Table at the Edgewater
99 W Plant St
Winter Garden, FL 34787
407.230.4837
chefstableattheedgewater.com

NORMAN VAN AKEN
Norman's
4012 Central Florida Pkwy
Orlando, FL 32837
407.393.4333
normans.com

PANAMA CITY BEACH

KEN DUENAS
Café Thirty-A
3899 E Scenic Hwy 30A
Seagrove Beach, FL 32459
850.231.2166
cafethirtya.com

PAUL STELLATO
Firefly
535 Richard Jackson Blvd
Panama City Beach, FL 32407
850.249.3359
fireflypcb.com

PENSACOLA

GREGG MCCARTHY
The Grand Marlin
400 Pensacola Beach Blvd
Pensacola Beach, FL 32561
850.677.9153
thegrandmarlin.com

IRV MILLER
Jackson's Steakhouse
400 S Palafox St
Pensacola, FL 32502
850.469.9898
jacksons.goodgrits.com

FRANK TAYLOR
The Global Grill
27 S Palafox Pl
Pensacola, FL 32501
850.469.9966
dineglobalgrill.com

POMPANO BEACH

JOSEPH PARSONS
JoJo's Tacos
216 Commercial Blvd
Lauderdale-by-the-Sea, FL 33308
954.835.5561
jojostacos.com

OLIVER SAUCY
Café Maxx
2601 E Atlantic Blvd
Pompano Beach, FL 33062
954.782.0606
cafemaxx.com

PORT ST. LUCIE

MICHAEL PERRIN
11 Maple Street
3224 NE Maple Ave
Jensen Beach , FL 34957
772.334.7714
11maplestreet.net

PUNTA GORDA

JEANIE ROLAND
The Perfect Caper
121 E Marion Ave
Punta Gorda, FL 33950
941.505.9009
theperfectcaper.com

SARASOTA

RAYMOND ARPKE
Euphemia Haye
5540 Gulf of Mexico Dr
Longboat Key, FL 34228
941.383.3633
euphemiahaye.com

DEREK BARNES
Derek's Culinary
Casual Restaurant
514 Central Ave
Sarasota, FL 34236
941.366.6565
dereks-sarasota.com

RYAN BOEVE
Pomona Bistro and Wine Bar
481 N Orange Ave
Sarasota, FL 34236
941.706.1677
pomonabistroandwine.com

LAN BRADEEN
Melange

1568 Main St
Sarasota, FL 34236
941.953.7111
melangesarasota.com

DINO CARTA
Sarasota, FL

FRANCIS CASCIATO
Libby's Café + Bar

1917 S Osprey Ave
Sarasota, FL 34236
941.487.7300
libbyscafebar.com

HARRY CHRISTENSEN
Harry's Continental Kitchens

525 Saint Judes Dr
Longboat Key, FL 34228
941.383.0777
harryskitchen.com

DYLAN ELHAJOUI
Mozaic

1377 Main St
Sarasota, FL 34236
941.951.6272
mozaicsarasota.com

JUSTIN FIELDS
Roy's

2001 Siesta Dr
Sarasota, FL 34239
941.952.0109
roysrestaurant.com

JEREMY HAMMOND-CHAMBERS
Innovative Dining

Sarasota, FL
941.373.5678
innovative-dining.com

CHRISTIAN HERSHMAN
State Street
Eating House + Cocktails

1533 State St
Sarasota, FL 34236
941.951.1533
statestreetsrq.com

TOMMY KLAUBER
Pattigeorge's

4120 Gulf of Mexico Dr
Longboat Key, FL 34228
941.383.5111
pattigeorges.com

JOSE MARTINEZ
Maison Blanche

2605 Gulf of Mexico Dr
Longboat Key, FL 34228
941.383.8088
themaisonblanche.com

MASAKI MATSUNAE
VIZEN Sushi & Fusion

6559 Gateway Ave
Sarasota, FL 34231
941.926.0830
vizen-sarasota.com

PAUL MATTISON
Mattison's

7275 S Tamiami Trail
Sarasota, FL 34231
941.921.3400
mattisons.com

STEVE PHELPS
Indigenous

239 S Links Ave
Sarasota, FL 34236
941.706.4740
indigenoussarasota.com

JAMIL PINEDA
Michael's on East

1212 East Ave S
Sarasota, FL 34239
941.366.0007
bestfood.com

YSAAC SANCHEZ
Selva Grill

1345 Main St
Sarasota, FL 34236
941.362.4427
selvagrill.com

DARWIN SANTA MARIA
Darwin's on 4th

1525 4th St
Sarasota, FL 34236
941.343.2165
darwinson4th.com

TALLAHASSEE

DAVID GWYNN
Cypress Restaurant

320 E Tennessee St
Tallahassee, FL 32301
850.513.1100
cypressrestaurant.com

KEVIN STOUT
Food Glorious Food

1950 Thomasville Rd
Tallahassee, FL 32303
850.224.7279
foodgloriousfood.com

TERRY WHITE
Sage

3534 Maclay Blvd S
Tallahassee, FL 32312
850.270.9396
sagetallahassee.com

TAMPA

FERRELL ALVAREZ
Café Dufrain

707 Harbour Post Dr
Tampa, FL 33602
813.275.9701
cafedufrain.com

GREG BAKER
The Refinery

5137 N Florida Ave
Tampa, FL 33603
813.237.2000
thetamparefinery.com

GERALDO BAYONA
Columbia Restaurant

2117 E 7th Ave
Tampa, FL 33605
813.248.4961
columbiarestaurant.com

MARTY BLITZ
Mise en Place

442 W Kennedy Blvd #110
Tampa, FL 33606
813.254.5373
miseonline.com

RICHARD BOTTINI
Six Tables Tampa

4267 Henderson Blvd
Tampa, FL 33629
813.207.0527
sixtablestampa.com

TED DORSEY
Boca

901 W Platt St
Tampa, FL 33606
813.254.7070
bocatampa.com

CHRIS FERNANDEZ
Red Mesa

4912 4th St N
St. Petersburg, FL 33703
727.527.8728
redmesarestaurant.com

KORY FOLTZ
Oystercatchers

2900 Bayport Dr
Tampa, FL 33607
813.207.6815
oystercatchersrestaurant.com

TYSON GRANT
Parkshore Grill

300 Beach Dr NE
St. Petersburg, FL 33701
727.896.3463
parkshoregrill.com

ZACK GROSS
Z Grille

104 2nd St S
St. Petersburg, FL 33701
727.822.9600
zgrille.net

HABTEAB HAMDE
Bern's Steak House

1208 S Howard Ave
Tampa, FL 33606
813.251.2421
bernssteakhouse.com

CHAD JOHNSON
SideBern's

2208 W Morrison Ave
Tampa, FL 33606
813.258.2233
sideberns.com

FELICIA LACALLE
Samba Room

1502 S Howard Ave
Tampa, FL 33606
813.251.4022
sambatampa.com

TONY MANGIAFICO
Gratzzi Italian Grille

211 2nd St S
St. Petersburg, FL 33701
727.623.9037
gratzzigrille.com

ROBERT MASSON
717 South

717 S Howard Ave
Tampa, FL 33606
813.250.1661
717south.com

CHAD MCCOLGIN
Boca

901 W Platt St
Tampa, FL 33606
813.254.7070
bocatampa.com

ERIC MCHUGH
The Refinery

5137 N Florida Ave
Tampa, FL 33603
813.237.2000
thetamparefinery.com

GARY MORAN
Wimauma

4205 S MacDill Ave
Tampa, FL 33611
813.498.0494
wimaumafoods.com

ERIC NERI
Maritana Grille

3400 Gulf Blvd
Tampa, FL 33706
727.360.1882
loewshotel.com

BT NGUYEN
Restaurant BT

2507 S MacDill Ave #B
Tampa, FL 33629
813.258.1916
restaurantbt.com

COURTNEY ORWIG
SideBern's

2208 W Morrison Ave
Tampa, FL 33606
813.258.2233
sideberns.com

FELIX PIEDRA
Vizcaya

10905 N Dale Mabry Hwy
Tampa, FL 33618
803.968.7400
vizcayarestaurante.com

TOMMY TANG
Yummy House

2202 W Waters Ave
Tampa, FL 33610
813.915.2828
yummyhousetampa.com

RENE VALENZUELA
Taco Bus

913 E Hillsborough Ave
Tampa, FL 33603
813.232.5889
taco-bus.com

KEITH WILLIAMSON
Tampa, FL

WEST PALM BEACH

JOSEPH CLARK
Sushi Jo

319 Belvedere Rd #112
West Palm Beach, FL 33405
561.868.7893
sushijo.com

CLAY CONLEY
Buccan

350 S County Rd
Palm Beach, FL 33480
561.833.3450
clayconley.com

OSCAR DE LA CRUZ
Portobello Cucina Italiana

351 S U.S. 1
Jupiter, FL 33477
561.748.3224
portobellojupiter.com

MARCELLO FIORENTINO
Marcello's La Sirena

6316 S Dixie Hwy
West Palm Beach, FL 33405
561.585.3128
lasirenaonline.com

NORBERT GOLDNER
Café L'Europe

331 S County Rd
Palm Beach, FL 33480
561.655.4020
cafeleurope.com

ADAM HERVIEUX
3800 Ocean

3800 N Ocean Dr
Riviera Beach, FL 33404
561.340.1795
3800oceanrestaurant.com

JIM LEIKEN
Café Boulud

301 Australian Ave
Palm Beach, FL 33480
561.655.6060
danielnyc.com

JEAN-PIERRE LEVERRIER
Chez Jean-Pierre

132 N County Rd
Palm Beach, FL 33480
561.833.1171
chezjean-pierre.com

CARLO SERNAGLIA
Vagabondi Restaurant

319 Belvedere Rd
West Palm Beach, FL 33405
561.249.2281
vagabondirestaurant.com

ANTHONY SICIGNANO
The Breakers Hotel

1 S County Rd
Palm Beach, FL 33480
561.655.6611
thebreakers.com

ALPHARETTA

DARIN HIEBEL
di Paolo

8560 Holcomb Bridge Rd
Alpharetta, GA 30022
770.587.1051
dipaolorestaurant.com

JOE AHN
SOHO Atlanta

4300 Paces Ferry Rd
Atlanta, GA 30339
770.801.0069
sohoatlanta.com

CHAD CLEVENGER
Alma Cocina

191 Peachtree St NE
Atlanta, GA 30303
404.968.9662
alma-atlanta.com

ATHENS

HUGH ACHESON
Five & Ten

1653 S Lumpkin St
Athens, GA 30606
706.546.7300
fiveandten.com

DREW BELLINE
No. 246

129 E Ponce de Leon Ave
Decatur, GA 30030
678.399.8246
no246.com

CHAD CRETE
The Iberian Pig

121 Sycamore St
Decatur, GA 30030
404.371.8800
iberianpigatl.com

MATT PALMERLEE
The Branded Butcher

225 N Lumpkin St
Athens, GA 30601
706.850.5152
facebook.com/thebrandedbutcher

RICHARD BLAIS
The Spence

75 5th St NW
Atlanta, GA 30308
404.892.9111
thespenceatl.com

LAURA CULBREATH
Kyma

3085 Piedmont Rd NE
Atlanta, GA 30305
404.262.0702
buckheadrestaurants.com

ATLANTA

JAMIE ADAMS
Veni Vidi Vici

41 14th St NW
Atlanta, GA 30309
404.875.8424
buckheadrestaurants.com

ANGUS BROWN
Octopus Bar

560 Gresham Ave
Atlanta, GA 30316
404.627.9911
octopusbaratl.com

SHANE DEVEREUX
The Lawrence

905 Juniper St
Atlanta, GA 30309
404.961.7177
thelawrenceatlanta.com

MARLA ADAMS
Babette's Café

573 N Highland Ave NE
Atlanta, GA 30307
404.523.9121
babettescafe.com

ANDY CARSON
Bacchanalia

1198 Howell Mill Rd NW
Atlanta, GA 30318
404.365.0410
starprovisions.com

GARY DONLICK
Bistro Niko

3344 Peachtree Rd
Atlanta, GA 30326
404.261.6456
buckheadrestaurants.com

SHAUN DOTY
Bantam + Biddy

1544 Piedmont Rd
Atlanta, GA 30324
404.907.3496
bantamandbiddy.com

ADAM EVANS
The Optimist

914 Howell Mill Rd
Atlanta, GA 30318
404.477.6260
theoptimistrestaurant.com

RON EYESTER
Rosebud Restaurant

1397 N Highland Ave NE
Atlanta, GA 30306
404.347.9747
rosebudatlanta.com

FORD FRY
JCT Kitchen & Bar

1198 Howell Mill Rd #18
Atlanta, GA 30318
404.355.2252
jctkitchen.com

KEVIN GILLESPIE
Gunshow

924 Garrett St SE #B
Atlanta, GA 30316
chefkevingillespie.com

CHRIS HALL
Local Three Kitchen & Bar

3290 Northside Pkwy NW
Atlanta, GA 30327
404.968.2700
localthree.com

CLIFFORD HARRISON
Bacchanalia

1198 Howell Mill Rd NW
Atlanta, GA 30318
404.365.0410
starprovisions.com

ATSUSHI HAYAKAWA
Sushi House Hayakawa

5979 Buford Hwy NE #A-10
Atlanta, GA 30340
770.986.0010
atlantasushibar.com

E.J. HODGKINSON
JCT Kitchen & Bar

1198 Howell Mill Rd #18
Atlanta, GA 30318
404.355.2252
jctkitchen.com

JOSH HOPKINS
White Oak Kitchen & Cocktails

270 Peachtree St
Atlanta, GA 30303
whiteoakkitchen.com

LINTON HOPKINS
Restaurant Eugene

2277 Peachtree Rd NE
Atlanta, GA 30309
404.355.0321
restauranteugene.com

PETER KAISER
Twist

3500 Peachtree Rd NE
Atlanta, GA 30326
404.869.1191
h2sr.com

PANO KARATASSOS
Kyma

3085 Piedmont Rd NE
Atlanta, GA 30305
404.262.0702
buckheadrestaurants.com

GERRY KLASKALA
Aria

490 E Paces Ferry Rd NE
Atlanta, GA 30305
404.233.7673
aria-atl.com

RICHARD LEE
Davio's

3500 Peachtree Rd NE
Atlanta, GA 30326
404.844.4810
davios.com

TAKA MORIUCHI
Taka

375 Pharr Rd NE #600
Atlanta, GA 30305
404.869.2802
takasushiatlanta.com

TODD MUSSMAN
Muss & Turner's

1675 Cumberland Pkwy SE #309
Smyrna, GA 30080
770.434.1114
mussandturners.com

TOMO NAITO
Tomo

3630 Peachtree Rd NE #140
Atlanta, GA 30326
404.835.2708
tomorestaurant.com

KEVIN OUZTS
The Spotted Trotter Charcuterie

1610 Hosea L Williams Dr NE
Atlanta, GA 30317
404.254.4958
thespottedtrotter.com

HECTOR SANTIAGO
Atlanta, GA

JAY SWIFT
4th & Swift

621 N Ave NE
Atlanta , GA 30308
678.904.0160
4thandswift.com

ROBERT PHALEN
One Eared Stag

1029 Edgewood Ave NE
Atlanta, GA 30307
404.525.4479
oneearedstag.com

STEVEN SATTERFIELD
Miller Union

999 Brady Ave NW
Atlanta, GA 30318
678.733.8550
millerunion.com

MARC TAFT
Chicken and the Egg

800 Whitlock Ave NW #124
Atlanta, GA 30064
678.388.8813
chickandtheegg.com

ANN PRICE
Ann's Snack Bar

1615 Memorial Dr SE
Atlanta, GA 30317
404.687.9207
annssnackbar.com

SCOTT SERPAS
Serpas Restaurant

659 Auburn Ave NE #501
Atlanta, GA 30312
404.688.0040
serpasrestaurant.com

CHIP ULBRICH
South City Kitchen Midtown

1144 Crescent Ave NE
Atlanta, GA 30309
404.873.7358
southcitykitchen.com

ANNE QUATRANO
Bacchanalia

1198 Howell Mill Rd NW
Atlanta, GA 30318
404.365.0410
starprovisions.com

STEPHEN SHARP
Blue Ridge Grill

1261 W Paces Ferry Rd NW
Atlanta, GA 30327
404.233.5030
blueridgegrill.com

HILARY WHITE
The Hil

9110 Selborne Ln #110
Palmetto, GA 30268
770.463.6040
thehil.com

KEVIN RATHBUN
Rathbun's

112 Krog St NE
Atlanta, GA 30307
404.524.8280
kevinrathbun.com

RYAN SMITH
Empire State South

999 Peachtree St NE #140
Atlanta, GA 30309
404.541.1105
empirestatesouth.com

TYLER WILLIAMS
Woodfire Grill

1782 Cheshire Bridge Rd
Atlanta, GA 30324
404.347.9055
woodfiregrill.com

CRAIG RICHARDS
Ecco

40 7th St NE
Atlanta, GA 30306
404.347.9555
ecco-atlanta.com

ZEB STEVENSON
Livingston

659 Peachtree St NE
Atlanta, GA 30308
404.897.5000
livingstonatlanta.com

IAN WINSLADE
Murphy's

997 Virginia Ave NE
Atlanta, GA 30306
404.872.0904
murphys-atlanta-restaurant.com

GUY WONG
Miso Izakaya

619 Edgewood Ave SE
Atlanta, GA 30312
678.701.0128
misoizakaya.com

AUGUSTA

HEINZ SOWINSKI
La Maison on Telfair

404 Telfair St
Augusta, GA 30901
706.722.4805
lamaisontelfair.com

SEAN WIGHT
Frog Hollow Tavern

1282 Broad St
Augusta, GA 30901
706.364.6906
froghollowtavern.com

BLUE RIDGE

POLINA WALKER
Blue Ridge Brewery

187 Depot St
Blue Ridge, GA 30513
706.632.6611
blueridgebrewery.com

CLARKESVILLE

MARC BADON
Glen-Ella Springs Inn

1789 Bear Gap Rd
Clarkesville, GA 30523
706.754.7295
glenella.com

CLAYTON

JAMIE ALLRED
Lake Rabun Hotel & Restaurant

35 Andrea Ln
Lakemont, GA 30552
706.782.4946
lakerabunhotel.com

DAVID DARUGH
Beechwood Inn

220 Beechwood Dr
Clayton, GA 30525
706.782.5485
beechwoodinn.ws

GAYLE DARUGH
Beechwood Inn

220 Beechwood Dr
Clayton, GA 30525
706.782.5485
beechwoodinn.ws

JENNY WILSON
Fromage & Other Fine Foods

31 Earl St
Clayton, GA 30525
706.212.7349
fromageclayton.com

ROSWELL

ERIC BALDERRAMA
Bistro VG

70 W Crossville Rd
Roswell, GA 30075
770.993.1156
bistrovg.com

SAVANNAH

VINCENT BURNS
The Olde Pink House

23 Abercorn St
Savannah, GA 31401
912.232.4286
plantersinnsavannah.com

HERVÉ DIDAILLER
Papillote

218 W Broughton St
Savannah, GA 31401
912.232.1881
papillote-savannah.com

CHRISTOPHER DINELLO
Alligator Soul

114 Barnard St
Savannah, GA 31401
912.232.7899
alligatorsoul.com

BLAKE ELSINGHORST
Café 37

205 E 37th St
Savannah, GA 31401
912.236.8533
cafe37.com

CHARLES FERGUSON
Belford's of Savannah

315 W Saint Julian St
Savannah, GA 31401
912.233.2626
belfordssavannah.com

GERALD GREEN
Garibaldi Café

315 W Congress St
Savannah, GA 31401
912.232.7118
garibaldisavannah.com

BRIAN HANSON
Vic's on the River

26 E Bay St
Savannah, GA 31401
912.721.1000
vicsontheriver.com

ROBERTO LEOCI
Leoci's Trattoria

606 Abercorn St
Savannah, GA 31401
912.335.7027
leocis.com

PATRICK MCNAMARA
Noble Fare

321 Jefferson St
Savannah, GA 31401
912.443.3210
noblefare.com

NICK MUELLER
Chef Nick Mueller & Co

438 Kessler Lp
Guyton, GA 31312
912.728.8150
chefnick.net

CHRISTOPHER J. NASON
Sapphire Grill

110 W Congress St
Savannah, GA 31401
912.443.9962
sapphiregrill.com

BRANDY WILLIAMSON
Local 11ten

1110 Bull St
Savannah, GA 31401
912.790.9000
local11ten.com

KELLY YAMBOR
Elizabeth on 37th

105 E 37th St
Savannah, GA 31401
912.236.5547
elizabethon37th.net

ST. SIMONS ISLAND

DAVE SNYDER
Halyards Restaurant

55 Cinema Ln
St. Simons, GA 31522
912.638.9100
halyardsrestaurant.com

DANIEL ZEAL
Georgian Room

100 Cloister Dr
Sea Island, GA 31561
912.638.3611
seaisland.com

THOMASVILLE

SCOTT FOSTER
Liam's Restaurant

113 E Jackson St
Thomasville, GA 31792
229.226.9944
liamsthomasville.com

WOODSTOCK

MICHAEL BOLOGNA
Vingenzo's

105 E Main St #100
Woodstock, GA 30188
770.924.9133
vingenzos.com

INGREDIENT: SEAWEED

HAWAII

PETER ABARCAR JR.
Hapuna Beach Prince Hotel

62-100 Kauna'Oa Dr
Kohala Coast, HI 96743
808.880.1111
princeresortshawaii.com

ALLEN HESS
Canoe House

68-1400 Mauna Lani Dr
Waikoloa, HI 96743
808.885.6622
maunalani.com

ANNIE ROESLER
Annie's Island Fresh Burgers

79-7460 Mamalahoa Hwy #105
Kealakekua, HI 96750
808.324.6000
anniesislandfreshburgers.com

DAVID ABRAHAMS
Red Water Café

65-1299 Kawaihae Rd
Waimea, HI 96743
808.885.9299
redwatercafe.com

NOAH HESTER
Blue Dragon Restaurant

61-3616 Kawaihae Rd
Waimea, HI 96743
808.882.7771
bluedragonrestaurant.com

MOSES TAVARES
Cafe Pesto

61-3665 Hawaii 270
Kawaihae, HI 96743
808.882.1071
cafepesto.com

JAMES BABIAN
Four Seasons Resort Hualalai

72-100 Ka'upulehu Dr
Kailua-Kona, HI 96740
808.325.8000
fourseasons.com

KENICHI KANADA
Kenichi Pacific

78-6831 Alii Dr #125
Kailua-Kona, HI 96740
808.322.6400
kenichihawaii.com

NORIO YAMAMOTO
Monstera Noodles & Sushi

68-1330 Mauna Lani Dr #111
Kohala Coast, HI 96743
808.887.2711
monsterasushi.com

SANDY BARR RIVERA
Hawaii Community College

200 W Kawili St
Hilo, HI 96732
808.934.2562
hawaii.edu

JOSHUA KETNER
Hilo Bay Café

315 Makaala St #109
Hilo, HI 96720
808.935.4939
hilobaycafe.com

KAUAI

JEAN-MARIE JOSSELIN
Josselin's Tapas Bar & Grill

2829 Ala Kalanikaumaka
Koloa, HI 96756
808.742.7117
josselins.com

SAM CHOY
Kai Lanai

78-6831 Alii Dr #1000
Kailua-Kona, HI 96740
808.333.3434
samchoy.com

PETER MERRIMAN
Merriman's

65-1227 Opelo Rd
Kamuela, HI 96743
808.885.6822
merrimanshawaii.com

MATT SMITH
Luau

1571 Poipu Rd
Koloa, HI 96756
808.742.1234
granthyattkauai.com

HI

MAUI

ISAAC BANCACO
Pineapple Grill

200 Kapalua Dr
Kapalua, HI 96761
808.669.9600
cohnrestaurants.com

MARK ELLMAN
Mala Ocean Tavern

1307 Front St
Lahaina, HI 96761
808.667.9394
malaoceantavern.com

BEVERLY GANNON
Hali'imaile General Store

900 Haliimaile Rd
Makawao, HI 96768
808.572.2666
bevgannonrestaurants.com

JAY LEDEE
Japengo

200 Nohea Kai Dr
Ka'anapali, HI 96761
808.667.4727
maui.hyatt.com

CAMERON LEWARK
Spago

3900 Wailea Alanui Dr
Maui, HI 96753
808.874.8000
fourseasons.com

MICHAEL LOFARO
Humuhumunukunukuapua'a

3850 Wailea Alanui Dr
Wailea-Makena, HI 96753
800.888.6100
grandwailea.com

JAMES MCDONALD
I'O Restaurant

505 Front St
Lahaina, HI 96761
808.661.8422
iomaui.com

SCOTT MCGILL
T S Restaurants

2530 Kekaa Dr
Lahaina, HI 96761
808.667.4800
tsrestaurants.com

JURG MUNCH
Lahaina Grill

127 Lahainaluna Rd
Lahaina, HI 96761
808.667.5117
lahainagrill.com

NEIL MURPHY
Merriman's

1 Bay Club Pl
Lahaina, HI 96761
808.669.6400
merrimanshawaii.com

NICHOLAS PORRECA
Ferraro's Bar e Ristorante

3900 Wailea Alanui Dr
Maui, HI 96753
808.874.8000
fourseasons.com

SHELDON SIMEON
Star Noodle

286 Kupuohi St
Maui, HI 96761
808.667.5400
starnoodle.com

JOJO VASQUEZ
The Plantation House

2000 Plantation Club Dr
Lahaina, HI 96761
808.669.6299
theplantationhouse.com

AKIRA WATANABE
Sushi Paradise

1215 S Kihei Rd
Kihei, HI 96753
808.879.3751

OAHU

BRIAN CHAN
Restaurant Epic

1131 Nuuanu Ave
Honolulu, HI 96817
808.587.7877
restaurantepichawaii.com

RON DE GUZMAN
Stage Restaurant

1250 Kapiolani Blvd
Honolulu, HI 96814
808.237.5429
stagerestauranthawaii.com

VIKRAM GARG
La Mer

2199 Kalia Rd
Honolulu, HI 96815
808.923.2311
halekulani.com

ED KENNEY
Town

3435 Waialae Ave
Honolulu, HI 96816
808.735.5900
townkaimuki.com

MANABU KIKUCHI
Sushi Izakaya Gaku

1329 S King St
Honolulu, HI 96814
808.589.1329

DAVE KODAMA
Sansei

2552 Kalakaua Ave
Honolulu, HI 96815
808.931.6286
sanseihawaii.com

GEORGE MAVROTHALASSITIS
Chef Mavro

1969 S King St
Honolulu, HI 96826
808.944.4714
chefmavro.com

RUSSELL SIU
3660 on the Rise

3660 Waialae Ave
Honolulu, HI 96816
808.737.1177
3660.com

ALAN TAKASAKI
Le Bistro

5730 Kalanianaole Hwy
Honolulu, HI 96821
808.373.7990

WADE UEOKA
Alan Wong's

1857 S King St #208
Honolulu, HI 96826
808.949.1939
alanwongs.com

ALAN WONG
Alan Wong's

1857 S King St #208
Honolulu, HI 96826
808.949.1939
alanwongs.com

ROY YAMAGUCHI
Roy's

226 Lewers St
Honolulu, HI 96815
808.923.7697
roysrestaurant.com

BOISE

JOHN BERRYHILL
Berryhill & Co.

121 N 9th St #102
Boise, ID 83702
208.387.3553
johnberryhillrestaurants.com

RICHARD LANGSTON
Café Vicino

808 W Fort St
Boise, ID 83702
208.472.1463
cafevicino.com

ANDREW MAYER
Boise, ID

WILEY EARL
Fork

199 N 8th St
Boise, ID 83702
208.287.1700
boisefork.com

TRAVIS LEVI
Bardenay

610 W Grove St
Boise, ID 83702
208.426.0538
bardenay.com

CHRIS MCDONALD
The Arid Club

1137 W River St
Boise, ID 83702
208.343.4631
aridclub.org

LUIS FLORES
Chandlers Steakhouse

981 W Grove St
Boise, ID 83702
208.383.4300
chandlersboise.com

ANDREA MARICICH
Salt Tears Coffeehouse & Noshery

4714 W State St
Boise, ID 83703
208.275.0017
salttears.com

MATT VILLEGAS
Plaza Grill

1109 Main St
Boise, ID 83702
208.343.4611
owyheeplaza.com

DAVID KNICKREHM
Bella Aquila

775 S Rivershore Ln
Eagle, ID 83616
208.938.1900
bellaaquilarestaurant.com

ENRIQUE MARTINEZ
Barbacoa

276 Bobwhite Ct
Boise, ID 83706
208.338.5000
barbacoa-boise.com

GINO VUELO
Gino's Italian Restaurant

3015 W McMillan Rd
Boise, ID 83646
208.887.7710

COEUR D'ALENE

GREG LAMM
Boise, ID

SHIGE MATSUZAWA
Shige Japanese Cuisine

100 N 8th St # 215
Boise, ID 83702
208.338.8423

ADAM HEGSTED
Coeur d'Alene Casino and Resort

37914 S Hwy 95
Worley, ID 83876
208.769.2600
cdacasino.com

LAURENT ZIROTTI
Fleur de Sel

4365 E Inverness Dr
Post Falls, ID 83854
208.777.7600
fleur-de-sel.weebly.com

NAMPA

PAUL BEVERLEY
Simple Sushi

1214 1st St S
Nampa, ID 83651
208.463.4663
simplesushibar.com

DUSTAN BRISTOL
Brick 29 Bistro

320 11th Ave S
Nampa, ID 83651
208.468.0029
brick29.com

SUN VALLEY

JOHN MURCKO
Sun Valley Resort

2 Sun Valley Rd
Sun Valley, ID 83353
208.622.2800
sunvalley.com

TWIN FALLS

MARK OWSLEY
St. Luke's Magic Valley

801 Pole Line Rd W
Twin Falls, ID 83301
208.814.0605
stlukesonline.org

FERMENTATION

Innovating with this ancient form of preservation, experimentation is key to getting the brew just right.

CARBONDALE

LASSE SORENSEN
Tom's Place

17107 N U.S. 51
De Soto, IL 62924
618.867.3033
tomsplacedesoto.com

CHAMPAIGN

JESSICA GORIN
Big Grove Tavern

1 E Main St
Champaign, IL 61820
217.239.3505
biggrovetavern.com

CHICAGO

GRANT ACHATZ
Alinea

1723 N Halsted St
Chicago, IL 60614
312.867.0110
alinearestaurant.com

JOSE LUIS AGUILAR
South Barrington, IL

JOHN ANDERES
Telegraph

2601 N Milwaukee Ave
Chicago, IL 60647
773.292.9463
telegraphwinebar.com

AUGIE ARIFI
Café Lucci

609 Milwaukee Ave
Glenview, IL 60025
847.729.2268
cafelucci.com

GARY BACA
Joe's Seafood, Prime Steak &
Stone Crab

10 E Grand Ave
Chicago, IL 60611
312.379.5637
joes.net

JEROME BACLE
Courtright's

8989 Archer Ave
Chicago, IL 60480
708.839.8000
courtrights.com

JIMMY BANNOS JR.
The Purple Pig

500 N Michigan Ave
Chicago, IL 60611
312.464.1744
thepurplepigchicago.com

RICK BAYLESS
Topolobampo

445 N Clark St
Chicago, IL 60654
312.661.1434
fronterakitchens.com

DAVID BERAN
Next

953 W Fulton Market
Chicago, IL 60607
312.226.0858
nextrestaurant.com

MARC BERNARD
Big Bowl

60 E Ohio St
Chicago, IL 60611
312.951.1888
bigbowl.com

JOHNNY BESCH
Le Bistro Bordeaux

618 Church St
Evanston, IL 60201
847.424.1483
lebistrobordeaux.com

DUNCAN BIDDULPH
Rootstock

954 N California Ave
Chicago, IL 60622
773.292.1616
rootstockbar.com

GREG BIGGERS
Café des Architectes

20 E Chestnut St
Chicago, IL 60611
312.324.4063
cafedesarchitectes.com

MYCHAEL BONNER
Di Pescara

601 N Milwaukee Ave
Wheeling, IL 60090
847.777.6878
di-pescara.com

HOMARO CANTU
Moto Restaurant

945 W Fulton Market
Chicago, IL 60607
312.491.0058
motorestaurant.com

MICHAEL CARLSON
Schwa

1466 N Ashland Ave
Chicago, IL 60622
773.252.1466
schwarestaurant.com

PATRICK CASSATA
The Bank

121 W Front St
Wheaton, IL 60187
630.665.2265
thebankwheaton.com

MATT CHASSEUR
Alinea

1723 N Halsted St
Chicago, IL 60614
312.867.0110
alinearestaurant.com

MICHAEL CHENG
Sun Wah BBQ

5039 N Broadway
Chicago, IL 60640
773.769.1254
sunwahbbq.com

JOHN CHIAKULAS
foodlife

835 N Michigan Ave
Chicago, IL 60611
312.335.3663
foodlifechicago.com

JOHN COLETTA
Quartino

626 N State St
Chicago, IL 60654
312.698.5000
quartinochicago.com

FEDERICO COMACCHIO
Coco Pazzo

300 W Hubbard St
Chicago, IL 60654
312.836.0900
cocopazzochicago.com

LUCA CORAZZINA
312 Chicago

136 N La Salle St
Chicago, IL 60602
312.696.2420
312chicago.com

DAVID DIGREGORIO
Osteria Via Stato

620 N State St
Chicago, IL 60654
312.642.8450
osteriaviastato.com

ADAM DITTMER
Bistro Campagne

4518 N Lincoln Ave
Chicago, IL 60625
773.271.6100
bistrocampagne.com

CURTIS DUFFY
Grace

652 W Randolph St
Chicago, IL 60661
312.234.9494
grace-restaurant.com

CHRISTIAN ECKMANN
Lettuce Entertain You

116 Sheridan St
Chicago, IL 60640
773.878.7340
leye.com

GRAHAM ELLIOT
Graham Elliot

217 W Huron St
Chicago, IL 60654
312.624.9975
grahamelliot.com

JOSE LUIS ESPINO
Chicago, IL

RICHIE FARINA
Moto Restaurant

945 W Fulton Market
Chicago, IL 60607
312.491.0058
motorestaurant.com

DIRK FLANIGAN
The Gage

24 S Michigan Ave
Chicago, IL 60603
312.372.4243
thegagechicago.com

PHILLIP FOSS
El Ideas

2419 W 14th St
Chicago, IL 60608
312.226.8144
elideas.com

CURTIS GAMBLE
Bread & Wine

3732 W Irving Park Rd
Chicago, IL 60618
773.866.5266
breadandwinechicago.com

CARLOS GAYTAN
Mexique

1529 W Chicago Ave
Chicago, IL 60642
312.850.0288
mexiquechicago.com

MARK GROSZ
Oceanique

505 Main St
Evanston, IL 60202
847.864.3435
oceanique.com

SARAH GRUENEBERG
Spiaggia

980 N Michigan Ave
Chicago, IL 60612
312.280.3300
spiaggiarestaurant.com

LEE GUIDRY
SUSHISAMBA

504 N Wells St
Chicago, IL 60654
312.595.2300
sushisamba.com

JASON HAMMEL
Lula Café

2537 N Kedzie Blvd
Chicago, IL 60647
773.489.9554
lulacafe.com

KEVIN HICKEY
Allium

120 E Delaware Pl
Chicago, IL 60611
312.799.4900
alliumchicago.com

JOHN HOGAN
Keefer's Restaurant

20 W Kinzie St
Chicago, IL 60654
312.467.9525
keefersrestaurant.com

TREVOR HOYTE
IPO

172 W Adams St
Chicago, IL 60603
312.917.5608
iporestaurant.com

TONY HU
Lao Sze Chuan

2172 S Archer Ave
Chicago, IL 60616
312.326.5040
tonygourmetgroup.com

BRIAN HUSTON
The Publican

837 W Fulton Market
Chicago, IL 60607
312.733.9555
thepublicanrestaurant.com

JUN ICHIKAWA
Mirai Sushi

2020 W Division St
Chicago, IL 60622
773.862.8500
miraisushi.com

STEPHANIE IZARD
Girl and the Goat

809 W Randolph St
Chicago, IL 60607
312.492.6262
girlandthegoat.com

RICHARD JAMES
Frontera Grill

445 N Clark St
Chicago, IL 60654
312.661.1434
fronterakitchens.com

J. JOHO
Everest

440 S La Salle St #40
Chicago, IL 60605
312.663.8920
chefjoho.com

PAUL KAHAN
Blackbird

619 W Randolph St
Chicago, IL 60661
312.715.0708
blackbirdrestaurant.com

JOEL KAZOUINI
Chez Joel Bistro

1119 W Taylor St
Chicago, IL 60607
312.226.6479
chezjoelbistro.com

BILL KIM
Urban Belly

3053 N California Ave
Chicago, IL 60618
773.583.0500
urbanbellychicago.com

EDWARD KIM
Ruxbin

851 N Ashland Ave
Chicago, IL 60622
312.624.8509
ruxbinchicago.com

MATTHEW KIRKLEY
L2O

2300 N Lincoln Park W
Chicago, IL 60614
773.868.0002
l2orestaurant.com

MICHAEL KORNICK
DMK Burger Bar

2954 N Sheffield Ave
Chicago, IL 60657
773.360.8686
dmkburgerbar.com

JONCARL LACHMAN
HB Home Bistro

3404 N Halsted St
Chicago, IL 60657
773.661.0299
homebistrochicago.com

MICHAEL LACHOWICZ
Restaurant Michael

64 Green Bay Rd
Winnetka, IL 60093
847.441.3100
restaurantmichael.com

JUSTIN LARGE
Big Star

1531 N Damen Ave
Chicago, IL 60622
773.235.4039
bigstarchicago.com

RYAN LAROCHE
NoMI

800 N Michigan Ave
Chicago, IL 60611
312.239.4030
hyatt.com

THOMAS LENTS
Sixteen

401 N Wabash Ave
Chicago, IL 60611
312.588.8030
sixteenchicago.com

DALE LEVITSKI
Sprout

1417 W Fullerton Ave
Chicago, IL 60614
773.348.0706
sproutrestaurant.com

KATHLEEN LEWIS
The Cellar Bistro

132 N Hale St
Wheaton, IL 60187
630.653.6299
thecellarbistro.com

ROLAND LICCIONI
Les Nomades

222 E Ontario St
Chicago, IL 60611
312.649.9010
lesnomades.net

JAY LOVELL
Lovell's of Lake Forest

915 S Waukegan Rd
Lake Forest , IL 60045
847.234.8013
lovellsoflakeforest.com

CHRIS MACCHIA
The Florentine

151 W Adams St
Chicago, IL 60603
312.660.8866
e2hospitality.com

MAURO MAFRICI
Pelago Ristorante

201 E Delaware Pl
Chicago, IL 60611
312.280.0700
pelagorestaurant.com

TONY MANTUANO
Spiaggia

980 N Michigan Ave
Chicago, IL 60611
312.280.3300
spiaggiarestaurant.com

ANTHONY MARTIN
Tru

676 N Saint Clair St
Chicago, IL 60611
312.202.0001
trurestaurant.com

SAUL MAYA
Il Poggiolo

8 E 1st St
Hinsdale, IL 60521
630.734.9400
ilpoggiolohinsdale.com

RYAN MCCASKEY
Acadia

1639 S Wabash Ave
Chicago, IL 60616
312.360.9500
acadiachicago.com

ANDY MOTTO
Quince

1625 Hinman Ave #102
Evanston, IL 60201
847.570.8400
quincerestaurant.net

ANDRES PADILLA
Topolobampo

445 N Clark St
Chicago, IL 60654
312.661.1434
rickbayless.com

PATRICK MCLAUGHLIN
Parker's Restaurant & Bar

1000 31st St
Downers Grove, IL 60515
630.960.5700
selectrestaurants.com

CARRIE NAHABEDIAN
NAHA

500 N Clark St
Chicago, IL 60654
312.321.6242
naha-chicago.com

CHRIS PANDEL
Balena

1633 N Halsted St
Chicago, IL 60614
312.867.3888
balenachicago.com

MARK MENDEZ
Vera

1023 W Lake St
Chicago, IL 60607
312.243.9770
verachicago.com

VICTOR NEWGREN
Lawry's The Prime Rib

100 E Ontario St
Chicago, IL 60611
312.787.5000
lawrysonline.com

B.K. PARK
Chicago, IL

MATTHIAS MERGES
Yusho

2853 N Kedzie Ave
Chicago, IL 60618
773.904.8558
yusho-chicago.com

CHRIS NUGENT
goosefoot

2656 W Lawrence Ave
Chicago, IL 60625
773.942.7547
goosefoot.net

MICHAEL PAULSEN
Abigail's American Bistro

493 Roger Williams Ave
Highland Park, IL 60035
847.780.4862
abigails493.com

CORY MORRIS
Mercat a la Planxa

638 S Michigan Ave
Chicago, IL 60605
312.765.0524
mercatchicago.com

EDGAR OJEDA
Wildfire

159 W Erie St
Chicago, IL 60654
312.787.9000
wildfirerestaurant.com

VICTOR PERDUE
Viaggio

1330 W Madison St
Chicago, IL 60607
312.829.3333
viaggiochicago.com

BRYAN MOSCATELLO
Storefront Company

1941 W North Ave
Chicago, IL 60622
773.661.2609
thestorefrontcompany.com

DANIEL OVANIN
Glen Prairie

1250 Roosevelt Rd
Glen Ellyn, IL 60137
630.613.1250
glenprairie.com

SERENA PERDUE
Niche

14 S 3rd St
Chicago, IL 60134
630.262.1000
nichegeneva.com

LAURA PIPER
Trattoria No. 10
10 N Dearborn St #1
Chicago, IL 60602
312.984.1718
trattoriaten.com

ROBERT REYNAUD
Vivere
71 W Monroe St
Chicago, IL 60603
312.332.4040
vivere-chicago.com

NATHAN SEARS
Vie
4471 Lawn Ave #100
Western Springs, IL 60558
708.246.2082
vierestaurant.com

RYAN POLI
Tavernita
151 W Erie St
Chicago, IL 60654
312.274.1111
tavernita.com

RICHARD ROETTGEN
Chicago, IL

MIKE SHEERIN
Trenchermen
2039 W North Ave
Chicago, IL 60647
773.661.1540
trenchermen.com

DAVID POSEY
Blackbird
619 W Randolph St
Chicago, IL 60661
312.715.0708
blackbirdrestaurant.com

MASSIMO SALATINO
Francesca's Restaurants
Chicago, IL
773.334.8368
miafrancesca.com

PATRICK SHEERIN
Trenchermen
2039 W North Ave
Chicago, IL 60647
773.661.1540
trenchermen.com

TONY PRIOLO
Piccolo Sogno
464 N Halsted St #1
Chicago, IL 60642
312.421.0077
piccolosognorestaurant.com

PRISCILA SATKOFF
Salpicon
1252 N Wells St
Chicago, IL 60610
312.988.7811
salpicon.com

BRUCE SHERMAN
North Pond
2610 N Cannon Dr
Chicago, IL 60614
773.477.5845
northpondrestaurant.com

DOUG PSALTIS
RPM Italian Restaurant
52 W Illinois St
Chicago, IL 60654
312.222.1888
rpmitalian.com

CRAIG SCHOETTLER
Chicago, IL

DEREK SIMCIK
Atwood Café
1 W Washington St
Chicago, IL 60602
312.368.1900
atwoodcafe.com

MOOSAH REAUME
Pump Room
1301 N State Pkwy
Chicago, IL 60610
312.229.6740
pumproom.com

ZOE SCHOR
Ada Street
1664 Ada St
Chicago, IL 60642
773.697.7069
adastreetchicago.com

LARRY SMITH
Winnetka, IL

ART SMITH
Table Fifty-Two

52 W Elm St
Chicago, IL 60610
312.573.4000
tablefifty-two.com

BRENDAN SODIKOFF
Au Cheval

800 W Randolph St
Chicago, IL 60607
312.929.4580
aucheval.tumblr.com

MARK SPARACINO
Prosecco

710 N Wells St
Chicago, IL 60610
312.951.9500
prosecco.us.com

SANTIAGO SUAREZ
1776

397 W Virginia St
Crystal Lake, IL 60014
815.356.1776
1776restaurant.com

CARY TAYLOR
The Southern

1840 W North Ave
Chicago, IL 60622
773.342.1840
thesouthernchicago.com

GIUSEPPE TENTORI
GT Fish and Oyster

531 N Wells St
Chicago, IL 60654
312.929.3501
gtoyster.com

HEATHER TERHUNE
Sable Kitchen & Bar

505 N State St
Chicago, IL 60654
312.755.9704
sablechicago.com

CHAO THAPTHIMKUNA
Union Sushi + Barbeque Bar

230 W Erie St
Chicago, IL 60654
312.662.4888
eatatunion.com

SHIN THOMPSON
Bonsoiree

2728 W Armitage Ave
Chicago, IL 60647
773.486.7511
bon-soiree.com

RICK TRAMONTO
Tramonto's Steak & Seafood

601 N Milwaukee Ave
Wheeling, IL 60090
847.777.6575
ricktramonto.com

CHARLIE TROTTER
Chicago, IL

COLIN TURNER
Tin Fish

18201 S Harlem Ave
Tinley Park, IL 60477
708.532.0200
tinfishrestaurant.com

JARED VAN CAMP
Nellcote

833 W Randolph St
Chicago, IL 60607
312.432.0500
nellcoterestaurant.com

TANAPAT VANNOPAS
Seven Ocean

122 N Marion St
Berwyn, IL 60301
708.524.7979
sevenoceanoakpark.com

LUIS VAZQUEZ
Café Ba-Ba-Reeba

2024 N Halsted St
Chicago, IL 60614
773.935.5000
cafebabareeba.com

JASON VINCENT
Nightwood

2119 S Halsted St
Chicago, IL 60608
312.526.3385
nightwoodrestaurant.com

PAUL VIRANT
Vie Restaurant

4471 Lawn Ave
Chicago, IL 60558
708.246.2082
vierestaurant.com

JARED WENTWORTH
Longman & Eagle

2657 N Kedzie Ave
Chicago, IL 60647
773.276.7110
longmanandeagle.com

ERICK WILLIAMS
MK

868 N Franklin St
Chicago, IL 60610
312.482.9179
mkchicago.com

ERLING WU-BOWER
Avec

615 W Randolph St
Chicago, IL 60661
312.377.2002
avecrestaurant.com

TAKASHI YAGIHASHI
Takashi

1952 N Damen Ave
Chicago, IL 60647
773.772.6170
takashichicago.com

CARLOS YSAGUIRRE
Anteprima

5316 N Clark St
Chicago, IL 60640
773.506.9990
anteprimachicago.net

ANDREW ZIMMERMAN
Sepia

123 N Jefferson St
Chicago, IL 60661
312.441.1920
sepiachicago.com

DOMINIC ZUMPANO
Market House on the Square

655 Forest Ave
Lake Forest , IL 60045
847.234.8800
themarkethouse.com

RANDY ZWEIBAN
Province

161 N Jefferson St
Chicago, IL 60661
312.669.9900
provincerestaurant.com

EDWARDSVILLE

SLADE ROSS
Erato

126 Main St
Edwardsville, IL 62025
618.307.3203
eratoonmain.com

ADAM WASHBURN
Craft Chophouse

210 S Buchanan St
Edwardsville, IL 62025
618.307.9300
craft-chophouse.com

EFFINGHAM

NIALL CAMPBELL
Firefly Grill

1810 Avenue of Mid-America
Effingham, IL 62401
217.342.2002
ffgrill.com

GALENA

STEVE DOWE
Perry Street Brasserie

124 N Commerce St
Galena, IL 61036
815.777.3773
perrystreetbrasserie.com

GALESBURG

BILL EGENLAUF
Chez Willy's

41 S Seminary St
Galesburg, IL 61401
309.341.4141
chezwillys.com

HERRIN

DAVID HAYS
Mary's Restaurant

509 S Park Ave
Herrin, IL 62948
618.942.2742
marysfinedining.com

PEORIA

JOSH ADAMS
June

4450 N Prospect Rd
Peoria Heights, IL 61616
877.682.5863
junerestaurant.com

RYAN DUNKLE
Two25

225 NE Adams St
Peoria, IL 61612
309.282.7777
two25peoria.com

ROCK ISLAND

RACHID BOUCHAREB
Le Figaro

708 2nd Ave
Rock Island, IL 61201
309.786.4944
lefigarorestaurant.com

SHEFFIELD

ERAN SALZMANN
Z Best Café

129 S Main St
Sheffield, IL 61361
815.454.2425
zbestcafe.com

SPRINGFIELD

JORDAN COFFEY
American Harvest Eatery

3241 W Iles Ave
Springfield, IL 62711
217.546.8300
americanharvesteatery.com

132

BERNARD CRETIER
Le Vichyssois

220 W Rand Rd
Lakemoor, IL 60051
815.385.8221
levichyssois.com

LENNIE FERRIGNO
Bella Milano

4525 Wabash Ave
Springfield, IL 62711
217.547.0011
bellamilanos.com

MICHAEL HIGGINS
Maldaner's

222 S 6th St
Springfield, IL 62701
217.522.4313
maldaners.com

JOHN KIDD
Sebastian's Hideout

221 S 5th St
Springfield, IL 62701
217.789.8988
sebastianshideout.com

AUGUST MROZOWSKI
Augie's Front Burner

109 S 5th St
Springfield, IL 62701
217.544.6979
augiesfrontburner.com

ROBB WYSS
Illini Country Club

1601 Illini Rd
Springfield, IL 62704
217.546.4614
illinicc.net

 INDIANA

BLOOMINGTON

DANIEL ORR
FARMbloomington

108 E Kirkwood Ave
Bloomington, IN 47408
812.323.0002
farm-bloomington.com

DAVID TALLENT
Restaurant Tallent

208 N Walnut St
Bloomington, IN 47404
812.330.9801
restauranttallent.com

FORT WAYNE

MATTHEW NOLOT
Eddie Merlot's

1502 Illinois Rd S
Fort Wayne, IN 46804
260.459.2222
eddiemerlots.com

INDIANAPOLIS

ABBI ADAMS
Bluebeard

653 Virginia Ave
Indianapolis, IN 46203
317.686.1580
bluebeardindy.com

JOHN ADAMS
Bluebeard

653 Virginia Ave
Indianapolis, IN 46203
317.686.1580
bluebeardindy.com

ELI ANDERSON
Indianapolis, IN

DEBBIE BENNETT
Yokohama

67 N Madison Ave
Greenwood, IN 46141
317.859.1888
yokohamagreenwood.com

NEAL BROWN
The Libertine

38 E Washington St
Indianapolis, IN 46204
317.631.3333
libertineindy.com

DENIS DE STAIC
Woodstock Club

1301 W 38th St
Indianapolis, IN 46208
317.926.3348
woodstockclub.com

DAN DUNVILLE
10-01 Food & Drink

1001 Broad Ripple Ave
Indianapolis, IN 46220
317.253.1001
1001fooddrink.com

MICAH FRANK
Black Market

922 Massachusetts Ave
Indianapolis, IN 46202
317.822.6757
blackmarketindy.net

GREG HARDESTY
Recess

4907 N College Ave
Indianapolis, IN 46205
317.925.7529
recessindy.com

TYLER HERALD
Patachou, Inc.

4923 N College Ave #25
Indianapolis, IN 46205
317.202.0765
patachouinc.com

JOSEPH HEWETT
The Indigo Duck

39 E Court St
Franklin, IN 46131
317.560.5805
theindigoduck.com

ERIN KEM
R Bistro

888 Massachusetts Ave
Indianapolis, IN 46204
317.423.0312
rbistro.com

IN

REGINA MEHALLICK
R bistro

888 Massachusetts Ave
Indianapolis, IN 46204
317.423.0312
rbistro.com

THOMAS MELVIN
Mo's

47 S Pennsylvania St
Indianapolis, IN 46204
317.624.0720
mosindy.net

RYAN NELSON
Late Harvest Kitchen

8605 River Crossing
Indianapolis, IN 46240
317.663.8063
lateharvestkitchen.com

STEVEN J. OAKLEY
Oakleys Bistro

1464 W 86th St
Indianapolis, IN 46260
317.824.1231
oakleysbistro.com

LAYTON ROBERTS
Meridian

5694 N Meridian St
Indianapolis, IN 46208
317.466.1111
meridianonmeridian.com

ANASS SENTISSI
Saffron Cafe

621 Fort Wayne Ave
Indianapolis, IN 46204
317.917.0131
saffroncafe-indy.com

CHUTIKAN SOUVANNACHACK
Siam Square

936 Virginia Ave
Indianapolis, IN 46203
317.636.8424
siamsquareindy.com

MERRILLVILLE

SAM CHUNG
Asparagus

7876 Broadway
Merrillville, IN 46410
219.794.0000
asparagusrestaurant.com

TAMMY PHAM
Asparagus

7876 Broadway
Merrillville, IN 46410
219.794.0000
asparagusrestaurant.com

ROANOKE

AARON BUTTS
Joseph Decuis

191 N Main St
Roanoke, IN 46783
260.672.1715
josephdecuis.com

VALPARAISO

NICOLE BISSONNETTE
Bistro 157

157 W Lincoln Way
Valparaiso, IN 46383
219.462.0992
bistro157.net

WESTFIELD

CRAIG BAKER
The Local Eatery & Pub

14655 N Gray Rd
Westfield, IN 46062
317.218.3786
localeateryandpub.com

CEDAR FALLS

CHRIS MEYERS
Ferrari's Ristorante

1521 Technology Pkwy
Cedar Falls, IA 50613
319.277.1385
barmuda.com

CHANCEY VOYSEY
Bourbon Street

314 Main St
Cedar Falls, IA 50613
319.266.5285
barmuda.com

CEDAR RAPIDS

MON SAYASIT
Daniel Arthur's

822 3rd Ave SE
Cedar Rapids, IA 52404
319.362.9341
danielarthurs.net

MATT STEIGERWALD
Lincoln Café

117 1st St NW
Mt. Vernon, IA 52314
319.895.4041
foodisimportant.com

IAN TRASK
Daniel Arthur's

821 3rd Ave SE
Cedar Rapids, IA 52403
319.362.9340
danielarthurs.net

DECORAH

ANDY BONNET
Rubaiyat

117 W Water St
Decorah, IA 52101
563.382.9463
rubaiyatrestaurant.com

JUSTIN SCARDINA
La Rana Bistro

120 Washington St
Decorah, IA 52101
563.382.3067
laranabistro.com

DES MOINES

DAVID BARUTHIO
Baru Sixty-Six

6587 University Ave
Des Moines, IA 50324
515.277.6627
baru66.com

BRIAN DENNIS
801 ChopHouse

801 Grand Ave #200
Des Moines, IA 50309
515.288.6000
801chophouse.com

GEORGE FORMARO
Centro

1003 Locust S
Des Moines, IA 50309
515.248.1780
centrodesmoines.com

JED HOFFMAN
Trostel's Dish

12851 University Ave #400
Des Moines, IA 50325
515.221.3474
dishtrostels.com

DOMINIC IANNARELLI
Splash

303 Locust St
Des Moines, IA 50309
515.244.5686
splash-seafood.com

ENOSH KELLEY
Bistro Montage

2724 Ingersoll Ave
Des Moines, IA 50312
515.557.1924
bistromontage.com

JOSH MCCURNIN
Fleming's

150 S Jordan Creek Pwy
West Des Moines, IA 50266
515.457.2916
flemingssteakhouse.com

ANDY SCHUMACHER
Des Moines, IA

DUBUQUE

RYAN NORMAN
The Copper Kettle

2987 Jackson St
Dubuque, IA 52001
563.845.0567
facebook.com/1fooddubuque

IOWA CITY

JAMES ADRIAN
Atlas World Grill

127 Iowa Ave
Iowa City, IA 52240
319.341.7700
atlasiowacity.com

TONY CARTER-WALSH
One Twenty Six

126 E Washington St
Iowa City, IA 52240
319.887.1909
onetwentysix.net

ANDY DIEP
Konomi

843 Quarry Rd #140
Coralville, IA 52241
319.351.2880
konomigrill.com

BRYAN HERZIC
Orchard Green

521 S Gilbert St
Iowa City, IA 52240
319.354.1642
orchardgreenrestaurant.com

BRADY MCDONALD
Basta

121 Iowa Ave
Iowa City, IA 52240
319.337.2010
bastaiowacity.com

ERIC MCDOWELL
Chef's Table

223 E Washington St
Iowa City, IA 52240
319.337.0490
chefstableiowacity.com

KATY MEYER
Trumpet Blossom Café

310 E Prentiss St
Iowa City, IA 52240
319.248.0077
trumpetblossom.com

CHRISTIAN PROCHASKA
Iowa City, IA

DAVID WIESENECK
Motley Cow Café

160 N Linn St
Iowa City, IA 52245
319.688.9177
motleycowcafe.com

DARREN XIE
Iowa City, IA

ROOT TO LEAF
Using the whole vegetable is both flavorful and economical.

KANSAS CITY

PHILIP QUILLEC
Café Provence

3936 W 69th Terrace
Prairie Village, KS 66208
913.384.5998
kcconcept.com

CARL THORNE-THOMSEN
Story

3931 W 69th Terrace
Prairie Village, KS 66208
913.236.9955
storykc.com

DAN UCHE
Bristol Seafood Grill

5400 W 119th St
Leawood, KS 66209
913.663.5777
bristolseafoodgrill.com

LAWRENCE

KEN BAKER
Pachamama's

800 New Hampshire St
Lawrence, KS 66044
785.841.0990
pachamamas.com

MICHAEL BEARD
715

715 Massachusetts St
Lawrence, KS 66044
785.856.7150
715mass.com

MANHATTAN

SCOTT BENJAMIN
4 Olives Wine Bar

3033 Anderson Ave
Manhattan, KS 66503
785.539.1295
fourolives.biz

CADELL BYNUM
Harry's Restaurant

418 Poyntz Ave
Manhattan, KS 66502
785.537.1300
harrysmanhattan.com

WICHITA

BOBBY LANE
Chester's Chophouse & Wine Bar

1550 N Webb Rd
Wichita, KS 67206
316.201.1300
chesterschophouse.com

JAKE LIPPINCOTT
The Petroleum Club

100 N Broadway St
Wichita, KS 67202
316.262.6471
petroleumclub.com

AARON WHITCOMB
Newport Grill

1900 N Rock Rd
Wichita, KS 67206
316.636.9555
newportgrillwichita.com

COVINGTON

MATT BUSCHLE
Virgil's Café

710 Fairfield Ave
Bellevue, KY 41073
859.491.3287
virgilscafe.com

STEPHEN WILLIAMS
Bouquet

519 Main St
Covington, KY 41011
859.491.7777
bouquetrestaurant.com

LEXINGTON

COLE ARIMES
Coles 735 Main

735 E Main St
Lexington, KY 40502
859.266.9000
coles735main.com

JEREMY ASHBY
AZUR

3070 Lakecrest Cir #550
Lexington, KY 40513
859.296.1007
azurrestaurant.com

MATT COMBS
Sal's Chophouse

3373 Tates Creek Rd
Lexington, KY 40502
859.269.9922
bluegrasshospitality.com

ALAN LAMOUREUX
Malone's

3735 Palomar Centre Dr
Lexington, KY 40513
859.977.2620
bluegrasshospitality.com

JONATHAN LUNDY
Jonathan at Gratz Park

120 W 2nd St
Lexington, KY 40507
859.252.4949
jagp.info

OUITA MICHEL
Holly Hill Inn

426 N Winter St
Midway, KY 40347
859.846.4732
hollyhillinn.com

JORDAN NOEL
Lexington, KY

BRIAN SURBAUGH
Table Three Ten Restaurant

310 W Short St
Lexington, KY 40507
859.309.3901
table-three-ten.com

LOUISVILLE

BOBBY BENJAMIN
La Coop

732 E Market St
Louisville, KY 40202
502.410.2888
coopbistro.com

ADAM BURRESS
Hammerheads

921 Swan St
Louisville, KY 40204
502.365.1112
louisvillehammerheads.com

KATHY CARY
Lilly's

1147 Bardstown Rd
Louisville, KY 40204
502.451.0447
lillyslapeche.com

S. DEAN CORBETT
Corbett's Restaurant

5050 Norton Healthcare Blvd
Louisville, KY 40241
502.327.5058
corbettsrestaurant.com

ANTHONY LAMAS
Seviche

1538 Bardstown Rd
Louisville, KY 40205
502.473.8560
sevicherestaurant.com

EDWARD LEE
610 Magnolia

610 W Magnolia Ave
Louisville, KY 40208
502.636.0783
610magnolia.com

ANNIE PETTRY
Decca Restaurant

812 E Market St
Louisville, KY 40206
502.749.8128
deccarestaurant.com

JOHN VARANESE
Varanese

2106 Frankfort Ave
Louisville, KY 40206
502.899.9904
varanese.com

BRIAN LYNCH
Louisville, KY

KEVIN RICE
Louisville, KY

LEVON WALLACE
Proof on Main

702 W Main St
Louisville, KY 40202
502.217.6360
proofonmain.com

FERNANDO MARTINEZ
Guaca-Mole

9921 Ormsby Station Rd
Louisville, KY 40223
502.365.4822

DAVID SCALES
Lilly's

1147 Bardstown Rd
Louisville, KY 40204
502.451.0447
lillyslapeche.com

SHAWN WARD
Jack Fry's Restaurant

1007 Bardstown Rd
Louisville, KY 40204
502.452.9244
jackfrys.com

COBY MING
Harvest Restaurant

624 E Market St
Louisville, KY 40202
502.384.9090
harvestlouisville.com

TROY SCHUSTER
211 Clover Lane

211 Clover Ln
Louisville, KY 40207
502.896.9570
211cloverlane.com

JOSH MOORE
Volare

2300 Frankfort Ave
Louisville, KY 40206
502.894.4446
volare-restaurant.com

MICHAEL TON
Basa

2244 Frankfort Ave
Louisville, KY 40206
502.896.1016
basarestaurant.net

HIKO NAKANISHI
hiko-A-mon

1115 Herr Ln #130
Louisville, KY 40222
502.365.1651
hikoamon.com

BRUCE UCAN
Mayan Café

813 E Market St
Louisville, KY 40206
502.566.0651
themayancafe.com

BATON ROUGE

SAMMY CHENEVERT
The Little Village

447 3rd St
Baton Rouge, LA 70801
225.218.6685
littlevillagebr.com

NATHAN GRESHAM
Galatoire's Bistro

17451 Perkins Rd
Baton Rouge, LA 70810
225.753.4864
galatoires.com

MARVIN HENDERSON
Tsunami

100 Lafayette St
Baton Rouge, LA 70801
225.346.5100
servingsushi.com

JAIME HERNANDEZ
Juban's Creole Restaurant

3739 Perkins Rd
Baton Rouge, LA 70808
225.346.8422
jubans.com

DALE MOUGEOT
Louisiana Bayou Bistro

441 S Vaughan St
Brusly, LA 70719
225.749.6354
labayoubistro.com

COLT PATIN
Louisiana Culinary Institute

10550 Airline Hwy
Baton Rouge, LA 70816
225.769.8820
lci.edu

SCOTT VARNEDOE
Stroubes Seafood and Steak

107 3rd St
Baton Rouge, LA 70801
225.448.2830
stroubes.com

HOUMA

LINDSAY R. MASON
Cristiano Ristorante

724 High St
Houma, LA 70360
985.223.1130
cristianoristorante.com

KEVIN TEMPLET
Fremin's Restaurant

402 W 3rd St
Thibodaux, LA 70301
985.449.0333
fremins.net

LAFAYETTE

MANNY AUGELLO
Jolie's Louisiana Bistro

507 W Pinhook Rd
Lafayette, LA 70503
337.706.8544
jolieslouisianabistro.com

NASH BARRECA
Nash's Restaurant

101 E 2nd St
Lafayette, LA 70518
337.839.9333
nashsrestaurant.com

BRIAN BLANCHARD
iMonelli Restaurant

4017 Johnston St
Lafayette, LA 70503
337.989.9291
imonelli.com

WILLIAM BRIAND
Cochon

921 Camellia Blvd
Lafayette, LA 70508
337.993.9935
cochonlafayette.com

JEREMY CONNER
Village Café

1 Degaulle Square
Lafayette, LA 70508
337.981.8085
villagecafelafayette.com

COLLIN CORMIER
Viva La Waffle

200 Belle Chasse Dr
Lafayette, LA 70506
337.288.4685
vivalawaffle.com

JUSTIN GIROUARD
The French Press

214 E Vermilion St
Lafayette, LA 70501
337.233.9449
thefrenchpresslafayette.com

HOLLY GOETTING
Charley G's

3809 S Ambassador Caffery Pkwy
Lafayette, LA 70503
337.981.0108
charleygs.com

KEVIN HAWKINS
Pamplona Tapas Bar

631 Jefferson St
Lafayette, LA 70501
337.232.0070
pamplonatapas.com

MAZEN HIJAZI
Mazen Grill

5818 Johnston St
Lafayette, LA 70503
337.769.4440
mazens.com

PAUL LE
Bonsai

4409 Ambassador Caffery Pkwy
Lafayette, LA 70508
337.993.3330
bonsaisushibar.com

HEATH LEMOINE
Zea Rotisserie and Grill

235 Doucet Rd
Lafayette, LA 70503
337.406.0013
zearestaurants.com

CHAD PHARES
Phares

3502 Ambassador Caffery Pkwy
Lafayette, LA 70503
337.504.3002
pharesrestaurant.net

ERNEST PREJEAN
Prejean's Restaurant

3480 NE Evangeline Thruway
Lafayette, LA 70507
337.896.3247
prejeans.com

ROBERT SANDBERG
Jefferson Street Pub

500 Jefferson St
Lafayette, LA 70501
337.232.5040
jeffersonstreetpub.com

MICHAEL YEN
Dozo Restaurant

4702 Johnston St
Lafayette, LA 70503
337.993.9588
dozolafayette.com

LAKE CHARLES

MOHAMED CHETTOUH
La Truffe Sauvage

815 W Bayou Pines Dr
Lake Charles, LA 70601
337.439.8364
thewildtruffle.com

MONROE

CORY BAHR
Restaurant Cotton

101 N Grand St
Monroe, LA 71201
318.325.0818
restaurantcotton.com

NEW IBERIA

NICK LANDRY
Bruce Foods Corporation

1653 Old Spanish Trail
New Iberia, LA 70563
337.365.8101
brucefoods.com

NEW ORLEANS

BRIAN ARMOUR
Dante's Kitchen

736 Dante St
New Orleans, LA 70118
504.861.3121
danteskitchen.com

PAUL ARTIGUES
Green Goddess

307 Exchange Pl
New Orleans, LA 70130
504.301.3347
greengoddessnola.com

RENE BAJEUX
Rene Bistrot

700 Tchoupitoulas St
New Orleans, LA 70130
504.613.2350
renebistrotneworleans.com

CHRIS BARBATO
Café Adelaide

300 Poydras St
New Orleans, LA 70130
504.595.3305
cafeadelaide.com

JOHN BESH
Besh Restaurant Group

301 Tchoupitoulas St
New Orleans, LA 70130
504.299.9777
chefjohnbesh.com

ADAM BIDERMAN
The Company Burger

4600 Freret St
New Orleans, LA 70115
504.267.0320
thecompanyburger.com

PAOLO CENNI
Ristorante da Piero

401 Williams Blvd
Kenner, LA 70062
504.469.8585
ristorantedapiero.net

MATTHEW FARMER
Apolline

4729 Magazine St
New Orleans, LA 70115
504.894.8869
apollinerestaurant.com

SCOTT BOSWELL
Stella!

1032 Chartres St
New Orleans, LA 70116
504.587.0091
restaurantstella.com

LEAH CHASE
Dooky Chase's

2301 Orleans Ave
New Orleans, LA 70119
504.821.0600
dookychaserestaurant.com

CHIP FLANAGAN
Ralph's On the Park

900 City Park Ave
New Orleans, LA 70119
504.488.1000
ralphsonthepark.com

CARLOS BRICENO
New Orleans, LA

MICHAEL CONSTANTINI
Satsuma

3218 Dauphine St
New Orleans, LA 70117
504.304.5962
satsumacafe.com

TENNEY FLYNN
GW Fins

808 Bienville St
New Orleans, LA 70112
504.581.3467
gwfins.com

DAVID BRIDGES
Upperline

1413 Upperline St
New Orleans, LA 70115
504.891.9822
upperline.com

CHRIS DEBARR
Serendipity

3700 Orleans Ave
New Orleans, LA 70119
504.407.0818
serendipitynola.com

JOHN FOLSE
Restaurant R'evolution

777 Bienville St
New Orleans, LA 70130
225.644.6000
jfolse.com

FRANK BRIGTSEN
Brigtsen's

723 Dante St
New Orleans, LA 70118
504.861.7610
brigtsens.com

JUSTIN DEVILLIER
La Petite Grocery

4238 Magazine St
New Orleans, LA 70115
504.891.3377
lapetitegrocery.com

ADOLFO GARCIA
La Boca

857 Fulton St
New Orleans, LA 70130
504.525.8205
labocasteaks.com

AARON BURGAU
Patois

6078 Laurel St
New Orleans, LA 70118
504.895.9441
patoisnola.com

DANIEL ESSES
The Three Muses

536 Frenchmen St
New Orleans, LA 70116
504.252.4801
thethreemuses.com

HAO GONG
Sake Cafe

2830 Magazine St
New Orleans, LA 70115
504.894.0033
sakecafeuptown.us

ANTHONY GRAY
New Orleans, LA

KOMEI HORIMOTO
Horinoya

920 Poydras St
New Orleans, LA 70112
504.561.8914

JOSH LASKAY
NOLA

534 Saint Louis St
New Orleans, LA 70130
504.522.6652
emerilsrestaurants.com

RAY GRUEZKE
Rue 127

127 N Carrollton Ave
New Orleans, LA 70119
504.483.1571
rue127.com

RICHARD HUGHES
The Pelican Club

312 Exchange Pl
New Orleans, LA 70130
504.523.1504
pelicanclub.com

DONALD LINK
Herbsaint

701 Saint Charles Ave
New Orleans, LA 70130
504.524.4114
herbsaint.com

MICHAEL GULOTTA
August

301 Tchoupitoulas St
New Orleans, LA 70130
504.299.9777
restaurantaugust.com

TONY HUSTAD
Nuvolari's

246 Girod St
Mandeville, LA 70448
985.626.5619
nuvolaris.com

DUKE LOCICERO
Café Giovanni

117 Decatur St
New Orleans, LA 70130
504.529.2154
cafegiovanni.com

BEN HAMMOND
Cochon

930 Tchoupitoulas St
New Orleans, LA 70130
504.588.2123
cochonrestaurant.com

EMERIL LAGASSE
Emeril's

800 Tchoupitoulas St
New Orleans, LA 70130
504.528.9393
emerils.com

ERICK LOOS IV
La Provence

25020 U.S. 190
Lacombe, LA 70445
985.626.7662
laprovencerestaurant.com

ALEX HARRELL
Sylvain

625 Chartres St
New Orleans, LA 70130
504.265.8123
sylvainnola.com

BRIAN LANDRY
Borgne

601 Loyola Ave
New Orleans, LA 70113
504-613-3860
borgnerestaurant.com

PHILLIP LOPEZ
Root

200 Julia St
New Orleans, LA 70130
504.252.9480
rootnola.com

JOHN HARRIS
Lilette

3637 Magazine St
New Orleans, LA 70115
504.895.1636
liletterestaurant.com

BRIAN LARSON
Clancy's

6100 Annunciation St
New Orleans, LA 70118
504.895.1111
clancysneworleans.com

EMAN LOUBIER
Dante's Kitchen

736 Dante St
New Orleans, LA 70118
504.861.3121
danteskitchen.com

CHRIS LUSK
Restaurant R'evolution

777 Bienville St
New Orleans, LA 70130
504.553.2277
revolutionnola.com

MAI NGUYEN
Ba Mien Restaurant

13235 Chef Menteur Hwy
New Orleans, LA 70129
504.255.0500
bamien.com

MATT REGAN
Lüke

333 Saint Charles Ave
New Orleans, LA 70130
504.378.2840
lukeneworleans.com

GERARD MARAS
New Orleans Cooking Experience

1519 Carondelet St
New Orleans, LA 70130
504.430.5274

MILES PRESCOTT
Rio Mar

800 S Peters St
New Orleans, LA 70130
504.525.3474
riomarseafood.com

GREG REGGIO
Zea's Rotisserie and Grill

1525 Saint Charles Ave
New Orleans, LA 70130
504.520.8100
zearestaurants.com

NICK MARTIN
A Mano

870 Tchoupitoulas St
New Orleans, LA 70130
504.208.9280
amanonola.com

PAUL PRUDHOMME
K-Paul's Louisiana Kitchen

416 Chartres St
New Orleans, LA 70130
504.596.2530
chefpaul.com

MICHAEL REGUA SR.
Antoine's Restaurant

713 Saint Louis St
New Orleans, LA 70130
504.581.4422
antoines.com

BRADLEY MCGEHEE
Ye Olde College Inn

3000 S Carrollton Ave
New Orleans, LA 70118
504.866.3683
collegeinn1933.com

BARUCH RABASA
Atchafalaya

901 Louisiana Ave
New Orleans, LA 70115
504.891.9626
atchafalayarestaurant.com

JACQUES SALEUN
Chateau du Lac Bistro

2037 Metairie Rd
Metairie, LA 70001
504.831.3773
chateaudulacbistro.com

TORY MCPHAIL
Commander's Palace

1403 Washington Ave
New Orleans, LA 70130
504.899.8221
commanderspalace.com

JARED RALLS
La Boca

857 Fulton St
New Orleans, LA 70130
504.525.8205
labocasteaks.com

ANTHONY SCANIO
Delmonico

1300 Saint Charles Ave
New Orleans, LA 70130
504.525.4937
emerilsrestaurants.com

MICHAEL NELSON
GW Fins

808 Bienville St
New Orleans, LA 70112
504.581.3467
gwfins.com

LAZONE RANDOLPH
Brennan's

417 Royal St
New Orleans, LA 70130
504.525.9711
brennansneworleans.com

IAN SCHNOEBELEN
Iris

321 N Peters St
New Orleans, LA 70130
504.299.3944
irisneworleans.com

ALON SHAYA
Domenica

123 Baronne St
New Orleans, LA 70112
504.648.6020
domenicarestaurant.com

STEPHEN STRYJEWSKI
Cochon

930 Tchoupitoulas St
New Orleans, LA 70130
504.588.7675
cochonrestaurant.com

SHREVEPORT

GIUSEPPE BRUCIA
Ristorante Giuseppe

4800 Line Ave
Shreveport, LA 71106
318.869.4548
ristorantegiuseppe.com

MICHAEL SICHEL
Galatoire's

209 Bourbon St
New Orleans, LA 70130
504.525.2021
galatoires.com

MITSUKO TANNER
Little Tokyo

1340 S Carrollton Ave
New Orleans, LA 70118
504.861.6088
littletokyonola.com

ANTHONY FELAN
Wine Country Bistro & Bottle Shop

4801 Line Ave
Shreveport, LA 71106
318.629.9463
winecountrynet.com

DAVID SLATER
Emeril's

800 Tchoupitoulas St
New Orleans, LA 70130
504.528.9393
emerilsrestaurants.com

R.J. TSAROV
Delachaise

3442 Saint Charles Ave
New Orleans, LA 70115
504.895.0858
thedelachaise.com

STEVE MYLAR
The Mabry House

1540 Irving Pl
Shreveport, LA 71101
318.227.1121

DAVID SOLAZZO
Ristorante del Porto

501 E Boston St
Covington , LA 70433
985.875.1006
delportoristorante.com

ALLISON VINES-RUSHING
MiLa

817 Common St
New Orleans, LA 70112
504.412.2580
milaneworleans.com

SUSAN SPICER
Bayona

430 Dauphine St
New Orleans, LA 70112
504.525.4455
bayona.com

SUE ZEMANICK
Gautreau's

1728 Soniat St
New Orleans, LA 70115
504.899.7397
gautreausrestaurant.com

MICHAEL STOLTZFUS
Coquette

2800 Magazine St
New Orleans, LA 70115
504.265.0421
coquette-nola.com

NATHANIAL ZIMET
Boucherie

8115 Jeannette St
New Orleans, LA 70118
504.862.5514
boucherie-nola.com

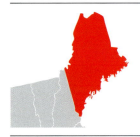 MAINE

BAR HARBOR

ALLISON MARTIN
The Burning Tree

69 Otter Creek Dr
Mt. Desert, ME 04660
207.288.9331

KEVIN NORLANDER
Reading Room

7 Newport Dr
Bar Harbor, ME 04609
207.288.3351
barharborinn.com

CASSADY PAPPAS
Havana

318 Main St
Bar Harbor, ME 04609
207.288.2822
havanamaine.com

MARK RAMPACEK
Eden

321 Main St
Bar Harbor, ME 04609
207.288.4422
barharborvegetarian.com

KYLE YARBOROUGH
Mache Bistro

135 Cottage St
Bar Harbor, ME 04609
207.288.0447
machebistro.com

PORTLAND

JONATHAN CARTWRIGHT
The White Barn Inn

37 Beach Ave
Kennebunk Beach, ME 04043
207.967.2321
whitebarninn.com

CHAD CONLEY
Gather

189 Main St
Yarmouth, ME 04096
207.847.3250
gathermaine.com

STEVE CORRY
Five Fifty-Five

555 Congress St
Portland, ME 04101
207.761.0555
fivefifty-five.com

KRISTA KERN DESJARLAIS
Bresca

111 Middle St
Portland, ME 04101
207.772.1004
restaurantbresca.com

ROB EVANS
DuckFat

43 Middle St
Portland, ME 04101
207.774.8080
duckfat.com

CLARK FRASIER
Arrows Restaurant

41 Berwick Rd
Ogunquit, ME 03907
207.361.1100
arrowsrestaurant.com

MARK GAIER
Arrows Restaurant

41 Berwick Rd
Ogunquit, ME 03907
207.361.1100
arrowsrestaurant.com

CHRISTOPHER GEER
Vignola Cinque Terre

10 Dana St
Portland, ME 04101
207.772.1330
vignolamaine.com

MITCHELL GEROW
The East Ender

47 Middle St
Portland, ME 04101
207.879.7669
eastenderportland.com

MATT GINN
Five Fifty-Five

555 Congress St
Portland, ME 04101
207.761.0555
fivefifty-five.com

SAM HAYWARD
Fore Street

288 Fore St
Portland, ME 04101
207.775.2717
forestreet.biz

IAN HAYWARD
Petite Jacqueline

190 State St
Portland, ME 04101
207.553.7044
bistropj.com

JASON KENNEDY
Black Tie Company

1 Union Wharf
Portland, ME 04101
207.761.6665
theblacktieco.com

LARRY MATTHEWS JR.
Back Bay Grill

65 Portland St
Portland, ME 04101
207.772.8833
backbaygrill.com

MASA MIYAKE
Miyake

468 Fore St
Portland, ME 04101
207.871.9170
miyakerestaurants.com

LEE SKAWINSKI
Vignola Cinque Terre

10 Dana St
Portland, ME 04101
207.772.1330
vignolamaine.com

HARDING LEE SMITH
The Front Room

73 Congress St
Portland, ME 04101
207.773.3366
hardingleesmith.com

PETER SUELTENFUSS
Grace

15 Chestnut St
Portland, ME 04101
207.828.4422
restaurantgrace.com

ANDREW TAYLOR
Hugo's

88 Middle St
Portland, ME 04101
207.774.8538
hugos.net

DAVID TURIN
David's 388

388 Cottage Rd
South Portland, ME 04106
207.347.7388
davids388.com

MIKE WILEY
Hugo's

88 Middle St
Portland, ME 04101
207.774.8538
hugos.net

JASON WILLIAMS
The Well at Jordan's Farm

21 Wells Rd
Cape Elizabeth, ME 04107
207.831.9350
jordansfarm.wix.com/thewell

ROCKLAND

BRIAN HILL
Shepherd's Pie

18 Central St
Rockport, ME 04856
207.236.8500
shepherdspierockport.com

MELISSA KELLY
Primo

2 S Main St
Rockland, ME 04841
207.596.0770
primorestaurant.com

KEIKO SUZUKI STEINBERGER
Suzuki

419 Main St
Rockland, ME 04841
207.596.7447
suzukisushi.com

ANNAPOLIS

RUSSELL BROWN
O'Learys Seafood

310 3rd St
Annapolis, MD 21403
410.263.0884
olearysseafood.com

PHILIP SOKOLOWSKI
The Severn Inn

1993 Baltimore Annapolis Blvd
Annapolis, MD 21409
410.349.4000
severninn.com

JAIME AYALA
Ranazul

8171 Maple Lawn Blvd
Fulton, MD 20759
301.498.9666
ranazul.us

JEAN-LOUIS EVENNOU
Café Normandie

185 Main St
Annapolis, MD 21401
410.263.3382
cafenormandie.com

JOSEPH TIS
Paladar Latin Kitchen

1905 Towne Centre Blvd #100
Annapolis, MD 21401
410.897.1022
paladarlatinkitchen.com

CHRIS BECKER
Fleet Street Kitchen

1012 Fleet St
Baltimore, MD 21202
410.244.5830
fleetstreetkitchen.com

BRENDAN KEEGAN JR.
Brasserie Brightwell

206 N Washington St
Annapolis, MD 21601
410.819.3838
brasseriebrightwell.com

KEN UPTON
Ken's Creative Kitchen

980 Awald Rd #201
Annapolis, MD 21403
410.268.3222
kenscreativekitchen.com

BRIAN BOSTON
The Milton Inn

14833 York Rd
Sparks, MD 21152
410.771.4366
miltoninn.com

ALFREDO MALINIS JR.
Level Small Plates Lounge

69 West St
Annapolis, MD 21404
410.268.0003
levelsmallplateslounge.com

KAREN WILLIAMS
Back Porch Café

980 Awald Rd #102
Annapolis, MD 21403
410.268.3222
kenscreativekitchen.com

CHRIS CLUNE
b bistro

1501 Bolton St
Baltimore, MD 21217
410.383.8600
b-bistro.com

BALTIMORE

ARTURO OTTAVIANO
Osteria 177

177 Main St
Annapolis, MD 21401
410.267.7700
osteria177.com

JASON AMBROSE
Salt

2127 E Pratt St
Baltimore, MD 21231
410.276.5480
salttavern.com

PATRICK CROOKS
Roy's

720 Aliceanna St
Baltimore, MD 21202
410.659.0099
roysrestaurant.com

BILL CROUSE
Baltimore, MD

JAMIE FORSYTHE
Baltimore, MD

JON KOHLER
Pairings Bistro

2105 Laurel Bush Rd #108
Bel Air, MD 21015
410.569.5006
pairingsbistro.com

LINWOOD DAME
Linwoods

25 Crossroads Dr
Owings Mills, MD 21117
410.356.3030
linwoods.com

CHAD GAUSS
The Food Market

1017 W 36th St
Baltimore, MD 21211
410.366.0606
thefoodmarketbaltimore.com

CHRIS LEWIS
Iron Bridge

10435 Maryland 108
Columbia, MD 21044
410.997.3456
ironbridgewines.com

MATTHEW DAY
Woodberry Kitchen

2010 Clipper Park Rd #126
Baltimore, MD 21211
410.464.8000
woodberrykitchen.com

MICHAEL GETTIER
Antrim 1844's
Smokehouse Restaurant

30 Trevanion Rd
Taneytown, MD 21787
410.756.6812
antrim1844.com

KING LIN
Sushi Sono

10215 Wincopin Cir
Columbia, MD 21044
410.997.6131
sushisonomd.com

THOMAS DEVINE
Linwoods

25 Crossroads Dr
Owings Mills, MD 21117
410.356.3030
linwoods.com

SPIKE GJERDE
Woodberry Kitchen

2010 Clipper Park Rd #126
Baltimore, MD 21211
410.464.8000
woodberrykitchen.com

BRETT LOCKARD
Blue Hill Tavern

938 S Conkling St
Baltimore, MD 21224
443.388.9363
bluehilltavern.com

MARC DIXON
Bistro Blanc

3800 Ten Oaks Rd
Glenelg, MD 21737
410.489.7907
bistroblancmd.com

ERIC HOUSEKNECHT
Thames Street Oyster House

1728 Thames St
Baltimore, MD 21231
443.449.7726
thamesstreetoysterhouse.com

SUGUNYA LUNZ
The Kings
Contrivance Restaurant

10150 Shaker Dr
Columbia, MD 21046
410.995.0500
greatfoodmd.com

THOMAS DUNKLIN
B&O American Brasserie

2 N Charles St
Baltimore, MD 21201
443.692.6172
bandorestaurant.com

JONAH KIM
PABU

725 Aliceanna St
Baltimore, MD 21202
410.223.1460
pabuizakaya.com

JULIAN MARUCCI
Cinghiale

822 Lancaster St
Baltimore, MD 21202
410.547.8282
cgeno.com

MICHAEL MATASSA
Alchemy

1011 W 36th St
Baltimore, MD 21211
410.366.1163
alchemyon36.com

MATTHEW SEIGMUND
The Oregon Grille

1201 Shawan Rd
Cockeysville, MD 21030
410.771.0505
theoregongrille.com

TAE STRAIN
Baltimore, MD

DAVE NEWMAN
The Brewer's Art

1106 N Charles St
Baltimore, MD 21201
410.547.6925
thebrewersart.com

JOHN SHIELDS
Gertrude's

10 Art Museum Dr
Baltimore, MD 21218
410.889.3399
gertrudesbaltimore.com

KARIN TIFFANY
Peter's Inn

504 S Ann St
Baltimore, MD 21231
410.675.7313
petersinn.com

DARREN POOLE
Old South Country Club

699 Maryland 408
Lothian, MD 20711
410.741.6037
oldsouthcountryclub.org

JILL SNYDER
Clementine

5402 Harford Rd
Baltimore, MD 21214
410.444.1497
bmoreclementine.com

AUDIEL VERA
Kali's Court Restaurant

1606 Thames St
Baltimore, MD 21231
410.276.4700
kaliscourt.com

ROB REHMERT
Catonsville Gourmet

829 Frederick Rd
Catonsville, MD 21228
410.788.0005
catonsvillegourmet.com

FRANCESCO SORRENTINO
Trattoria Alberto

1660 Crain Hwy S
Glen Burnie, MD 21061
410.761.0922
trattoriaalberto.com

JANE VIETCH
Henninger's Tavern

1812 Bank St
Baltimore, MD 21231
410.342.2172
henningerstavern.com

JAY ROHLFING
Linwoods

25 Crossroads Dr
Owings Mills, MD 21117
410.356.3030
linwoods.com

PAULINE SPILIADIS
The Black Olive

814 S Bond St
Baltimore, MD 21231
410.276.7141
theblackolive.com

ANDREW WEINZIRL
Maggie's Farm

4341 Harford Rd
Baltimore, MD 21214
410.254.2376
maggiesfarmmd.com

JESSE SANDLIN
Vino Rosina

507 S Exeter St
Baltimore, MD 21202
410.528.8600
vinorosina.com

TED STELZENMULLER
Jack's Bistro

3123 Elliott St
Baltimore, MD 21224
410.878.6542
jacksbistro.com

CHAD WELLS
Baltimore, MD

JASON WHITE
Rams Head Shore House

800 Main St
Stevensville, MD 21666
410.643.2466
ramsheadtavern.com

CINDY WOLF
Charleston

1000 Lancaster St
Baltimore, MD 21202
410.332.7373
charlestonrestaurant.com

BETHESDA

DANE SEWLALL
Black's Bar & Kitchen

7750 Woodmont Ave
Bethesda, MD 20814
301.652.5525
blacksbarandkitchen.com

CAMBRIDGE

IAN CAMPBELL
Bistro Poplar

535 Poplar St
Cambridge, MD 21613
410.228.4884
bistropoplar.com

EASTON

JORDAN LLOYD
Bartlett Pear Inn

28 S Harrison St
Easton, MD 21601
410.770.3300
bartlettpearinn.com

LISA MACDOUGAL
Pope's Tavern at the Oxford Inn

504 S Morris St
Oxford, MD 21645
410.226.5220
oxfordinn.net

DAVID MCCALLUM
Tilghman Island Inn

21384 Coopertown Rd
Tilghman, MD 21671
410.886.2141
tilghmanislandinn.com

DANIEL POCHRON
The Inn at Perry Cabin

308 Watkins Ln
St. Michaels, MD 21663
410.745.2200
perrycabin.com

CALEB TAYLOR
Sherwood's Landing

308 Watkins Ln
St. Michaels, MD 21663
410.745.2200
perrycabin.com

FREDERICK

RIC ADE
Ayse

6 N East St
Frederick, MD 21701
240.651.5155
aysemeze.com

STEVE HARTZELL
The Tasting Room

101 N Market St
Frederick, MD 21701
240.379.7772
thetastingroomrestaurant.com

ADAM HARVEY
The Wine Kitchen

50 Carroll Creek Way
Frederick, MD 21701
301.663.6968
thewinekitchen.com

GRAEME RITCHIE
Volt

228 N Market St
Frederick, MD 21701
301.696.8658
voltrestaurant.com

JASON ROUTZAHN
The Silver Maple Restaurant & Wine Bar

5018 Old National Pike
Frederick, MD 21702
301.371.3125
silvermaplerestaurant.com

BRYAN VOLTAGGIO
Volt

228 N Market St
Frederick, MD 21701
301.696.8658
voltrestaurant.com

JACK WALKER
Firestone's Culinary Tavern

105 N Market St
Frederick, MD 21701
301.663.0330
firestonesrestaurant.com

GAITHERSBURG

JOSEPH ZAKA
Le Palais

304 Main St #100
Gaithersburg, MD 20878
301.947.4051
restaurantlepalais.com

LEONARDTOWN

BRENDAN CAHILL
The Front Porch

22770 Washington St
Leonardtown, MD 20650
301.997.1009
thefrontporchsomd.com

OCEAN CITY

JULIUS ADAM SANDERS
Jules Fine Dining

11805 Coastal Hwy
Ocean City, MD 21842
410.524.3396
ocjules.com

POTOMAC

FRANCIS LAYRLE
Bezu

9812 Falls Rd #106
Potomac, MD 20854
301.299.3000
bezurestaurant.com

SILVER SPRING

DIANA DAVILA
Jackie's Restaurant

8081 Georgia Ave
Silver Spring, MD 20910
301.565.9700
jackiesrestaurant.com

PEDRO MATAMOROS
Silver Spring, MD

ED WITT
8407 kitchen bar

8407 Ramsey Ave
Silver Spring, MD 20910
301.587.8407
8407kb.com

 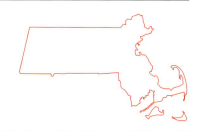
ARLINGTON

PAUL TURANO
Tryst Restaurant

689 Massachusetts Ave
Arlington, MA 02476
781.641.2227
trystrestaurant.com

BOSTON

JAMIE BISSONNETTE
Toro

1704 Washington St
Boston, MA 02118
617.536.4300
toro-restaurant.com

JOSHUA BREEN
Terramia Ristorante

98 Salem St
Boston, MA 02113
617.523.3112
terramiaristorante.com

BILL BRODSKY
City Landing

255 State St
Boston, MA 02109
617.725.0305
citylanding.com

SEAN CALLAHAN
Ten Tables

597 Centre St
Jamaica Plain, MA 02130
617.524.8810
tentables.net

PATRICK CAMPBELL
No. 9 Park

9 Park St
Boston, MA 02108
617.742.9991
no9park.com

MICHELE CARTER
The Butcher Shop

522 Tremont St
Boston, MA 02118
617.423.4800
thebutchershopboston.com

JOANNE CHANG
Myers + Chang

1145 Washington St
Boston, MA 02118
617.542.5200
myersandchang.com

TIM CUSHMAN
O Ya

9 East St
Boston, MA 02111
617.654.9900
oyarestaurantboston.com

CHARLES DRAGHI
Erbaluce

69 Church St
Boston, MA 02116
617.426.6969
erbaluce-boston.com

JOSE DUARTE
Taranta

210 Hanover St
Boston, MA 02113
617.720.0052
tarantarist.com

DAVID DUBOIS
The Franklin Café

278 Shawmut Ave
Boston, MA 02118
617.350.0010
franklincafe.com

TODD ENGLISH
Olives

10 City Square
Charlestown, MA 02129
617.242.1999
toddenglish.com

CHRIS GOULD
Uni Sashimi Bar

370 Commonwealth Ave
Boston, MA 02215
617.536.7200
unisashimibar.com

GORDON HAMERSLEY
Hamersley's Bistro

553 Tremont St
Boston, MA 02116
617.423.2700
hamersleysbistro.com

SCOTT HEBERT
Troquet

140 Boylston St
Boston, MA 02116
617.695.9463
troquetboston.com

ANDY HUSBANDS
Tremont 647

647 Tremont St
Boston, MA 02118
617.266.4600
tremont647.com

MARISA IOCCO
Gennaro's 5 North Square

5 North Square
Boston, MA 02113
617.720.1050
5northsquare.com

MICHAEL LEVITON
Lumière

1293 Washington St
Boston, MA 02465
617.244.9199
lumiererestaurant.com

KEVIN LONG
Red Lantern

39 Stanhope St
Boston, MA 02116
617.262.3900
redlanternboston.com

BARBARA LYNCH
No. 9 Park

9 Park St
Boston, MA 02108
617.742.9991
no9park.com

COLIN LYNCH
Menton

354 Congress St
Boston, MA 02210
617.737.0099
mentonboston.com

JAMIE MAMMANO
Mistral Bistro

223 Columbus Ave
Boston, MA 02116
617.867.9300
mistralbistro.com

FRANK MCCLELLAND
L'Espalier

774 Boylston St
Boston, MA 02199
617.262.3023
lespalier.com

DIDIER MONTAROU
Miel Brasserie Provencale

510 Atlantic Ave
Boston, MA 02210
617.217.5151
intercontinentalboston.com

KEN ORINGER
Clio

370 Commonwealth Ave
Boston, MA 02215
617.536.7200
cliorestaurant.com

STEPHEN OXAAL
B&G Oysters

550 Tremont St
Boston, MA 02116
617.423.0550
bandgoysters.com

TING SAN
Oishii

1166 Washington St
Boston, MA 02118
617.482.8868
oishiiboston.com

MARK SAPIENZA
Cafe Fleuri

250 Franklin St
Boston, MA 02110
617.451.1900
boston.langhamhotels.com

MICHAEL SCHLOW
Radius

8 High St
Boston, MA 02110
617.426.1234
radiusrestaurant.com

JEREMY SEWALL
Eastern Standard

528 Commonwealth Ave
Boston, MA 02215
617.532.9100
easternstandardboston.com

LYDIA SHIRE
Scampo

215 Charles St
Boston, MA 02114
617.536.2100
scampoboston.com

MANUEL SIFNUGEL
Masona Grill

4 Corey St
West Roxbury, MA 02132
617.323.3331
masonagrill.com

ROBERT SISCA
Bistro du Midi

272 Boylston St
Boston, MA 02116
617.426.7878
bistrodumidi.com

ADAM WILLIAMS
Lucca

226 Hanover St
Boston, MA 02113
617.742.9200
luccaboston.com

BROOKLINE

NELSON COGNAC
Cognac Bistro

455 Harvard St
Brookline, MA 02446
617.232.5800
cognacbistrooysterbar.com

CAMBRIDGE

JODY ADAMS
Rialto

1 Bennett St
Cambridge, MA 02138
617.661.5050
rialto-restaurant.com

BRANDON ARMS
Garden at the Cellar

991 Massachusetts Ave
Cambridge, MA 02138
617.475.0045
gardenatthecellar.com

JASON BOND
Bondir

279 Broadway #A
Cambridge, MA 02139
617.661.0009
bondircambridge.com

DANTE DE MAGISTRIS
dante

40 Edwin H Land Blvd
Cambridge, MA 02141
617.497.4200
restaurantdante.com

MARY DUMONT
Harvest

44 Brattle St
Cambridge, MA 02138
617.868.2255
harvestcambridge.com

BARRY MAIDEN
Hungry Mother

233 Cardinal Medeiros Ave
Cambridge, MA 02141
617.499.0090
hungrymothercambridge.com

TIM MASLOW
Strip-T's

93 School St
Watertown, MA 02472
617.923.4330
stripts.com

TONY MAWS
Craigie on Main

853 Main St
Cambridge, MA 02139
617.497.5511
craigieonmain.com

ANTHONY MAZZOTTA
Catalyst

300 Technology Square
Cambridge, MA 02139
617.576.3000
catalystrestaurant.com

PETER MCCARTHY
EVOO

350 3rd St
Cambridge, MA 02142
617.661.3866
evoorestaurant.com

CASSIE PIUMA
Oleana

134 Hampshire St
Cambridge, MA 02139
617.661.0505
oleanarestaurant.com

ANA SORTUN
Oleana

134 Hampshire St
Cambridge, MA 02139
617.661.0505
oleanarestaurant.com

PHILLIP TANG
East by Northeast

1128 Cambridge St
Cambridge, MA 02139
617.876.0286
exnecambridge.com

JASPER WHITE
Summer Shack

149 Alewife Brook Pkwy
Cambridge, MA 02140
617.520.9500
summershackrestaurant.com

TIM WIECHMANN
T.W. Food

377 Walden St
Cambridge, MA 02138
617.864.4745
twfoodrestaurant.com

CAPE COD

BILL ATWOOD
The Red Pheasant Inn

905 Main St
Dennis, MA 02638
508.385.2133
redpheasantinn.com

SHAREEF BADAWY
The Brewster Fish House

2208 Main St
Brewster, MA 02631
508.896.7867
brewsterfish.com

KEVIN CROWELL
Détente

15 Winter St
Edgartown, MA 02539
508.627.8810
detentemv.com

MICHAEL DEAN
Victor's

175 Bradford St Ext
Provincetown, MA 02657
508.487.1777
victorsptown.com

FREDERIC FEUFEU
Bleu

10 Market St
Mashpee, MA 02649
508.539.7907
bleurestaurant.com

MACGREGOR B. HAY
Mac's Shack

91 Commercial St
Wellfleet, MA 02667
508.349.6333
macsseafood.com

TOBY HILL
Hyannis Port, MA

ERIC JANSEN
Blackfish

17 Truro Center Rd
Truro, MA 02666
508.349.3399

MARTHA KANE
Fin

800 Main St
Dennis, MA 02638
508.385.2096
fincapecod.com

RUTH MANCHESTER
Bramble Inn

2019 Main St
Brewster, MA 02631
508.896.7644
brambleinn.com

EREZ PINHAS
ABBA

89 Old Colony Way
Orleans, MA 02653
508.255.8144
abbarestaurant.com

DOUGLAS RAMLER
Cape Sea Grille

31 Sea St
Harwich Port, MA 02646
508.432.4745
capeseagrille.com

PHILIPPE RISPOLI
PB Boulangerie Bistro

15 Lecount Hollow Rd
South Wellfleet, MA 02663
508.349.1600
pbboulangeriebistro.com

ANTHONY SILVESTRI
Ocean House

425 Old Wharf Rd
Dennis Port, MA 02639
508.394.0700
oceanhouserestaurant.com

YUJI WATANABE
Inaho

157 Route 6A
Yarmouth Port, MA 02675
508.362.5522
inahocapecod.com

CONCORD

CHRIS CHUNG
AKA Bistro

145 Lincoln Rd
Lincoln, MA 01773
781.259.9920
akabistrolincoln.com

CAROLYN JOHNSON
80 Thoreau

80 Thoreau St
Concord, MA 01742
978.318.0008
80thoreau.com

GREAT BARRINGTON

PETER PLATT
The Old Inn on the Green

134 New Marlboro Branch Rd
New Marlborough, MA 01230
413.229.7924
oldinn.com

DAN SMITH
John Andrews Restaurant

1 Blunt Rd
Great Barrington, MA 01230
413.528.3469
jarestaurant.com

ADAM ZIEMINSKI
Café Adam

325 Stockbridge Rd #4
Great Barrington, MA 01230
413.528.7786
cafeadam.org

HINGHAM

PAUL WAHLBERG
Alma Nove

22 Shipyard Dr
Hingham, MA 02043
781.749.3353
almanovehingham.com

LENOX

ARNAUD COTAR
Blantyre

16 Blantyre Rd
Lenox, MA 01240
413.637.3556
blantyre.com

ERIC PERCY
Church Street Café

65 Church St
Lenox, MA 01240
413.637.2745
churchstreetlenox.com

BJORN SOMLO
Nudel

37 Church St
Lenox, MA 01240
413.551.7183
nudelrestaurant.com

FRANK TESSIER
Chez Nous Bistro

150 Main St
Lee, MA 01238
413.243.6397
cheznousbistro.com

JEFFREY THOMPSON
The Dining Room at Wheatleigh

11 Hawthorne Rd
Lenox, MA 01240
413.637.0610
wheatleigh.com

MARTHA'S VINEYARD

MAX EAGAN
Lambert's Cove Inn

90 Manaquayak Rd
West Tisbury, MA 02575
508.693.2298
lambertscoveinn.com

MEDFIELD

BRENDAN PELLEY
Zebra's Bistro and Wine Bar

21 North St
Medfield, MA 02052
508.359.4100
zebrasbistro.com

NANTUCKET

GABRIEL FRASCA
Straight Wharf

6 Harbor Square
Nantucket, MA 02554
508.228.4499
straightwharfrestaurant.com

AMANDA LYDON
Straight Wharf

6 Harbor Square
Nantucket, MA 02554
508.228.4499
straightwharfrestaurant.com

LIAM MACKEY
The Pearl

12 Federal St
Nantucket, MA 02554
508.228.9701
thepearlnantucket.com

STEPHEN MARCAURELLE
Boarding House

12 Federal St
Nantucket, MA 02554
508.228.9622
boardinghousenantucket.com

KYLE ZACHARY
TOPPER'S

120 Wauwinet Rd
Nantucket, MA 02554
508.228.8768
wauwinet.com

NATICK

EDWARD HOFFEY
Sel de la Terre

1245 Worcester St
Natick, MA 01760
508.650.1800
seldelaterre.com

TORU OGA
Oga's Japanese Cuisine

915 Worcester St
Natick, MA 01760
508.653.4338
ogasnatick.com

NEW ASHFORD

SUZANNE CHAMPAGNE IVY
The Mill on the Floss

342 Route 7
New Ashford, MA 01237
413.458.9123
millonthefloss.com

NEWTON

DAVID PUNCH
Sycamore.

755 Beacon St
Newton, MA 02459
617.244.4445
sycamorenewton.com

MING TSAI
Blue Ginger

583 Washington St
Wellesley, MA 02482
781.283.5790
ming.com

SALEM

ANTONIO BETTENCOURT
62 Restaurant & Wine Bar

62 Wharf St
Salem, MA 01970
978.744.0062
62restaurant.com

SCITUATE

ROBIN KING
Restaurant ORO

162 Front St
Scituate, MA 02066
781.378.2465
restaurantoro.com

JURG KUMMER
Barker Tavern

21 Barker Rd
Scituate, MA 02066
781.545.6533
barkertavern.com

SUNDERLAND

DEBORAH SNOW
Blue Heron
Restaurant & Catering

112 N Main St
Sunderland, MA 01375
413.665.2102
blueherondining.com

WALTHAM

RICHARD BARRON
Il Capriccio

888 Main St
Waltham, MA 02453
781.894.2234
ilcapricciowaltham.com

WESTWOOD

STEVE LACOUNT
Chiara Bistro

569 High St
Westwood, MA 02090
781.461.8118
chiarabistro.com

ANN ARBOR

EVE ARONOFF
Frita Batidos

117 W Washington St
Ann Arbor, MI 48104
734.761.2882
fritabatidos.com

CRAIG COMMON
The Common Grill

112 S Main St
Chelsea, MI 48118
734.475.0470
commongrill.com

THAD GILLIES
Logan

115 W Washington St
Ann Arbor, MI 48104
734.327.2312
logan-restaurant.com

BRANDON JOHNS
Grange Kitchen & Bar

118 W Liberty St
Ann Arbor, MI 48104
734.995.2107
grangekitchenandbar.com

JIM LEONARDO
Vinology

110 S Main St
Ann Arbor, MI 48104
734.222.9841
vinowinebars.net

BRENDAN MCCALL
Mani Osteria & Bar

341 E Liberty St
Ann Arbor, MI 48104
734.769.6700
maniosteria.com

DUC TANG
Pacific Rim

114 W Liberty St
Ann Arbor, MI 48104
734.662.9303
pacificrimbykana.com

ALEX YOUNG
Zingerman's Roadhouse

2501 Jackson Ave
Ann Arbor, MI 48103
734.663.3663
zingermansroadhouse.com

BENTON HARBOR

JENNY DRILON
Bentwood Tavern

600 W Water St
New Buffalo, MI 49117
269.469.1699
bentwoodtavern.com

ELTON MAN
Point O'Woods

1516 Roslyn Rd
Benton Harbor , MI 49022
269.944.1433
pointowoods.com

CHAD MILLER
Soe Café

12868 Red Arrow Hwy
Sawyer, MI 49125
269.426.4878
soe-cafe.com

TIMOTHY SIZER
Timothy's

16220 Lakeshore Rd
Union Pier, MI 49129
269.469.0900
timothysrestaurant.com

RYAN THORNBURG
Bistro on the Boulevard

521 Lake Blvd
St. Joseph, MI 49085
269.983.6600
theboulevardinn.com

JOHNPAUL VERHAGE
Tabor Hill Restaurant & Winery

185 Mount Tabor Rd
Buchanan, MI 49107
800.283.3363
taborhill.com

DETROIT

STEVE ALLEN
Steve & Rocky's

43150 Grand River Ave
Novi, MI 48375
248.374.0688
steveandrockys.com

CHRISTIAN BORDEN
Brizola

555 E Lafayette Blvd
Detroit, MI 48226
313.309.2499
greektowncasino.com

MILOS CIHELKA
Southfield, MI

LUCIANO DEL SIGNORE
Bacco Ristorante

29410 Northwestern Hwy
Southfield, MI 48034
248.356.6600
baccoristorante.com

QUIRT EDWARDS
Andiamo's

400 Renaissance Center
Detroit, MI 48243
313.567.6700
andiamoitalia.com

KEVIN ENRIGHT
Oakland Community College

2480 Opdyke Rd
Bloomfield Hills, MI 48304
248.341.2000
oaklandcc.edu

CHRIS FRANZ
The Rattlesnake Club Restaurant

300 River Pl Dr
Detroit, MI 48207
313.567.4400
rattlesnakedetroit.com

DINO GROSSI
Volare Ristorante

49115 Pontiac Trail
Wixom, MI 48393
248.960.7771
ristorantevolare.com

PAUL GROSZ
Cuisine

670 Lothrop Rd
Detroit, MI 48202
313.872.5110
cuisinerestaurant.com

ADAM HIGHTOWER
Gastronomy

1 Towne Square
Southfield, MI 48076
248.864.4410
theepicureangroup.com

ANDREW HOLLYDAY
Roast

1128 Washington Blvd
Detroit, MI 48226
313.961.2500
roastdetriot.com

AARON KOIVU
Forest Grill

735 Forest Ave
Birmingham, MI 48009
248.258.9400
theforestgrill.com

DAVE MANCINI
Supino Pizzeria

2457 Russell St
Detroit, MI 48207
313.567.7879
supinopizzeria.com

LORRAINE PLATMAN
Sweet Lorraine's

29101 Greenfield Rd
Southfield, MI 48076
248.559.5985
sweetlorraines.com

BRIAN POLCYN
Forest Grill

735 Forest Ave
Birmingham, MI 48009
248.258.9400
theforestgrill.com

JAMES RIGATO
The Root Restaurant & Bar

340 Town Center Blvd
White Lake, MI 48386
248.698.2400
therootrestaurant.com

ZACHARY STOTZ
Atlas Global Bistro

3111 Woodward Ave
Detroit, MI 48201
313.831.2241
atlasglobalbistro.com

JOHN SUMMERVILLE
The Lark

6430 Farmington Rd
West Bloomfield Township, MI
48322
248.661.4466
thelark.com

FRANK TURNER
Northern Lakes Seafood Company

39495 Woodward Ave
Bloomfield Hills, MI 48304
248.646.7900
theepicureangroup.com

DON YAMAUCHI
MotorCity Casino Hotel

2901 Grand River Ave
Detroit, MI 48201
313.237.6732
motorcitycasino.com

GRAND RAPIDS

MATTHEW MILLAR
Reserve

201 Monroe Ave NW
Grand Rapids, MI 49503
616.855.9463
reservegr.com

HOLLAND

BRIAN WOODS
Butch's Restaurant

44 E 8th St #110
Holland, MI 49423
616.396.8227
butchs.net

KALAMAZOO

ADAM WATTS
Rustica

236 S Kalamazoo Mall
Kalamazoo, MI 49007
269.492.0247
rusticakzoo.com

MARQUETTE

NATHAN MILESKI
Northern Michigan University

1401 Presque Isle Ave
Marquette, MI 49855
906.227.2295
nmu.edu

TOM WAHLSTROM
Elizabeth's Chophouse

113 S Front St
Marquette, MI 49855
906.228.0900
elizabethschophouse.com

TRAVERSE CITY

MYLES ANTON
Trattoria Stella

1200 W 11th St
Traverse City, MI 49684
231.929.8989
stellatc.com

JENNIFER BLAKESLEE
The Cooks' House

115 Wellington St
Traverse City, MI 49686
231.946.8700
thecookshouse.net

DAN MARSH
Red Ginger

237 E Front St
Traverse City, MI 49684
231.944.1733
eatatginger.com

ERIC PATTERSON
The Cooks' House

115 Wellington St
Traverse City, MI 49686
231.946.8700
thecookshouse.net

OFFAL
Used in traditional and gourmet cuisine, offal is not for the faint of heart.

DULUTH

SCOTT GRADEN
Scenic Café

5461 N Shore Dr
Duluth, MN 55804
218.525.6274
sceniccafe.com

GRAND MARAIS

JUDI BARSNESS
Grand Marais, MN

HARMONY

STEPHEN LARSON
QUARTER/quarter

25 Center St E
Harmony, MN 55939
507.886.5500
quarterquarter.com

MINNEAPOLIS

BEN JACOBY
Craftsman

4300 E Lake St
Minneapolis, MN 55406
612.722.0175
craftsmanrestaurant.com

PATRICK ATANALIAN
Sanctuary

903 Washington Ave S
Minneapolis, MN 55415
612.339.5058
sanctuaryminneapolis.com

ISAAC BECKER
112 Eatery

112 N 3rd St
Minneapolis, MN 55401
612.343.7696
112eatery.com

PAUL BERGLUND
The Bachelor Farmer

50 2nd Ave N
Minneapolis, MN 55401
612.206.3920
thebachelorfarmer.com

THOMAS BOEMER
Corner Table

4257 Nicollet Ave
Minneapolis, MN 55409
612.823.0011
cornertablerestaurant.com

STEVEN BROWN
Tilia

2726 W 43rd St
Minneapolis, MN 55410
612.354.2806
tiliampls.com

JIM CHRISTIANSEN
Union

731 Hennepin Ave
Minneapolis, MN 55403
612.455.6690
unionmpls.com

MIKE DECAMP
La Belle Vie

510 Groveland Ave
Minneapolis, MN 55403
612.874.6440
labellevie.us

DOUG FLICKER
Piccolo

4300 Bryant Ave S
Minneapolis, MN 55409
612.827.8111
piccolompls.com

VINCENT FRANCOUAL
Vincent - A Restaurant

1100 Nicollet Ave
Minneapolis, MN 55403
612.630.1189
vincentarestaurant.com

ERICK HARCEY
Victory 44

2203 N 44th Ave
Minneapolis, MN 55412
612.588.2228
victory-44.com

JOSH HILL
Manny's Steakhouse

825 Marquette Ave S
Minneapolis, MN 55402
612.339.9900
mannyssteakhouse.com

KIMINOBU ICHIKAWA
Origami
30 N 1st St
Minneapolis, MN 55401
612.333.8430
origamirestaurant.com

ADAM KING
Café Lurcat
1624 Harmon Pl
Minneapolis, MN 55403
612.486.5500
cafelurcat.com

MICHAEL MACKAY
Citizen Cafe
2403 E 38th St
Minneapolis, MN 55406
612.729.1122
thecitizencafe.com

TIM MCKEE
La Belle Vie
510 Groveland Ave
Minneapolis, MN 55403
612.874.6440
labellevie.us

TYGE NELSON
Chino Latino
2916 Hennepin Ave S
Minneapolis, MN 55408
612.824.7878
chinolatino.com

MIKE PHILLIPS
Green Ox Meat Co.
Minneapolis, MN

VIXAYSAK PHOMMACHANH
Tiger Sushi II
2841 Lyndale Ave
Minneapolis, MN 55408
612.874.1800
tigersushiusa.com

T.J. RAWITZER
Masu Sushi & Robata
330 E Hennepin Ave
Minneapolis, MN 55414
612.332.6278
masusushiandrobata.com

JACK RIEBEL
Butcher & the Boar
1121 Hennepin Ave
Minneapolis, MN 55403
612.238.8888
butcherandtheboar.com

ALEXANDER ROBERTS
Restaurant Alma
528 SE University Ave
Minneapolis, MN 55414
612.379.4909
restaurantalma.com

LANDON SCHOENEFELD
HauteDish
119 Washington Ave N
Minneapolis, MN 55401
612.338.8484
haute-dish.com

SEAN SHERMAN
Black Sheep Chefs Catering
Minneapolis, MN
612.486.2433
blacksheepchefs.com

JAY SPARKS
Masa
1070 Nicollet Mall
Minneapolis, MN 55403
612.338.6272
masa-restaurant.com

PETER STINE
Minneapolis, MN

SCOTT THOLE
McCormick & Schmick's
800 Nicollet Mall
Minneapolis, MN 55402
612.338.3300
mccormickandschmicks.com

ADAM VICKERMAN
Café Levain
4762 Chicago Ave S
Minneapolis, MN 55407
612.823.7111
cafelevain.com

SAMEH WADI
Saffron Restaurant & Lounge
123 N 3rd St
Minneapolis, MN 55401
612.746.5533
saffronmpls.com

ROBERT WHOLFEIL
The Oceanaire Seafood Room
50 S 6th St
Minneapolis, MN 55403
612.333.2277
theoceanaire.com

JAMES WINBERG
Travail Kitchen and Amusements

4154 W Broadway Ave
Robbinsdale, MN 55422
763.535.1131
facebook.com/Travailkitchen

STEWART WOODMAN
Heidi's

2903 Lyndale Ave S
Minneapolis, MN 55408
612.354.3512
heidismpls.com

ROCHESTER

GREG JAWORSKI
NOSH Restaurant & Bar

310 S Washington St
Lake City, MN 55041
651.345.2425
noshrestaurant.com

BRYCE LAMB
Sontes

4-3rd St SW
Rochester, MN 55902
507.292.1628
sontes.com

ST. PAUL

WYATT EVANS
W.A. Frost & Co.

374 Selby Ave
St. Paul, MN 55102
651.224.5715
wafrost.com

J.D. FRATZKE
Strip Club Meat & Fish

378 Maria Ave
St. Paul, MN 55106
651.793.6247
domeats.com

RUSSELL KLEIN
Meritage

410 Saint Peter St
St. Paul, MN 55102
651.222.5670
meritage-stpaul.com

LENNY RUSSO
Heartland Restaurant

289 E 5th St
St. Paul, MN 55101
651.699.3536
heartlandrestaurant.com

DEEP SOUTH
Coast to coast chefs are embracing Southern techniques and cuisine.

GREENWOOD

TAYLOR RICKETTS
Delta Bistro

117 Main St
Greenwood, MS 38930
662.455.9575
deltabistro.com

DAN BLUMENTHAL
BRAVO!

4500 Interstate 55 Frontage Rd #244
Jackson, MS 39211
601.982.8111
bravobuzz.com

DAVID FERRIS
Babalu Tacos & Tapas

622 Duling Ave
Jackson, MS 39216
601.366.5757
babalums.com

GULFPORT

BILL VRAZEL
Vrazel's Fine Food Restaurant

3206 W Beach Blvd
Gulfport, MS 39501
228.863.2229
vrazels.com

ANDY COOK
Ridgeland, MS

KARL GORLINE
BRAVO!

4500 Interstate 55 Frontage Rd #244
Jackson, MS 39211
601.982.8111
bravobuzz.com

HATTIESBURG

NITCHAKAMOL RISE
Jutamas Thai Restaurant

910 Timothy Ln
Hattiesburg, MS 39401
601.584.8583

STEPHEN D'ANGELO
Jackson, MS

MATT JOHNSON
Walker's Drive-In

3016 N State St
Jackson, MS 39216
601.982.2633
walkersdrivein.com

ROBERT ST. JOHN
Purple Parrot Café

3810 Hardy St
Hattiesburg, MS 39402
601.264.0656
purpleparrotcafe.net

ALEX EATON
Table 100

100 Ridge Way
Flowood, MS 39232
601.420.4202
tableonehundred.com

NICK WALLACE
King Edward Hotel

235 W Capitol St
Jackson , MS 39201
601.353.5464
kingedwardhoteljackson.com

JACKSON

NICK APOSTLE
Nick's

3000 Old Canton Rd
Jackson, MS 39216
601.981.8017
nicksrestaurant.com

DEREK EMERSON
Walker's Drive-In

3016 N State St
Jackson, MS 39216
601.982.2633
walkersdrivein.com

OCEAN SPRINGS

FRANK MAISANO
Maisano's Fine Wine and Spirits

1622 Bienville Blvd
Ocean Springs, MS 39564
228.872.9590
maisanosfinewine.com

OXFORD

VISHWESH BHATT
Snack Bar

721 N Lamar Blvd
Oxford, MS 38655
662.236.6363
citygroceryonline.com

JOHN CURRENCE
City Grocery

152 Courthouse Square
Oxford , MS 38655
662.232.8080
citygroceryonline.com

JESSE HOUSTON
City Grocery

152 Courthouse Square
Oxford, MS 38655
662.232.8080
citygroceryonline.com

JOEL MILLER
Ravine

53 County Road 321
Oxford, MS 38655
662.234.4555
oxfordravine.com

JON MYRICK
Proud Larry's

211 S Lamar Blvd
Oxford, MS 38655
662.236.0050
proudlarrys.com

STARKVILLE

TY THAMES
Restaurant Tyler

100 E Main St
Starkville, MS 39759
662.324.1014
restauranttyler.com

COLUMBIA

MIKE ODETTE
Sycamore

800 E Broadway
Columbia, MO 65201
573.874.8090
sycamorerestaurant.com

MARK SULLTROP
44 Stone Public House

3910 Peachtree Dr
Columbia, MO 65203
573.443.2726
44stonepub.com

KANSAS CITY

RAY COMISKEY
Capital Grille

4740 Jefferson St
Kansas City, MO 64112
816.531.8345
thecapitalgrille.com

MICHAEL FOUST
The Farmhouse

300 Delaware St
Kansas City, MO 64105
816.569.6032
eatatthefarmhouse.com

COLBY GARRELTS
bluestem

900 Westport Rd
Kansas City, MO 64111
816.561.1101
bluestemkc.com

BRADLEY GILMORE
Gram & Dun

600 Ward Pkwy
Kansas City, MO 64112
816.389.2900
gramanddun.com

DEBBIE GOLD
The American Restaurant

200 E 25th St #400
Kansas City, MO 64108
816.545.8000
theamericankc.com

TED HABIGER
Room 39

1719 W 39th St
Kansas City, MO 64111
816.753.3939
rm39.com

HOWARD HANNA
The Rieger Hotel
Grill and Exchange

1924 Main St
Kansas City, MO 64108
816.471.2177
theriegerkc.com

INGRID HANRIOT
Café des Amis

1121/2 Main St
Parkville, MO 64152
816.587.6767
cafedesamiskc.com

MARTIN HEUSER
Affare

1911 Main St
Kansas City, MO 64108
816.298.6182
affarekc.com

JONATHAN JUSTUS
Justus Drugstore

106 W Main St
Smithville, MO 64089
816.532.2300
drugstorerestaurant.com

EMMANUEL LANGLADE
Aixois Bistro

251 E 55th St
Kansas City, MO 64113
816.333.3305
aixois.com

MARVIN LEWIS
Jasper's

1201 W 103rd St
Kansas City, MO 64114
816.941.6600
jasperskc.com

JENNIFER MALONEY
Café Sebastienne

4420 Warwick Blvd
Kansas City, MO 64111
816.561.7740
kemperart.org

TRAVIS NAPIER
Bristol Seafood Grill

51 E 14th St
Kansas City, MO 64106
816.448.6007
bristolseafoodgrill.com

JONATHAN NUÑEZ
Michael Smith

1900 Main St
Kansas City, MO 64108
816.842.2202
michaelsmithkc.com

ALEX POPE
The Local Pig

2618 Guinotte Ave
Kansas City, MO 64120
816.200.1639
thelocalpig.com

MANO RAFAEL
Le Fou Frog

400 E 5th St
Kansas City, MO 64106
816.474.6060
lefoufrog.com

TATE ROBERTS
EBT

1310 Carondelet Dr #100
Kansas City, MO 64114
816.942.8870
ebtrestaurant.com

PATRICK RYAN
Port Fonda

4141 Pennsylvania Ave
Kansas City, MO 64111
816.216.6462
portfondakc.com

MICHAEL SMITH
Michael Smith

1900 Main St
Kansas City, MO 64108
816.842.2202
michaelsmithkc.com

DAN SWINNEY
Lidia's

101 W 22nd St
Kansas City, MO 64108
816.221.3722
lidias-kc.com

CELINA TIO
Julian

6227 Brookside Plaza
Kansas City, MO 64113
816.214.8454
juliankc.com

JOE WEST
bluestem

900 Westport Rd
Kansas City, MO 64111
816.561.1101
bluestemkc.com

ST. LOUIS

ADAM ALTNETHER
Niche

7734 Forsyth Blvd
Clayton, MO 63105
314.773.7755
nichestlouis.com

BRANDON BENACK
Truffles

9202 Clayton Rd
St. Louis, MO 63124
314.567.9100
todayattruffles.com

JON BERGER
Napoli 2

1054 Town and Country Crossing Dr
Town and Country, MO 63017
636.256.9998
napoli2.com

VINCENT BOMMARITO
Tony's

410 Market St
St. Louis, MO 63102
314.231.7007
tonysstlouis.com

CHRIS BORK
Blood & Sand

1500 Saint Charles St
St. Louis, MO 63103
314.241.7263
bloodandsandstl.com

WILLIAM CARDWELL
Cardwell's at the Plaza

94 Plaza Frontenac
St. Louis, MO 63131
314.997.8885
billcardwell.com

RAY CARPENTER
Prime 1000

1000 Washington Ave
St. Louis, MO 63101
314.241.1000
prime1000.com

GERARD CRAFT
Craft Restaurants

4584 Laclede Ave
St. Louis, MO 63108
314.361.1200

MATT DAUGHADAY
Taste

4584 Laclede Ave
St. Louis, MO 63108
314.361.1200
tastebarstl.com

JOSH GALLIANO
MX Movies

618 Washington Ave
St. Louis, MO 63101
314.222.2994
facebook.com/MXSTLMovies

CHRISTOPHER LEE
Hendrick's BBQ

1200 S Main St
St. Charles, MO 63301
636.724.8600
hendricksbbq.com

CHRISTOPHER DESENS
Culinary Institute of St. Louis

2700 N Lindbergh Blvd
St. Louis, MO 63114
877.226.2433
ci-stl.com

ADAM GNAU
Acero

7266 Manchester Rd
St. Louis, MO 63143
314.644.1790
fialafood.com

BEN LESTER
Mosaic Restaurants

1001 Washington Ave
St. Louis, MO 63101
314.621.6001
mosaicrestaurants.com

ANTHONY DEVOTI
Five Bistro

5100 Daggett Ave
St. Louis, MO 63110
314.773.5553
fivebistro.com

JUSTIN HAIFLEY
The Tavern Kitchen and Bar

2961 Dougherty Ferry Rd
St. Louis, MO 63122
636.825.0600
tavernstl.com

IVY MAGRUDER
Vin de Set

2017 Chouteau Ave
St. Louis, MO 63103
314.241.8989
vindeset.com

JODIE FERGUSON
Table Three

16765 Main St
Wildwood, MO 63040
636.458.4333
table-three.com

CARL HAZEL
Eleven Eleven Mississippi

1111 Mississippi Ave
St. Louis, MO 63104
314.241.9999
1111-m.com

ELISE MENSING
Brasserie by Niche

4580 Laclede Ave
St. Louis, MO 63108
314.454.0600
brasseriebyniche.com

JIMMY FIALA
The Crossing

7823 Forsyth Blvd
Clayton, MO 63105
314.721.7375
fialafood.com

CHRIS JANEK
Franco

1535 S 8th St
St. Louis, MO 63104
314.436.2500
eatatfranco.com

NICHOLAS MILLER
Harvest

1059 S Big Bend Blvd
St. Louis, MO 63117
314.645.3522
harveststlouis.com

DOMINIC GALATI
Dominic's on the Hill

5101 Wilson Ave
St. Louis, MO 63110
314.771.1632
dominicsrestaurant.com

KORY KIM
Clayton, MO

AIDAN MURPHY
Old Warson Country Club

9841 Old Warson Rd
St. Louis, MO 63124
314.968.0840
oldwarson.com

KEVIN NASHAN
Sidney Street Café

2000 Sidney St
St. Louis, MO 63104
314.771.5777
sidneystreetcafe.com

MATT OWENS
Bristol Seafood Grill

2314 Technology Dr
O'Fallon, MO 63368
636.625.6350
bristolseafoodgrill.com

VITO RACANELLI JR.
Mad Tomato Italian Kitchen

8000 Carondelet Ave
Clayton, MO 63105
314.932.5733
madtomatostl.com

JOSH ROLAND
Salt

4356 Lindell Blvd
St. Louis, MO 63108
314.932.5787
enjoysalt.com

LOU ROOK
Annie Gunn's

16806 Chesterfield Airport Rd
Chesterfield, MO 63005
636.532.7684
anniegunns.com

CLAUS SCHMITZ
Mosaic Restaurants

1001 Washington Ave
St. Louis, MO 63101
314.621.6001
mosaicrestaurants.com

AARON TEITELBAUM
Herbie's Vintage 72

405 N Euclid Ave
St. Louis, MO 63108
314.769.9595
herbies.com

JASON TILFORD
Milagro Modern Mexican

20 Allen Ave #130
Webster Groves, MO 63119
314.962.4300
milagromodernmexican.com

QUI TRAN
Mai Lee

8396 Musick Memorial Dr
Brentwood, MO 63144
314.645.2835
maileerestaurant.com

TAMI TRINH
Pho Grand

3195 S Grand Blvd
St. Louis, MO 63118
314.664.7435
phogrand.com

CASSY VIRES
Home Wine Kitchen

7322 Manchester Rd
Maplewood, MO 63143
314.802.7676
homewinekitchen.com

MIKE WARHOVER
Modesto

5257 Shaw Ave
St. Louis, MO 63110
314.772.8272
modestotapas.com

ANDY WHITE
Schlafly Tap Room

2100 Locust St
St. Louis, MO 63103
314.241.2337
schlafly.com

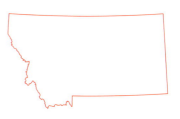

BIG SKY

ERIC STENBERG
Big Sky, MT

BIGFORK

FABRIZIO MOROLDO
Moroldo's Ristorante Italiano

7951 Montana 35
Bigfork, MT 59911
406.837.2720
moroldo-restaurant.com

BILLINGS

KARL KUROKAWA
Juliano's

2912 7th Ave N
Billings, MT 59101
406.248.6400
julianosrestaurant.wordpress.com

DARBY

JACOB LEATHERMAN
Triple Creek Ranch

5551 W Fork Rd
Darby, MT 59829
406.821.4600
triplecreekranch.com

GALLATIN GATEWAY

CHRIS KIMMEL
Buck's T-4 Lodge

46625 U.S. 191
Gallatin Gateway, MT 59730
406.995.4111
buckst4.com

MISSOULA

PEARL CASH
Pearl Cafe

231 E Front St
Missoula, MT 59802
406.541.0231
pearlcafe.us

SCOTT GILL
Scotty's Table

131 S Higgins Ave #U3
Missoula, MT 59802
406.549.2790
scottystable.net

WALKER HUNTER
Burns St. Bistro

1500 Burns St
Missoula, MT 59802
406.543.0719
burnsstbistro.com

DOMINICK MARTIN
Red Bird

111 N Higgins Ave
Missoula, MT 59802
406.549.2906
redbirdrestaurant.com

ABE RISHO
Silk Road

515 S Higgins Ave
Missoula, MT 59801
406.541.0752
silkroadcatering.com

JIM TRACEY
Red Bird

111 N Higgins Ave
Missoula, MT 59802
406.549.2906
redbirdrestaurant.com

WHITEFISH

ANDY BLANTON
Cafe Kandahar

3824 Big Mountain Rd
Whitefish, MT 59937
406.862.6247
cafekandahar.com

INGREDIENT: HOMEMADE VINEGAR

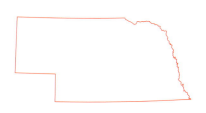

KEARNEY

CARLOS POCHE
Kearney, NE

CLAYTON CHAPMAN
The Grey Plume

220 S 31st Ave #3101
Omaha, NE 68131
402.763.4447
thegreyplume.com

PAUL KULIK
The Boiler Room

1110 Jones St
Omaha, NE 68102
402.916.9274
theboilerroomrestaurant.com

LINCOLN

TRAVIS GREEN
Dish

1100 E O St
Lincoln, NE 68508
402.475.9475
dishdowntown.com

JOHN ENGLER
The Grey Plume

220 S 31st Ave #3101
Omaha, NE 68131
402.763.4447
thegreyplume.com

GEORGE LIAO
Wave Bistro

4002 N 144th St
Omaha, NE 68116
402.496.8812
wavebistrorestaurant.com

BRANDON HARPSTER
The Single Barrel

130 N 10th St
Lincoln, NE 68508
402.904.4631
thesinglebarrel.com

CEDRIC FICHEPAIN
Le Voltaire

569 N 155th Plaza
Omaha, NE 68154
402.934.9374
levoltaireomaha.com

JOEL MAHR
Lot 2

6207 Maple St
Omaha, NE 68104
402.504.4200
lot2benson.com

OMAHA

DARRELL AULD
Twisted Cork Bistro

10730 Pacific St
Omaha, NE 68114
402.932.1300
twistedcorkbistro.com

LIONEL HAVE
Executive Chef Catering

Omaha, NE
402.598.2207
executivechefcatering.org

BOBBY MEKINEY
M's Pub

422 S 11th St
Omaha, NE 68102
402.342.2550
mspubomaha.com

TOM BUDER
Blue Sushi Sake Grill

416 S 12th St
Omaha, NE 68102
402.408.5566
bluesushisakegrill.com

JESSICA JOYCE
Block 16

1611 Farnam St
Omaha, NE 68102
402.342.1220
block16omaha.com

DARIO SCHICKE
Dario's Brasserie

4920 Underwood Ave
Omaha, NE 68132
402.933.0799
dariosbrasserie.com

JON SEYMOUR
V. Mertz

1022 Howard St
Omaha, NE 68102
402.345.8980
vmertz.com

PAUL URBAN
Block 16

1611 Farnam St
Omaha, NE 68102
402.342.1220
block16omaha.com

GLENN WHEELER
Spencer's

102 S 10th St
Omaha, NE 68102
402.280.8888
spencersforsteaksandchops.com

MILTON YIN
Hiro 88

1308 Jackson St
Omaha, NE 68102
402.933.5168
hiro88.com

SOUTH SIOUX CITY

RYAN DEVITT
Kahill's

385 E 4th St
South Sioux City, NE 68776
402.494.5025
kahills.net

GARDNERVILLE RANCHOS

YVES GIGOT
La Ferme

2291 Main St
Gardnerville, NV 89460
775.783.1004
lafermegenoa.com

RICHARD LACOUNTE
1862 David Walley's
Restaurant and Saloon

2001 Foothill Rd
Genoa, NV 89411
888.737.1862
1862davidwalleysrestaurant
andsaloon.com

BRADLEY NUSS
Stateline, NV

FRANK STAGNARO
Edgewood

100 Lake Pkwy
Stateline, NV 89449
877.708.6862
edgewoodtahoe.com

LAS VEGAS

MARIO ANDREONI
Panevino Ristorante

246 Via Antonio Ave
Las Vegas, NV 89119
702.222.2400
panevinolasvegas.com

MARK ANTHONY
Las Vegas, NV

702.236.3280
chefmarkanthony.com

AKIRA BACK
Yellowtail

3600 S Las Vegas Blvd
Las Vegas, NV 89109
702.730.3900
lightgroup.com

JAVIER BARAJAS
Lindo Michoacan

2655 E Desert Inn Rd
Las Vegas, NV 89121
702.735.6828
lindomichoacan.com

STEVE BENJAMIN
L'Atelier de Joel Robuchon

3799 S Las Vegas Blvd
Las Vegas, NV 89109
702.891.7358
joel-robuchon.net

TIM BERES
T-Bones Chophouse

11011 W Charleston Blvd
Las Vegas, NV 89135
702.797.7576
sclv.com

GENO BERNARDO
Nove Italiano

4321 W Flamingo Rd
Las Vegas, NV 89103
702.942.6832
palms.com

FRED BIELAK
Michael's Gourmet Room

9777 S Las Vegas Blvd
Las Vegas, NV 89183
702.796.7111
southpointcasino.com

STEVE BLANDINO
Charlie Palmer Steak

3960 S Las Vegas Blvd
Las Vegas, NV 89119
702.632.5120
charliepalmer.com

GIANCARLO BOMPAROLA
Siena Italian Authentic Trattoria

9500 W Sahara Ave
Las Vegas, NV 89117
702.360.3358
sienaitalian.com

ARNAULD BRIAND
Ventano Italian Grill and Seafood

191 S Arroyo Grande Blvd
Henderson, NV 89012
702.944.4848
ventanoitalian.com

NICOLE BRISSON
Carnevino

3325 S Las Vegas Blvd
Las Vegas, NV 89109
701.789.4141
carnevino.com

CARLOS BUSCAGLIA
Due Forni

3555 S Town Center Dr #105
Las Vegas, NV 89135
702.586.6500
dueforni.com

NEIL CAMPBELL
Sterling's Seafood Steakhouse

407 N Virginia St
Las Vegas, NV 89501
800.687.8733
silverlegacyreno.com

MATHIEU CHARTRON
Guy Savoy

3570 S Las Vegas Blvd
Las Vegas, NV 89109
702.731.7110
caesarspalace.com

GERALD CHIN
Las Vegas, NV

SAIPIN CHUTIMA
Lotus of Siam

953 E Sahara Ave #A5
Las Vegas, NV 89104
702.735.3033
saipinchutima.com

HEATH CICERELLI
Emeril's New Orleans Fish House

3799 S Las Vegas Blvd
Las Vegas , NV 89109
702.891.7374
mgmgrand.com

TODD CLORE
Todd's Unique Dining

4350 E Sunset Rd
Henderson, NV 89014
702.259.8633
toddsunique.com

CHRIS CONLON
Light Group

6276 S Rainbow Blvd #120
Las Vegas, NV 89118
702.693.8300
lightgroup.com

JACOB CORONADO
Addiction

455 E Harmon Ave
Las Vegas, NV 89019
702.369.5400
rumorvegas.com

JOSH CRAIN
American Fish

3730 S Las Vegas Blvd
Las Vegas, NV 89109
877.230.2742
michaelmina.net

BRAD CRUZ
Carve

5255 Boulder Hwy
Las Vegas, NV 89122
702.856.5300
eastsidecannery.com

BARRY DAKAKE
N9NE Steakhouse

4321 W Flamingo Rd
Las Vegas, NV 89103
702.933.9900
n9nesteak.com

PAUL DEL FAVERO
Mesa Grill

3570 S Las Vegas Blvd
Las Vegas , NV 89109
702.731.7110
mesagrill.com

CHAD ELLIS
Petra Greek Taverna

440 S Rampart Blvd
Las Vegas, NV 89145
702.534.0200
petragreektaverna.com

MITSUO ENDO
Aburiya Raku

5030 Spring Mountain Rd
Las Vegas, NV 89146
702.367.3511
raku-grill.com

MIMMO FERRARO
Ferraro's

4480 Paradise Rd
Las Vegas, NV 89169
702.364.5300
ferraroslasvegas.com

RICHARD GIBSON
Battista's Hole in the Wall

4041 Audrie St
Las Vegas, NV 89109
702.732.1424
battistaslasvegas.com

MICHAEL GOODMAN
Verandah

3960 S Las Vegas Blvd
Las Vegas , NV 89119
702.632.5121
fourseasons.com

STEPHEN HOPCRAFT
STK

3708 S Las Vegas Blvd
Las Vegas, NV 89109
702.698.7990
stkhouse.com

ROBERT KIRCHHOFF
Craftsteak

3799 S Las Vegas Blvd
Las Vegas, NV 89109
702.891.7318
craftrestaurantsinc.com

SEAN GRIFFIN
Prime Steakhouse

3600 S Las Vegas Blvd
Las Vegas , NV 89109
702.693.8865
bellagio.com

BRIAN HOWARD
Comme Ca

3708 S Las Vegas Blvd
Las Vegas, NV 89109
702.698.7910
commecarestaurant.com

ERIC KLEIN
Spago

3500 S Las Vegas Blvd
Las Vegas, NV 89109
702.369.6300
wolfgangpuck.com

FERNANDO GUERRERO
Del Frisco's

3925 Paradise Rd
Las Vegas , NV 89169
702.796.0063
delfriscos.com

MATTHEW HURLEY
CUT

3325 S Las Vegas Blvd
Las Vegas, NV 89109
702.607.6300
wolfgangpuck.com

TACHO KNEELAND
Cabo Wabo Cantina

3663 S Las Vegas Blvd
Henderson, NV 89109
702.385.2226
cabowabocantina.com

CARLOS GUÍA
The Country Club

3131 Las Vegas Blvd S
Las Vegas, NV 89109
702.770.3463
wynnlasvegas.com

CHRISTOPHER JOHNS
South Point Hotel Casino

9777 Las Vegas Blvd S
Las Vegas, NV 89183
702.796.7111
southpointcasino.com

JOSEPH KUDRAK
T-Bones Chophouse

11011 W Charleston Blvd
Las Vegas, NV 89135
702.797.7576
sclv.com

TODD HARRINGTON
Central by Michel Richard

3570 S Las Vegas Blvd
Las Vegas, NV 89109
702.650.5921
centrallv.com

WES KENDRICK
Table 34

600 E Warmsprings Rd
Las Vegas, NV 89119
702.263.0034
table34lasvegas.com

GEORGES LAFORGE
Pamplemousse Le Restaurant

400 E Sahara Ave
Las Vegas, NV 89104
702.733.2066
pamplemousserestaurant.com

DEVIN HASHIMOTO
Mizumi

3131 Las Vegas Blvd S
Las Vegas, NV 89109
702.770.3463
wynnlasvegas.com

HIEW GUN KHONG
Jasmine

3600 S Las Vegas Blvd
Las Vegas, NV 89109
702.693.8865
bellagio.com

CLAUDE LE TOHIC
Joel Robuchon

3799 S Las Vegas Blvd
Las Vegas, NV 89109
702.891.7925
joel-robuchon.net

KYLE LONDERGAN
Postrio

3377 S Las Vegas Blvd
Las Vegas , NV 89109
702.796.1110
wolfgangpuck.com

MICHAEL MINOR
Border Grill

3950 S Las Vegas Blvd
Las Vegas, NV 89119
702.632.7403
bordergrill.com

JASON NEVE
B&B Ristorante

3355 S Las Vegas Blvd
Las Vegas, NV 89109
702.266.9977
bandbristorante.com

TERRY LYNCH
Mon Ami Gabi

3655 S Las Vegas Blvd
Las Vegas, NV 89109
702.944.4224
monamigabi.com

TOM MOLONEY
Aquaknox

3355 S Las Vegas Blvd
Las Vegas , NV 89109
702.414.3772
aquaknox.net

CHRIS NOBLE
35 Steaks + Martinis

4455 Paradise Rd
Las Vegas, NV 89169
702.693.5207
hardrockhotel.com

BRIAN MASSIE
Diablo's Cantina

3770 S Las Vegas Blvd
Las Vegas, NV 89109
702.730-7979
lightgroup.com

RICK MOONEN
Rick Moonen's RM Seafood

3930 S Las Vegas Blvd
Las Vegas, NV 89119
702.632.9300
rmseafood.com

BRYAN OGDEN
Las Vegas, NV

SHAWN MCCLAIN
Sage

3730 S Las Vegas Blvd
Las Vegas, NV 89109
877.230.2742
arialasvegas.com

ROBERT MOORE
Jean-Georges Steakhouse

3730 S Las Vegas Blvd
Las Vegas, NV 89158
702.590.8638
arialasvegas.com

JUAN ORTEGA
Casa di Amore

2850 E Tropicana Ave
Las Vegas , NV 89121
702.433.4967
casadiamore.com

ANTHONY MEIDENBAUER
The Barrymore

99 Convention Center Dr
Las Vegas , NV 89109
702.407.5303
barrymorelv.com

KURTESS MORTENSON
Bally's

3645 Las Vegas Blvd S
Las Vegas, NV 89109
877.603.4390
ballyslasvegas.com

LUCIANO PELLEGRINI
Valentino

3355 S Las Vegas Blvd
Las Vegas, NV 89109
702.414.3000
valentinorestaurants.com

DAVE MIDDLETON
Marche Bacchus

2620 Regatta Dr
Las Vegas, NV 89128
702.804.8008
marchebacchus.com

HIRO NAKANO
Sen of Japan

8480 W Desert Inn Rd #F1
Las Vegas, NV 89117
702.871.7781
senofjapan.com

JULIO PERAZA
American Fish

3730 S Las Vegas Blvd
Las Vegas, NV 89109
877.230.2742
michaelmina.net

IAN PINKNEY
Las Vegas, NV

BRYAN PODGORSKI
Bouchon Bistro

3355 S Las Vegas Blvd
Las Vegas, NV 89109
702.414.6200
bouchonbistro.com

VINCENT POUESSEL
Aureole

3950 S Las Vegas Blvd
Las Vegas, NV 89119
702.632.7401
charliepalmer.com

MARK PURDY
Alize

4321 W Flamingo Rd
Las Vegas, NV 89103
702.951.7000
alizelv.com

GIANPAOLO PUTZU
Canaletto Ristorante Veneto

3377 S Las Vegas Blvd
Las Vegas, NV 89109
702.733.0070
ilfornaio.com

VIVEK RAWAT
MOzen Bistro

3752 S Las Vegas Blvd
Paradise, NV 89158
702.590.8888
mandarinoriental.com

BRUNO RIOU
Mix Lounge

3950 S Las Vegas Blvd
Las Vegas, NV 89119
702.632.9500
mandalaybay.com

JOEL ROBUCHON
Joel Robuchon

3799 S Las Vegas Blvd
Las Vegas, NV 89109
702.891.7925
joel-robuchon.com

ANDRE ROCHAT
Andre's

3770 S Las Vegas Blvd
Las Vegas, NV 89109
702.798.7151
andrelv.com

SEAN ROE
Table 10

3327 S Las Vegas Blvd
Las Vegas, NV 89109
702.607.6363
emerilsrestaurants.com

JOHN ROMINE
Silverado

9777 S Las Vegas Blvd
Las Vegas , NV 89183
702.796.7111
southpointcasino.com

DAN ROSSI
Scarpetta

3708 S Las Vegas Blvd
Las Vegas, NV 89109
702.698.7960
scottconant.com

PASCAL SANCHEZ
Twist

3752 S Las Vegas Blvd
Las Vegas, NV 89109
888.881.9367
mandarinoriental.com

GUY SAVOY
Guy Savoy

3570 S Las Vegas Blvd
Las Vegas, NV 89109
702.731.7110
guysavoy.com

JOHN SCHENK
Strip House

3667 S Las Vegas Blvd
Las Vegas, NV 89109
702.737.5200
striphouse.com

THEO SCHOENEGGER
Sinatra

3131 Las Vegas Blvd S
Las Vegas, NV 89109
702.770.3463
wynnlasvegas.com

WAYNE SCHUMAKER
Mastro's Ocean Club

3720 S Las Vegas Blvd
Las Vegas, NV 89109
702.798.7115
mastrosrestaurants.com

JULIAN SERRANO
Julian Serrano

3730 S Las Vegas Blvd
Las Vegas, NV 89109
702.590.8520
arialasvegas.com

DARRIN SHINAGAWA
Roy's

620 E Flamingo Rd
Las Vegas, NV 89119
702.691.2053
roysrestaurant.com

MATTHEW SILVERMAN
Vintner Grill

10100 W Charleston Blvd
Las Vegas, NV 89135
702.214.5590
vglasvegas.com

JOHN SIMMONS
Firefly

3900 Paradise Rd
Las Vegas, NV 89169
702.369.3971
fireflylv.com

DAVE SIMMONS
Lawry's The Prime Rib

4043 Howard Hughes Pkwy
Las Vegas, NV 89169
702.893.2223
lawrysonline.com

DAVID SNYDER
Wynn Las Vegas

3121 Las Vegas Blvd S
Las Vegas, NV 89109
702.770.7000
wynnlasvegas.com

ROBERT SOLANO
Mundo

495 S Grand Central Pkwy
Las Vegas, NV 89106
702.270.4400
mundolasvegas.com

CHARLIE SOLE
Las Vegas, NV

DAVID SOMMELLA
China Grill

3950 S Las Vegas Blvd
Las Vegas, NV 89119
702.632.7404
mandalaybay.com

KEN TORRES
Gallagher's Steakhouse

3790 S Las Vegas Blvd
Las Vegas, NV 89109
702.740.6450
gallaghersnysteakhouse.com

PAUL VIGIL
Twin Creeks

3333 Blue Diamond Rd
Las Vegas , NV 89139
702.914.8564
silvertoncasino.com

MICHAEL VITANGELI
Osteria del Circo

3600 S Las Vegas Blvd
Las Vegas, NV 89109
702.693.8150
bellagio.com

TYLER WAKUTA
Roy's

8701 W Charleston Blvd
Las Vegas, NV 89117
702.838.3620
roysrestaurant.com

DAVID WALZOG
SW Steakhouse

3131 Las Vegas Blvd S
Las Vegas, NV 89109
702.770.3463
wynnlasvegas.com

RICHARD WELLS
Canal Street

4500 W Tropicana Ave
Las Vegas , NV 89103
702.365.7550
orleanscasino.com

DALTON WILSON
DW Bistro

6115 S Fort Apache Rd #112
Las Vegas, NV 89148
702.527.5200
dwbistro.com

HERB WILSON
SUSHISAMBA

3327 S Las Vegas Blvd
Las Vegas, NV 89109
702.607.0700
sushisamba.com

MING YU
Wing Lei

3131 Las Vegas Blvd S
Las Vegas, NV 89109
702.770.3463
wynnlasvegas.com

RENO

JOE BELL
Wild River Grille

17 S Virginia St #180
Reno, NV 89501
775.284.7455
bestrenorestaurant.com

TROY CANNAN
Lulou's
1470 S Virginia St
Reno, NV 89502
775.329.9979

IVAN FONTANA
Midtown Eats
719 S Virginia St
Reno, NV 89501
775.324.3287
midtowneatsreno.com

NATALIE SELLERS
4th Street Bistro
3065 W 4th St
Reno, NV 89523
775.323.3200
4thstbistro.com

IVANO CENTEMERI
La Strada
345 N Virginia St
Reno, NV 89501
775.348.9297
eldoradoreno.com

ALBERTO GAZZOLA
La Vecchia
3005 Skyline Blvd #160
Reno, NV 89509
775.825.1113
lavecchiareno.com

DAVID SILVERMAN
Silver Peak Restaurant & Brewery
124 Wonder St
Reno, NV 89502
775.324.1864
silverpeakbrewery.com

KAIMI COONRAD
The Cheese Board
247 California Ave
Reno, NV 89509
775.323.3115
cheeseboardcatering.com

BILL GILBERT
Beaujolais Bistro
130 West St
Reno, NV 89501
775.323.2227
beaujolaisbistro.com

DAVID STERN
SoDo
275 Hill St
Reno, NV 89501
775.322.2710
sodoreno.com

BEN DEINKEN
The Brewere's Cabinet
475 S Arlington Ave
Reno, NV 89501
775.348.7481
thebrewerscabinet.com

CLINT JOLLY
Great Thyme Catering
Reno, NV
775.453.0847
greatthyme.com

AURIANE UGALDE
775 Gastropub
5162 Meadowood Mall Cir
Reno, NV 89502
775.828.0775
775gastropub.com

JEAN-PIERRE DOIGNON
Le Bistro Café
120 Country Club Dr #29
Incline Village, NV 89451
775.831.0800
lebistrorestaurant.net

RICK KOPLAU
Lone Eagle Grille
111 Country Club Dr
Incline Village, NV 89451
775.886.6899
loneeaglegrille.com

MARK ESTEE
Campo
50 N Sierra St
Reno, NV 89501
775.737.9555
camporeno.com

B.J. MUELLER
Sauce Wagon
160 W Liberty St
Reno, NV 89501
775.622.6615
saucewagon.com

 NEW HAMPSHIRE

CENTER HARBOR

SCOTT OULLETTE
Canoe Restaurant

232 Whittier Hwy
Center Harbor, NH 03226
603.253.4762
magicfoodsrestaurantgroup.com

CONCORD

SUNNY CHUNG
Sunny's Table

11 Depot St
Concord, NH 03301
603.225.8181
sunnystable.com

JOSHUA DUDA
Lake Sunapee Country Club

100 Country Club Ln
New London, NH 03257
603.526.6040
lakesunapeecc.com

COREY FLETCHER
Granite Restaurant

96 Pleasant St
Concord, NH 03301
603.227.9000
graniterestaurant.com

DOVER

EVAN HENNESSEY
Stages at One Washington

1 Washington St #325
Dover, NH 03820
603.842.4077
stages-dining.com

MANCHESTER

MICHAEL T. BUCKLEY
Michael Timothy's Dining Group

207 Main St
Nashua, NH 03060
603.424.0995
buckleysgreatsteaks.com

STUART CAMERON
Hanover Street Chophouse

149 Hanover St
Manchester, NH 03101
603.644.2467
hanoverstreetchophouse.com

BENJAMIN KNACK
Bedford Village Inn

2 Olde Bedford Way
Bedford, NH 03110
603.472.2001
bedfordvillageinn.com

ZACK MARTINEAU
Copper Door

15 Leavy Dr
Bedford, NH 03110
603.488.2677
copperdoorrestaurant.com

JEFFREY PAIGE
Cotton

75 Arms St
Manchester, NH 03101
603.622.5488
cottonfood.com

MATT TROTTIER
Tek-Nique

170 Route 101
Bedford, NH 03110
603.488.5629
restaurantteknique.com

PORTSMOUTH

JOHN HARRINGTON
Thirsty Moose Tap House

21 Congress St
Portsmouth, NH 03801
603.427.8645
thirstymoosetaphouse.com

PETER KOGE
Sake

141 Congress St
Portsmouth, NH 03801
603.431.1822
portsmouthsake.com

SIMON LAMPERT
Four

189 State St
Portsmouth, NH 03801
603.319.1547
fouronstate.com

JETHRO LOICHLE
Ristorante Massimo

59 Penhallow St
Portsmouth, NH 03801
603.436.4000
ristorantemassimo.com

MATT LOUIS
Moxy

106 Penhallow St
Portsmouth, NH 03801
603.319.8178
moxyrestaurant.com

EVAN MALLETT
Black Trumpet

29 Ceres St
Portsmouth, NH 03801
603.431.0887
blacktrumpetbistro.com

DESIRE MOONSAMY
Hagan's Grill

6 High St
Hampton, NH 03842
603.926.5668
hagansgrill.com

MARTY RUMLY
Jumpin' Jay's Fish Café

150 Congress St
Portsmouth, NH 03801
603.766.3474
jumpinjays.com

MARK SEGAL
100 Club

100 Market St
Portsmouth, NH 03801
603.766.4100
onehundredclub.com

GREGG SESSLER
Cava

10 Commercial Alley
Portsmouth, NH 03801
603.319.1575
cavatapasandwinebar.com

ALLAMUCHY TOWNSHIP

STEPHEN SCHWARTZINGER
Mattar's Bistro

1115 County Rd 517
Allamuchy Township, NJ 07820
908.852.2300
mattars.com

ATLANTIC CITY

GUISEPPE BIANCALANA
Café 2825

2825 Atlantic Ave
Atlantic City, NJ 08401
609.344.6913
cafe2825.com

COSIMO CASSANO
Girasole

3108 Pacific Ave
Atlantic City, NJ 08401
609.345.5554
girasoleac.com

FRANK DOUGHERTY
Dock's Oyster House

2405 Atlantic Ave
Atlantic City, NJ 08401
609.345.0092
docksoysterhouse.com

JEFF GOTTA
Carmine's

2801 Pacific Ave
Atlantic City, NJ 08401
609.572.9300
carminesnyc.com

NERY HERNANDEZ
Buddakan

1 Atlantic Ocean
Atlantic City, NJ 08401
609.674.0100
buddakanac.com

GEOFF JOHNSON
Roman Grill

199 New Rd
Linwood, NJ 08221
609.926.3030
romangrill.com

KEVIN KELLY
Steve & Cookies By the Bay

9700 Amherst Ave
Margate, NJ 08402
609.823.1163
steveandcookies.com

FERNANDO MASCI
Il Mulino New York

1000 Boardwalk
Atlantic City, NJ 08401
609.449.6006
ilmulino.com

ROSALBA MORICI
Girasole

3108 Pacific Ave
Atlantic City, NJ 08401
609.345.5554
girasoleac.com

LUKE PALLADINO
Luke Palladino

1333 New Rd
Northfield, NJ 08225
609.646.8189
lukepalladino.com

CARMEN RONE
Tomatoes

9300 Amherst Ave
Margate, NJ 08402
609.822.7535
tomatoesmargate.com

CHRIS SCARDUZIO
Mia

2100 Pacific Ave
Atlantic City, NJ 08401
609.441.2345
miaac.com

SERGIO SOTO
Gallagher's Steakhouse

1133 Boardwalk
Atlantic City, NJ 08401
609.340.6555
arkrestaurants.com

JOSEPH TUCKER
Catch

2401 Atlantic Ave
Longport, NJ 08403
609.822.3474
main.catch2401.com

CAMDEN

JOE BROWN
Melange Café

18 Tanner St
Haddonfield, NJ 08033
856.354.1333
melangerestaurants.com

SAMUEL GIUMARELLO
Giumarello's
Restaurant & G Bar Lounge

329 Haddon Ave
Haddon Township, NJ 08108
856.858.9400
giumarellos.com

PASQUALE MASTERS
Pasta Pomodoro

700 County Route 561
Voorhees, NJ 08043
856.782.7430
pastapomodoronj.com

FRANCISCO CABRERA
El Sitio

729 Haddon Ave
Collingswood, NJ 08108
856.240.1217
elsitiocollingswood.com

DANIEL HOVER
Ritz Seafood

910 Haddonfield-Berlin Rd
Voorhees, NJ 08043
856.566.6650
ritzseafood.com

MATTHEW MCELMOYL
Oliver a bistro

218 Farnsworth Ave
Bordentown, NJ 08505
609.298.7177
oliverabistro.com

ALEX CAPASSO
Blackbird Dining Establishment

714 Haddon Ave
Collingswood, NJ 08108
856.854.3444
blackbirdnj.com

MASAHARU ITO
Fuji

116 Kings Hwy E
Haddonfield, NJ 08033
856.354.8200
fujirestaurant.com

ROBERT MINNITI
Bacio Catering

75 E Main St
Moorestown, NJ 08057
856.780.5402
bcater.com

MANISH CHOPRA
Cross Culture

208 Kings Hwy E
Haddonfield, NJ 08033
856.428.4343
crossculturerestaurant.net

FRED KELLERMANN
Elements Café

517 Station Ave
Haddon Heights, NJ 08035
856.546.8840
elementscafe.com

NUNZIO PATRUNO
Nunzio Ristorante Rustico

706 Haddon Ave
Collingswood, NJ 08108
856.858.9840
nunzios.net

MARIO DIVENTURA
Filomena Lakeview

1738 County Rd 706
Deptford, NJ 08096
856.228.4235
filomenalakeview.com

JUSTIN KUNKEL
Kunkel's Seafood & Steakhouse

920 Kings Hwy
Haddon Heights, NJ 08035
856.547.1225
kunkelsrestaurant.com

JOHN PILARZ
Anthony's Creative Italian Cuisine

512 Station Ave
Haddon Heights, NJ 08035
856.310.7766
anthonyscuisine.com

VINCENT FANARI
Dream Cuisine Café

1990 Marlton Pike E
Cherry Hill, NJ 08003
856.751.2800
dreamcuisinecafe.net

FRANCO LOMBARDO
Sapori

601 Haddon Ave
Collingswood, NJ 08108
856.858.2288
sapori.info

MARIANNE POWELL
A Little Café

118 White Horse Rd
Camden, NJ 08043
856.784.3344
alittlecafenj.com

JOSHUA REEVES
Barnsboro Inn

699 Main St
Sewell, NJ 08080
856.468.3557
barnsboroinn.com

CHRIS SAMMONS
Zinc Café

679 Stokes Rd
Medford, NJ 08055
609.953.9462
zinccafenj.com

ROBIN WINZINGER
Robin's Nest

2 Washington St
Mt. Holly, NJ 08060
609.261.6149
robinsnestmountholly.com

FLEMINGTON

ANTHONY BUCCO
The Ryland Inn

111 Old Hwy 28
Whitehouse Station, NJ 08889
908.534.4011
rylandinnnj.com

CHRIS CONNORS
Anton's at the Swan

43 S Main St
Lambertville, NJ 08530
609.397.1960
antons-at-the-swan.com

BRIAN HELD
Brian's

9 Klines Ct
Lambertville, NJ 08530
609.460.4148
brianslambertville.com

CHRISTOPHER HIRSHEIMER
Canal House Cooking

6 Coryell St
Lambertville, NJ 08530
815.777.8477
thecanalhouse.com

MATT MCPHERSON
Matt's Red Rooster Grill

22 Bloomfield Ave
Flemington, NJ 08822
908.788.7050
mattsredroostergrill.com

MARK MILLER
Hamilton's Grill Room

8 Coryell St
Lambertville, NJ 08530
609.397.4343
hamiltonsgrillroom.com

DE ANNA PATERRA
DeAnna's Restaurant

54 N Franklin St
Lambertville, NJ 08530
609.397.8957
deannasrestaurant.com

FREEHOLD

YOSHI
Arisu

167 U.S. Hwy 9
Englishtown, NJ 07726
732.536.7874
arisunj.com

ANDREW ARANEO
Drew's Bayshore Bistro

28 E Front St
Keyport, NJ 07735
732.739.9219
bayshorebistro.com

GIOVANNI ATZORI
Undici

11 W River Rd
Rumson, NJ 07760
732.842.3880
undicirestaurant.com

CHRIS BRANDL
Brandl.

703 Belmar Plaza
Belmar, NJ 07719
732.280.7501
brandlrestaurant.com

RON CAUDILL
Raven and the Peach

740 River Rd #100
Fair Haven, NJ 07704
732.747.4666
ravenandthepeach.net

JOSEPH CETRULO
Stella Marina

800 Ocean Ave
Asbury Park, NJ 07712
732.775.7776
stellamarinarestaurant.com

IAN COOPER
Manasquan, NJ

TERRY ELEFTHERIOU
Shipwreck Grill

720 Ashley Ave
Brielle, NJ 08730
732.292.9380
shipwreckgrill.com

CHRIS ESTELLE
Asbury Park, NJ

TAKA HIRAI
Taka

632 Mattison Ave
Asbury Park, NJ 07712
732.775.1020
takaapnj.com

STEFFAN MANNO
Giamano's Ristorante

301 Main St
Bradley Beach, NJ 07720
732.775.4275
giamanos.com

DARRYL FEENEY
red

46 English Plaza
Red Bank, NJ 07701
732.741.3232
rednj.com

PAUL HOLZHEIMER
Porta

911 Kingsley St
Asbury Park, NJ 07712
732.776.7661
pizzaporta.com

ULISSES NOVA
Metropolitan Café

8 E Main St
Freehold, NJ 07728
732.780.9400
metrocafenj.com

DOMINIQUE FILONI
Avenue

23 Ocean Ave
Long Branch, NJ 07740
732.759.2900
leclubavenue.com

BRIAN IMBRIALE
The Wine Bar

40 1st Ave
Atlantic Highlands, NJ 07716
732.291.1377
ahwinebar.com

JOHN PANEBIANCO
Brando's Citi Cucina

162 Main St
Asbury Park, NJ 07712
732.774.2222
brandosnj.com

SCOTT GIORDANO
Whispers

200 Monmouth Ave
Spring Lake, NJ 07762
732.974.9755
whispersrestaurant.com

BOBBY JOHNSON
Clementine's

306 Main St
Avon-by-the-Sea, NJ 07717
732.988.7979
clementinesavon.com

CASEY PESCE
d'jeet?

637 Broad St
Shrewsbury, NJ 07702
732.224.8887
djeetcatering.com

NICHOLAS HARARY
Restaurant Nicholas

160 New Jersey 35
Red Bank, NJ 07701
732.345.9977
restaurantnicholas.com

BRIAN KATZ
10th Ave Burrito Co.

801 Belmar Plaza
Belmar, NJ 07719
732.280.1515
tenthaveburrito.com

JOE PISACRETA
Il Giardinello Ristorante

1232 New Jersey 166
Asbury Park, NJ 08753
732.286.9111
ilgiardinello.com

MATTHEW HIGGINS
La Cipollina Ristorante

16 W Main St
Freehold, NJ 07728
732.308.3830
lacipollina.com

MICHAEL KRIKORIAN
Copper Canyon

51 1st Ave
Atlantic Highlands, NJ 07716
732.291.8444
thecoppercanyon.com

ALEX ROGERS
The Inlet Café

3 Cornwall St
Highlands, NJ 07732
732.872.9764
inletcafe.com

HACKENSACK

JOE ROMANOWSKI
Bay Ave Trattoria

122 Bay Ave
Highlands, NJ 07732
732.872.9800
bayavetrattoria.com

MARILYN SCHLOSSBACH
Langosta Lounge

1000 Ocean Ave
Asbury Park, NJ 07712
732.455.3275
langostalounge.com

NICHOLAS WILKINS
Restaurant Nicholas

160 New Jersey 35
Red Bank, NJ 07701
732.345.9977
restaurantnicholas.com

SHUENN YANG
Yumi

1120 Ocean Ave
Sea Bright, NJ 07760
732.212.0881
yumirestaurant.com

ERIC YEGELWEL
Nicchio

1000 Main St
Belmar, NJ 07719
732.280.1132
nicchiorestaurant.com

MATTHEW ZAPPOLI
Tre Amici

628 Ocean Ave
Long Branch, NJ 07740
732.571.8922
treamicinj.com

PETER ANGELAKOS
Bacari Grill

800 Ridgewood Rd
Washington Township, NJ 07676
201.358.6330
bacarigrill.com

GASPARD CALOZ
Madeleine's Petit Paris

416 Tappan Rd
Northvale, NJ 07647
201.767.0063
madeleinespetitparis.com

STEVE CHRISTIANSON
St. Eve's

611 N Maple Ave
Ho-Ho-Kus, NJ 07423
201.857.4717
stevesnj.com

THOMAS CISZAK
Chakra

144 W State Route 4
Paramus, NJ 07652
201.556.1530
chakrarestaurant.com

RONNY COHEN
White Manna Hamburgers

358 River St
Hackensack, NJ 07601
201.342.0914

ALEX DAKU
Le Jardin

1257 River Rd
Edgewater, NJ 07020
201.224.9898
lejardinnj.com

HANS EGG
The Saddle River Inn

2 Barnstable Ct
Saddle River, NJ 07458
201.825.4016
saddleriverinn.com

MATTHEW GAVZIE
MK Valencia

228 Main St
Ridgefield Park, NJ 07660
201.373.0228
ridgefieldparkrestaurant.com

GEORGE GEORGIADES
Varka Estiatorio

30 N Spruce St
Ramsey, NJ 07446
201.995.9333
varkarestaurant.com

GINO GJEVUKAJ
Dimora

100 Piermont Rd
Norwood, NJ 07648
201.750.5000
dimoraristorante.com

ALEX GORANT
AXIA Taverna

18 Piermont Rd
Tenafly, NJ 07670
201.569.5999
axiataverna.com

JOHN HALLIGAN
The Park Steakhouse

151 Kinderkamack Rd
Park Ridge, NJ 07656
201.930.1300
theparksteakhouse.com

KEVIN KOHLER
Café Panache

130 E Main St
Ramsey, NJ 07446
201.934.0030
cafepanachenj.com

CARLO ORLANDO
A Mano Pizza

24 Franklin Ave
Ridgewood, NJ 07450
201.493.2000
amanopizza.com

DENIS WHITTON
Harvest Bistro

252 Schraalenburgh Rd
Closter, NJ 07624
201.750.9966
harvestbistro.com
Jersey City

CRAIG LEVY
RoCCA

203 Rock Rd
Glen Rock, NJ 07452
201.670.4945
roccaitalianrestaurant.com

KEVIN PORTSCHER
Village Green Restaurant

36 Prospect St
Ridgewood, NJ 07450
201.445.2914
villagegreenrestaurant.com

BRYAN GREGG
Jersey City, NJ

PETER LORIA
Café Matisse

167 Park Ave
Rutherford, NJ 07070
201.935.2995
cafematisse.com

WILLIAM ROANE
McCormick & Schmick's

175 Riverside Square Mall
Hackensack, NJ 07601
201.968.9410
mccormickandschmicks.com

MATTIAS GUSTAFSSON
Madame Claude Cafe

364 1/2 4th St
Jersey City, NJ 07302
201.876.8800
madameclaudecafe.com

JOHN MARSANO
The Brick House

179 Godwin Ave
Wyckoff, NJ 07481
201.848.1211
thebrickhousewyckoff.com

ANDREW RODRIGUEZ
Ho-Ho-Kus Inn

1 E Franklin Turnpike
Ho-Ho-Kus, NJ 07423
201.445.4115
hohokusinn.com

ARCHIE MEJIA
Sabor Latin Bistro

8809 River Rd
North Bergen, NJ 07047
201.945.6663
saborlatinbistro.com

FRED MORTATI
A Mano Pizza

24 Franklin Ave
Ridgewood, NJ 07450
201.493.2000
amanopizza.com

SETH WARSHAW
Etc. Steakhouse

1409 Palisade Ave
Teaneck, NJ 07666
201.357.5677
etcsteakhouse.com

RODNEY PETERSEN
Amanda's

908 Washington St
Hoboken, NJ 07030
201.798.0101
amandasrestaurant.com

CHRISTINE NUNN
Picnic, The Restaurant

14-25 Plaza Rd
Fair Lawn, NJ 07410
201.796.2700
picnictherestaurant.com

ADAM WEISS
Esty Street

86 Spring Valley Rd
Park Ridge, NJ 07656
201.307.1515
estystreet.com

ANTHONY PINO
Bin 14

1314 Washington St
Hoboken, NJ 07030
201.963.9463
bin14.com

MORRISTOWN

ADRIANA POLITIS
GP's

24 69th St
Guttenberg, NJ 07093
201.861.6588
gpsrestaurant.com

MARICEL PRESILLA
Cucharamama

233 Clinton St
Hoboken, NJ 07030
201.420.1700
cucharamama.com

CHRIS SIVERSEN
Maritime Parc

84 Audrey Zapp Dr
Jersey City, NJ 07305
201.413.0050
maritimeparc.com

BILL SPITZ
Bistro La Source

85 Morris St
Jersey City, NJ 07302
201.209.1717
bistrolasource.com

KEN TRICKILO
Liberty House

76 Audrey Zapp Dr
Jersey City, NJ 07305
201.395.0300
libertyhouserestaurant.com

WALLY WEAVER
3 Forty Grill

340 Sinatra Dr
Hoboken, NJ 07030
201.217.3406
3fortygrill.com

MICHAEL CHU
Ming II

3 Speedwell Ave
Morristown, NJ 07960
973.871.2323
ming2morristown.com

DAVID DRAKE
Alice's Restaurant

24 Nolans Point Park Rd
Lake Hopatcong, NJ 07849
973.663.9600
alicesrestaurantnj.com

ANTONIO GRANDE
Il Capriccio

633 New Jersey 10
Whippany, NJ 07981
973.884.9176
ilcapriccio.com

NATALE GRANDE
Il Capriccio

633 New Jersey 10
Whippany, NJ 07981
973.884.9176
ilcapriccio.com

JAMES LAIRD
Restaurant Serenade

6 Roosevelt Ave
Chatham, NJ 07928
973.701.0303
restaurantserenade.com

BROOKS NICKLAS
Rosemary and Sage

26 Paterson-Hamburg Turnpike
Riverdale, NJ 07457
973.616.0606
rosemaryandsage.com

JEFFREY OREL
Rod's Steak & Seafood Grille

1 Convent Rd
Morristown, NJ 07960
973.539.6666
rodssteak.com

RALPH PERROTTI
LuNello's Montville Inn

167 U.S. Hwy 202
Montville, NJ 07045
973.541.1234
montvilleinn.com

MATTHEW PIERONE
The Gourmet Café

136 Baldwin Rd
Parsippany, NJ 07054
973.316.0088
njgourmetcafe.com

DAVID PRUSIN
David Todd's City Tavern

150 South St
Morristown, NJ 07960
973.993.8066
davidtoddscitytavern.com

JOHN SCHAEFER
Tabor Road Tavern

510 Tabor Rd
Morris Plains, NJ 07950
973.267.7004
taborroadtavern.com

MANOP SUTIPAYAKUL
Origin

10 South St
Morristown, NJ 07960
973.971.9933
originthai.com

KEVIN TAKAFUJI
Blue Morel

2 Whippany Rd
Morristown, NJ 07960
973.451.2619
bluemorel.com

FREDY UMANZOR
Tim Schafer's Cuisine

82 Speedwell Ave
Morristown, NJ 07960
973.538.3330
timschafersrestaurant.com

NEW BRUNSWICK

J.R. BELT
Stage Left

5 Livingston Ave
New Brunswick, NJ 08901
732.828.4444
stageleft.com

ANDREA DIMEGLIO
Luca's Ristorante

2019 New Jersey 27
North Brunswick, NJ 08873
732.297.7676
lucasristorante.com

BRIAN KARLUK
Steakhouse 85

85 Church St
New Brunswick, NJ 08901
732.247.8585
steakhouse85.com

BRUCE LEFEBVRE
The Frog and the Peach

29 Dennis St
New Brunswick, NJ 08901
732.846.3216
frogandpeach.com

JUSTIN QUINT
Clydz

55 Paterson St
New Brunswick, NJ 08901
732.846.6521
clydz.com

IRA SIEGEL
Just

2280 U.S. Hwy 9
Old Bridge Township, NJ 08857
732.707.4800
justrestaurantnj.com

ALEX STOTLER
Due Mari

78 Albany St
New Brunswick, NJ 08901
732.296.1600
duemarinj.com

NEWARK

JOE ALBERGO
Rose Mediterranean

435 Bloomfield Ave
Caldwell, NJ 07006
973.403.7673
rosemediterranean.com

MITCHELL ALTHOLZ
The Manor

111 Prospect Ave
West Orange, NJ 07052
973.731.2360
themanorrestaurant.com

ZOD ARIFAI
Blu

554 Bloomfield Ave
Montclair, NJ 07042
973.509.2202
restaurantblu.com

CLAUDE BROWNE
Basilico

324 Millburn Ave
Millburn, NJ 07041
973.379.7020
basilicomillburn.com

HUMBERTO CAMPOS JR.
Restaurant Lorena's

168 Maplewood Ave
Maplewood, NJ 07040
973.763.4460
restaurantlorena.com

MICHAEL CARRINO
Pig & Prince

1 Lackawanna Plaza
Montclair, NJ 07042
973.233.1006
pigandprince.com

RYAN DEPERSIO
Fascino

331 Bloomfield Ave
Montclair, NJ 07042
973.233.0350
fascinorestaurant.com

ARIANE DUARTE
CulinAriane

33 Walnut St
Montclair, NJ 07042
973.744.0533
culinariane.com

TRE GHOSHAL
Adara

77 Walnut St
Montclair, NJ 07042
973.783.0462
restaurantadara.com

ALEXANDRE GOMES
Mompou Tapas

77 Ferry St
Newark, NJ 07105
973.578.8114
mompoutapas.com

LANCE KNOWLING
Indigo Kitchen

615 Bloomfield Ave
Montclair, NJ 07042
973.707.2950
lanceknowling.com

FRANCESCO PALMIERI
The Orange Squirrel

412 Bloomfield Ave
Bloomfield, NJ 07003
973.337.6421
theorangesquirrel.com

JUAN ANDRES PLACENCIA
Costanera Restaurant

511 Bloomfield Ave
Montclair, NJ 07042
973.337.8289
costaneranj.com

ANTHONY PUCCIARELLO
Cielo

168 Passaic Ave
Fairfield, NJ 07004
973.808.1414
cielonj.com

DAN RICHER
Arturo's Osteria & Pizzeria

180 Maplewood Ave
Maplewood, NJ 07040
973.378.5800
arturosnj.com

ADAM ROSE
Nico Kitchen and Bar

1 Center St
Newark, NJ 07102
973.642.1226
nicokitchenbar.com

LOUIS SEGER
Lu Nello

182 Stevens Ave
Cedar Grove, NJ 07009
973.837.1660
lunello.com

CHARLES TUTINO
Verjus Restaurant

1790 Springfield Ave
Maplewood, NJ 07040
973.378.8990
verjusrestaurant.com

HEINRICH K. AICHEM
Black Forest Inn

249 U.S. Hwy 206
Stanhope, NJ 07874
973.347.3344
blackforestinn.com

ANDRE DE WAAL
Andre's

188 Spring St
Newton, NJ 07860
973.300.4192
andresrestaurant.com

MICHAEL WEISSHAUPT
Restaurant Latour

1 Wild Turkey Way
Hamburg, NJ 07419
973.827.5996
crystalgolfresort.com

PATERSON

JOSE AVILES
Paterson, NJ

CARLO CARBONARO
Bottagra

80 Wagaraw Rd
Hawthorne, NJ 07506
973.423.4433
bottagra.com

JOSE VELEZ
Toscania Trattoria

75 Main St
Little Falls, NJ 0424
973.256.2984
toscanianj.com

POINT PLEASANT

KRISTOPHER GREENE
Atlantic Bar & Grill

10 Central Ave
Seaside Park, NJ 08752
732.854.1588
atlanticbarandgrillnj.com

MIKE JURUSZ
709

709 Arnold Ave
Point Pleasant, NJ 08742
732.295.0709
709pointbeach.com

ARTIE KEENAN
Bay Head Yacht Club

111 Metcalf St
Bay Head, NJ 08742
732.899.2085
bayheadyachtclub.com

PRINCETON

CHRISTOPHER ALBRECHT
Eno Terra

4484 New Jersey 27
Kingston, NJ 08528
609.497.1777
enoterra.com

WILL MOONEY
The Brothers Moon

7 W Broad St
Hopewell, NJ 08525
609.333.1330
brothersmoon.com

JIM WEAVER
Tre Piani

120 Rockingham Row
Princeton, NJ 08540
609.452.1515
trepiani.com

SOMERVILLE

TIM AMOROSO
Witherspoon Grill

57 Witherspoon St
Princeton, NJ 08088
609.924.6011
bluepoint.jmgroupprinceton.com

MANUEL PEREZ
The Peacock Inn

20 Bayard Ln
Princeton, NJ 08540
609.924.1707
peacockinn.com

JUSTIN BRAUN
Rocky Hill, NJ

SCOTT ANDERSON
elements

163 Bayard Ln
Princeton, NJ 08540
609.924.0078
elementsprinceton.com

SALVATORE SCARLATA
Vidalia

21 Phillips Ave
Lawrenceville, NJ 08648
609.896.4444
eatatvidalia.com

BILL DORRLER
Osteria Morini

107 Morristown Rd
Bernardsville, NJ 07924
908.221.0040
osteriamorini.com

FRANK CAPONI
Medittera

29 Hulfish St
Princeton, NJ 08542
609.252.9680
mediterrarestaurant.com

CRAIG SHELTON
Aeon Hospitality Holdings, LLC

Princeton, NJ
aeonhospitalityholdings.com

MARK FARRO
Uproot Restaurant

9 Mount Bethel Rd
Warren, NJ 07059
908.834.8194
uprootrestaurant.com

CHRIS GRACIANO
Witherspoon Grill

57 Witherspoon St
Princeton, NJ 08088
609.924.6011
bluepoint.jmgroupprinceton.com

BOBBY TRIGG
The Ferry House

32 Witherspoon St
Princeton, NJ 08540
609.924.2488
theferryhouse.com

DAVID FELTON
Ninety Acres

2 Main St
Peapack, NJ 07977
908.901.9500
natirar.com

MARIO MANGONE
Chambers Walk Café & Catering

2667 Main St
Lawrenceville, NJ 08648
609.896.5995
chamberswalk.com

EDGAR URIAS
Blue Point Grill

258 Nassau St
Princeton, NJ 08542
609.921.1211
bluepoint.jmgroupprinceton.com

COREY HEYER
The Bernard's Inn

27 Mine Brook Rd
Bernardsville, NJ 07924
908.766.0002
bernardsinn.com

MELISSA HILL
twofiftytwo

252 Somerville Rd
Bedminster, NJ 07921
908.234.9093
twofiftytworestaurant.com

SCOTT HOWLETT
Sublime

12 Lackawanna Ave
Peapack, NJ 07934
908.781.1888
sublimenj.com

KEVIN KNEVALS
Osteria Morini

107 Morristown Rd
Bernardsville, NJ 07924
908.221.0040
osteriamorini.com

ALLAN RUSSO
Sette

7 Mine Brook Rd
Bernardsville, NJ 07924
908.502.5054
settecucina.com

FILIPPO RUSSO
Da Filippo's Ristorante

132 E Main St
Somerville, NJ 08876
908.218.0110
dafilippos.com

JOHN TOCCI
Water & Wine

141 Stirling Rd
Watchung, NJ 07069
908.755.9344
visitwaterandwine.com

UNION

KARA DECKER
A Toute Heure

232 Centennial Ave
Cranford, NJ 07016
908.276.6600
atouteheure.com

ANDREW DICATALDO
Patria

169 W Main St
Rahway, NJ 07065
732.943.7531
patrianj.com

BILL HENDRA
Huntley Taverne

3 Morris Ave
Summit, NJ 07901
908.273.3166
thehuntleytaverne.com

BRUCE JOHNSON
Roots Steakhouse

401 Springfield Ave
Summit, NJ 07901
908.273.0027
rootssteakhouse.com

JOSEPH MASTRELLA
Luciano's Ristorante

1579 Main St
Rahway, NJ 07065
732.815.1200
lucianosristorante.com

C.J. REYCRAFT JR.
Chez Catherine

431 North Ave W
Westfield, NJ 07090
908.654.4011
chezcatherine.com

FRANK RIZZO
The Italian Pantry Bistro

13 Eastman St
Cranford, NJ 07016
908.272.7790
theitalianpantrybistro.com

ED STONE
Baltusrol Golf Club

201 Shunpike Rd
Springfield , NJ 07081
973.376.1900
baltusrol.org

PETER TURSO
Ursino

1075 Morris Ave
Union, NJ 07083
908.249.4099
ursinorestaurant.com

GEORGE VASTARDIS
Limani Seafood Grill

235 North Ave W
Westfield, NJ 07090
908.233.0052
limaniwestfieldnj.com

WILDWOOD

CARL MESSICK
Peter Shields Inn & Restaurant

1301 Beach Ave
Cape May, NJ 08204
609.884.9090
petershieldsinn.com

ANTHONY MICARI
The Ebbitt Room

25 Jackson St
Cape May, NJ 08204
609.884.5700
virginiahotel.com

CLAUDE POTTIER
Claude's Restaurant

100 Olde New Jersey Ave
North Wildwood, NJ 08260
609.522.0400
claudesrestaurant.com

ALBUQUERQUE

JOHN APODACA JR.
Indigo Crow Café

4515 Corrales Rd
Corrales, NM 87048
505.898.7000
indigocrowcafe.com

KEVIN BLADERGROEN
Blades' Bistro

221 Hwy 165 #L
Placitas, NM 87043
505.771.0695
bladesbistro.com

CASEY BOWER
Artichoke Café

424 Central Ave SE
Albuquerque, NM 87102
505.243.0200
artichokecafe.com

RYAN HALLUM
Marcello's Chophouse

2201 Q St
Albuquerque, NM 87110
505.837.2467
marcelloschophouse.com

LELAND HAROLD
Forque Kitchen and Bar

330 Tijeras Ave NW
Albuquerque, NM 87102
505.843.2700
albuquerque.hyatt.com

CLAUS HJORTKJAER
Brasserie La Provence

3001 Central Ave NE
Albuquerque, NM 87106
505.254.7644
laprovencenobhill.com

JENNIFER JAMES
Jennifer James 101

4615 Menaul Blvd NE
Albuquerque, NM 87110
505.884.3860
jenniferjames101.com

CHRISTOPHER POPE
Zinc Wine Bar & Bistro

3009 Central Ave NE
Albuquerque, NM 87106
505.254.9462
zincabq.com

MARC QUINONES
Bien Shur

30 Rainbow Rd
Albuquerque, NM 87113
800.526.9366
sandiacasino.com

KA'AINOA RAVEY
Farm & Table

8917 4th St NW
Albuquerque, NM 87114
505.503.7124
farmandtablenm.com

SAM REED
Corn Maiden

1300 Tuyuna Trail
Bernalillo, NM 87004
505.867.1234
tamaya.hyatt.com

RICHARD WINTERS
Farina Pizzeria

510 Central Ave SE
Albuquerque, NM 87102
505.243.0130
farinapizzeria.com

SANTA FE

JAMES CAMPBELL CARUSO
La Boca

72 W Marcy St
Santa Fe, NM 87501
505.982.3433
labocasf.com

MARK CONNELL
Tomme

229 Galisteo St
Santa Fe, NM 87501
505.820.2253
tommesf.com

CHARLES DALE
Terra

198 State Road 592
Santa Fe, NM 87506
505.946.5700
fourseasons.com

ERIC DISTEFANO
Coyote Café

132 W Water St
Sante Fe, NM 87501
505.983.1615
coyotecafe.com

SHOHKO FUKUDA
Shohko Café

321 Johnson St
Santa Fe, NM 87501
505.982.9708
shohkocafe.com

ESTEVAN GARCIA
Santa Fe, NM

KATHARINE KAGEL
Café Pasqual's

121 Don Gaspar Ave
Santa Fe, NM 87501
505.983.9340
pasquals.com

TOM KERPON
Tanti Luce 221

221 Shelby St
Santa Fe, NM 87501
505.988.2355
tantiluce221.com

MARK KIFFIN
The Compound Restaurant

653 Canyon Rd
Santa Fe, NM 87501
505.982.4353
compoundrestaurant.com

NELLI MALTEZOS
Trattoria Nostrani

304 Johnson St
Santa Fe, NM 87501
505.983.3800
trattorianostrani.com

MARK MILLER
Santa Fe, NM

LOUIS MOSKOW
315 Restaurant & Wine Bar

315 Old Santa Fe Trail
Santa Fe, NM 87501
505.986.9190
315santafe.com

FERNANDO OLEA
Santa Fe, NM

MARTIN RIOS
Restaurant Martin

526 Galisteo St
Santa Fe, NM 87501
505.820.0919
restaurantmartinsantafe.com

EDUARDO RODRIGUEZ
Coyote Café

132 W Water St
Santa Fe, NM 87501
505.983.1615
coyotecafe.com

TAOS

LESLEY B. FAY
Graham's Grille

106 Paseo del Pueblo Norte
Taos, NM 87571
575.751.1350
grahamstaos.com

GIN HATTORI
Sushi a la Hattori

1405 Paseo del Pueblo Norte
Taos , NM 87571
575.737.5123
taosdining.com

FREDERICK MULLER
El Meze Restaurant

1017 Paseo del Pueblo Norte
Taos, NM 87571
575.751.3337
elmeze.com

AMERICAN CAVIAR
American aquafarms are raising caviar that rivals the Caspian's finest.

BC|A NEW YORK

ALBANY

JASPER ALEXANDER
Hattie's

45 Phila St
Saratoga Springs, NY 12866
518.584.4790
hattiesrestaurant.com

MICHAEL CUNNINGHAM
Provence

1475 Western Ave
Albany, NY 12203
518.689.7777
milano-restaurant.com

MARK GRAHAM
Max London's

466 Broadway
Saratoga Springs, NY 12866
518.587.3535
maxlondons.com

JASON BAKER
Adventure in Food Trading

381 Broadway
Menands, NY 12204
518.436.7603
adventureinfood.com

DANIEL DARVES-BORNOZ
Milano Restaurant

594 New Loudon Rd
Albany, NY 12110
518.783.3334
milano-restaurant.com

HARRY HATZIPARASKEVAS
Athos

1814 Western Ave
Albany, NY 12203
518.608.6400
athosrestaurant.com

FABRIZIO BAZZANI
Chianti II

18 Division St
Saratoga Springs, NY 12866
518.580.0025
chiantiristorante.com

BRIAN DONALDSON
Nove

707 Saratoga Rd
Saratoga Springs, NY 12831
518.583.8877
novesaratoga.com

BRAD HOLUB
Longfellow's

500 Union Ave
Saratoga Springs, NY 12866
518.587.0108
longfellows.com

DOMINIQUE BRIALY
Epicurean Bistro

579 Troy-Schenectady Rd
Latham, NY 12110
518.786.8272
epicurean-ny.com

BRADY DUHAME
Angelo's Prime Bar + Grill

30 Clifton Country Rd
Clifton Park, NY 12065
518.631.6500
angelosprimebarandgrill.com

JEREMY KEOUGH
Maestro's

353 Broadway
Saratoga Springs, NY 12866
518.580.0312
maestrosatthevandam.com

DOMINIC COLOSE
Wine Bar

417 Broadway
Saratoga Springs, NY 12866
518.584.8777
thewinebarofsaratoga.com

SANDRA FOSTER
Village Pizzeria and Ristorante

2727 New York 29
Middle Grove, NY 12850
518.882.9431
villagepizzeria.com

SCOTT KRAUSE
MezzaNotte

2026 Western Ave
Albany, NY 12203
518.689.4433
mezzanottealbany.com

JOHN LAPOSTA
Maestro's

353 Broadway
Saratoga Springs, NY 12866
518.580.0312
maestrosatthevandam.com

DALE MILLER
Sperry's

30 1/2 Caroline St
Saratoga Springs, NY 12866
518.584.9618
sperrysrestaurant.com

MICHAEL NICCOLI
Century House

997 New Loudon Rd
Latham, NY 12110
518.785.0834
thecenturyhouse.com

MARLA ORTEGA
illium Cafe

9 Broadway
Troy, NY 12180
518.273.7700
illiumcafe.com

JAIME ORTIZ
Angelo's 677 Prime

677 Broadway
Albany, NY 12207
518.427.7463
677prime.com

PAUL OZIMEK
Taste

45 Beaver St
Albany, NY 12207
518.694.3322
tastealbany.com

JORDAN PATREGNANI
Capriccio

26 Henry St
Saratoga Springs, NY 12866
518.587.9463
capricciosaratoga.com

DAVID PEDINOTTI
One Caroline Street Bistro

1 Caroline St
Saratoga Springs, NY 12866
518.587.2026
onecaroline.com

GARRETT PENISTAN
One Caroline Street Bistro

1 Caroline St
Saratoga Springs, NY 12866
518.587.2026
onecaroline.com

WIDJIONO "YONO" PURNOMO
Yono's

25 Chapel St
Albany, NY 12210
518.436.7747
yonos.com

JIM RUA
Café Capriccio

49 Grand St
Albany, NY 12207
518.465.0439
cafecapriccio.com

JASON SAUNDERS
Prime at Saratoga National

458 Union Ave
Saratoga Springs, NY 12866
518.583.4653
golfsaratoga.com

LARRY SCHEPICI
Jack's Oyster House

42 State St
Albany, NY 12207
518.465.8854
jacksoysterhouse.com

MICHAEL ST. JOHN
Albany's Scrimshaw

660 Albany Shaker Rd
Albany, NY 12211
518.869.8100
desmondhotelsalbany.com

FRANK TARDIO
Angelo's Tavolo

1 Glen Ave
Albany, NY 12302
518.374.7262
angelostavolo.com

COURTNEY WITHEY
Aperitivo Bistro

426 State St
Schenectady, NY 12305
518.579.3371
aperitivobistro.com

ROSLYN ZECCHINI
Boca Bistro

541 Broadway
Saratoga Springs, NY 12866
518.581.2401
bocabistro.com

BREWSTER

GEORGE SEITZ
Arch

1292 New York 22
Brewster, NY 10509
845.279.5011
archrestaurant.com

BROOKLYN

JOHNATHAN ADLER
Franny's

295 Flatbush Ave
Brooklyn, NY 11217
718.230.0221
frannysbrooklyn.com

SAUL BOLTON
Saul Restaurant

140 Smith St
Brooklyn, NY 11201
718.935.9844
saulrestaurant.com

MARCO CHIRICO
Marco Polo Ristorante

345 Court St
Brooklyn, NY 11231
718.852.5015
marcopoloristorante.com

DANNY AMEND
Franny's

295 Flatbush Ave
Brooklyn, NY 11217
718.230.0221
frannysbrooklyn.com

RICCARDO BUITONI
Aurora

70 Grand St
Brooklyn, NY 11249
718.388.5100
aurorabk.com

SHEA CRAWFORD
Belleville Bistro

330 5th St
Brooklyn, NY 11215
718.832.9777
bellevillebistro.com

TODD ANDREWS
Anella

222 Franklin St
Brooklyn, NY 11222
718.389.8102
anellabrooklyn.com

MIMMO CAPPIELLO
Baci and Abbracci

204 Grand St
Brooklyn, NY 11211
718.599.6599
baciny.com

ANDREA DAL MONTE
Campo De Fiori

187 5th Ave
Brooklyn, NY 11217
347.763.0933
pizzacampodefiori.com

MICHAEL AYOUB
Fornino

187 Bedford Ave
Brooklyn, NY 11211
718.384.6004
forninopizza.com

JOE CARROLL
Fette Sau

354 Metropolitan Ave
Brooklyn, NY 11211
718.963.3404
fettesaubbq.com

YVON DE TASSIGNY
St. Anselm

355 Metropolitan Ave
Brooklyn, NY 11211
718.384.5054

MICHELE BALDACCI
Locanda Vini E Olii

129 Gates Ave
Brooklyn, NY 11238
718.622.9202
locandavinieolii.com

FRANK CASTRONOVO
Prime Meats

465 Court St
Brooklyn, NY 11231
718.254.0327
frankspm.com

DOMENICO DEMARCO
Di Fara Pizza

1424 Ave J
Brooklyn, NY 11230
718.258.1367
difara.com

JUSTIN BAZDARICH
Speedy Romeo

376 Classon Ave
Brooklyn, NY 11238
718.230.0061
speedyromeo.com

SEBASTIEN CHAMARET
Le Comptoir

251 Grand St
Brooklyn, NY 11211
718.486.3300
lecomptoirny.com

CAROLINE FIDANZA
Saltie

378 Metropolitan Ave
Brooklyn, NY 11211
718.387.4777
saltieny.com

SAM FILLORAMO
Mile End

97A Hoyt St
Brooklyn, NY 11217
718.852.7510
mileenddeli.com

ERIC FRANCOU
Radegast Hall & Biergarten

113 N 3rd St
Brooklyn, NY 11211
718.963.3973
radegasthall.com

NEIL GANIC
Petite Crevette

144 Union St
Brooklyn, NY 11231
718.855.2632

JACQUES GAUTIER
Palo Santo

652 Union St
Brooklyn, NY 11215
718.636.6311
palosanto.us

JOHN GIBSON
Stonehome Wine Bar

87 Lafayette Ave
Brooklyn, NY 11217
718.624.9443
stonehomewinebar.com

DAVID GOULD
Roman's

243 Dekalb Ave
Brooklyn, NY 11205
718.622.5300
romansnyc.com

ABDOUL GUEYE
A Bistro on Dekalb

250 Dekalb Ave
Brooklyn, NY 11205
347.384.2972
abistrodekalb.com

RAFAEL HASID
Miriam

79 5th Ave
Brooklyn, NY 11217
718.622.2250
miriamrestaurant.com

BRANDON HOY
Blanca

261 Moore St
Brooklyn, NY 11206
646.703.2715
blancanyc.com

JOE ISIDORI
Arthur on Smith

276 Smith St
Brooklyn, NY 11231
718.360.2340
arthuronsmith.com

RYAN JARONIK
Benchmark Restaurant

339 2nd St
Brooklyn, NY 11215
718.965.7040
benchmarkrestaurant.com

SOHUI KIM
Good Fork

391 Van Brunt St
Brooklyn, NY 11231
718.643.6636
goodfork.com

ANNA KLINGER
Al Di La

248 5th Ave
Brooklyn, NY 11215
718.783.4565
aldilatrattoria.com

BRIAN LETH
Vinegar Hill House

72 Hudson Ave
Brooklyn, NY 11201
718.522.1018
vinegarhillhouse.com

BRET MACRIS
Rosewater

787 Union St
Brooklyn, NY 11215
718.783.3800
rosewaterrestaurant.com

JASON MARCUS
Traif

229 S 4th St
Brooklyn, NY 11211
347.844.9578
traifny.com

ANTHONY MARZUILLO
Soigne

486 6th Ave
Brooklyn, NY 11215
718.369.4814
soignebrooklyn.com

BRADFORD MCDONALD
Colonie

127 Atlantic Ave
Brooklyn, NY 11201
718.855.7500
colonienyc.com

SASHA MIRANDA
Miranda

80 Berry St
Brooklyn, NY 11211
718.387.0711
mirandarestaurant.com

CARLO MIRARCHI
Roberta's

261 Moore St
Brooklyn, NY 11206
718.417.1118
robertaspizza.com

BOB MOREN
Walter Foods

253 Grand St
Brooklyn, NY 11211
718.387.8783
walterfoods.com

CONO MORENA
Verde on Smith

216 Smith St
Brooklyn, NY 11201
718.222.1525
verdeonsmith.com

ANTONIO MORICHINI
Bevacco

60 Henry St
Brooklyn, NY 11201
718.624.1444
bevacco.com

ROBERT NEWTON
Seersucker

329 Smith St
Brooklyn, NY 11231
718.422.0444
seersuckerbrooklyn.com

JOSEPH OGRODNEK
Battersby

255 Smith St
Brooklyn, NY 11231
718.852.8321
battersbybrooklyn.com

TIM OLTMAN
Jack the Horse

66 Hicks St
Brooklyn, NY 11201
718.852.5084
jackthehorse.com

SHARON PACHTER
The Grocery

288 Smith St
Brooklyn, NY 11231
718.596.3335
thegroceryrestaurant.com

GREGORY PENALOZA
Bogota Latin Bistro

141 5th Ave
Brooklyn, NY 11217
718.230.3805
bogotabistro.com

MIKE POIARKOFF
Char No.4

196 Smith St
Brooklyn, NY 11201
718.643.2106
charno4.com

CARLO PULIXI
Convivium Osteria

68 5th Ave
Brooklyn, NY 11217
718.857.1833
convivium-osteria.com

SEAN QUINN
Chadwick's

8822 3rd Ave
Brooklyn, NY 11209
718.833.9855
chadwicksny.com

ED QUISH
Egg

135 N 5th St
Brooklyn, NY 11211
718.302.5151
pigandegg.com

CESAR RAMIREZ
Chef's Table at Brooklyn Fare

200 Schermerhorn St
Brooklyn, NY 11201
718.243.0050
brooklynfare.com

SEAN REMBOLD
Diner

85 Broadway
Brooklyn, NY 11211
718.486.3077
dinernyc.com

JOSH SHARKEY
Bark

474 Bergen St
Brooklyn, NY 11217
718.789.1939
barkhotdogs.com

DAVID SHEA
Applewood

501 11th St
Brooklyn, NY 11215
718.788.1810
applewoodny.com

PETER SHELSKY
Shelsky's Smoked Fish

251 Smith St
Brooklyn, NY 11231
718.855.8817
shelskys.com

ADAM SHEPARD
Lunetta

116 Smith St
Brooklyn, NY 11201
718.488.6269
lunetta-ny.com

ALEX SIDOROV
Okeanos

314 7th Ave
Brooklyn, NY 11215
347.725.4162
okeanosnyc.com

BRAD STEELMAN
River Café

1 Water St
Brooklyn, NY 11201
718.522.5200
rivercafe.com

WALKER STERN
Battersby

255 Smith St
Brooklyn, NY 11231
718.852.8321
battersbybrooklyn.com

DALE TALDE
Talde

369 7th Ave
Brooklyn, NY 11215
347.916.0031
taldebrooklyn.com

ZAHRA TANGORRA
Brucie

234 Court St
Brooklyn, NY 11201
347.987.4961
brucienyc.com

GUILLAUME THIVET
Cadaqués

188 Grand St
Brooklyn, NY 11211
718.218.7776
cadaquesny.com

MARIA VELEZ
Mojito's Cuban Cuisine

82 Washington Ave
Brooklyn, NY 11205
718.797.3100
mojitocubancuisine.com

MOSES WENDEL
Pardes

497 Atlantic Ave
Brooklyn, NY 11217
718.797.3880
pardesrestaurant.com

KAZUO YOSHIDA
1 or 8

66 S 2nd St
Brooklyn, NY 11211
718.384.2152
oneoreightbk.com

BUFFALO

ZEFF BONSEY
Buffalo, NY

JOE CHAMBER
Russell's Steaks, Chops, and More

6675 Transit Rd
Williamsville, NY 14221
877.614.6835
salvatoresgrand.com

CHRISTOPHER DAIGLER
Encore

492 Pearl St
Buffalo, NY 14202
716.931.5001
encorebuffalo.com

THOMAS DIANA
Salvatore's Italian Gardens

6461 Transit Rd
Depew, NY 14043
716.683.7990
salvatores.net

STEVE GEDRA
Bistro Europa

484 Elmwood Ave
Buffalo, NY 14222
716.884.1100
europabuffalo.com

MARK HUTCHINSON
Hutch's

1375 Delaware Ave
Buffalo, NY 14209
716.885.0074
hutchsrestaurant.com

PAUL JENKINS
Tempo

581 Delaware Ave
Buffalo, NY 14202
716.885.1594
tempobuffalo.com

MARK MCGRANAHAN
E.B. Green's Steakhouse

2 Fountain Plaza
Buffalo, NY 14202
716.855.4870
ebgreens.com

BRIAN MIETUS
Bacchus Wine Bar and Restaurant

56 W Chippewa St
Buffalo, NY 14202
716.854.9463
ultimaterestaurants.com

ANDREW NUERNBERGER
Roycroft Inn

40 S Grove St
East Aurora, NY 14052
716.652.5552
roycroftinn.com

CARMELO RAIMONDI
Carmelo's Restaurant

425 Center St
Lewiston, NY 14092
716.754.2311
carmelos-restaurant.com

J.J. RICHERT
Torches

1141 Kenmore Ave
Kenmore, NY 14217
716.447.7915
torches1141.com

KEVIN RICHERT
Torches

1141 Kenmore Ave
Kenmore, NY 14217
716.447.7915
torches1141.com

CHRISTOPHER SALVATI
Buffalo, NY

ADAM WAHLQUIST
Buffalo, NY

CHESTERTOWN

MATTHEW BOLTON
Friends Lake Inn

963 Friends Lake Rd
Chestertown, NY 12817
518.494.4751
friendslake.com

COLD SPRING

JOHN GUERRERO
Hudson House

2 Main St
Cold Spring, NY 10516
845.265.9355
hudsonhouseinn.com

EARLTON

DAMON BAEHREL
Damon Baehrel

776 County Highway 45
Earlton, NY 12058
518.269.1009
damonbaehrel.com

HECTOR

BRUD HOLLAND
Red Newt Bistro

3675 Tichenor Rd
Hector, NY 14841
607.546.4100
rednewt.com

HUDSON

BRIAN ALBERT
Old Chatham Country Store

639 Albany Turnpike
Old Chatham, NY 12136
518.794.6227
oldchathamcountrystore.com

MAX CENCI
Ca'Mea

333 Warren St
Hudson, NY 12534
518.822.0005
camearestaurant.com

BEN FREEMOLE
The Crimson Sparrow

746 Warren St
Hudson, NY 12534
518.671.6565
thecrimsonsparrow.com

JEFFREY GIMMEL
Swoon

340 Warren St
Hudson, NY 12534
518.822.8938
swoonkitchenbar.com

JOHN MCCARTHY
The Crimson Sparrow

746 Warren St
Hudson, NY 12534
518.671.6565
thecrimsonsparrow.com

TIMOTHY MEYERS
DABA

225 Warren St
Hudson, NY 12534
518.249.4631
dabahudson.com

JOSEPHINE PROUL
Local 111

111 Main St
Philmont, NY 12565
518.672.7801
local111.com

LORI SELDEN
Mexican Radio

537 Warren St
Hudson, NY 12534
518.828.7770
mexrad.com

DAVID WURTH
Crossroads Food Shop

2642 Route 23
Hillsdale, NY 12529
518.325.1461
crossroadsfoodshop.com

JOB YACUBIAN
Farmer's Wife

3 County Route 8
Ancramdale, NY 12503
518.329.5431
thefarmerswife.biz

HYDE PARK

DOMINICK CERRONE
Culinary Institue of America

1946 Campus Dr
Hyde Park, NY 12538
845.452.9600
ciachef.edu

DAVID KAMEN
Culinary Institute of America

1946 Campus Dr
Hyde Park, NY 12538
845.452.9600
ciachef.edu

GIANNI SCAPPIN
Caterina de Medici

946 Campus Dr
Hyde Park, NY 12538
845.471.6608
ciarestaurants.com

ALBERTO VANOLI
Culinary Institute of America

1946 Campus Dr
Hyde Park, NY 12538
845.452.9600
ciachef.edu

ITHACA

RICHARD AVERY
Simeon's on the Commons

224 E State St
Ithaca, NY 14850
607.272.2212
simeonsithaca.com

SETH GREGORY
Fine Line Bistro

404 W Martin Luther King Jr. St
Ithaca, NY 14850
607.277.1077
finelinebistro.com

DOUG GRUEN
Blue Stone

110 N Aurora St
Ithaca, NY 14850
607.272.2371
bluestoneithaca.com

DANO HUTNIK
Dano's Heuriger on Seneca

9564 Route 414
Ithaca, NY 14850
607.582.7555
danosonseneca.com

ANTHONY JORDAN
Taverna Banfi

130 Statler Dr
Ithaca, NY 14853
607.254.2565
tavernabanfi.com

KINGSTON

MARCUS GUILIANO
Aroma Thyme Bistro

165 Canal St
Ellenville, NY 12428
845.647.3000
aromathymebistro.com

KEVIN KATZ
Red Onion

1654 New York 212
Saugerties, NY 12477
845.679.1223
redonionrestaurant.com

PAUL KELLY
Milton, NY

JOSEPH KUMAR
Harvest Café

10 Main St #327
New Paltz, NY 12561
845.255.4205
harvesttablenp.com

DEVIN MILLS
Peekamoose

8373 New York 28
Big Indian, NY 12410
845.254.6500
peekamooserestaurant.com

PIERRE-LUC MOEYS
Oriole 9

9 Oriole Dr
Woodstock, NY 12498
845.679.5763
oriole9.com

GIUSEPPE NAPOLI
The Tavern at Diamond Mills

25 S Partition St
Saugerties, NY 12477
845.247.0700
diamondmillshotel.com

JOHN N. NOVI
Depuy Canal House Restaurant

1315 Main St
High Falls, NY 12440
845.687.7777
depuycanalhouse.net

RIC ORLANDO
New World Home Cooking Co.

1411 New York 212
Saugerties, NY 12477
845.246.0900
newworldhomecooking.com

KRIS ROBERTS
Kingston, NY

BONNIE SNOW
A Tavola Trattoria

46 Main St
New Paltz, NY 12561
845.255.1426
atavolany.com

NATHAN SNOW
A Tavola Trattoria

46 Main St
New Paltz, NY 12561
845.255.1426
atavolany.com

JESSICA WINCHELL
Global Palate

1746 Route 9W
West Park, NY 12429
845.384.6590
globalpalaterestaurant.com

LAKE PLACID

JARRAD LANG
View

77 Mirror Lake Dr
Lake Placid, NY 12946
518.302.3000
mirrorlakeinn.com

NATHAN RICH
Artisan's at Lake Placid Lodge

144 Lodge Way
Lake Placid, NY 12946
518.523.2700
lakeplacidlodge.com

PAUL SORGULE
Harvest America Ventures

28 Center St
Saranac Lake, NY 12983
518.524.5906
harvestamericaventures.com

LONG ISLAND

ALEX ALGIERI
Luce & Hawkins

400 S Jamesport Ave
Jamesport, NY 11947
631.722.2900
jedediahhawkinsinn.com

COLIN AMBROSE
Estia's Little Kitchen

1615 County Road 79
Sag Harbor, NY 11963
631.725.1045
estiaslittlekitchen.com

MATT BIRNSTILL
1770 House

143 Main St
East Hampton, NY 11937
631.324.1770
1770house.com

SEAN BLAKESLEE
Rare 650

650 Jericho Turnpike
Syosset, NY 11791
516.496.8000
rare650.com

SCOTT BRADLEY
Snaps

2010 Wantagh Ave
Wantagh, NY 11793
516.221.0029
snapsrestaurant.com

JAMES CARPENTER
East Hampton, NY

EFREM COLON
Patchogue, NY

JONATHAN CONTES
Mosaic

418 N Country Rd
St. James, NY 11780
631.584.2058
eatmosaic.com

STEVE DEL LIMA
Vitae Restaurant & Wine Bar

54 New St
Huntington, NY 11743
631.385.1919
vitaeli.com

DAVID DIAZ
Beaumarchais

409 W 13th St
East Hampton, NY 10014
212.675.2400
brasseriebeaumarchais.com

MICHAEL GINOR
Lola's

113 Middle Neck Rd
Great Neck, NY 11021
516.466.5666
restaurantlola.com

DOUGLAS GULIJA
Plaza Café

61 Hill St
Southhampton, NY 11968
631.283.9323
plazacafe.us

GERARD HAYDEN
North Fork Table and Inn

57225 Main Rd
Southold, NY 11971
631.765.0177
nofoti.com

WILLIAM HOLDEN
Market Bistro

519 N Broadway
Jericho, NY 11753
516.513.1487
marketbistroli.com

TAYLOR KNAPP
First and South

100 S St
Greenport, NY 11944
631.333.2200
firstandsouth.com

LARRY KOLAR
Backyard Restaurant at Sole East

90 Second House Rd
Montauk, NY 11954
631.668.9739
soleeast.com

TY KOTZ
Topping Rose House

1 County Road 79
Bridgehampton, NY 11932
631.537.0870
craftrestaurantsinc.com

RICHARD LANZA
Blackstone Steakhouse

10 Pinelawn Rd
Melville, NY 11747
631.271.7780
blackstonesteakhouse.com

GREG LING
The Riverhead Project

300 E Main St
Riverhead, NY 11901
631.284.9300
theriverheadproject.com

MAURIZIO MARFOGLIA
Tutto Il Giorno

6 Bay St
Sag Harbor, NY 11963
631.725.7009

MICHAEL MARONI
Maroni Cuisine

18 Woodbine Ave
Northport, NY 11768
631.757.4500
maronicuisine.com

MICHAEL MEEHAN
H2O Seafood Grill

215 W Main St
Smithtown, NY 11787
631.361.6464
h2oseafoodgrill.com

TODD MITGANG
South Edison

17 S Edison St
Montauk, NY 11954
631.668.4200
southedison.com

JAMES MOLLITOR
Galleria

238 Post Ave
Westbury, NY 11590
516.997.7373
galleriaristorante.com

MICHAEL MOSSALLAM
La Pace

51 Cedar Swamp Rd
Glen Cove, NY 11542
516.671.2970
lapaceglencove.com

KEITA NAKASHIMA
Sen

23 Main St
Sag Harbor, NY 11963
631.725.1774
senrestaurant.com

GUY REUGE
Mirabelle

150 Main St
Stony Brook, NY 11790
631.751.0555
threevillageinn.com

ELMER RUBIO
Chachama Grill

655 Montauk Hwy
East Patchogue, NY 11772
631.758.7640
chachamagrill.com

TOM SCHAUDEL
Jewel by Tom Schaudel

400 Broadhollow Rd
Melville, NY 11747
631.755.5777
jewelrestaurantli.com

NOAH SCHWARTZ
Noah's

136 Front St
Greenport, NY 11944
631.477.6720
chefnoahschwartz.com

JOHN SCUNZIANO
Islip, NY

JULIO VELAZQUEZ
Sage Bistro

2620 Merrick Rd
Bellmore, NY 11710
516.679.8928
bistrosage.com

CARMINE VIVOLO
Sempre Vivolo

696 Vanderbilt Motor Pkwy
Hauppauge, NY 11788
631.435.1737
semprevivolo.com

GARRETT WELLINS
Silver's

15 Main St
Southampton, NY 11968
631.283.6443
silversrestaurant.com

MIRKO ZAGAR
Mirko's

670 Montauk Hwy
Water Mill, NY 11976
631.726.4444
mirkosrestaurant.com

MANHATTAN

EINAT ADMONY
Balaboosta

214 Mulberry St
New York, NY 10012
212.966.7366
balaboostanyc.com

TOM ALLAN
New York, NY

RYAN ANGULO
Buttermilk Channel

524 Court St
New York, NY 11231
718.852.8490
buttermilkchannelnyc.com

MICHAEL ANTHONY
Gramercy Tavern

42 E 20th St
New York, NY 10003
212.477.0777
gramercytavern.com

MASASHI AOKI
Sushi of Gari 46

347 W 46th St
New York, NY 10036
212.957.0046
sushiofgari.com

CARLOS ARRIAGA
Alfama

214 E 52nd St
New York, NY 10022
212.759.5552
alfamanyc.com

EDWIN BALLANCO
Vitae

4 E 46th St
New York, NY 10017
212.682.3562
vitaenyc.com

JULIETA BALLESTEROS
Crema

111 W 17th St
New York, NY 10011
212.691.4477
cremarestaurante.com

DAVID BANK
Land Thai Kitchen

450 Amsterdam Ave
New York, NY 10024
212.501.8121
landthaikitchen.com

DAN BARBER
Blue Hill at Stone Barns

75 Washington Pl
New York, NY 10011
212.539.1776
bluehillfarm.com

SERENA BASS
Lido

2168 8th Ave
New York, NY 10026
646.490.8575
lidoharlem.com

LIDIA BASTIANICH
Felidia

243 E 58th St
New York, NY 10022
212.758.1479
felidia-nyc.com

MARIO BATALI
Babbo

110 Waverly Pl
New York, NY 10011
212.777.0303
babbonyc.com

IVAN BEACCO
Acqua at Peck Slip

21 Peck Slip
New York, NY 10038
212.349.4433
acquarestaurantnyc.com

JEREMY BEARMAN
Rouge Tomate

10 E 60th St
New York, NY 10022
646.237.8977
rougetomatenyc.com

CHRIS BEISCHER
The Mercer Kitchen

99 Prince St
New York, NY 10012
212.966.5454
themercerkitchen.com

ED BELLANCO
Vitae

4 E 46th St
New York, NY 10017
212.682.3562
vitaenyc.com

PEDRO BENITEZ
Frankie and Johnnie's

32 W 37th
New York, NY 10018
212.947.8940
frankieandjohnnies.com

JONATHAN BENNO
Lincoln Ristorante

142 W 65th St
New York, NY 10023
212.359.6500
lincolnristorante.com

MATTEO BERGAMINI
SD26

19 E 26th St
New York, NY 10010
212.265.5959
sd26ny.com

JEAN-MICHEL BERGOUGNOUX
L'Absinthe Brasserie

227 E 67th St
New York, NY 10065
212.794.4950
labsinthe.com

ROBERT BERRY
New York, NY

PHILIPPE BERTINEAU
Benoit Bistro

60 W 55th St
New York, NY 10019
646.943.7373
benoitny.com

RAWIA BISHARA
Tanoreen

7523 3rd Ave
New York, NY 11209
718.748.5600
tanoreen.com

ABRAM BISSELL
NoMad

1170 Broadway
New York, NY 10001
212.796.1500
thenomadhotel.com

JOSH BLAKELY
New York, NY

APRIL BLOOMFIELD
The Spotted Pig

314 W 11th St
New York, NY 10014
212.620.0393
thespottedpig.com

MATTEO BOGLIONE
White and Church

281 Church St
New York, NY 10013
212.226.1607
whiteandchurch.com

SIMONE BONELLI
Giano

126 E 7th St
New York, NY 10009
212.673.7200
gianonyc.com

CHRISTOPHE BONNEGRACE
Cercle Rouge

241 W Broadway
New York, NY 10013
212.226.6252
cerclerougeresto.com

ADAM BORDONARO
Astra

979 3rd Ave
New York, NY 10022
212.644.9394
charliepalmer.com

JIM BOTSACOS
Molyvos

871 7th Ave
New York, NY 10019
212.582.7500
molyvos.com

DAVID BOULEY
Bouley

163 Duane St
New York, NY 10013
212.964.2525
davidbouley.com

DANIEL BOULUD
DANIEL

60 E 65th St
New York, NY 10065
212.288.0033
danielnyc.com

ANTHONY BOURDAIN
Brasserie Les Halles

411 Park Ave S
New York, NY 10016
212-679-4111
leshalles.net

JOSH BOWEN
New York, NY

JIMMY BRADLEY
Red Cat

227 10th Ave
New York, NY 10011
212.242.1122
theredcat.com

TERRENCE BRENNAN
Picholine

35 W 64th St
New York, NY 10023
212.724.8585
picholinenyc.com

BRUCE BROMBERG
Blue Ribbon

97 Sullivan St
New York, NY 10012
212.229.0404
blueribbonrestaurants.com

ERIC BROMBERG
Blue Ribbon

97 Sullivan St
New York, NY 10012
212.229.0404
blueribbonrestaurants.com

ALTON BROWN
Food Network

75 9th Ave
New York, NY 10011
866.587.4653
altonbrown.com

JEAN FRANCOIS BRUEL
DANIEL

60 E 65th St
New York, NY 10065
212.288.0033
danielnyc.com

SCOTT BRYAN
Apiary

60 3rd Ave
New York, NY 10003
212.254.0888
apiarynyc.com

DAVID BURKE
David Burke Townhouse

133 E 61st St
New York, NY 10065
212.813.2121
davidburketownhouse.com

ROCCO CADOLINI
Roc
190A Duane St
New York, NY 10013
212.625.3333
rocrestaurant.com

FLOYD CARDOZ
North End Grill
104 N End Ave
New York, NY 10282
646.747.1600
northendgrillnyc.com

MICHAEL CETRULO
Scalini Fedeli
165 Duane St
New York, NY 10013
212.528.0400
scalinifedeli.com

P.J. CALAPA
Ai Fiori
400 5th Ave
New York, NY 10018
212.613.8660
aifiorinyc.com

ANDREW CARMELLINI
The Dutch
131 Sullivan St
New York, NY 10012
212.677.6200
thedutchnyc.com

AARON CHAMBERS
Boulud Sud
20 W 64th St
New York, NY 10023
212.595.1313
danielnyc.com

JOEY CAMPANARO
Little Owl
90 Bedford St
New York, NY 10014
212.741.4695
thelittleowlnyc.com

JENNIFER CARROLL
New York, NY

DAVID CHANG
Momofuku Noodle Bar
171 First Ave
New York, NY 10003
212.777.7773
momofuku.com

MARCO CANORA
Hearth
403 E 12th St
New York, NY 10009
646.602.1300
restauranthearth.com

KIM CARROLL
Fette Sau
354 Metropolitan Ave
New York, NY 11211
718.963.3404
fettesaubbq.com

FUSHING CHEUNG
Fu Sushi
182 Ave B #1
New York, NY 10009
917.667.0075

JOSH CAPON
Lure Fishbar
142 Mercer St
New York, NY 10012
212.431.7676
chefcapon.com

AMORETTE CASAUS
Ardesia
510 W 52nd St
New York, NY 10019
212.247.9191
ardesia-ny.com

HOK CHIN
Duo
72 Madison Ave
New York, NY 10016
212.686.7272
duonewyork.com

ROBERT CAPORUSCIO
Kesté Pizza and Vino
271 Bleecker St
New York, NY 10014
212.243.1500
kestepizzeria.com

CESARE CASELLA
Salumeria Rosi
283 Amsterdam Ave
New York, NY 10023
212.877.4801
salumeriarosi.com

PETER CHO
The Breslin Bar & Dining Room
16 W 29th St
New York, NY 10001
212.679.1939
thebreslin.com

GIUSEPPE COLADONATO
La Masseria
235 W 48th St #2
New York, NY 10036
212.582.2111
lamasserianyc.com

GABRIEL CRUZ
Forty Four
44 W 44th St
New York, NY 10036
212.944.8844
royaltonhotel.com

CHRISTIAN DELOUVRIER
La Mangeoire
1008 2nd Ave
New York, NY 10022
212.759.7086
lamangeoire.com

TOM COLICCHIO
Craft
43 E 19th St
New York, NY 10003
212.780.0880
craftrestaurantsinc.com

ANDY D'AMICO
Nice Matin
201 W 79th St
New York, NY 10024
212.873.6423
nicematinnyc.com

SYLVAIN DELPIQUE
New York, NY

ELI COLLINS
DBGB
299 Bowery
New York, NY 10003
212.933.5300
danielnyc.com

JAMES DANGLER
2 West
2 West St
New York, NY 10004
917.790.2525
ritzcarlton.com

CHRISTOPHER DELUNA
La Fonda Del Sol
200 Park Ave
New York, NY 10166
212.867.6767
patinagroup.com

SCOTT CONANT
Scarpetta
355 West 14th St
New York, NY 10014
212.691.0555
scottconant.com

RICCARDO DARDHA
Bread and Tulips
365 Park Ave S
New York, NY 10016
212.532.9100
breadandtulipsnyc.com

HAROLD DIETERLE
Kin Shop
469 6th Ave
New York, NY 10011
212.675.4295
kinshopnyc.com

EMANUEL CONCAS
Mercato
352 W 39th St
New York, NY 10018
212.643.2000
mercatonyc.com

FRANK DE CARLO
Peasant
194 Elizabeth St
New York, NY 10012
212.965.9511
peasantnyc.com

ROCCO DISPIRITO
New York, NY

FRANK CRISPO
Crispo Restaurant
240 W 14th St
New York, NY 10011
212.229.1818
crisporestaurant.com

GIADA DE LAURENTIS
Food Network
75 9th Ave
New York, NY 10011
866.587.4653
giadadelaurentiis.com

JOSEPH DOBIAS
JoeDoe
45 E 1st St
New York, NY 10003
212.780.0262
chefjoedoe.com

JOHN DOHERTY
Wolfpack Hospitality

515 W 20th St 4W
New York, NY 10011
866.580.2499
wolfpackhospitality.com

ALAIN DUCASSE
Benoit Bistro

60 W 55th St
New York, NY 10019
646.943.7373
benoitny.com

WYLIE DUFRESNE
wd~50

50 Clinton St
New York, NY 10002
212.477.2900
wd-50.com

LAURENCE EDELMAN
Left Bank

117 Perry St
New York, NY 10014
212.727.1170
leftbankmanhattan.com

JOSH EDEN
August

359 Bleecker St
New York, NY 10014
212.929.8727
augustny.com

JOSH ELLIOTT
Third Avenue Alehouse

1644 3rd Ave
New York, NY 10128
212.360.6106

ALFREDO ESCOBAR
Fred's at Barney's New York

660 Madison Ave
New York, NY 10065
212.833.2200
barneys.com

BRAD FARMERIE
PUBLIC

210 Elizabeth St
New York, NY 10012
212.343.7011
public-nyc.com

MICHAEL FERRARO
Delicatessen

54 Prince St
New York, NY 10012
212.226.0211
delicatessennyc.com

BOBBY FLAY
Mesa Grill

102 5th Ave
New York, NY 10011
212.807.7400
mesagrill.com

MARC FORGIONE
Marc Forgione

134 Reade St
New York, NY 10013
212.941.9401
marcforgione.com

JOSEPH FORTUNATO
Extra Virgin

259 W 4th St
New York, NY 10014
212.691.9359
extravirginrestaurant.com

JOHN FRASER
Dovetail

103 W 77th St
New York, NY 10024
212.362.3800
dovetailnyc.com

AMANDA FREITAG
New York, NY

RON GALLO
JoJo

160 E 64th St
New York, NY 10021
212.223.5656
jojorestaurantnyc.com

HALAVI GAZALA
Gazala's

380 Columbus Ave
New York, NY 10024
212.873.8880
gazalasplace.com

PAUL GERARD
Exchange Alley

424 E 9th St
New York, NY 10009
212.228.8525
exchangealleynyc.com

MICHAEL GERSHKOVICH
Mike's Bistro

228 W 72nd St #1
New York, NY 10023
212.799.3911
mikesbistro.com

MARCUS GLEADOW-WARE
Aureole

135 W 42nd St
New York, NY 10036
212.319.1660
charliepalmer.com

MARKUS GLOCKER
Restaurant Gordon Ramsay
at the London NYC

151 W 54th St
New York, NY 10019
212.468.8888
gordonramsay.com

VITO GNAZZO
Il Gattopardo

33 W 54th St #1
New York, NY 10019
212.246.0412
ilgattopardonyc.com

CRUZ GOLER
Lupa

170 Thompson St
New York, NY 10012
212.982.5089
luparestaurant.com

JOHN GREELEY
21 club

21 W 52nd St
New York, NY 10019
212.582.7200
21club.com

ALEX GUARNASCHELLI
Butter

415 Lafayette St
New York, NY 10003
212.253.2828
butterrestaurant.com

KURT GUTENBRUNNER
Wallse

344 W 11th St
New York, NY 10014
212.352.2300
kg-ny.com

GABRIELLE HAMILTON
Prune

54 E 1st St
New York, NY 10003
212.677.6221
prunerestaurant.com

PETER HANSEN
New York, NY

LEE HANSON
Minetta Tavern

113 MacDougal St
New York, NY 10012
212.475.3850
minettatavernny.com

RYAN HARDY
New York, NY

SYLVAIN HARRIBEY
Gaby Restaurant

45 W 45th St
New York, NY 10036
212.354.8844
gabynyrestaurant.com

GLENN HARRIS
Jane

100 W Houston St
New York, NY 10012
212.254.7000
janerestaurant.com

ERIC HAUGEN
The Lamb's Club

132 W 44th St
New York, NY 10036
212.997.5262
thelambsclub.com

SAM HAZEN
Veritas

43 E 20th St #1
New York, NY 10003
212.353.3700
veritas-nyc.com

ABE HIROKI
En Japanese Brasserie

435 Hudson St
New York, NY 10014
212.647.9196
enjb.com

LAUREN HIRSCHBERG
CraftBar

900 Broadway
New York, NY 10003
212.461.4300
craftrestaurantsinc.com

DAVID HONEYSETT
Raoul's

180 Prince St
New York, NY 10012
212.966.3518
raouls.com

FLORIAN V. HUGO
Brasserie Cognac

1740 Broadway
New York, NY 10019
212.757.3600
cognacrestaurant.com

PATTI JACKSON
I Trulli

122 E 27th St
New York, NY 10016
212.481.7372
itrulli.com

GAVIN KAYSEN
Café Boulud

20 E 76th St
New York, NY 10021
212.772.2600
danielnyc.com

DANIEL HUMM
Eleven Madison Park

11 Madison Ave
New York, NY 10010
212.889.0905
elevenmadisonpark.com

JAMES JERMYN
Maloney and Porcelli

37 E 50th St
New York, NY 10022
212.750.2233
maloneyandporcelli.com

JAMES KENT
Eleven Madison Park

11 Madison Ave
New York, NY 10010
212.889.0905
elevenmadisonpark.com

HUNG HUYNH
Catch

21 9th Ave
New York, NY 10014
212.392.5978
emmgroupinc.com

MARCUS JERNMARK
Aquavit

65 E 55th St
New York, NY 10022
212.307.7311
aquavit.org

VIKAS KHANNA
Junoon

27 W 24th St
New York, NY 10010
212.490.2100
junoonnyc.com

RENÉ IBARRA
La Cerveceria

65 2nd Ave
New York, NY 10003
212.777.6965
lacervecerianyc.com

ELI KAIMEH
Per Se

10 Columbus Cir
New York, NY 10019
212.823.9335
perseny.com

HOONI KIM
Danji

346 W 52nd St
New York, NY 10019
212.586.2880
danjinyc.com

SHU IKEDA
Yakitori Torishin

1193 1st Ave
New York, NY 10065
212.988.8408
torishinny.com

LAURENT KALKOTOUR
DB Bistro Moderne

55 W 44th St
New York, NY 10036
212.391.2400
danielnyc.com

RICHARD KING
Hundred Acres, Five Points

38 MacDougal St
New York, NY 10012
212.475.7500
hundredacresnyc.com

SANDY INGBER
Grand Central Oyster Bar

87 E 42nd St
New York, NY 10017
212.490.6650
oysterbarny.com

SHIGEMI KAWAHARA
Ippudo

65 4th Ave
New York, NY 10003
212.388.0088
ippudony.com

NIKKI KING BENNETT
Pure Food and Wine

54 Irving Pl
New York, NY 10003
212.477.1010
purefoodandwine.com

JAKE KLEIN
Morrell Wine Bar and Café

1 Rockefeller Plaza
New York, NY 10020
212.688.9370
morrellwinebar.com

DAN KLUGER
ABC Kitchen

35 E 18th St
New York, NY 10003
212.475.5829
abckitchennyc.com

CRAIG KOKETSU
Quality Meats

57 W 58th St
New York, NY 10019
212.371.7777
qualitymeatsnyc.com

SOTOHIRO KOSUGI
Soto

357 6th Ave
New York, NY 10014
212.414.3088
sotonyc.com

GABRIEL KREUTHER
The Modern

9 W 53rd St
New York, NY 10019
212.333.1220
themodernnyc.com

HIDEO KURIBARA
Ushiwakamaru

136 W Houston St
New York, NY 10012
212.228.4181
ushiwakamarunyc.com

MARK LADNER
Del Posto

85 10th Ave
New York, NY 10011
212.497.8090
delposto.com

MATT LAMBERT
The Musket Room

265 Elizabeth St
New York, NY 10012
musketroom.com

PIERRE LANDET
La Marina

348 Dyckman St
New York, NY 10034
212.567.6300
lamarinanyc.com

FRANK LANGELLO
Babbo

110 Waverly Pl
New York, NY 10011
212.777.0303
babbonyc.com

LOUIS LANZA
Citrus Bar and Grill

320 Amsterdam Ave
New York, NY 10023
212.595.0500
citrusnyc.com

MARK LAPICO
Jean-Georges

1 Central Park W
New York, NY 10023
212.299.3900
jean-georges.com

KEVIN LASKO
Park Avenue

100 E 63rd St
New York, NY 10065
212.644.1900
parkavenyc.com

JASON LAWLESS
Tocqueville

1 E 15th St
New York, NY 10003
212.647.1515
tocquevillerestaurant.com

EDDY LEROUX
DANIEL

60 E 65th St
New York, NY 10065
212.288.0033
danielnyc.com

PAUL LIEBRANDT
Corton

239 W Broadway
New York, NY 10013
212.219.2777
cortonnyc.com

MATTHEW LIGHTNER
Atera

77 Worth St
New York, NY 10013
212.226.1444
ateranyc.com

KYUNG UP LIM
Michael's

24 W 55th St
New York, NY 10019
212.767.0555
michaelsnewyork.com

CARLOS LLAGUNO
Les Halles

411 Park Ave S
New York, NY 10016
212.679.4111
leshalles.net

ANITA LO
Annisa

13 Barrow St
New York, NY 10014
212.741.6699
annisarestaurant.com

MICHAEL LOMONACO
Porter House

10 Columbus Cir
New York, NY 10019
212.823.9500
porterhousenewyork.com

PINO LUONGO
Morso Restaurant Café

420 E 59th St
New York, NY 10022
212.759.2706
morso-nyc.com

STEPHEN LYLE
Henry's

2745 Broadway
New York, NY 10025
212.866.0600
henrysnyc.com

PRESTON MADSON
Isa

191 Chrystie St
New York, NY 10002
212.420.0012
freemansrestaurant.com

WALDY MALOUF
High Heat pizza, burgers & tap

154 Bleecker St
New York, NY 10012
212.300.4446
highheatnyc.com

JOHN MARSH
Greensquare Tavern

5 W 21st St
New York, NY 10010
212.929.2468
greensquaretavern.com

JOHNATHAN MASSE
Le Parisien

163 E 33rd St
New York, NY 10016
212.889.5489
leparisiennyc.com

PHILIPPE MASSOUD
ilili

236 5th Ave
New York, NY 10001
212.683.2929
ililinyc.com

HEMANT MATHUR
Tulsi

211 E 46th St
New York, NY 10017
212.888.0820
tulsinyc.com

NOBU MATSUHISA
Nobu

105 Hudson St
New York, NY 10013
212.219.0500
noburestaurants.com

MICHELE MAZZA
Il Mulino Uptown

37 E 60th St
New York, NY 10065
212.750.3270
ilmulino.com

BRENDAN MCHALE
Tasting Table

New York, NY
tastingtable.com

JULIAN MEDINA
Toloache

251 W 50th St
New York, NY 10019
212.581.1818
toloachenyc.com

HENRY MEER
City Hall

131 Duane St
New York, NY 10013
212.227.7777
cityhallnewyork.com

JEHANGIR MEHTA
Graffiti

224 E 10th St
New York, NY 10002
212.464.7743
graffitinyc.com

DANNY MENA
Hecho en Dumbo

354 Bowery
New York, NY 10012
212.937.4245
hechoendumbo.com

GEORGE MENDES
Aldea

31 W 17th St
New York, NY 10011
212.675.7223
aldearestaurant.com

NOAH METNICK
La Grenouille

3 E 52nd St
New York, NY 10022
212.752.1495
la-grenouille.com

DANNY MEYER
Union Square Hospitality

24 Union Square E
New York, NY 10003
212.228.3585
ushgnyc.com

STEVE MEYERS
Docks Oyster Bar

633 3rd Ave
New York, NY 10017
212.986.8080
docksoysterbar.com

NOBUHIKO MIKAMI
Japonica

100 University Pl
New York, NY 10003
212.243.7752
japonicanyc.com

JUNYA MIURA
Yopparai

151 Rivington St
New York, NY 10002
212.777.7253
yopparainyc.com

HAROLD MOORE
COMMERCE

50 Commerce St
New York, NY 10014
212.524.2301
commercerestaurant.com

MARCO MOREIRA
Tocqueville

1 E 15th St
New York, NY 10003
212.647.1515
tocquevillerestaurant.com

MASAHARU MORIMOTO
Morimoto

88 10th Ave
New York, NY 10011
212.989.8883
morimotonyc.com

PIETRO MOSCONI
Monte's Trattoria

97 MacDougal St
New York, NY 10012
212.228.9194
montestrattorianyc.com

HARRISON MOSHER
Alta

64 W 10th St
New York, NY 10011
212.505.7777
altarestaurant.com

SEAMUS MULLEN
Tertulia

359 6th Ave
New York, NY 10014
646.559.9909
tertulianyc.com

CHRIS MULLER
Le Bernardin

155 W 51st St
New York, NY 10019
212.554.1515
le-bernardin.com

MELISSA MULLER DAKA
Eolo

190 7th Ave
New York, NY 10011
646.225.6606
eolonewyork.com

MASAKI NAKAYAMA
Mr ROBATA

1674 Broadway
New York, NY 10019
646.321.6682
mrrobata.com

VINCENT NARGI
The Odeon

145 W Broadway
New York, NY 10013
212.233.0507
theodeonrestaurant.com

RIAD NASR
Balthazar

80 Spring St
New York, NY 10012
212.965.1414
balthazarny.com

AKHTAR NAWAB
La Esquina

114 Kenmare St
New York, NY 10012
646.613.1333
esquinanyc.com

JOE NG
Red Farm

529 Hudson St
New York, NY 10014
212.792.9700
redfarmnyc.com

KELLIE NGUYEN-RABANIT
Le Colonial

149 E 57th St
New York, NY 10022
212.752.0808
lecolonialnyc.com

ANN NICKINSON
Kitchenette

156 Chambers St
New York, NY 10007
212.267.6740
kitchenetterestaurant.com

FORTUNATO NICOTRA
Felidia

243 E 58th St
New York, NY 10022
212.758.1479
felidia-nyc.com

NILS NOREN
Marcus Samuelsson Group

2036 5th Ave
New York, NY 10035
212.319.3080
samuelssongroup.com

ANDY NUSSER
Casa Mono

52 Irving Pl
New York, NY 10003
212.253.2773
casamononyc.com

MELISSA O'DONNELL
Salt Bar

29 Clinton St
New York, NY 10002
212.979.8471
saltnyc.com

BILLY OLIVA
Delmonico's

56 Beaver St
New York, NY 10004
212.509.1144
delmonicosny.com

SISHA ORTUZAR
Riverpark

450 E 29th St
New York, NY 10016
212.729.9790
riverparknyc.com

KAAN OZDEMIR
New York, NY

GIGIO PALAZZO
Pala Pizza

198 Allen St
New York, NY 10002
212.614.7252
palapizza.com

CHARLIE PALMER
Aureole

135 W 42nd St
New York, NY 10036
212.319.1660
charliepalmer.com

PAM PANYASIRI
Pam Real Thai

404 W 49th St
New York, NY 10019
212.333.7500
pamrealthaifood.com

DAVID PASTERNACK
Esca

402 W 43rd St
New York, NY 10036
212.564.7272
esca-nyc.com

FRANCIS PEABODY
Olio Pizza e Più

3 Greenwich Ave
New York, NY 10011
212.243.6546
olionyc.com

ZAKARY PELACCIO
Fatty Crab

643 Hudson St
New York, NY 10014
212.352.3592
fattycrew.com

JACQUES PÉPIN
The International Culinary Center

462 Broadway
New York, NY 10013
888.324.2433
internationalculinarycenter.com

PETER PETTI
Sojourn

244 E 79th St
New York, NY 10021
212.537.7745
sojournrestaurant.com

KING PHOJANAKONG
Kuma Inn

113 Ludlow St
New York, NY 10002
212.353.8866
kumainn.com

STEVEN PICKER
Good Restaurant

89 Greenwich Ave
New York, NY 10014
212.691.8080
goodrestaurantnyc.com

BEN POLLINGER
Oceana

120 W 49th St
New York, NY 10020
212.759.5941
oceanarestaurant.com

ALFRED PORTALE
Gotham Bar and Grill

12 E 12th St
New York, NY 10003
212.620.4020
gothambarandgrill.com

TRAVIS POST
Yunnan Kitchen

79 Clinton St
New York, NY 10002
212.253.2527
yunnankitchen.com

MICHAEL PSILAKIS
Kefi

505 Columbus Ave
New York, NY 10024
212.873.0200
michaelpsilakis.com

CARMEN QUAGLIATA
Union Square Cafe

21 E 16th St
New York, NY 10003
212.243.4020
unionsquarecafe.com

JOE QUINTANA
Rosa Mexicano

9 E 18th St
New York, NY 10003
212.533.3350
rosamexicano.com

ALEXANDRA RAIJ
Txikito

240 9th Ave
New York, NY 10001
212.242.4730
txikitonyc.com

JOSEPH REALMUTO
Nick & Toni's Café

100 W 67th St
New York, NY 10023
212.496.4000
nickandtoniscafe.com

OLIVIER REGINENSI
New York, NY

ANTHONY RICCO
Spice Market

403 W 13th St
New York, NY 10014
212.675.2322
spicemarketnewyork.com

ADRIANO RICCO
STK Midtown

1114 Avenue of the Americas
New York, NY 10036
646.624.2455
stkhouse.com

ERIC RIPERT
Le Bernardin

155 W 51st St
New York, NY 10019
212.554.1515
le-bernardin.com

MISSY ROBBINS
A Voce

41 Madison Ave
New York, NY 10010
212.545.8555
avocerestaurant.com

BILL RODGERS
Keens Steakhouse

72 W 36th St
New York, NY 10018
212.947.3636
keens.com

MATT ROJAS
Rouge et Blanc

48 MacDougal St
New York, NY 10012
212.260.5757
rougeetblancnyc.com

MICHAEL ROMANO
Union Square Café

21 E 16th St
New York, NY 10003
212.243.4020
unionsquarecafe.com

KAMAL ROSE
Tribeca Grill

375 Greenwich St
New York, NY 10013
212.941.3900
myriadrestaurantgroup.com

ANTHONY SASSO
Casa Mono

52 Irving Pl
New York, NY 10003
212.253.2773
casamononyc.com

MASATO SHIMIZU
15 East Restaurant

15 E 15th St
New York, NY 10003
212.647.0015
15eastrestaurant.com

LUIGI RUSSO
Il Postino

337 E 49th St
New York, NY 10017
212.688.0033
ilpostinony.com

JESSE SCHENKER
Recette

328 W 12th St
New York, NY 10014
212.414.3000
recettenyc.com

JASMINE SHIMODA
Degustation

239 E 5th St
New York, NY 10003
212.979.1012

MARCUS SAMUELSSON
Red Rooster

310 Lenox Ave
Harlem, NY 10027
212.792.9001
redroosterharlem.com

DALE SCHNELL
KTCHN

508 W 42nd St
New York, NY 10036
212.868.2999
ktchnnyc.com

BARBARA SIBLEY
La Palapa

77 Saint Marks Pl
New York, NY 10003
212.777.2537
lapalapa.com

AARON SANCHEZ
Tacombi

267 Elizabeth St
New York, NY 10012
917.727.0179
chefaaronsanchez.com

VINOD SHARMA
Seva

30-7 34th St
New York, NY 11103
718.626.4440
sevarestaurant.com

JUSTIN SMILLIE
Il Buco Alimentari

52 Great Jones St
New York, NY 10012
212.837.2622
ilbuco.com

RICHARD SANDOVAL
Maya

1191 1st Ave
New York, NY 10065
212.585.1818
richardsandoval.com

CHRIS SHEA
David Burke Kitchen

23 Grand St
New York, NY 10013
212.201.9119
davidburkekitchen.com

RITA SODI
I Sodi

105 Christopher St
New York, NY 10014
212.414.5774
isodinyc.com

CHRIS SANTOS
Stanton Social

99 Stanton St
New York, NY 10002
212.995.0099
thestantonsocial.com

DAVID SHIM
Kristalbelli

8 W 36th St
New York, NY 10018
212.290.2211
kristalbelli.com

CHIKARA SONO
Kyo Ya

94 E 7th St
New York, NY 10009
212.982.4140

ANGELO SOSA
Añejo

668 10th Ave
New York, NY 10036
212.920.4770
anejonyc.com

MARK SPANGENTHAL
Kutsher's Tribeca

186 Franklin St
New York, NY 10013
212.431.0606
kutsherstribeca.com

JEREMY SPECTOR
Brindle Room

277 E 10th St
New York, NY 10009
212.529-9702
brindleroom.com

JOHN STAGE
Dinosaur Bar B Que

700 W 125th St
New York, NY 10027
212.694.1777
dinosaurbarbque.com

T.J. STEELE
New York, NY

RENE STEIN
Seasonal

132 W 58th St
New York, NY 10019
212.957.5550
seasonalnyc.com

NEVILLE STODDART JR.
Markt

676 6th Ave
New York, NY 10010
212.727.3314
marktrestaurant.com

ALEX STUPAK
Empellon Cocina

105 1st Ave
New York, NY 10003
212.780.0999
empellon.com

MASA TAKAYAMA
Masa

10 Columbus Cir
New York, NY 10019
212.823.9800
masanyc.com

COLT TAYLOR
One if by Land, Two if by Sea

17 Barrow St
New York, NY 10014
212.255.8649
oneifbyland.com

BILL TELEPAN
Telepan

72 W 69th St
New York, NY 10023
212.580.4300
telepan-ny.com

GABE THOMPSON
Dell'anima

38 8th Ave
New York, NY 10014
212.366.6633
dellanima.com

AKIKO THURNAUER
Family Recipe

231 Eldridge St
New York, NY 10002
212.529.3133
familyrecipeny.com

JASON TILMANN
Triomphe

49 W 44th St
New York, NY 10036
212.453.4233
triomphe-newyork.com

DHEERAJ TOMAR
Devi

8 E 18th St
New York, NY 10003
212.691.1300
devinyc.com

TAKASHI TOMONO
Sushi of Gari

402 E 78th St
New York, NY 10075
212.517.5340
sushiofgari.com

LAURENT TOURONDEL
Arlington Club

1032 Lexington Ave
New York, NY 10021
212.249.5700
arlingtonclubny.com

JAMES TRACEY
Craft

43 E 19th St
New York, NY 10003
212.780.0880
craftrestaurantsinc.com

MANUEL TREVINO
Marble Lane

355 W 16th St
New York, NY 10011
212.229.2336
marblelane.com

MATTHEW TROPEANO
La Silhouette

362 W 53rd St
New York, NY 10019
212.581.2400
la-silhouettenyc.com

TOSHI UEKI
Blue Ribbon Sushi

119 Sullivan St
New York, NY 10012
212.343.0404
blueribbonrestaurants.com

TOM VALENTI
Ouest

2315 Broadway
New York, NY 10024
212.580.8700
ouestny.com

CIRO VERDE
Da Ciro

229 Lexington Ave
New York, NY 10016
212.532.1636
daciro.com

MARC VIDAL
Boqueria

171 Spring St
New York, NY 10012
212.343.4255
boquerianyc.com

CEDRIC VONGERICHTEN
Perry St.

176 Perry St
New York, NY 10014
212.352.1900
jean-georges.com

JEAN-GEORGES VONGERICHTEN
Jean Georges

1 Central Park W
New York, NY 10023
212.299.3900
jean-georges.com

DAVID WALTUCK
Ark Restaurant Group

485 10th Ave
New York, NY 10018
212.206.8800
arkrestaurants.com

JASON WANG
Xian Famous Foods

81 Saint Marks Pl
New York, NY 10003
212.786.2068
xianfoods.com

JONATHAN WAXMAN
Barbuto

775 Washington St
New York, NY 10014
212.924.9700
barbutonyc.com

JASON WEINER
Almond

12 E 22nd St
New York, NY 10010
212.228.7557
almondnyc.com

COLIN WHIDDON
La Grenouille

3 E 52nd St
New York, NY 10022
212.752.0652
la-grenouille.com

MICHAEL WHITE
Marea

240 Central Park S
New York, NY 10019
212.582.5100
marea-nyc.com

JODY WILLIAMS
Buvette

42 Grove St
New York, NY 10014
212.255.3590
ilovebuvette.com

DAMON WISE
New York, NY

SIMPSON WONG
Wong

7 Cornelia St
New York, NY 10014
212.989.3399
wongnewyork.com

CHRIS WYMAN
Scarpetta

355 W 14th St
New York, NY 10014
212.691.0555
scarpettanyc.com

ISAO YAMADA
Brushstroke

30 Hudson St
New York, NY 10013
212.791.3771
brushstrokenyc.com

NAOMICHI YASUDA
Sushi Yasuda

204 E 43rd St
New York, NY 10017
212.972.1001
sushiyasuda.com

ORHAN YEGEN
Sip Sak

928 2nd Ave
New York, NY 10022
212.583.1900
orhanyegen.com

JUNG YIM
JUNGSIK

2 Harrison St
New York, NY 10013
212.219.0900
jungsik.kr

GEOFFREY ZAKARIAN
National Bar and Dining Room

557 Lexington Ave
New York, NY 10022
212.715.2400
geoffreyzakarian.com

GALEN ZAMARRA
Mas (farmhouse)

39 Downing St
New York, NY 10014
212.255.1790
masfarmhouse.com

GREGORY ZAPANTIS
Kellari Taverna

19 W 44th St
New York, NY 10036
212.221.0144
kellari.us

NEW CITY

ANTHONY ACCOMANDO
Antoine McGuire's

19 Main St
Haverstraw, NY 10927
845.429.4121
antoinemcguires.com

DOUG CHI NGUYEN
Wasabi

110 Main St
Nyack, NY 10960
845.358.7977
wasabichi.com

GEORGE DEMARSICO
Xaviars

506 Piermont Ave
Piermont, NY 10968
845.359.7007
xaviars.com

ANTHONY DEVANZO
Velo Bistro

12 N Broadway
Nyack, NY 10960
845.353.7667
velonyack.com

ANDREW GARRITANO
Il Fresco

15 Kings Hwy
Orangeburg, NY 10962
845.398.0200
il-fresco.com

JEFF KAUFMAN
Hudson House

134 Main St
Nyack, NY 10960
845.353.1355
hudsonhousenyack.com

MARCELLO RUSSODIVITO
Marcello's Ristorante

21 Lafayette Ave
Suffern, NY 10901
845.357.9108
marcellosgroup.com

PHILIPPE SCOUARNEC
Freelance Café

506 Piermont Ave
Piermont, NY 10968
845.365.3250
xaviars.com

POUGHKEEPSIE

HANS BAUMANN
Canterbury Brook Inn

331 Main St
Cornwall, NY 12518
845.534.9658
thecanterburybrookinn.com

HERVE BOCHARD
Café Les Baux

152 Church St
Millbrook, NY 12545
845.677.8166
cafelesbaux.com

FRANCESCO BUITONI
Mercato

61 E Market St
Red Hook, NY 12571
845.758.5879
mercatoredhook.com

JAMES CARTER
Lakeview House

343 Lakeside Rd
Newburgh, NY 12550
845.566.7100
thelakeviewhouse.com

MEGAN FELLS
The Artist's Palate

307 Main St
Poughkeepsie, NY 12601
845.483.8074
theartistspalate.biz

EDUARDO LAURIA
Aroma Osteria

114 Old Post Rd
Wappingers Falls, NY 12590
845.298.6790
aromaosteriarestaurant.com

DANIEL CROCCO
Brasserie 292

292 Main St
Poughkeepsie, NY 12601
845.473.0292
brasserie292.com

CLAUDE GUERMONT
Le Pavillon

230 Salt Point Turnpike
Poughkeepsie, NY 12603
845.473.2525

IRA LEE
Twisted Soul

47 Raymond Ave
Poughkeepsie, NY 12603
845.454.2770
twistedsoulconcepts.com

JOSEPH DALU
Le Petit Bistro

8 E Market St
Rhinebeck, NY 12572
845.876.7400
lepetitbistro.com

WAYNE HOMSI
Il Barilotto

1113 Main St
Fishkill, NY 12524
845.897.4300
ilbarilottorestaurant.com

SERGE MADIKIAN
Serevan

6 Autumn Ln
Amenia, NY 12501
845.373.9800
serevan.com

WESLEY DIER
Local

38 W Market St
Rhinebeck, NY 12572
845.876.2214
thelocalrestaurantandbar.com

MICHEL JEAN
Stissing House

7801 S Main St
Pine Plains, NY 12567
518.398.8800
stissinghouse.com

SHANNON MCKINNEY
McKinney and Doyle
Fine Foods Cafe

10 Charles Colman Blvd
Pawling, NY 12564
845.855.3875
mckinneyanddoyle.com

MICHAEL DIMARTINO
Landmark Tavern

526 New York 94
Warwick, NY 10990
845.986.5444
landmarkinnwarwick.com

THOMAS KACHERSKI
Crew Restaurant and Bar

2290 South Rd
Poughkeepsie, NY 12601
845.462.8900
crewrestaurant.com

RIFO MURTOVIC
Café Amarcord

276 Main St
Beacon, NY 12508
845.440.0050
cafeamarcord.net

CHARLES FELLS
The Artist's Palate

307 Main St
Poughkeepsie, NY 12601
845.483.8074
theartistspalate.biz

EDWARD KOWALSKI
Lola's

131 Washington St
Poughkeepsie, NY 12601
845.471.8555
lolascafeandcatering.com

REI PERAZA
Panzur

69 Broadway
Tivoli, NY 12583
845.757.1071
panzur.com

BRIAN PSKOWSKI
Ward's Bridge Inn

135 Ward St
Montgomery, NY 12549
845.457.1300
wardsbridgeinn.com

SEADON SHOUSE
Glenmere Mansion

634 Pine Hill Rd
Chester, NY 10918
845.469.1900
glenmeremansion.com

MARK STRAUSMAN
Pine Plains, NY

JOEL TROCINO
Amici's

35 Main St
Poughkeepsie, NY 12601
845.452.4700
amicis-restaurant.com

FRED WHITTLE
50 Front Street

50 Front St
Newburgh, NY 12250
845.562.7111
50frontstreet.com

KRISTA WILD
Wildfire Grill

74 Clinton St
Montgomery, NY 12549
845.457.3770
wildfireny.com

CATHERINE WILLIAMS
Crave

129 Washington St
Poughkeepsie, NY 12601
845.452.3501
craverestaurantandlounge.com

DOLPH ZUEGER
Chateau Hathorn

33 Hathorn Rd
Warwick, NY 10990
845.986.6099
chateauhathorn.com

QUEENS

DANNY BROWN
Danny Brown Wine Bar
104-02 Metropolitan Ave
Forest Hills, NY 11375
718.261.2144
dannybrownwbk.com

GIANNA CERBONE-TEOLI
Manducatis Rustica

46-33 Vernon Blvd
Long Island City, NY 11101
718.937.1312
manducatisrustica.com

MARIO DICHIARA
Il Poeta

98-04 Metropolitan Ave
Forest Hills, NY 11375
718.544.4223
ilpoetarestaurant.com

HERBERT DUARTE
Saffron

16150 Cross Bay Blvd
Queens, NY 11414
347.392.4152
saffronrestaurantnewyork.com

LUIS ENRIQUEZ
Giardino

44-37 Douglaston Pkwy
Queens, NY 11363
718.428.1090
giardinos.com

PETER GIANNAKAS
Ovelia Psistaria Bar

34-01 30th Ave
Queens, NY 11103
718.721.7217
ovelia-nyc.com

IAN KAPITAN
Alobar

46-42 Vernon Blvd
Long Island City, NY 11101
718.752.6000
alobarnyc.com

JAMES KNOWLES
Chateau Steakhouse

185-01 Union Turnpike
Fresh Meadows, NY 11366
718.454.3000
chateausteakhouse.com

MINA NEWMAN
Cristo's Steak House

41-08 23rd Ave
Astoria, NY 11105
718.777.8400
facebook.com/ChristosSteakHouse

RORY O'FARRELL
Cavo

42-18 31st Ave
Queens, NY 11103
718.721.1001
cavoastoria.com

GEORGE RALLIS
Hell Gate Social

12-21 Astoria Blvd
Astoria, NY 11102
718.204.8313
hellgatesocial.com

ROCCO SACRAMONE
Trattoria L'incontro

21-76 31st St
Astoria, NY 11105
718.721.3532
trattorialincontro.com

ALEX SCHINDLER
LIC Market

21-52 44th Dr
Queens, NY 11101
718.361.0013
licmarket.com

KATSUYUKI SEO
Katsuno

103-01 Metropolitan Ave
Forest Hills, NY 11375
718.575.4033
katsunorestaurnt.com

ARDIAN SKENDERI
Taverna Kyclades

33-07 Ditmars Blvd
Astoria, NY 11105
718.545.8666
tavernakyclades.com

ALBERTO TANAKA
Shiro of Japan

80-40 Cooper Ave
Queens, NY 11385
718.326.8704
shiroofjapan.com

MICHELLE VIDO
Vesta Trattoria

21-02 30th Ave
Astoria, NY 11102
718.545.5550
vestavino.com

GIUSEPPE VITERALE
Ornella Trattoria Italiana

29-17 23rd Ave
Queens, NY 11105
718.777.9477
ornellatrattoria.com

JASON ZUKAS
Tazzina

75-01 88th St
Glendale, NY 11385
718.275.1306
tazzinany.com

ROCHESTER

ALEX BACON
Nolan's on the Lake

130 Lakeshore Dr
Canandaigua, NY 14424
585.905.0201
nolansonthelake.com

WARREN BACON
Nolan's on the Lake

130 Lakeshore Dr
Canandaigua, NY 14424
585.905.0201
nolansonthelake.com

CHRIS BRANDT
Next Door Bar and Grill

3220 Monroe Ave
Rochester, NY 14618
585.249.4575
nextdoorbarandgrill.com

WILLIAM BURKLE
Bistro 135

135 W Commercial St
Rochester, NY 14445
585.662.5555
bistro135.net

JAMES PAWL KANE
Edibles

704 University Ave
Rochester, NY 14607
585.271.4910
ediblesrochester.com

DAN MARTELLO
Good Luck

50 Anderson Ave
Rochester, NY 14607
585.340.6161
restaurantgoodluck.com

ARTHUR ROGERS
Lento

274 N Goodman St
Rochester, NY 14607
585.271.3470
lentorestaurant.com

GINO RUGGIERO
2 Vine

24 Winthrop St
Rochester, NY 14607
585.454.6020
2vine.com

MIKE SCHNUPP
Tavern 58 at Gibbs

58 University Ave
Rochester, NY 14605
585.546.5800
tavern58.com

MIKE SOKOLSKI
New York Wine
and Culinary Center

800 S Main St
Canandaigua, NY 14424
585.394.7070
nywcc.com

LUIS VASQUEZ
Mendon House

1369 Pittsford-Mendon Rd
Mendon , NY 14506
585.624.7370
themendonhouse.com

STATEN ISLAND

STEFANO SENA
Bocelli

1250 Hylan Blvd
Staten Island, NY 10305
718.420.6150
bocellirest.com

SYRACUSE

MARC ALBINO
Rosalie's Cucina

841 W Genesee St
Skaneateles, NY 13152
315.685.2200
rosaliescucina.com

VINCENT BARCELONA
Harvest on Hudson

1 River St
Hastings, NY 10706
914.478.2800
harvest2000.com

WILLIAM COLLINS
Syracuse University

323 S Crouse Ave
Syracuse, NY 13244
315.443.4156
syr.edu

SCOTT FRATANGELO
Harvest on Hudson

1 River St
Hastings, NY 10706
914.478.2800
harvest2000.com

KEVIN GENTILE
Gentile's

313 N Geddes St
Syracuse, NY 13204
315.474.8258
gentilesrestaurant.com

VERONA

JEFFREY HERRING
Pino Bianco

5218 Patrick Rd
Verona, NY 13478
315.361.7711
turningstone.com

MICHAEL ZMIGRODSKI
Wildflowers at Turning Stone

5218 Patrick Rd
Verona, NY 13478
315.361.8620
turningstone.com

WHITE PLAINS

SERGIO ARIAS
Caffe Azzurri

20 N Central Ave
Hartsdale, NY 10530
914.358.5248
caffeazzurri.com

ALBERT ASTUDILLO
La Cremaillere

46 Bedford-Banksville Rd
Bedford, NY 10506
914.234.9647
cremaillere.com

RAY BALIDEMAJ
Alba's Restaurant

400 N Main St
Port Chester, NY 10573
914.937.2236
albasrestaurant.com

JEAN MARC CABRIOL
Rye, NY

NICOLA CRISTIANI
Lusardi's Larchmont

1885 Palmer Ave
Larchmont, NY 10538
914.834.5555
lusardislarchmont.com

DAVID DIBARI
Cookery

39 Chestnut St
Dobbs Ferry, NY 10522
914.305.2336
thecookeryrestaurant.com

MIKE DONNELLY
Café of Love

38 E Main St
Mt. Kisco, NY 10549
914.242.1002
cafeofloveny.com

JOSEPH ENGONGORO
Trevi Ristorante

11 Taylor Square
West Harrison, NY 10604
914.949.5810
treviofharrison.com

RICH FOSHAY
Wobble Café

21 Campwoods Rd #102
Ossining, NY 10562
914.762.3459
wobblecafe.com

ERIC GABRYNOWICZ
Restaurant North

386 Main St
Armonk, NY 10504
914.273.8686
restaurantnorth.com

SHEA GALLANTE
Italian Kitchen

698 Saw Mill River Rd
Ardsley, NY 10502
914.693.5400
ik-ny.com

BRIAN GALVIN
Ocean House

49 N Riverside Ave
Croton-on-Hudson, NY 10520
914.271.0702
oceanhouseoysterbar.com

JOHN GENDY
Halstead Avenue Bistro

123 Halstead Ave
Harrison, NY 10528
914.777.1181
halsteadbistro.com

ANTHONY GONCALVES
42

1 Renaissance Square
White Plains, NY 10601
914.761.4242
42therestaurant.com

PAUL HARRISON
Westchester Restaurant Group

74 1/2 Pondfield Rd
Bronxville, NY 10708
914.337.1200
thewrgonline.com

ROBERT HORTON
An American Bistro

296 Columbus Ave
Tuckahoe, NY 10707
914.793.0807
anamericanbistro.com

ENRIQUE ITURRALDE
Posto 22

22 Division St
New Rochelle, NY 10801
914.235.2464
posto22.com

RAYMOND JACKSON
New Rochelle, NY

MATTHEW KARP
Plates

121 Myrtle Blvd
Larchmont, NY 10538
914.834.1244
platesonthepark.com

PETER KELLY
x2o Xaviars on the Hudson

71 Water Grant St
Yonkers, NY 10701
914.965.1111
xaviars.com

ETHAN KOSTBAR
Moderne Barn

430 Bedford Rd
Armonk, NY 10504
914.730.0001
modernebarn.com

JEAN-CLAUDE LANCHAIS
Hive Living Room + Bar

80 W Red Oak Ln
White Plains, NY 10604
914.696.2782
renaissancewestchester.com

MARC LIPPMAN
Crabtree's Kittle House

11 Kittle Rd
Chappaqua, NY 10514
914.666.8044
kittlehouse.com

MANNY LOZANO
Bistro Rollin

142 Fifth Ave
Pelham, NY 10803
914.633.0780
bistrorollin.com

ANDREW MASCIANGELO
Savona

2 Chase Rd
Scarsdale, NY 10583
914.798.0550
savonarestaurant.com

PHILLIP MCGRATH
Iron Horse Grill

20 Wheeler Ave
Pleasantville, NY 10570
914.741.0717
ironhorsegrill.com

JEREMY MCMILLAN
Bedford Post - the Farmhouse

954 Old Post Rd
Bedford, NY 10506
914.234.7800
bedfordpostinn.com

ANDRE MOLLE
Le Chateau

1410 New York 35
South Salem, NY 10590
914.533.6631
lechateauny.com

FORTUNATO MULTARI
Mamma Rosa Italian Restaurant

252 Route 100
Somers, NY 10589
914.232.8080
mammarosaristorante.com

JOE SASSO
Sam's

50 Gedney Way
White Plains, NY 10605
914.949.0978
samsofgedneyway.com

PIETRO SICILIANO
Tombolino Ristorante

356 Kimball Ave
Yonkers, NY 10704
914.237.1266
tombolinoristorante.com

ALEX SZE
Juniper

575 Warburton Ave
Hastings-on-Hudson, NY 10706
914.478.2542
juniperhastings.com

JOSEPH TRAMA
Grace's Table

324 Central Ave
White Plains, NY 10606
914.684.8855
graces-table.com

ERIC ULBRICH
Vox

721 Titicus Rd
North Salem, NY 10560
914.669.5450
voxnorthsalem.com

CHRIS VERGARA
Meritage

1505 Weaver St
Scarsdale, NY 10583
914.472.8484
meritagerestaurant.net

MARCH WALKER
Birdsall House

970 Main St
Peekskill, NY 10566
914.930.1880
birdsallhouse.net

WINDHAM

STEPHANE DESGACHES
Bistro Brie & Bordeaux

5386 New York 23
Windham, NY 12496
518.734.4911
bistrobrieandbordeaux.com

HERITAGE BREEDS
Renewed fascination with heritage breeds is encouraging their preservation.

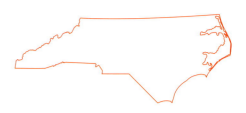

ASHEVILLE

ADAM ANSON
Fig Bistro

18 Brook St
Asheville, NC 28803
828.277.0889
figbistro.com

ADAM BANNASCH
Zambra

85 W Walnut St
Asheville, NC 28801
828.232.1060
zambratapas.com

KATIE BUTTON
Curate

11 Biltmore Ave
Asheville, NC 28801
828.239.2946
curatetapasbar.com

BRIAN CANIPELLI
Cucina 24

24 Wall St
Asheville, NC 28801
828.254.6170
cucina24restaurant.com

MEHERWAN IRANI
Chai Pani

22 Battery Park Ave
Asheville, NC 28801
828.254.4003
chaipani.net

ELLIOTT MOSS
The Admiral

400 Haywood Rd
Asheville, NC 28806
828.252.2541
theadmiralnc.com

JASON SELLERS
Plant

165 Merrimon Ave
Asheville, NC 28801
828.258.7500
plantisfood.com

JACOB SESSOMS
Table

48 College St
Asheville, NC 28801
828.254.8980
tableasheville.com

JOE SKULLY
Corner Kitchen

3 Boston Way
Asheville, NC 28803
828.274.2439
thecornerkitchen.com

BRIAN SONOSKUS
Tupelo Honey Café

12 College St
Asheville, NC 28801
828.255.4863
tupelohoneycafe.com

BANNER ELK

BILL GREENE
Artisanal

1200 Dobbins Rd
Banner Elk, NC 28604
828.898.5395
artisanalnc.com

ANDREW LONG
Simplicity at the Mast Farm Inn

2543 Broadstone Rd
Banner Elk, NC 28604
828.963.5857
themastfarminn.com

STAN CHAMBERLAIN
Crippen's

239 Sunset Dr
Blowing Rock, NC 28605
828.295.3487
crippens.com

MICHAEL FOREMAN
Bistro Roca

143 Wonderland Trail
Blowing Rock, NC 28605
828.295.4008
bistroroca.com

MATT PROCTOR
Storie Street

1167 Main St
Blowing Rock, NC 28605
828.295.7075
storiestreetgrille.com

BOONE

EDWIN BLOODWORTH
The Gamekeeper

3005 Shulls Mill Rd
Boone, NC 28607
828.963.7400
gamekeeper-nc.com

KEN GORDON
The Gamekeeper

3005 Shulls Mill Rd
Boone, NC 28607
828.963.7400
gamekeeper-nc.com

CASHIERS

JOHN FLEER
Canyon Kitchen

94 Lonesome Valley Rd
Cashiers, NC 28774
828.743.7967
lonesomevalley.com

CHARLOTTE

JIM ALEXANDER
Zebra

4521 Sharon Rd
Charlotte, NC 28211
704.442.9525
zebrarestaurant.net

MAJID AMOORPOUR
Bistro La Bon

1322 Central Ave
Charlotte, NC 28205
704.333.4646
bistrolabon.com

GENE BRIGGS
Blue

206 N College St
Charlotte, NC 28202
704.927.2583
bluecharlotte.com

TOM CONDRUN
The Liberty

1812 South Blvd
Charlotte, NC 28203
704.332.8830
thelibertycharlotte.com

TOMMY DYRNESS
Upstream

6902 Phillips Place Ct
Charlotte, NC 28210
704.556.7730
harpersgroup.com

JON FORTES
Mimosa Grill

327 S Tryon St
Charlotte, NC 28202
704.343.0700
harpersgroup.com

MARC JACKSINA
Halcyon

500 S Tryon St
Charlotte, NC 28202
704.910.0865
halcyonflavors.com

JOE KINDRED
Rooster's

150 N College St
Charlotte, NC 28202
704.370.7667
roosterskitchen.com

JAMIE LYNCH
5Church

127 N Tryon St
Charlotte, NC 28202
704.919.1322
5church.com

KERRY MOFFETT
Good Food on Montford

1701 Montford Dr
Charlotte, NC 28209
704.525.0881
goodfoodonmontford.com

BRUCE MOFFETT
Barrington's

7822 Fairview Rd
Charlotte, NC 28226
704.364.5755
barringtonsrestaurant.com

JIM NOBLE
King's Kitchen

129 W Trade St
Charlotte, NC 28202
704.375.1990
kingskitchen.org

CASSIE PARSONS
Harvest Moon Grille

235 N Tryon St
Charlotte, NC 28202
704.342.1193
harvestmoongrillecharlotte.com

JAY POUND
Soul Gastrolounge

1500 Central Ave
Charlotte, NC 28205
704.348.1848
soulgastrolounge.com

SCOTT WALLEN
Wolfgang Puck Pizza Bar

6706-C Philips Place Ct
Charlotte, NC 28210
704.295.0101
wolfgangpuck.com

TREY WILSON
Customshop

1601 Elizabeth Ave
Charlotte, NC 28204
704.333.3396
customshopfood.com

DURHAM

JIM ANILE
Revolution

107 W Main St
Durham, NC 27701
919.956.9999
revolutionrestaurant.com

BEN BARKER
Durham , NC

COLIN BEDFORD
Fearrington House

2000 Fearrington Village Center
Fearrington Village, NC 27312
919.542.2121
fearrington.com

JASON CUNNINGHAM
Fairview Dining Room

3001 Cameron Blvd
Durham, NC 27705
919.490.0999
washingtondukeinn.com

CHARLIE DEAL
Jujube

1201 Raleigh Rd
Chapel Hill, NC 27517
919.960.0555
jujuberestaurant.com

SCOTT HOWELL
Nana's

2514 University Dr #104
Durham, NC 27707
919.493.8545
nanasdurham.com

SHANE INGRAM
Four Square

2701 Chapel Hill Rd
Durham, NC 27707
919.401.9877
foursquarerestaurant.com

MATT KELLY
Vin Rouge

2010 Hillsborough Rd
Durham, NC 27705
919.416.0466
vinrougerestaurant.com

GLENN LOZUKE
Durham, NC

SEAN MCCARTHY
One

100 Meadowmont Village Cir
Chapel Hill, NC 27517
919.537.8207
one-restaurant.com

JUSTIN RAKES
Durham, NC

ANDREA REUSING
Lantern

423 W Franklin St
Chapel Hill, NC 27516
919.969.8846
lanternrestaurant.com

MARCO SHAW
Piedmont

401 Foster St
Durham, NC 27701
919.683.1213
piedmontrestaurant.com

BILL SMITH
Crook's Corner

610 W Franklin St
Chapel Hill, NC 27516
919.929.7643
crookscorner.com

AARON VANDEMARK
Panciuto

110 S Churton St
Hillsborough, NC 27278
919.732.6261
panciuto.com

TOM WHITAKER
Fearrington House

2000 Fearrington Village Center
Fearrington Village, NC 27312
919.542.2121
fearrington.com

TODD WHITNEY
Vin Rouge

2010 Hillsborough Rd
Durham, NC 27705
919.416.0466
vinrougerestaurant.com

GREENSBORO

CHRIS BLACKBURN
Josephine's Bistro

2417 Spring Garden St
Greensboro, NC 27403
336.285.6590
josephinesbistro.com

MICHAEL HARKENREADER
Undercurrent

327 Battleground Ave
Greensboro, NC 27401
336.370.1266
undercurrentrestaurant.com

GRAHAM HEATON
Table 16

600 S Elm St
Greensboro, NC 27406
336.279.8525
table16restaurant.com

LEIGH HESLING
Green Valley Grill

622 Green Valley Rd
Greensboro, NC 27408
336.854.2015
greenvalleygrill.com

GEORGE NEAL
1618

1618 W Friendly Ave
Greensboro, NC 27403
336.235.0898
1618concepts.com

JAY PIERCE
Lucky 32

1421 Westover Terrace
Greensboro, NC 27408
336.370.0707
lucky32.com

KINSTON

VIVIAN HOWARD
Chef and the Farmer

120 W Gordon St
Kinston, NC 28501
252.208.2433
chefandthefarmer.com

MURPHY

JAMES REAUX
Murphy's Chophouse

140 Valley River Ave
Murphy, NC 28906
828.835.3287
murphyschophouse.com

OUTER BANKS

ANDREW DONOVAN
The Brine and Bottle

7531 S Virginia Dare Trail
Nags Head, NC 27959
252.715.1818
thebrineandbottle.com

DONNY KING
Ocean Boulevard
Bistro and Martini Bar

4700 N Virginia Dare Trail
Kitty Hawk, NC 27949
252.261.2546
obbistro.com

TRAVIS LEE ROBINSON
The Left Bank

1461 Duck Rd
Kitty Hawk, NC 27949
866.860.3979
thesanderling.com

SAM MCGANN
Blue Point

1240 Duck Rd
Duck, NC 27949
252.261.8090
thebluepoint.com

PINEHURST

MARK ELLIOTT
Elliott's on Linden

905 Linden Rd
Pinehurst, NC 28374
910.215.0775
elliottsonlinden.com

RALEIGH

JUSTIN BURDETT
Ruka's Table

163 Main St
Highlands, NC 28741
828.526.3636
highlandsrestaurantgroup.com

JOHN CHILDERS
Herons

100 Woodland Pond Dr
Cary, NC 27513
919.447.4200
theumstead.com

ASHLEY CHRISTENSEN
Poole's

426 S McDowell St
Raleigh, NC 27601
919.832.4477
poolesdowntowndiner.com

JEREMY CLAYMAN
Raleigh, NC

SCOTT CRAWFORD
Herons

100 Woodland Pond Dr
Cary, NC 27513
919.447.4200
theumstead.com

SERGE FALCOZ-VIGNE
518 West

518 W Jones St
Raleigh, NC 27603
919.829.2518
518west.com

SEAN FOWLER
Mandolin

2519 Fairview Rd
Raleigh, NC 27608
919.322.0365
mandolinraleigh.com

STEVEN GREENE
An Cuisine

2800 Renaissance Park Pl
Cary, NC 27513
919.677.9229
ancuisines.com

TONY HOPKINS
Buku

110 E Davie St
Raleigh, NC 27601
919.834.6963
bukuraleigh.com

BRENT HOPKINS
Gravy

135 S Wilmington St
Raleigh, NC 27601
919.896.8513
gravyraleigh.com

JOSH HUGHES
An Cuisine

2800 Renaissance Park Pl
Cary, NC 27513
919.677.9229
ancuisines.com

SCOTT JAMES
Midtown Grille

4421-115 Six Forks Rd
Raleigh, NC 27609
919.782.9463
themidtowngrille.com

WOL KIM
Mura

4121 Main at North Hills St #110
Raleigh, NC 27609
919.781.7887
muranorthhills.com

JOHN KORZEKWINSKI
J. Betski's

10 W Franklin St #120
Raleigh, NC 27604
919.833.7999
jbetskis.com

MICHAEL LEE
Sono

319 Fayetteville St #101
Raleigh, NC 27601
919.521.5328
sonoraleigh.com

DAVID MAO
David's Dumpling & Noodle Bar

1900 Hillsborough St
Raleigh, NC 27607
919.239.4536
ddandnb.com

WALTER ROYAL
Angus Barn

9401 Glenwood Ave
Raleigh, NC 27617
919.787.3505
angusbarn.com

DANIEL SCHURR
Second Empire

330 Hillsborough St
Raleigh, NC 27603
919.829.3663
second-empire.com

MATT SCOFIELD
Sitti

137 S Wilmington St
Raleigh, NC 27601
919.239.4070
sitti-raleigh.com

JASON SMITH
18 Seaboard

18 Seaboard Ave #100
Raleigh, NC 27604
919.861.4318
18seaboard.com

MASATOSHI TSUJIMURA
Waraji

5910 Duraleigh Rd
Raleigh, NC 27612
919.783.1883
warajijapaneserestaurant.com

DAVID WIMMERS
Saint Jacques

6112 Falls of Neuse Rd
Raleigh, NC 27609
919.862.2770
saintjacquesfrenchcuisine.com

SANFORD

CHAD BLACKWELDER
Steele Pig

133 S Steele St
Sanford, NC 27330
919.777.9963
thesteelepig.com

SOUTHERN PINES

PREM NATH
195

195 Bell Ave
Southern Pines, NC 28387
910.692.7110
195pinehurstdining.com

CURT SHELVEY
Curt's Cucina

515 SE Broad St
Southern Pines, NC 28387
910.725.1868
curtscucina.com

WILMINGTON

CHARIN CHOTI
Big Thai

1319 Military Cutoff Rd
Wilmington, NC 28405
910.256.6588
bigthaiwilmington.com

MARC COPENHAVER
Wilmington, NC

LEE GROSSMAN
Bento Box

1121 Military Cutoff Rd
Wilmington, NC 28405
910.509.0774
bentoboxsushi.com

KYLE MCKNIGHT
Manna

123 Princess St
Wilmington, NC 28401
910.763.5252
mannaavenue.com

JOHN-MIKE REHM
University of North Carolina -
Wilmington

601 S College Rd
Wilmington, NC 28403
910.962.3000
uncw.edu

KEITH RHODES
Catch

6623 Market St
Wilmington, NC 28405
910.799.3847
catchwilmington.com

SHAWN WELLERSDICK
Port Land Grille

1908 Eastwood Rd
Wilmington, NC 28403
910.256.6056
portlandgrille.com

JOSH WOO
Yo Sake

33 S Front St
Wilmington, NC 28401
910.763.3172
yosake.com

WINSTON-SALEM

JOHN BOBBY
Noble's Grille

380 Knollwood St
Winston-Salem, NC 27103
336.777.8477
noblesgrille.com

TIM GRANDINETTI
Spring House

450 N Spring St
Winston-Salem, NC 27101
336.293.4797
springhousenc.com

JANIS KARATHANAS
Mozelle's Fresh Southern Bistro

878 W 4th St
Winston-Salem, NC 27101
336.703.5400
mozelles.com

FREDDY LEE
Bernardin's

901 W 4th St
Winston-Salem, NC 27101
336.725.6666
bernardinsfinedining.com

BILL SMITH
Fabian's

1100 Reynolda Rd
Winston-Salem, NC 27104
336.723.7700
fabiansrestaurant.com

JOHN THARP
Bleu Restaurant & Bar

3425 Frontis St
Winston-Salem, NC 27103
336.760.2026
bleurestaurantandbar.com

BISMARCK

STUART TRACY
The Pirogue Grille

121 N 4th St
Bismarck, ND 58501
701.223.3770
piroguegrille.com

FARGO

RYAN NITSCHKE
HoDo Restaurant

101 Broadway
Fargo, ND 58102
701.478.6969
hoteldonaldson.com

MICHAEL WALD
Maxwells

1380 9th St E
West Fargo, ND 58078
701.277.9463
maxwellsnd.com

ERIC WATSON
Mezzaluna

309 Roberts St N
Fargo, ND 58102
701.364.9479
dinemezzaluna.com

NICK WEINHANDL
HoDo Restaurant

101 Broadway
Fargo, ND 58102
701.478.6969
hoteldonaldson.com

GRAND FORKS

SCOTT FRANZ
The Toasted Frog

124 N 3rd St
Grand Forks, ND 58201
701.772.3764
toastedfrog.com

INGREDIENT: RADISHES

AKRON

ZACH CONOVER
The Leopard

600 N Aurora Rd
Aurora , OH 44202
330.562.2111
theleopardrestaurant.com

ATHENS

JEREMY GRAVES
Athens, OH

CANTON

CARL FALCONE
Bender's Tavern

137 Court Ave SW
Canton, OH 44702
330.453.8424
bendersrestaurant.com

CHUCK ROLLINS
Hart Mansion

411 N Main St
Minerva, OH 44657
330.868.4278
hartmansionrestaurant.com

JOSH SCHORY
Lucca

228 4th St NW
Canton, OH 44702
330.456.2534
luccadowntown.com

CINCINNATI

NAT BLANFORD
Embers

8170 Montgomery Rd
Cincinnati, OH 45236
513.984.8090
embersrestaurant.com

MARK BODENSTEIN
Nicholson's Gastropub

625 Walut St
Cincinnati, OH 45202
513.564.9111
nicholsonspub.com

MICHELLE BROWN
Jag's Steak and Seafood

5980 W Chester Rd
West Chester, OH 45069
513.860.5353
jags.com

TERRY CARTER
Terry's Turf Club

4618 Eastern Ave
Cincinnati, OH 45226
513.533.4222

CHARLIE CHOI
Dancing Wasabi

3520 Edwards Rd
Cincinnati, OH 45208
513.533.4444
dancingwasabihydepark.com

DAVID COOK
Daveed's Next

8944 Columbia Rd
Loveland, OH 45140
513.683.2665
daveedsnext.com

JON CORCORAN
Mitchell's Fish Market

9456 Water Front Dr
West Chester, OH 45069
513.779.5292
mitchellsfishmarket.com

JEAN-ROBERT DE CAVEL
Jean-Robert's Table

713 Vine St
Cincinnati, OH 45202
513.621.4777
jrtable.com

DAVID FALK
Boca

3200 Madison Rd
Cincinnati, OH 45209
513.542.2022
boca-restaurant.com

JULIE FRANCIS
Nectar Restaurant

1000 Delta Ave
Cincinnati, OH 45208
513.929.0525
dineatnectar.com

STEVEN GEDDES
Local 127

413 Vine St
Cincinnati, OH 45202
513.721.1345
mylocal127.com

HARVEY GERMAIN
Tony's

12110 Montgomery Rd
Cincinnati, OH 45140
513.677.1993
tonysofcincinnati.com

JIMMY GIBSON
Jimmy G's

435 Elm St
Cincinnati, OH 45202
513.621.8555
jimmy-gs.com

TODD KELLY
Orchids at Palm Court

35 W 5th St
Cincinnati, OH 45202
513.564.6465
orchidsatpalmcourt.com

DR. JOHN KINSELLA
Smart Chefs, LLC

4634 Laurel View Dr
Cincinnati, OH 45244
513.846.1175
smartchefsllc.biz

JUSTIN LEIDENHEIMER
Carlo & Johnny

9769 Montgomery Rd
Montgomery, OH 45242
513.936.8600
jeffruby.com

JEREMY LIEB
Boca

3200 Madison Rd
Cincinnati, OH 45209
513.542.2022
boca-restaurant.com

JEREMY LUERS
Cincinnati, OH

OWEN MAASS
Cumin Eclectic Cuisine

3520 Erie Ave
Cincinnati, OH 45208
513.871.8714
cuminrestaurant.com

BLAKE MAIER
Cincinnati, OH

CRISTIAN PIETOSO
Via Vite

520 Vine St
Cincinnati, OH 45202
513.721.8483
viaviterestaurant.com

JASON ROSE
Jeff Ruby's

700 Walnut St
Cincinnati, OH 45202
513.784.1200
jeffruby.com

JOSE SALAZAR
The Palace

601 Vine St
Cincinnati, OH 45202
513.381.3000
palacecincinnati.com

DANIEL STOLTZ
Nicola's

1420 Sycamore St
Cincinnati, OH 45202
513.721.6200
nicolasrestaurant.com

DAVE TAYLOR
La Poste

3410 Telford St
Cincinnati, OH 45220
513.281.3663
laposteeatery.com

DANIEL WRIGHT
Abigail Street

1214 Vine St
Cincinnati, OH 45202
513.421.4040
abigailstreet.com

CLEVELAND

MATTHEW ANDERSON
Umami

42 N Main St
Chagrin Falls, OH 44022
440.247.8600
umamichagrinfalls.com

MICHAEL ANNANDONO
Michaelangelo's

2198 Murray Hill Rd
Cleveland, OH 44106
216.721.0300
mangelos.com

BEN BEBENROTH
Spice Kitchen and Bar

5800 Detroit Ave
Cleveland, OH 44102
216.961.9637
spicekitchenandbar.com

JOHN D'AMICO
Chez Francois

555 Main St
Vermilion, OH 44089
440.967.0630
chezfrancois.com

HEATHER HAVILAND
Lucky's Café

777 Starkweather Ave
Cleveland, OH 44113
216.622.7773
luckyscafe.com

JONATHAN BENNETT
Red Restaurant Group

3355 Richmond Rd
Cleveland, OH 44122
216.831.5599
redrestaurantgroup.com

JOHN DEJOY
John Palmer's Bistro 44

7590 Fredle Dr
Painesville, OH 44077
440.350.0793
johnpalmers.com

JEFF JARRETT
Amp 150

4277 W 150th St
Cleveland, OH 44135
216.706.8787
amp150.com

DANTE BOCCUZZI
Dante

2247 Professor Ave
Tremont, OH 44113
216.274.1200
restaurantdante.us

ANDREW DOMBROWSKI
Cowell & Hubbard

1305 Euclid Ave
Cleveland, OH 44115
216.479.0555
cowellhubbard.com

DOUGLAS KATZ
Fire Food & Drink

13220 Shaker Square
Cleveland, OH 44120
216.921.3473
firefoodanddrink.com

ADAM BOSTWICK
Cleveland, OH

MATT FISH
Melt Bar & Grilled

13463 Cedar Rd
Cleveland Heights, OH 44118
216.965.0988
meltbarandgrilled.com

MELISSA KHOURY
Washington Place Bistro

2203 Cornell Rd
Cleveland, OH 44106
216.791.6500
washingtonplacelittleitaly.com

ZACK BRUELL
L'Albatros

11401 Bellflower Rd
Cleveland, OH 44106
216.791.7880
albatrosbrasserie.com

ANDREW GORSKI
Tremont Tap House

2572 Scranton Rd
Cleveland, OH 44113
216.298.4451
tremonttaphouse.com

ZACH LADNER
Giovanni's Ristorante

25550 Chagrin Blvd
Cleveland, OH 44122
216.831.8625
giovanniscleveland.com

DEREK CLAYTON
Lola

2058 E 4th St
Cleveland, OH 44115
216.621.5652
lolabistro.com

MATT HARLAN
B-Spot

28699 Chagrin Blvd
Woodmere, OH 44122
216.292.5567
bspotburgers.com

ADAM LAMBERT
Bar Cento

1948 W 25th St
Cleveland, OH 44113
216.274.1010
barcento.com

MATTHEW MATHLAGE
Light Bistro

2801 Bridge Ave
Cleveland, OH 44113
216.771.7130
lightbistro.com

PAUL MINNILLO
Flour

34205 Chagrin Blvd
Moreland Hills, OH 44022
216.464.3700
flourrestaurant.com

BRETT MONTGOMERY
Sans Souci

24 Public Square
Cleveland, OH 44113
216.902.4095
sanssoucicleveland.com

JAMES MOWCOMBER
Lolita

900 Literary Rd
Cleveland, OH 44113
216.771.5652
lolitarestaurant.com

MATTHEW MYTRO
Flour

34205 Chagrin Blvd
Moreland Hills, OH 44022
216.464.3700
flourrestaurant.com

MICHAEL NOWAK
The Black Pig

1865 W 25th St
Cleveland, OH 44113
216.862.7551
theblackpigcleveland.com

JUSTIN OFANDISKI
Dante

2247 Professor Ave
Tremont, OH 44113
216.274.1200
restaurantdante.us

BRIAN OKIN
Cleveland, OH

ANTHONY ROMANO
Players on Madison

14523 Madison Ave
Lakewood, OH 44107
216.226.5200
playersonmadison.com

VYTAURAS SASNAUSKAS
Americano

1 Bratenahl Pl
Cleveland, OH 44108
216.541.3900
americanocleveland.com

JONATHON SAWYER
Greenhouse Tavern

2038 E 4th St
Cleveland, OH 44115
216.443.0511
thegreenhousetavern.com

STEVE SCHIMOLER
Crop Bistro & Bar

2537 Lorain Ave
Cleveland, OH 44113
216.696.2767
cropbistro.com

TOM SCHRENK
Table 45

9801 Carnegie Ave
Cleveland, OH 44106
216.707.4045
tbl45.com

KAREN SMALL
Flying Fig

2523 Market Ave
Cleveland, OH 44113
216.241.4243
theflyingfig.com

MARC STANDEN
Blue Point Grille

700 W Saint Clair Ave
Cleveland, OH 44113
216.875.7827
hospitalityrestaurants.com

MICHAEL SYMON
Lola Bistro

2058 E 4th St
Cleveland, OH 44115
216.621.5652
lolabistro.com

BRANDON WALUKAS
Spice Kitchen + Bar

5800 Detroit Ave
Cleveland, OH 44102
216.961.9637
spicekitchenandbar.com

ROCCO WHALEN
Fahrenheit

2417 Professor Ave
Cleveland, OH 44113
216.781.8858
fahrenheittremont.com

ERIC WILLIAMS
Momocho

1835 Fulton Rd
Cleveland, OH 44113
216.694.2122
momocho.com

COLUMBUS

DENVER ADKINS
The Top Steak House

2891 E Main St
Columbus, OH 43209
614.231.8238
thetopsteakhouse.com

MIKE BLACK
Due Amici

67 E Gay St
Columbus, OH 43215
614.224.9373
due-amici.com

RICHARD BLONDIN
The Refectory

1092 Bethel Rd
Columbus, OH 43220
614.451.9774
therefectoryrestaurant.com

PETER CHAPMAN
The Pearl

641 N High St
Columbus, OH 43215
614.227.0151
thepearlcolumbus.com

JEREMY COOK
Columbus, OH

NATE CROCKETT
Elevator Brewery
and Draught Haus

161 N High St
Columbus, OH 43215
614.228.0500
elevatorbrewing.com

JOHN DORNBACK
Basi Italia

811 Highland St
Columbus, OH 43215
614.294.7383
basi-italia.com

BRETT FIFE
Lindey's

169 E Beck St
Columbus, OH 43206
614.228.4343
lindeys.com

WILLIAM FUGITT
Gallerie Bar & Bistro

401 N High St
Columbus, OH 43215
614.384.8600
hiltoncolumbusdowntown.com

JAMIE GEORGE
Z Cucina di Spirito

1368 Grandview Ave
Columbus, OH 43212
614.486.9200
zcucina.com

OLIVIA GIESLER
M

2 Miranova Pl
Columbus, OH 43215
614.629.0000
matmiranova.com

BILL GLOVER
Sage American Bistro

2653 N High St
Columbus, OH 43202
614.267.7243
sageamericanbistro.com

MATT GOINGS
Mitchell's Steakhouse

1408 Polaris Pkwy
Columbus, OH 43004
614.888.2467
mitchellssteakhouse.com

HARTMUT HANDKE
Handke's

Columbus, OH

ROBERT HARRISON
De Novo

201 S High St
Columbus, OH 43215
614.222.8830
denovobistro.com

BRIAN HINSHAW
Cameron Mitchell Restaurants

515 Park St
Columbus, OH 43215
614.621.3663
cameronmitchell.com

TODD HUDSON
The Wildflower Café

207 E Main St
Mason, OH 45040
513.492.7514

TRAVIS HYDE
Ella

266 E Main St
New Albany, OH 43054
614.855.4600
ella-restaurant.com

MIKE KIMURA
Kihachi

2667 Federated Blvd
Columbus, OH 43235
614.764.9040

MATTHEW LITZINGER
L'Antibes

772 N High St
Columbus, OH 43215
614.291.1666
lantibes.com

RICK LOPEZ
Knead

505 N High St
Columbus, OH 43215
614.228.6323
kneadonhigh.com

LARRY MACDONALD
Cap City Fine Diner

1299 Olentangy River Rd
Columbus, OH 43212
614.291.3663
capcityfinediner.com

DAVE MACLENNAN
Basi Italia

811 Highland St
Columbus, OH 43215
614.294.7383
basi-italia.com

BRIAN PAWLAK
DeepWood

511 N High St
Columbus, OH 43215
614.221.5602
deepwoodrestaurant.com

KENT RIGSBY
Rigsby's Kitchen

698 N High St
Columbus, OH 43215
614.461.7888
rigsbyskitchen.com

HUBERT SEIFERT
SPAGIO

1295 Grandview Ave
Columbus, OH 43212
614.486.1114
spagio.com

ALANA SHOCK
Alana's

2333 N High St
Columbus, OH 43202
614.294.6783
alanas.com

THOMAS SMITH
The Worthington Inn

649 High St
Worthington, OH 43085
614.885.2600
worthingtoninn.com

DAVID TETZLOFF
G. Michael's

595 S 3rd St
Columbus, OH 43215
614.464.0575
gmichaelsbistro.com

PETE VITT
Lemongrass Fusion Bistro

641 N High St
Columbus, OH 43215
614.224.1414
lemongrassfusion.com

JARED YAZVAC
Mitchell's Ocean Club

4002 Easton Town Center
Columbus, OH 43219
614.416.2582
mitchellsoceanclub.com

PAUL YOW
Natalie's

79 S 4th St
Columbus, OH 43215
614.228.5199
nataliesdowntown.com

DAYTON

DOMINIQUE FORTIN
C'est Tout

2600 Far Hills Ave
Dayton, OH 45419
937.298.0022
cesttoutbistro.com

ANNE KEARNEY
Rue Dumaine

1061 Miamisburg Centerville Rd
Dayton, OH 45459
937.610.1061
ruedumainerestaurant.com

KEITH TAYLOR
Savona

79 S Main St
Centerville, OH 45458
937.610.9835
savonadayton.com

LISBON

RANDY PERRINO
Lock 24

42087 State Route 154
Lisbon, OH 44432
330.420.0464
thelock24.com

SANDUSKY

CESARE AVALLONE
Zinc Brasserie

142 Columbus Ave
Sandusky, OH 44870
419.502.9462
zincbrasserie.net

TOLEDO

MICHAEL BULKOWSKI
Toledo, OH

ROB CAMPBELL
Revolution Grille

5333 Monroe Ave
Toledo, OH 43623
419.841.0070
revolutiongrille.com

AARON WEIBLE
Sweetwater Chophouse

211 Carpenter Rd
Defiance, OH 43512
419.785.4434
sweetwaterchophouse.com

YOUNGSTOWN

TIM KING
The Upstairs

4500 Mahoning Ave
Youngstown, OH 44515
330.793.5577
theupstairsrestaurant.com

JONATHAN MAGER
Café Cimmento

12 E Boardman St
Youngstown, OH 44503
330.740.0166
cafecimmento.com

RESTAURANT FARMS
Chefs are growing their own ingredients controlling their supply of fresh flavor.

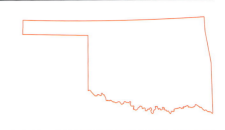

OKLAHOMA CITY

NICK BISHOP
The Mantel Wine Bar & Bistro

201 E Sheridan Ave
Oklahoma City, OK 73104
405.236.8040
themantelokc.com

CLAY FALKNER
Signature Grill

1317 E Danforth Rd
Edmond, OK 73034
405.330.4548
deepforkgrill.com

CALLY JOHNSON
Café 501

5825 NW Grand Blvd
Oklahoma City, OK 73118
405.844.1501
cafe501.com

ROBERT BLACK
A Good Egg Dining Group

601 NW 5th St
Oklahoma City, OK 73102
405.602.0184
goodeggdining.com

JONAS FAVELA
Metro Wine Bar & Bistro

6418 N Western Ave
Oklahoma City, OK 73116
405.840.9463
metrowinebar.com

RUSS JOHNSON
Ludivine

805 N Hudson Ave
Oklahoma City, OK 73102
405.778.6800
ludivineokc.com

ALAIN BUTHION
La Baguette Bistro

7408 N May Ave
Oklahoma City, OK 73116
405.840.3047
labaguettebistro.com

KURT FLEISCHFRESSER
The Coach House

6437 Avondale Dr
Nichols Hills, OK 73116
405.842.1000
thecoachhouseokc.com

JONATHAN KRELL
Stella

1201 N Walker Ave
Oklahoma City, OK 73103
405.235.2200
stellaokc.com

ANTHONY COMPAGNI
Benvenuti's Ristorante

105 W Main St
Norman, OK 73069
405.310.5271
benvenutisristorante.com

DAVID HENRY
The Coach House

6437 Avondale Dr
Nichols Hills, OK 73116
405.842.1000
thecoachhouseokc.com

CHRIS MCCABE
Red Prime Steak

504 N Broadway Ave
Oklahoma City, OK 73102
405.232.2626
redprimesteak.com

CHRISTINE DOWD
Aunt Pittypat's Catering

1515 N Portland
Oklahoma City, OK 73107
405.942.4000
auntpittypatscatering.com

VICTOR IZETA
Deep Fork Grill

5418 N Western Ave
Oklahoma City, OK 73118
405.848.7678
deepforkgrill.com

BRIAN MCGREW
Cheever's Café

2409 N Hudson Ave
Oklahoma City, OK 73103
405.525.7007
cheeverscafe.com

MANDY PARKHURST
Oklahoma City, OK

TIM INMAN
Stonehorse Café
1748 Utica Square
Tulsa, OK 74114
918.712.7470
stonehorsecafe.com

RYAN PARROTT
Local
2262 W Main St
Norman, OK 73069
405.928.5600
eatatlocal.com

ERIK REYNOLDS
SMOKE.
1542 E 15th St
Tulsa, OK 74120
918.949.4440
smoketulsa.com

JIMMY STEPNEY
Boulevard Steakhouse
505 South Blvd
Edmond, OK 73034
405.715.2333
boulevardsteakhouse.com

JUSTIN THOMPSON
Juniper
324 E 3rd St
Tulsa, OK 74120
918.794.1090
junipertulsa.com

JONATHON STRANGER
Ludivine
805 N Hudson Ave
Oklahoma City, OK 73102
405.778.6800
ludivineokc.com

PAUL WILSON
Juniper
324 E 3rd St
Tulsa, OK 74120
918.794.1090
junipertulsa.com

TULSA

SAM BRACKEN
The Canebrake
33241 E 732nd Rd
Wagoner, OK 74467
918.485.1807
thecanebrake.com

JAKUB HARTLIEB
Elements Steakhouse
8330 Riverside Pkwy
Tulsa, OK 74137
918.995.8335
riverspirittulsa.com

ASHLAND

ERIK BROWN
Amuse

15 N 1st St
Ashland, OR 97520
541.488.9000
amuserestaurant.com

ASTORIA

JOHN NEWMAN
Newmans at 988

988 S Hemlock St
Cannon Beach, OR 97110
503.436.1151
newmansat988.com

BEND

FABRICE BEAUDOIN
Meadows at the Lodge

17600 Center Dr
Sunriver, OR 97707
541.593.3740
sunriver-resort.com

JUSTIN COOK
Kanpai Sushi and Sake Bar

990 NW Newport Ave
Bend, OR 97701
541.388.4636
kanpai-bend.com

DEAN ECKER
The Lodge Restaurant

13899 Bishops Cap
Black Butte Ranch, OR 97759
541.595.1260
blackbutteranch.com

CLIFF ESLINGER
900 Wall Restaurant

900 NW Wall St
Bend, OR 97701
541.323.6295
900wall.com

ANDRES FERNANDEZ
Ariana

1304 NW Galveston Ave
Bend, OR 97701
541.330.5539
arianarestaurantbend.com

ARIANA FERNANDEZ
Ariana

1304 NW Galveston Ave
Bend, OR 97701
541.330.5539
arianarestaurantbend.com

STEVE HELT
Zydeco

919 Northwest Bond St
Bend, OR 97701
541.312.2899
zydecokitchen.com

JEFF HUNT
Spork

Bend, OR
541.390.0946
sporkbend.com

JOE KIM
5 Fusion and Sushi Bar

821 NW Wall St #100
Bend, OR 97701
541.323.2328
5fusion.com

GAVIN MCMICHAEL
Blacksmith Steakhouse

211 NW Greenwood Ave
Bend, OR 97701
541.318.0588
bendblacksmith.com

JURI SBANDATI
Trattoria Sbandati

1444 NW College Way
Bend, OR 97701
541.306.6825
trattoriasbandati.com

CORVALLIS

MITCH ROSENBAUM
Del Alma

136 SW Washington Ave #102
Corvallis, OR 97333
541.753.2222
delalmarestaurant.com

EUGENE

GABRIEL GIL
Soubise

Eugene, OR

BRENDAN MAHANEY
Belly

291 E 5th Ave
Eugene, OR 97401
541.687.8226
eatbelly.com

BEN NADOLNY
King Estate Winery

80854 Territorial Hwy
Eugene, OR 97405
541.942.9874
kingestate.com

STEPHANIE PEARL KIMMEL
Marche

296 E 5th Ave
Eugene, OR 97401
541.342.3612
marcherestaurant.com

ANDREW STONE
Ox and Fin

105 Oakway Center
Eugene, OR 97401
541.302.3000
oxandfin.com

GRANTS PASS

TIMOTHY KELLER
Grants Pass, OR

HOOD RIVER

KATHY WATSON
Nora's Table

110 5th St
Hood River, OR 97301
541.387.4000
norastable.com

NEWPORT

CHARLIE BRANFORD
Local Ocean Seafood

213 SE Bay Blvd
Newport, OR 97365
541.574.7959
localocean.net

SEAN MCCART
The Bay House

5911 SW Hwy 101
Lincoln City, OR 97367
541.996.3222
thebayhouse.org

JUSTIN WILLS
Restaurant Beck

2345 U.S. 101
Depoe Bay, OR 97341
541.765.3220
restaurantbeck.com

PORTLAND

DAVID ANDERSON
Genoa

2832 SE Belmont St
Portland, OR 97214
503.238.1464
genoarestaurant.com

JOBIE BAILEY
DOC

5519 NE 30th Ave
Portland, OR 97211
503.946.8592
docpdx.com

AARON BARNETT
St. Jack

2039 SE Clinton St
Portland, OR 97202
503.360.1281
stjackpdx.com

JASON BARWIKOWSKI
Woodsman Tavern

4537 SE Division St
Portland, OR 97206
971.373.8264
woodsmantavern.com

ERIC BECHARD
Thistle

228 NE Evans St
McMinnville, OR 97128
503.472.9623
thistlerestaurant.com

BEN BETTINGER
Imperial

410 SW Broadway
Portland, OR 97205
503.228.7222
imperialpdx.com

OSWALDO BIBIANO
Autentica

5507 NE 30th Ave
Portland, OR 97211
503.287.7555
autenticaportland.com

PHILIPPE BOULOT
Multnomah Athletic Club

1849 SW Salmon St
Portland, OR 97205
503.223.6251
themac.com

THOMAS BOYCE
Bluehour

250 NW 13th Ave
Portland, OR 97209
503.226.3394
bluehouronline.com

ANTHONY CAFIERO
Racion

1205 SW Washington St
Portland, OR 97205
971.276.8008
racionpdx.com

JEAN-JACQUES CHATELARD
Bistro Maison

729 NE 3rd St
McMinnville, OR 97128
503.474.1888
bistromaison.com

CHRIS CZARNECKI
Joel Palmer House

600 Ferry St
Dayton, OR 97114
503.864.2995
joelpalmerhouse.com

TONY DEMES
Noisette

1937 NW 23rd Pl
Portland, OR 97210
503.719.4599
noisetterestaurant.com

GREG DENTON
Ox

2225 NE Martin Luther King Jr Blvd
Portland, OR 97212
503.284.3366
oxpdx.com

CHRIS DIMINNO
Clyde Common

1014 SW Stark St
Portland, OR 97205
503.228.3333
clydecommon.com

SCOTT DOLICH
Park Kitchen

422 NW 8th Ave
Portland, OR 97209
503.223.7275
parkkitchen.com

DAVE FARRELL
Cabezon Restaurant
& Fish Market

5200 NE Sacramento St
Portland, OR 97213
503.284.6617
cabezonrestaurant.com

ERIC FERGUSON
Nick's Italian Café

521 NE 3rd St
McMinnville, OR 97128
503.434.4471
nicksitaliancafe.com

CHRISTOPHER FLANAGAN
Dundee Bistro

100 SW 7th St
Dundee, OR 97115
503.554.1650
dundeebistro.com

JASON FRENCH
Ned Ludd

3925 NE Martin Luther King Jr Blvd
Portland, OR 97212
503.288.6900
nedluddpdx.com

KEVIN GIBSON
Evoe

3731 SE Hawthorne Blvd
Portland, OR 97214
503.232.1010
pastaworks.com

JOHN GORHAM
Toro Bravo

120 NE Russell St
Portland, OR 97212
503.281.4464
torobravopdx.com

GREGORY GOURDET
Departure

525 SW Morrison St
Portland, OR 97204
503.802.5370
departureportland.com

TOMMY HABETZ
Trigger

128 NE Russell St
Portland, OR 97212
503.327.8234
triggerpdx.com

ZOE HACKETT
Cocotte

2930 NE Killingsworth St
Portland, OR 97211
503.227.2669
cocottepdx.com

GILBERT HENRY
Cuvee

214 W Main St
Carlton, OR 97111
503.852.6555
cuveedining.com

GREG HIGGINS
Higgins

1239 SW Broadway
Portland, OR 97205
503.222.9070
higginsportland.com

HIRO IKEGAYA
Mirakutei
536 E Burnside St
Portland, OR 97214
503.467.7501

CHRIS ISRAEL
Grüner
527 SW 12th Ave
Portland, OR 97205
503.241.7163
grunerpdx.com

SUNNY JIN
Jory
2525 Allison Ln
Newberg, OR 97132
503.554.2526
theallison.com

ERIC JOPPIE
Bar Avignon
2138 SE Division St
Portland, OR 97202
503.517.0808
baravignon.com

KATE KOO
Zilla Sake House
1806 NE Alberta St
Portland, OR 97211
503.288.8372
zillasakehouse.com

BRIAN LANDRY
Portland, OR

DOLAN LANE
clarklewis
1001 SE Water Ave #160
Portland, OR 97214
503.235.2294
clarklewispdx.com

GAVIN LEDSON
Jamison
900 NW 11th Ave
Portland, OR 97209
503.972.3330
jamisonpdx.com

PATRICK LEE-WARNER
Scratch
149 SW A Ave
Lake Oswego, OR 97034
503.697.1330
scratchfoodsllc.com

JENN LOUIS
Lincoln Restaurant
3808 N Williams Ave
Portland, OR 97227
503.288.6200
lincolnpdx.com

DAVID MACHADO
Nel Centro
1408 SW 6th Ave
Portland, OR 97202
503.484.1099
nelcentro.com

ALAN MANISCALCO
Ken's Artisan Pizza
304 SE 28th Ave
Portland, OR 97214
503.517.9951
kensartisan.com

JANIS MARTIN
Tanuki
8029 SE Stark St
Portland, OR 97215
503.477.6030
tanukipdx.com

RICH MEYER
Higgins
1239 SW Broadway
Portland, OR 97205
503.222.9070
higginsportland.com

BEN MEYER
Grain and Gristle
1473 NE Prescott St
Portland, OR 97211
503.298.5007
grainandgristle.com

DANIEL MONDOK
Paulee
1410 Oregon 99W
Dundee, OR 97115
503.538.7970
pauleerestaurant.com

RYOSHIRO MURATA
Murata
200 SW Market St #P105
Portland, OR 97201
503.227.0080

DAVID PADBERG
Raven and Rose
1331 SW Broadway
Portland, OR 97201
360.314.2002

VITALY PALEY
Paley's Place Bistro & Bar

1204 NW 21st Ave
Portland, OR 97209
503.243.2403
paleysplace.net

TRENT PIERCE
Wafu

3113 SE Division St
Portland, OR 97202
503.236.0205
wafupdx.com

NAOMI POMEROY
Beast

5425 NE 30th Ave
Portland, OR 97211
503.841.6968
beastpdx.com

BRIAN POOR
Portland City Grill

111 SW 5th Ave
Portland, OR 97204
503.450.0030
portlandcitygrill.com

ETHAN A. POWELL
The Parish

231 NW 11th Ave
Portland, OR 97209
503.227.2421
theparishpdx.com

WILLIAM PREISCH
The Bent Brick

1639 NW Marshall St
Portland, OR 97209
503.688.1655
thebentbrick.com

ANDY RICKER
Pok Pok

3226 SE Division St
Portland, OR 97202
503.232.1387
pokpokpdx.com

GABE ROSEN
Biwa

215 SE 9th Ave
Portland, OR 97214
503.239.8830
biwarestaurant.com

ALLEN ROUTT
The Painted Lady

201 S College St
Newberg, OR 97132
503.538.3850
thepaintedladyrestaurant.com

GABRIEL RUCKER
Le Pigeon

738 E Burnside St
Portland, OR 97214
503.546.8796
lepigeon.com

SAM SALTOS
Portland, OR

ADAM SAPPINGTON
Country Cat Dinner House

7937 SE Stark St
Portland, OR 97215
503.408.1414
thecountrycat.net

PATRICK SCHULTZ
Genoa

2832 SE Belmont St
Portland, OR 97214
503.238.1464
genoarestaurant.com

IAN SKOMSKI
Boxer Sushi

1524 SE 20th Ave
Portland, OR 97214
971.271.8635
boxersushi.com

DUANE SORENSON
The Woodsman Tavern

4537 SE Division St
Portland, OR 97206
971.373.8264
woodsmantavern.com

BRIAN SPANGLER
Apizza Scholls

4741 SE Hawthorne Blvd
Portland, OR 97215
503.233.1286
apizzascholls.com

ERIK VAN KLEY
Little Bird Bistro

219 SW 6th Ave
Portland, OR 97204
503.688.5952
littlebirdbistro.com

WILLIAM VOUNG
Ha VL

2738 SE 82nd Ave #102
Portland, OR 97266
503.772.0103

JOHANNA WARE
Smallwares

4605 NE Fremont St
Portland, OR 97213
971.229.0995
smallwarespdx.com

CATHY WHIMS
Nostrana

1401 SE Morrison St
Portland, OR 97214
503.234.2427
nostrana.com

KAT WHITEHEAD
Aviary

1733 NE Alberta St
Portland, OR 97211
503.287.2400
aviarypdx.com

RICK WIDMAYER
Screen Door

2337 E Burnside St
Portland, OR 97214
503.542.0880
screendoorrestaurant.com

AARON WOO
Natural Selection

3033 NE Alberta St
Portland, OR 97211
503.288.5883
naturalselectionpdx.com

JUSTIN WOODWARD
Castagna

1752 SE Hawthorne Blvd
Portland, OR 97214
503.231.7373
castagnarestaurant.com

ALEX YODER
Olympic Provisions

107 SE Washington St
Portland, OR 97214
503.954.3663
olympicprovisions.com

SALEM

DAVID ROSALES
La Capitale Resto

508 State St
Salem, OR 97301
503.585.1975
lacapitalesalem.com

ALLENTOWN

TYLER BAXTER
Cosmopolitan

22 N 6th St
Allentown, PA 18101
610.435.3540
ourcosmopolitan.com

LEE CHIZMAR
Bolete

1740 Seidersville Rd
Bethlehem, PA 18015
610.868.6505
boleterestaurant.com

FEDERICA MUGGENBURG
Hotel Bethlehem

437 Main St
Bethlehem, PA 18018
610.625.2219
hotelbethlehem.com

BELLEFONTE

JEREMIAH DICK
Miah's Cuisine

123 W Linn St
Bellefonte, PA 16823
814.932.7161

BLOOMSBURG

MATTHEW REVAK
Inn at Turkey Hill

991 Central Rd
Bloomsburg, PA 17815
570.387.1500
innatturkeyhill.com

CRESCO

MARK REINHARDT
Sand Spring Modern Cuisine

230 Sand Spring Rd
Cresco, PA 18326
570.595.3015
sandspringdining.com

ERIE

BERTRAND ARTIGUES
Bertrand's Bistro

18 N Park Row
Erie, PA 16501
814.871.6477
bertrandsbistro.com

DAN KERN
1201 Kitchen

1201 State St
Erie, PA 16501
814.464.8989
1201restaurant.com

HARRISBURG

ROBERT DACKO
Federal Taphouse

234 N 2nd St
Harrisburg, PA 17101
717.525.8077
federaltaphouse.com

JOHN REIS
The Golden Sheaf

1 N 2nd St
Harrisburg, PA 17101
717.237.6400
hiltonharrisburgdining.com

HAWLEY

GRANT GENZLINGER
The Settlers Inn

4 Main Ave
Hawley, PA 18428
570.226.2993
thesettlersinn.com

LANCASTER

TIM CARR
Carr's

50 W Grant St
Lancaster, PA 17603
717.299.7090
carrsrestaurant.com

MICHAEL CARSON
John J. Jeffries

300 Harrisburg Ave
Lancaster, PA 17603
717.431.3307
johnjjeffries.com

SEAN CAVANAUGH
John J. Jeffries

300 Harrisburg Ave
Lancaster, PA 17603
717.431.3307
johnjjeffries.com

CARL VITALE
Gibraltar

931 Harrisburg Ave
Lancaster, PA 17603
717.397.2790
kearesrestaurants.com

MILFORD

NANCIE SIMONET
Waterwheel

150 Water St
Milford, PA 18337
570.296.2383
waterwheelcafe.com

PHILADELPHIA

WALTER ABRAMS
Le Bec Fin

1523 Walnut St
Philadelphia, PA 19102
215.567.1000
lebecfin.com

CAROLYNN ANGLE
Standard Tap

901 N 2nd St
Philadelphia, PA 19123
215.238.0630
standardtap.com

DAVID ANSILL
Bar Ferdinand

1030 N 2nd St
Philadelphia, PA 19123
215.923.1313
barferdinand.com

KIONG BANH
Twenty Manning Grill

261 S 20th St
Philadelphia, PA 19103
215.731.0900
twentymanninggrill.com

JOHN BARRETT
Black Bass Hotel

3774 River Rd
Lumberville, PA 18933
215.297.9260
blackbasshotel.com

KYLE BEEBE
M Restaurant

231 S 8th St
Philadelphia, PA 19107
215.625.6666
mrestaurantphilly.com

ANTHONY BONETT
Moshulu

401 S Columbus Blvd
Philadelphia, PA 19106
215.923.2500
moshulu.com

DAVID BOYLE
Davio's

111 S 17th St
Philadelphia, PA 19103
215.563.4810
davios.com

JOHN BRANDT-LEE
Avalon

312 S High St
West Chester, PA 19382
610.436.4100
avalonrestaurant.net

PIERRE CALMELS
Bibou

1009 S 8th St
Philadelphia, PA 19147
215.965.8290
biboubyob.com

MICHAEL CAPPON
Isabella

382 E Elm St
Conshohocken, PA 19428
484.532.7470
barisabella.com

HAN CHIANG
Han Dynasty

108 Chestnut St
Philadelphia, PA 19106
215.922.1888
handynasty.net

JOE CICALA
Le Virtu

1927 E Passyunk Ave
Philadelphia, PA 19148
215.271.5626
levirtu.com

JONATHAN CICHON
Lacroix

210 W Rittenhouse Square
Philadelphia, PA 19103
215.790.2533
lacroixrestaurant.com

JASON CICHONSKI
Ela

627 S 3rd St
Philadelphia, PA 19147
267.687.8512
elaphilly.com

TONY CLARK
Serafina

130 S 18th St
Philadelphia, PA 19103
215.977.7755
serafinarestaurant.com

EBEN COPPLE
The Yardley Inn Restaurant & Bar

82 E Afton Ave
Yardley, PA 19067
215.493.3800
yardleyinn.com

ANDREW DEERY
Majolica

258 Bridge St
Phoenixville, PA 19460
610.917.0962
majolicarestaurant.com

MATT DELANO
Maggiano's

1201 Filbert St
Philadelphia, PA 19107
215.567.2020
maggianos.com

WILLIAM DISTEFANO
Fountain Restaurant

1 Logan Square
Philadelphia, PA 19103
215.963.1500
fourseasons.com/philadelphia

NICHOLAS ELMI
Rittenhouse Tavern

251 S 18th St
Philadelphia, PA 19103
215.732.2412
rittenhousetavern.com

PATRICK FEURY
Nectar

1091 Lancaster Ave
Berwyn, PA 19312
610.725.9000
tastenectar.com

JOSE GARCES
Amada

217-219 Chestnut St
Philadelphia, PA 19106
215.625.2450
amadarestaurant.com

CLARK GILBERT
Gemelli

4161 Main St
Philadelphia, PA 19127
215.487.1230
gemellionmain.com

PETER GILMORE
West Chester, PA

AL GRAFSTROM
La Fourno Ristorante

636 South St
Philadelphia, PA 19147
215.627.9000
lafourno.com

ZACH GRAINDA
White Dog Café

3420 Sansom St
Philadelphia, PA 19104
215.386.9224
whitedog.com

CHRISTOPHER GREWAY
Morimoto

723 Chestnut St
Philadelphia, PA 19106
215.413.9070
morimotorestaurant.com

MICHELE HAINES
Spring Mill Café

164 Barren Hill Rd
Conshohocken, PA 19428
610.828.2550
springmill.com

ROBERT HALPERN
Marigold Kitchen

501 S 45th St
Philadelphia, PA 19104
215.222.3699
marigoldkitchenbyob.com

MARTIN HAMANN
1862 by Martin Hamann

140 S Broad St
Philadelphia, PA 19102
215.563.6500
unionleague.org

SAM HO
Zento

132 Chestnut St
Philadelphia, PA 19106
215.925.9998
zentocontemporary.com

TAKAO IINUMA
Mai Cuisine

2 Penn Center
Philadelphia, PA 19102
215.523.5782
maicuisine.com

SAM JACOBSON
Sycamore

14 S Lansdowne Ave
Lansdowne, PA 19050
484.461.2867
sycamorebyo.com

AUGUSTO JALON
Augusto's

530 Madison Ave
Warminster, PA 18974
215.328.0556
augustocuisine.com

DAVID KATZ
Philadelphia, PA

WILL LANGLOIS
Stone Rose

822 Fayette St
Conshohoken, PA 19428
484.532.7300
thestoneroserestaurant.com

JEFF MICHAUD
Osteria

640 N Broad St
Philadelphia, PA 19130
215.763.0920
osteriaphilly.com

CHRIS KEARSE
Will

1911 East Passyunk Ave
Philadelphia, PA 19148
215.271.7683
willbyob.com

JOSH LAWLER
The Farm and Fisherman

1120 Pine St
Philadelphia, PA 19107
267.687.1555
thefarmandfisherman.com

JOHN MIMS
Daddy Mims'

150 Bridge St
Phoenixville, PA 19460
610.935.1800
daddymims.com

YONG KIM
Bluefin

2820 Dekalb Pike
East Norriton, PA 19401
610.277.3917
restaurantbluefin.com

ADAM LAZARICK
Philadelphia, PA

SAM NOH
Rouge

205 S 18th St
Philadelphia, PA 19103
215.732.6622
rouge98.com

BLAISE LABIK
Side Bar & Restaurant

10 E Gay St
West Chester, PA 19380
610.429.8297
sidebarandrestaurant.com

CALEB LENTCHNER
Marsha Brown

15 S Main St
New Hope, PA 18938
215.862.7044
marshabrownrestaurant.com

JOSHUA NOH
Alma de Cuba

1623 Walnut St
Philadelphia, PA 19103
215.988.1799
almadecubarestaurant.com

JEAN-MARIE LACROIX
Lacroix

210 W Rittenhouse Square
Philadelphia, PA 19103
215.790.2533
lacroixrestaurant.com

WILL MATHIAS
Carversville Inn

6205 Fleecydale Rd
Carversville, PA 18913
215.297.0900
carversvilleinn.com

TERRY OWENS
Redstone Grill

512 W Germantown Pike
Plymouth Meeting, PA 19462
610.941.4400
redstonegrill.com

BENNY LAI
Vietnam Café

816 S 47th St
Philadelphia, PA 19143
215.729.0260
eatatvietnam.com

BRENDAN MCGREW
Bourbon Blue

2 Rector St
Philadelphia, PA 19127
215.508.3360
bourbonblue.com

CHRIS PAINTER
Il Pittore

2025 Sansom St
Philadelphia, PA 19103
215.391.4900
ilpittore.com

GEORGES PERRIER
Philadelphia, PA

MARK PLESCHA
Charcoal

11 S Delaware Ave
Yardley, PA 19067
215.493.6394
charcoalbyob.com

ERIC PLESCHA
Charcoal

11 S Delaware Ave
Yardley, PA 19067
215.493.6394
charcoalbyob.com

JEFFREY POWER
Dettera

129 E Butler Ave
Philadelphia, PA 19002
215.643.0111
dettera.com

MITCH PRENSKY
Supper

926 South St
Philadelphia, PA 19147
215.592.8180
supperphilly.com

BEN PUCHOWITZ
Matyson

37 S 19th St
Philadelphia, PA 19103
215.564.2925
matyson.com

DAVID ROBINSON
Mile High Steak & Seafood

1102 Baltimore Pike
Glen Mills, PA 19342
610.361.0855
milehighss.com

CHIP ROMAN
Blackfish

119 Fayette St
Conshohocken, PA 19428
610.397.0888
blackfishrestaurant.com

DOUG RUNYEN
Fayette Street Grille

308 Fayette St
Conshohocken, PA 19428
610.567.0366
fayettestreetgrille.com

GEORGE SABATINO
Stateside

1536 E Passyunk Ave
Philadelphia, PA 19147
215.551.2500
statesidephilly.com

SYLVA SENAT
Tashan

777 S Broad St
Philadelphia, PA 19147
267.687.2170
mytashan.com

BRYAN SIKORA
A. Kitchen

135 S 18th St
Philadelphia, PA 19103
215.825.7030
akitchenphilly.com

MICHAEL SOLOMONOV
Zahav

237 Saint James Pl
Philadelphia, PA 19106
215.625.8800
zahavrestaurant.com

BRAD SPENCE
Amis

412 S 13th St
Philadelphia, PA 19147
215.732.2647
amisphilly.com

WALTER STAIB
City Tavern

138 S 2nd St
Philadelphia, PA 19106
215.413.1443
citytavern.com

DANIEL STERN
R2L

50 S 16th St
Philadelphia, PA 19102
215.564.5337
r2lrestaurant.com

STEPHAN STRYJEWSKI
Sola

614 W Lancaster Ave
Bryn Mawr, PA 19010
610.526.0123
solabyob.com

LEE STYER
Fond

1537 S 11th St
Philadelphia, PA 19148
215.551.5000
fondphilly.com

PITTSBURGH

HIROYUKI TANAKA
Zama

128 S 19th St
Philadelphia, PA 19103
215.568.1027
zamaphilly.com

JOHN TAUS
The Corner

102 S 13th St
Philadelphia, PA 19107
215.735.7500
thephillycorner.com

VINCENT TOTARO
Trattoria Totaro

639 Spring Mill Ave
Conshohocken, PA 19428
610.828.7050
trattoriaconshy.com

MARCIE TURNEY
Barbuzzo

110 S 13th St
Philadelphia, PA 19107
215.546.9300
barbuzzo.com

EVAN TURNEY
Varga Bar

941 Spruce St
Philadelphia, PA 19107
215.627.5200
vargabar.com

GIOVANNI VARALLO
Ristorante Pesto

1915 S Broad St
Philadelphia, PA 19148
215.336.8380
ristorantepesto.com

MARC VETRI
Vetri

1312 Spruce St
Philadelphia, PA 19107
215.732.3478
vetrifamily.com

NATHAN VOLZ
10 Arts Bistro & Lounge

10 Avenue of the Arts
Philadelphia, PA 19102
215.523.8273
10arts.com

JOSEPH WALTERS
Seven Stars Inn

300 Ridge Rd
Phoenixville, PA 19460
610.495.5205
sevenstarsinn.com

DAVE WALTI
Harvest Seasonal Grill and Wine Bar

549 Wilmington West Chester Pike
Glen Mills, PA 19342
610.358.1005
harvestseasonalgrill.com

JOHN WOLFERTH
Aperto

232 Woodbine Ave
Narberth, PA 19072
610.660.0160
apertobyob.com

ANDREW WOOD
Russet

1521 Spruce St
Philadelphia, PA 19102
215.546.1521
russetphilly.com

GREG ALAUZEN
Cioppino

2350 Railroad St
Pittsburgh, PA 15222
412.281.6593
cioppinoofpittsburgh.com

JAMILKA BORGES
Legume Bistro

214 N Craig St
Pittsburgh, PA 15213
412.621.2700
legumebistro.com

DONATO COLUCCIO
Donato's

46 Fox Chapel Rd
Pittsburgh, PA 15238
412.781.3700
donatosrestaurant.com

KEITH COUGHENOUR
Duquesne Club

325 6th Ave
Pittsburgh, PA 15222
412.391.1500
duquesne.org

RICHARD DESHANTZ
Meat & Potatoes

649 Penn Ave
Pittsburgh, PA 15222
412.325.7007
meatandpotatoespgh.com

DOUGLASS DICK
Pittsburgh, PA

KEITH FULLER
Root 174

1113 S Braddock Ave
Pittsburgh, PA 15218
412.243.4348
root174.com

TREVETT HOOPER
Legume Bistro

214 N Craig St
Pittsburgh, PA 15213
412.621.2700
legumebistro.com

LISA HYDE-GROSZ
The Pig and Truffle

202B Millersdale Rd
Greensburg, PA 15601
724.522.5354
pigandtruffle.com

ROGER LI
Tamari

3519 Butler St
Pittsburgh, PA 15201
412.325.3435
tamaripgh.com

BRIAN PEKARCIK
Spoon

134 S Highland Ave
Pittsburgh, PA 15206
412.362.6001
spoonpgh.com

MATTHEW PORCO
Sienna Sulla Piazza

22 Market Square
Pittsburgh, PA 15222
412.281.6363
siennapgh.com

ANTHONY PUPO
Willow

634 Camp Horne Rd
Pittsburgh, PA 15237
412.847.1007
willowpgh.com

DAVE RACICOT
314 Pasta & Prime

314 Allegheny River Blvd
Oakmont, PA 15139
412.828.7777
pastaandprime.com

JUSTIN SEVERINO
Cure

5336 Butler St
Pittsburgh, PA 15201
412.252.2595
curepittsburgh.com

KEVIN SOUSA
Salt of the Earth

5523 Penn Ave
Pittsburgh, PA 15206
412.441.7258
saltpgh.com

DEREK STEVENS
Eleven CK

1150 Smallman St
Pittsburgh, PA 15222
412.201.5656
elevenck.com

JOSEPH TAMBELLINI
Joseph Tambellini Restaurant

5701 Bryant St
Pittsburgh, PA 15206
412.665.9000
josephtambellini.com

JEREMY VOYTISH
Lidia's

1400 Smallman St
Pittsburgh, PA 15222
412.552.0150
lidias-pittsburgh.com

JASON WATTS
Kaya

2000 Smallman St
Pittsburgh, PA 15222
412.261.6565
bigburrito.com

SHOHOLA

PETER DANIEL
The Fork at Twin Lakes

814 Twin Lakes Rd
Shohola, PA 18458
570.296.8094
theforktl.com

WOMELSDORF

ERNIE RISSER
Risser's

4055 Conrad Weiser Pkwy
Womelsdorf, PA 19567
610.589.4570
rissersrestaurant.com

YORK

ANDRE EBERT
Accomac Inn

6330 River Dr
Hellam, PA 17406
717.252.1521
accomacinn.com

DARRELL TOBIN
York Blue Moon

361 W Market St
York, PA 17401
717.854.6664
bluemoonfresh.com

INGREDIENT: UNI

BRISTOL

RIZWAN AHMED
Hourglass Brasserie

382 Thames St
Bristol, RI 02809
401.396.9811
hourglassbrasserie.com

CHAMPE SPEIDEL
Persimmon

31 State St
Bristol, RI 02809
401.254.7474
persimmonbristol.com

NEWPORT

ALBERT BOUCHARD III
Restaurant Bouchard

505 Thames St
Newport, RI 02840
401.846.0123
restaurantbouchard.com

TYLER BURNLEY
Thames Street Kitchen

677 Thames St
Newport, RI 02840
401.846.9100
thamesstreetkitchen.com

JONATHAN CAMBRA
Boat House

227 Schooner Dr
Tiverton, RI 02878
401.624.6300
boathousetiverton.com

TED GIDLEY
The Clarke Cooke House

26 Bannister's Wharf
Newport, RI 02840
401.849.2900
bannistersnewport.com

KARSTEN HART
Castle Hill Inn

590 Ocean Ave
Newport, RI 02840
401.849.3800
castlehillinn.com

CHAD HOFFER
Thames Street Kitchen

677 Thames St
Newport, RI 02840
401.846.9100
thamesstreetkitchen.com

DANIEL KNERR
Black Pearl

Bannister's Wharf
Newport, RI 02840
401.846.5264
blackpearlnewport.com

BRIAN MANSFIELD
Newport Harbor Corporation

366 Thames St
Newport, RI 02840
401.848.7010
newportharbor.com

CASEY RILEY
Newport Harbor Corporation

366 Thames St
Newport, RI 02840
401.848.7010
newportharbor.com

JAKE ROJAS
Tallulah on Thames

464 Thames St
Newport, RI 02840
401.849.2433
tallulahonthames.com

LOU ROSSI
Castle Hill Inn

590 Ocean Ave
Newport, RI 02840
401.849.3800
castlehillinn.com

KEVIN THIELE
One Bellevue

1 Bellevue Ave
Newport, RI 02840
401.848.4824
hotelviking.com

PROVIDENCE

NEMO BOLIN
Cook & Brown Public House

959 Hope St
Providence, RI 02906
401.273.7275
cookandbrown.com

LUCIANO CANOVA
Trattoria Romana

3 Wake Robin Rd
Lincoln, RI 02865
401.333.6700
trattoria-romana.com

SIOBHAN MARÍA CHAVARRIA
Flan y Ajo

225 Westminster St
Providence, RI 02903
401.432.6656
flanyajo.com

NINO D'URSO
Capriccio

2 Pine St
Providence, RI 02903
401.421.1320
capriccios.com

RYAN ESCUDE
Ten Prime Steak and Sushi

55 Pine St
Providence, RI 02903
401.453.2333
tenprimesteakandsushi.com

MATTHEW GENNUSO
Chez Pascal

960 Hope St
Providence, RI 02906
401.421.4422
chez-pascal.com

GEORGE GERMON
Al Forno

577 S Main St
Providence, RI 02903
401.273.9760
alforno.com

JOHN GRANATA
Camille's

71 Bradford St
Providence, RI 02903
401.751.4812
camillesonthehill.com

DOUGLAS HIGLEY
New Rivers

7 Steeple St
Providence, RI 02903
401.751.0350
newriversrestaurant.com

MATT JENNINGS
Farmstead

186 Wayland Ave
Providence, RI 02906
401.274.7177
farmsteadinc.com

DAVE JOHNSON
Local 121

121 Washington St
Providence, RI 02903
401.274.2121
local121.com

FUMI KATO
Enn

600 George Washington Hwy
Lincoln, RI 02865
401.333.0366
ennri.com

SIMON KEATING
Circe

50 Weybosset St
Providence, RI 02903
401.437.8991
circerestaurantbar.com

TIMOTHY KELLY
Chapel Grille

Chapel View Blvd
Cranston, RI 02920
401.944.4900
chapelgrilleri.com

HARUKI KIBE
Haruki

172 Wayland Ave
Providence, RI 02906
401.223.0332
harukisushi.com

JOHANNE KILLEEN
Al Forno

577 S Main St
Providence, RI 02903
401.273.9760
alforno.com

BRIAN KINGSFORD
Bacaro

262 S Water St
Providence, RI 02903
401.751.3700
bacarorestaurant.net

PATRICK LOWNEY
Broadway Bistro

205 Broadway
Providence, RI 02903
401.331.2450
broadwaybistrori.com

CHRISTOPHER MAITLAND
15 Point Road Restaurant

15 Point Rd
Portsmouth, RI 02871
401.683.3138
15pointroad.com

JAMES MARK
North

3 Luongo Square
Providence, RI 02903
401.421.1100
foodbynorth.com

BRIAN O'DONNELL
Café Nuovo

1 Citizens Plaza
Providence, RI 02903
401.421.2525
cafenuovo.com

NICK RABAR
Avenue N

20 Newman Ave
Rumford, RI 02916
401.270.2836
avenuenamericankitchen.com

DARIUS SALKO
Tini

200 Washington St
Providence, RI 02903
401.383.2400
thetini.com

BENJAMIN SUKLE
The Dorrance

60 Dorrance St
Providence, RI 02903
401.521.6000
thedorrance.com

ANTHONY TARRO
Siena

238 Atwells Ave
Providence, RI 02903
401.521.3311
sienari.com

BRUCE TILLINGHAST
Providence, RI

MATTHEW VARGA
Gracie's

194 Washington St
Providence, RI 02903
401.272.7811
graciesprovidence.com

BEAU VESTAL
New Rivers

7 Steeple St
Providence, RI 02903
401.751.0350
newriversrestaurant.com

DEREK WAGNER
Nick's on Broadway

500 Broadway
Providence, RI 02909
401.421.0286
nicksonbroadway.com

SOUTH KINGSTOWN

KEVIN GAUDREAU
Trio

15 Kingstown Rd
Narragansett, RI 02882
401.792.4333
trio-ri.com

BRIAN HARTMAN
Manisses Restaurant

5 Spring St
Block Island, RI 02807
401.466.2421
blockislandresorts.com

PERRY RASO
Matunuck Oyster Bar

629 Succotash Rd
South Kingstown, RI 02879
401.783.4202
rhodyoysters.com

EVAN WARGO
Eli's

456 Chapel St
Block Island, RI 02807
401.466.5230
elisblockisland.com

WARWICK

JULES RAMOS
Warwick, RI

CHEF AS BUTCHER
Chefs are leaving the kitchen for the butcher shop, reviving this lost art.

AIKEN

REGAN BROWELL
The Willcox

100 Colleton Ave SW
Aiken, SC 29801
803.648.1898
thewillcox.com

LINDA ROONEY
Linda's Bistro

135 York St SE
Aiken , SC 29801
803.648.4853
lindasbistro-aiken.com

CRAIG DEIHL
Cypress

167 E Bay St
Charleston, SC 29401
843.727.0111
magnolias-blossom-cypress.com

JEREMY HOLST
Anson

12 Anson St
Charleston, SC 29401
843.577.0551
ansonrestaurant.com

JACQUES LARSON
Wild Olive

2867 Maybank Hwy
Johns Island, SC 29455
843.737.4177
wildoliverestaurant.com

MIKE LATA
FIG

232 Meeting St
Charleston, SC 29401
843.805.5900
eatatfig.com

CHARLESTON

JEREMIAH BACON
Macintosh

479B King St
Charleston, SC 29403
843.789.4299
themacintoshcharleston.com

SEAN BROCK
McCrady's & Husk

2 Unity Alley
Charleston, SC 29401
843.577.0025
mccradysrestaurant.com

BOB CARTER
Carter's Kitchen

148 Civitas St
Mt. Pleasant, SC 29464
843.284.0840
carterskitchenion.com

KEVIN JOHNSON
The Grocery

4 Cannon St
Charleston, SC 29403
843.302.8825
thegrocerycharleston.com

JOSHUA KEELER
Two Boroughs Larder

186 Coming St
Charleston, SC 29403
843.637.3722
twoboroughslarder.com

JEREMIAH LANGHORNE
McCrady's

2 Unity Alley
Charleston, SC 29401
843.577.0025
mccradysrestaurant.com

FRANK LEE
SNOB

192 E Bay St
Charleston, SC 29401
843.723.3424
mavericksouthernkitchens.com

JILL MATHIAS
Carolina's

10 Exchange St
Charleston, SC 29401
843.724.3800
carolinasrestaurant.com

FRANK MCMAHON
Hank's

10 Hayne St
Charleston, SC 29401
843.723.3474
hanksseafoodrestaurant.com

FRED NEUVILLE
Fat Hen

3140 Maybank Hwy
Johns Island, SC 29455
843.559.9090
thefathen.com

SARAH O'KELLEY
Glass Onion

1219 Savannah Hwy
Charleston, SC 29407
843.225.1717
ilovetheglassonion.com

PATRICK OWENS
Langdon's

778 S Shelmore Blvd
Mt. Pleasant, SC 29464
843.388.9200
theowensdininggroup.com

JOE PALMA
High Cotton

199 E Bay St
Charleston, SC 29401
843.724.3815
highcottoncharleston.com

NICO ROMO
Fish

442 King St
Charleston, SC 29403
843.722.3474
fishrestaurantcharleston.com

JASON STANHOPE
FIG

232 Meeting St
Charleston, SC 29401
843.805.5900
eatatfig.com

ROBERT STEHLING
Hominy Grill

207 Rutledge Ave
Charleston, SC 29403
843.937.0930
hominygrill.com

CHRIS STEWART
Glass Onion

1219 Savannah Hwy
Charleston, SC 29407
843.225.1717
ilovetheglassonion.com

NATHAN E. THURSTON
Stars

495 King St
Charleston, SC 29403
843.577.0100
starsrestaurant.com

STUART TRACY
Butcher & Bee

654 King St
Charleston, SC 29403
843.619.0202
butcherandbee.com

KEN VEDRINSKI
Trattoria Lucca

41-A Bogard St
Charleston, SC 29403
843.973.3323
luccacharleston.com

MICHELLE WEAVER
Charleston Grill

224 King St
Charleston, SC 29401
843.577.4522
charlestongrill.com

NATE WHITING
Tristan

10 Linguard St
Charleston, SC 29401
843.534.2155
tristandining.com

BOBBY YARBROUGH
Atlanticville

2063 Middle St
Sullivan's Island, SC 29482
843.883.9452
atlanticville.net

COLUMBIA

MIKE DAVIS
Terra

100 State St
West Columbia, SC 29169
803.791.3443
terrasc.com

BLYTHE KELLY
Cellar on Greene

2001 Greene St #D
Columbia, SC 29205
803.343.3303
cellarongreene.com

TIM PETERS
Motor Supply Co. Bistro

920 Gervais St
Columbia, SC 29201
803.256.6687
motorsupplycobistro.com

ALEX SUAUDOM DU MONDE
Baan Sawan Thai Bistro

2135 Devine St
Columbia, SC 29205
803.252.8992
baansawan.blogspot.com

FULVIO VALSECCHI
Ristorante Divino

803 Gervais St
Columbia, SC 29201
803.799.4550
ristorantedivino.com

GREENVILLE

JOE CLARKE
American Grocery Restaurant

732 S Main St
Greenville, SC 29601
864.232.7665
americangr.com

JOHN MALIK
Greenville, SC

chefjohnmalik.com

AARON MANTER
The Owl

728 Wade Hampton Blvd
Greenville, SC 29609
864.252.7015
facebook.com/OwlRestaurant

VICTORIA MOORE
The Lazy Goat

170 River Pl
Greenville, SC 29601
864.679.5299
thelazygoat.com

JOEY PEARSON
Nose Dive

116 S Main St
Greenville, SC 29601
864.373.7300
thenosedive.com

JASON SCHOLZ
Stella's Southern Bistro

684 Fairview Rd
Simpsonville, SC 29680
864.757.1212
stellasbistro.com

SPENCER THOMSON
Devereaux's

25 E Court St #100
Greenville, SC 29601
864.241.3030
devereauxsdining.com

HUY TRAN
Mekong

2013 Wade Hampton Blvd
Greenville, SC 29615
864.244.1314
mekongrestaurantsc.com

HILTON HEAD

RON ANDREWS
Brays Island Plantation

115 Brays Island Dr
Sheldon, SC 29941
843.846.3146
braysisland.org

YURI GOW
CQ's Restaurant

140 Lighthouse Rd
Hilton Head, SC 29928
843.671.2779
cqsrestaurant.com

ROBERT IRVINE
Robert Irvine's Eat

1000 William Hilton Pkwy #B6
Hilton Head Island, SC 29928
843.785.4850
eathhi.com

CHRISTOPHER JOHNSON
Michael Anthony's

37 New Orleans Rd #L
Hilton Head Island, SC 29928
843.785.6272
michael-anthonys.com

MATT JORDING
Sage Room Restaurant

81 Pope Ave #13
Hilton Head Island, SC 29928
843.785.5352
thesageroom.com

TONY POPE
Chechessee Creek Club

18 Chechessee Creek Dr
Okatie, SC 29909
843.987.7000
chechesseecreekclub.com

CLAYTON ROLLISON
WiseGuys

1513 Main St
Hilton Head Island, SC 29928
843.842.8866
wiseguyshhi.com

JOHN SOULIA
Hampton Hall Country Club

170 Hampton Hall Blvd
Bluffton, SC 29910
843.815.8730
hamptonhallclubsc.com

ROBERT WYSONG
Colleton River Plantation Club

60 Colleton River Dr
Bluffton, SC 29910
843.836.4400
colletonriverclub.com

SC

MYRTLE BEACH

BRAD DANIELS
Croissants Bistro & Bakery

3751 Robert N Grissom Pkwy
Myrtle Beach, SC 29577
843.448.2253
croissants.net

ANDREW GARDO
Sea Captain's House

3002 N Ocean Blvd
Myrtle Beach, SC 29577
843.448.8082
seacaptains.com

CURRY MARTIN
Aspen Grille

5101 N Kings Hwy
Myrtle Beach, SC 29577
843.449.9191
aspen-grille.com

PAWLEYS ISLAND

PIERCE CULLITON
Frank's Restaurant & Bar

10434 Ocean Hwy
Pawleys Island, SC 29585
843.237.3030
franksandoutback.com

CUSTER

NANCY GELLERMAN
Sage Creek Grille

611 Mount Rushmore Rd
Custer, SD 57730
605.673.2424
facebook.com/SageCreekGrille

RAPID CITY

M.J. ADAMS
The Corn Exchange

727 Main St
Rapid City, SD 57701
605.343.5070
cornexchange.com

PETER FRANKLIN
Delmonico Grill

609 W Main St
Rapid City, SD 57701
605.791.1664
delmonicogrill.biz

PAUL HERRINGER
Dakotah Steakhouse

1325 N Elk Vale Rd
Rapid City, SD 57703
605.791.1800
dakotahsteakhouse.com

BENJAMIN KLINKEL
Tally's Silver Spoon

530 6th St
Rapid City, SD 57701
605.342.7621
tallyssilverspoon.com

BEN PRUETT
Enigma Restaurant

445 Mount Rushmore Rd
Rapid City, SD 57701
605.716.0600
enigmarestaurant.com

SIOUX FALLS

CHAD HOWARD
Minerva's

301 S Phillips Ave
Sioux Falls, SD 57104
605.334.0386
minervas.net

KRISTINA KUEHN
K Restaurant

401 E 8th St
Sioux Falls, SD 57103
605.336.3315
k-restaurant.com

HAI LAM
Lam's Vietnamese Restaurant

1600 E Rice St
Sioux Falls, SD 57103
605.274.9898
lams-restaurant.com

NATHAN URINKO
Grille 26

1716 S Western Ave
Sioux Falls, SD 57105
605.444.1716
grille26.com

CARTER WEILAND
Parker's Bistro

210 S Main Ave
Sioux Falls, SD 57104
605.275.7676
parkersbistro.net

INGREDIENT: HONEY

 TENNESSEE

BRISTOL

CHRIS WALSH
The Troutdale Dining Room

412 6th St
Bristol, TN 37620
423.968.9099
thetroutdale.com

CHATTANOOGA

REBECCA BARON
St. John's Restaurant

1278 Market St
Chattanooga, TN 37403
423.266.4400
stjohnsrestaurant.com

ALEX CANALE
Chato Brasserie

200 Manufacturers Rd #101
Chattanooga, TN 37405
423.305.1352
chatodining.com

CHRIS CASTEEL
Chato Brasserie

200 Manufacturers Rd #101
Chattanooga, TN 37405
423.305.1352
chatodining.com

BICK JOHNSON
Bald Headed Bistro

201 Keith St SW
Cleveland, TN 37311
423.472.6000
baldheadedbistro.com

DANIEL LINDLEY
Alleia Restaurant

25 E Main St
Chattanooga, TN 37408
423.305.6990
alleiarestaurant.com

MATT MARCUS
Hennen's

193 Chestnut St
Chattanooga, TN 37402
423.634.5160
hennens.net

ERIK NIEL
Easy Bistro

203 Broad St
Chattanooga, TN 37402
423.266.1121
easybistro.com

EFREN ORMAZA
Terra Nostra Tapas & Wine Bar

105 Frazier Ave
Chattanooga, TN 37405
423.634.0238
terranostratapas.com

KNOXVILLE

CEDRIC COANT
Le Parigo

416 Clinch Ave W
Knoxville, TN 37902
865.525.9214
leparigo.net

JEFFREY DEALEJANDRO
The Crown & Goose

123 S Central St
Knoxville, TN 37902
865.524.2100
thecrownandgoose.com

JONATHAN GATLIN
Chez Liberty

5200 Kingston Pike
Knoxville, TN 37919
865.330.9862
chezliberty.com

HOLLY HAMBRIGHT
Holly's Eventful Dining

5032 Whittaker Dr #3
Knoxville, TN 37919
865.300.8071
hollyseventfuldining.com

JEEK KIM
Nama Sushi Bar

506 S Gay St
Knoxville, TN 37902
865.633.8539
namasushibar.com

JOSEPH LENN
The Barn Restaurant
at Blackberry Farm

1471 W Millers Cove Rd
Walland, TN 37886
865.380.2270
blackberryfarm.com

287

TN

MEMPHIS

DERON LITTLE
Seasons Café

12740 Kingston Pike
Knoxville, TN 37934
865.671.3679
seasons-cafe.com

KEITH BAMBRICK
McEwen's on Monroe

120 Monroe Ave
Memphis, TN 38103
901.527.7085
mcewensmemphis.com

JIMMY ISHII
Sekisui

25 S Belvedere Blvd
Memphis, TN 38104
901.725.0005
sekisuiusa.com

AMBER LLOYD
The Orangery

5412 Kingston Pike
Knoxville, TN 37919
865.588.2964
orangeryknoxville.com

KAREN CARRIER
The Beauty Shop Restaurant

966 S Cooper St
Memphis, TN 38104
901.272.7111
thebeautyshoprestaurant.com

ERLING JENSEN
Erling Jensen Restaurant

1044 S Yates Rd
Memphis, TN 38119
901.763.3700
ejensen.com

CHESTER MILLER
Bistro by the Tracks

215 Brookview Centre Way #109
Knoxville, TN 37919
865.558.9500
bistrobythetracks.com

MAC EDWARDS
The Elegant Farmer

262 S Highland St
Memphis, TN 38111
901.324.2221
theelegantfarmerrestaurant.com

WALLY JOE
ACRE Restaurant

690 S Perkins Rd
Memphis, TN 38117
901.818.2273
acrememphis.com

SHANE ROBERTSON
Northshore Brasserie

9430 S Northshore Dr
Knoxville, TN 37922
865.539.5188
northshorebrasserie.com

KELLY ENGLISH
Restaurant Iris

2146 Monroe Ave
Memphis, TN 38104
901.590.2828
restaurantiris.com

CULLEN KENT
Café Society

212 N Evergreen St
Memphis, TN 38112
901.722.2177
cafesocietymemphis.com

TERRY SAUNDERS
Ruth's Chris

950 Volunteer Landing Ln
Knoxville, TN 37915
865.546.4696
ruthschris.com

JOSÉ GUTIERREZ
River Oaks Restaurant

5871 Poplar Ave
Memphis, TN 38119
901.683.9305
riveroaksrestaurant.com

JACKSON KRAMER
Interim

5040 Sanderlin Ave
Memphis, TN 38117
901.818.0821
interimrestaurant.com

BART VAUGHAN
Foothills Milling Company

315 S Washington St
Maryville, TN 37804
865.977.8434
foothillsmillingcompany.com

MICHAEL HUDMAN
Andrew Michael Italian Kitchen

712 W Brookhaven Cir
Memphis, TN 38117
901.347.3569
andrewmichaelitaliankitchen.com

JODY MOYT
Owen Brennan's

6150 Poplar Ave
Memphis, TN 38119
901.761.0990
brennansmemphis.com

HOA NGUYEN
Saigon Le

51 N Cleveland St
Memphis, TN 38104
901.276.5326
saigon-le.com

CONNOR O'NEILL
eighty3

83 Madison Ave
Memphis, TN 38103
901.333.1224
eighty3memphis.com

MICHAEL PATRICK
Rizzo's Diner

106 E G.E. Patterson Ave
Memphis, TN 38103
901.523.2033
rizzosdiner.org

BEN SMITH
Tsunami

928 S Cooper St
Memphis, TN 38104
901.274.2556
tsunamimemphis.com

RYAN SPRUHAN
Chez Philippe

149 Union Ave
Memphis, TN 38103
901.529.4188
peabodymemphis.com

ANDREW TICER
Andrew Michael Italian Kitchen

712 W Brookhaven Cir
Memphis, TN 38117
901.347.3569
andrewmichaelitaliankitchen.com

RYAN TRIMM
Sweet Grass

937 S Cooper St
Memphis, TN 38104
901.278.0278
sweetgrassmemphis.com

FELICIA SUZANNE WILLETT
Felicia Suzanne

80 Monroe Ave #L1
Memphis, TN 38103
901.523.0877
feliciasuzanne.com

NASHVILLE

ERIK ANDERSON
The Catbird Seat

1711 Division St
Nashville, TN 37203
615.810.8200
thecatbirdseatrestaurant.com

JEREMY BARLOW
Sloco

2905 12th Ave S #104
Nashville, TN 37212
615.499.4793
slocolocal.com

TYLER BROWN
Capitol Grille

231 6th Ave N
Nashville, TN 37219
615.345.7116
capitolgrillenashville.com

YUN CHOO
Samurai Sushi

2209 Elliston Pl
Nashville, TN 37203
615.320.5438

JOSH HABIGER
The Catbird Seat

1711 Division St
Nashville, TN 37203
615.810.8200
thecatbirdseatrestaurant.com

PHILIP KRAJECK
Rolf and Daughters

700 Taylor St
Nashville, TN 37208
615.866.9897
rolfanddaughters.com

MATTHEW LACKEY
Flyte

718 Division St
Nashville, TN 37203
615.255.6200
flytenashville.com

DAVID MAXWELL
Miel Restaurant

343 53rd Ave N
Nashville, TN 37209
615.298.3663
mielrestaurant.com

JASON MCCONNELL
Red Pony Restaurant

408 Main St
Franklin, TN 37064
615.595.7669
RedPonyRestaurant.com

MARGOT MCCORMACK
Margot Café

1017 Woodland St
Nashville, TN 37206
615.227.4668
margotcafe.com

DEB PAQUETTE
Etch

303 Demonbreun St
Nashville, TN 37201
615.522.0685
etchrestaurant.com

EDGAR PENDLEY
Urban Grub

2506 12th Ave S
Nashville, TN 37204
615.679.9342
urbangrub.net

CHARLES PHILLIPS
1808 Grille

1808 W End Ave
Nashville, TN 37203
615.340.0012
1808grille.com

KEVIN RAMQUIST
F. Scott's Restaurant
and Jazz Bar

2210 Crestmoor Rd
Nashville, TN 37215
615.269.5861
fscotts.com

WILL UHLHORN
Table 3

3821 Green Hills Village Dr
Nashville, TN 37215
615.739.6900
table3nashville.com

BOB WAGGONER
Watermark

507 12th Ave S
Nashville, TN 37203
615.254.2000
watermark-restaurant.com

JAMIE WATSON
Café Fundamental

1115 Porter Rd
Nashville, TN 37206
615.915.0738
cafefundamental.com

TANDY WILSON
CITY HOUSE

1222 4th Ave N
Nashville, TN 37208
615.736.5838
cityhousenashville.com

AMARILLO

BRIAN MASON
BL Bistro

2203 S Austin St
Amarillo, TX 79109
806.355.7838
blbistro.com

WILL OWENS
Macaroni Joe's

1619 S Kentucky St
Amarillo, TX 79102
806.358.8990
macaronijoes.com

ARLINGTON

HANS BERGMANN
Cacharel

2221 E Lamar Blvd
Arlington, TX 76006
817.640.9981
cacharel.net

JOHN KLEIN
Sanford House

506 N Center St
Arlington, TX 76011
817.861.2129
thesanfordhouse.com

AUSTIN

KAYO ASAZU
Kome

4917 Airport Blvd
Austin, TX 78751
512.712.5700
kome-austin.com

TAKÉ ASAZU
Kome

4917 Airport Blvd
Austin, TX 78751
512.712.5700
kome-austin.com

JOHN BATES
Noble Pig

11815 620 N #4
Austin, TX 78750
512.382.6248
noblepigaustin.com

DAVID BULL
Congress

200 Congress Ave
Austin, TX 78701
512.827.2760
congressaustin.com

KELLY CASEY
Hudson's on the Bend

3509 Ranch Rd 620 N
Austin, TX 78734
512.266.1369
hudsonsonthebend.com

JAMIE CHOZET
The Mansion at Judges Hill

1900 Rio Grande
Austin, TX 78705
512.495.1800
mansionatjudgeshill.com

MITCHELL CIOHON
Chef Mitch

Austin, TX
262.443.0333
chef-mitch.com

SHAWN CIRKIEL
Olive & June

3411 Glenview Ave
Austin, TX 78703
512.467.9898
oliveandjune-austin.com

MAT CLOUSER
Swift's Attic

315 Congress Ave
Austin, TX 78701
512.482.8200
swiftsattic.com

TYSON COLE
Uchiko

4200 N Lamar Blvd
Austin, TX 78756
512.916.4808
uchiaustin.com

ANDREW CURREN
Easy Tiger

709 E 6th St
Austin, TX 78701
512.614.4972
easytigeraustin.com

MIKE DIAZ
Elizabeth Street Café

1501 S 1st St
Austin, TX 78704
512.291.2881
elizabethstreetcafe.com

JASON DONOHO
Alamo Drafthouse

320 E 6th St
Austin, TX 78701
512.476.1320
drafthouse.com

TODD DUPLECHAN
Lenoir

1807 S 1st St
Austin, TX 78704
512.215.9778
lenoirrestaurant.com

NED ELLIOT
Foreign and Domestic

306 E 53rd St
Austin, TX 78751
512.459.1010
fndaustin.com

AARON FRANKLIN
Franklin Barbecue

900 E 11th St
Austin, TX 78702
512.653.1187
franklinbarbecue.com

BRANDON FULLER
Café Josie

1200-B W 6th St
Austin, TX 78703
512.322.9226
cafejosie.com

TAKEHIKO FUSE
Musashino

3407 Greystone Dr
Austin, TX 78731
512.795.8593
musashinosushi.com

JOSEPH GALINDO
Wink Restaurant & Wine Bar

1014 N Lamar Blvd
Austin, TX 78703
512.482.8868
winkrestaurant.com

MARCOS GALVAN
Inn Above Onion Creek

4444 W F.M. 150
Kyle, TX 78640
512.268.1617
innaboveonioncreek.com

JONATHAN GELMAN
The Driskill

604 Brazos St
Austin, TX 78701
512.474.5911
driskillhotel.com

BRYCE GILMORE
Barley Swine

2024 S Lamar Blvd
Austin, TX 78704
512.394.8150
barleyswine.com

JACK GILMORE
Jack Allen's Kitchen

7720 Texas 71
Austin, TX 78735
512.852.8558
jackallenskitchen.com

JESSE GRIFFITHS
Dai Due Supper Club

Austin, TX
512.524.0688
daidueaustin.net

JAMIE GUTIERREZ
III Forks

111 Lavaca St
Austin, TX 78701
512.474.1776
3forks.com

HARVEY HARRIS
Siena Ristorante Toscano

6203 N Capital of Texas Hwy
Austin, TX 78731
512.349.7667
sienaaustin.com

JAMES HOLMES
Olivia

2043 S Lamar Blvd
Austin, TX 78704
512.804.2700
olivia-austin.com

JEFFREY HUNDELT
Mizu

3001 Ranch Rd 620 S
Austin, TX 78738
512.263.2801
mizuaustin.com

BEN HUSELTON
Paggi House

200 Lee Barton Dr
Austin, TX 78704
512.473.3700
paggihouse.com

FRANK JOHNSON
Roaring Fork

10850 Stonelake Blvd
Austin, TX 78759
512.342.2700
roaringfork.com

ALAN LAZARUS
Vespaio Ristorante

1610 S Congress Ave
Austin, TX 78704
512.441.6100
austinvespaio.com

JOHN LICHTENBERGER
Duchman Family Winery

13308 FM 150 W
Driftwood, TX 78619
512.858.1470
duchmanwinery.com

MARGARITO MACHADO
Carmelo's Restaurant

504 E 5th St
Austin, TX 78701
512.477.7497
carmelosrestaurant.com

HAROLD MARMULSTEIN
Salty Sow

1917 Manor Rd
Austin, TX 78722
512.391.2337
saltysow.com

WOLFGANG MURBER
Fabi and Rosi

509 Hearn St
Austin, TX 78703
512.236.0642
fabiandrosi.com

ZACK NORTHCUTT
Swift's Attic

315 Congress Ave
Austin, TX 78701
512.482.8200
swiftsattic.com

HEATHER OLDSTEIN
Bartlett's

2408 W Anderson Ln
Austin, TX 78757
512.451.7333
bartlettsaustin.com

RENE ORTIZ
La Condesa

400 W 2nd St
Austin, TX 78701
512.499.0300
lacondesa.com

MARK PAUL
Wink Restaurant & Wine Bar

1014 N Lamar Blvd
Austin, TX 78703
512.482.8868
winkrestaurant.com

ELMAR PRAMBS
Trio at Four Seasons

98 San Jacinto Blvd
Austin, TX 78701
512.685.8300
triorestaurantaustin.com

JOE PRIOR
Truluck's

400 Colorado St
Austin, TX 78701
512.482.9000
trulucks.com

DUSTIN PUSTKA
Jasper's

11506 Century Oaks Terrace
Austin, TX 78758
512.834.4111
kentrathbun.com

PAUL QUI
East Side King

1700 E 6th St
Austin, TX 78702
512.422.5884
eskaustin.com

STEVE RIAD
Tomodachi

4101 W Parmer Ln
Austin, TX 78727
512.821.9472
tomosushiaustin.com

RUBEN ROBLEDO
Perry's Steakhouse & Grille

114 W 7th St
Austin, TX 78701
512.474.6300
perryssteakhouse.com

RYAN SAMSON
Enoteca Vespaio

1610 S Congress Ave
Austin, TX 78704
512.441.7672
austinvespaio.com

PHILIP SPEER
Uchi + Uchiko

801 S Lamar Blvd
Austin, TX 78704
512.916.4808
uchiaustin.com

MATT UEMURA
North Modern Italian
11506 Century Oaks Terrace #124
Austin, TX 78758
512.339.4400
foxrc.com

ERICA WAKSMUNSKI
Congress
200 Congress Ave
Austin, TX 78701
512.827.2760
congressaustin.com

JOSH WATKINS
The Carillon
1900 University Ave
Austin, TX 78705
512.404.3655
thecarillonrestaurant.com

JACOB WEAVER
Haddington's
601 W 6th St
Austin, TX 78701
512.992.0204
haddingtonsrestaurant.com

ANDREW WISEHEART
Contigo
2027 Anchor Ln
Austin, TX 78723
512.614.2260
contigotexas.com

BAY CITY

SHAWN WATKINS
Fat Grass
1717 7th St
Bay City, TX 77414
979.244.7277
thefatgrass.com

BROWNSVILLE

SANDRA QUEZADA
Tunnel Bistro
2200 Boca Chica Blvd
Brownsville, TX 78521
956.550.8811

CARROLLTON

RICHARD CHAMBERLAIN
Chamberlain's Steakhouse
5330 Belt Line Rd
Addison, TX 75254
972.934.2467
chamberlainssteakhouse.com

KEITH HICKS
Buttons
15207 Addison Rd
Addison, TX 75001
972.503.2888
buttonsrestaurant.com

COLLEGE STATION

WADE BARKMAN
The Republic Steakhouse
701 University Dr E
College Station, TX 77840
979.260.4120
therepublic1836.com

CHRISTOPHER LAMPO
Christopher's World Grille
5001 Boonville Rd
Bryan, TX 77802
979.776.2181
christophersworldgrille.com

CORPUS CHRISTI

PENNEE CHANYAMAN
Thai Spice
523 N Water St
Corpus Christi, TX 78401
361.883.8884

KAREY JOHNSON
Glow
1815 Broadway St
Rockport, TX 78382
361.727.2644
glowrockport.com

LEZLIE KEEBLER
La Barataria
3500 Island Moorings Pkwy
Port Aransas, TX 78373
361.749.2212
labaratariarestaurantwinebar.com

TONY LAM
Vietnam
701 N Water St
Corpus Christi, TX 78401
361.853.2682
vietnam-restaurant.com

TIANA WORSHAM
Café Phoenix
229 Beach Ave
Port Aransas, TX 78373
361.749.9277

DALLAS

BRAD ALBERS
Eddie V's
4023 Oak Lawn Ave
Dallas, TX 75219
214.890.1500
eddiev.com

CARLO ALLESINA
La Fiorentina
4501 Cole Ave
Dallas, TX 75205
972.528.6170
lafiorentinadallas.com

NICK BADOVINUS
The Tried and True

2405 N Henderson Ave
Dallas, TX 75206
214.827.2405
neighborhoodservicesdallas.com

KLAUS BAUMBACH
Dallas, TX

JASON BIANCO
Palm

701 Ross Ave
Dallas, TX 75202
214.698.0470
thepalm.com

RICHARD BLANKENSHIP
Nick and Sam's Grill - Park Cities

8111 Preston Rd #150
Dallas, TX 75225
214.379.1111
nsgrillpc.com

SCOTT BLANKINSHIP
Triniti

1601 Elm St
Dallas, TX 75201
214.220.0403
clubcorp.com

CHERIF BRAHAMI
Rise No. 1

5360 W Lovers Ln #220
Dallas, TX 75209
214.366.9900
risesouffle.com

TIM BYRES
Smoke

901 Fort Worth Ave
Dallas, TX 75208
214.393.4141
smokerestaurant.com

JEAN-MARIE CADOT
Cadot

18111 Preston Rd #120
Dallas, TX 75252
972.267.5700
cadotrestaurant.com

MIGUEL CAUICH
Al Biernat's

4217 Oak Lawn Ave
Dallas, TX 75219
214.219.2201
albiernats.com

BRUNO DAVAILLON
Rosewood Mansion
on Turtle Creek

2821 Turtle Creek Blvd
Dallas, TX 75219
214.559.2100
rosewoodhotels.com

TIFFANY DERRY
Private Social

3232 McKinney Ave
Dallas, TX 75204
214.754.4744
privatesocial.com

GRAHAM DODDS
Central 214

5680 N Central Expy
Dallas, TX 75206
214.443.9339
central214.com

DEAN FEARING
Fearing's Restaurant

2121 McKinney Ave
Dallas, TX 75201
214.922.4848
fearingsrestaurant.com

OMAR FLORES
Driftwood

642 W Davis St
Dallas, TX 75208
214.942.2530
driftwood-dallas.com

GILBERT GARZA
Suze

4345 W NW Hwy
Dallas, TX 75220
214.350.6135
suzedallas.com

SCOTT GOTTLICH
Bijoux

5450 W Lovers Ln #225
Dallas, TX 75209
214.350.6100
bijouxrestaurant.com

NORMAN GRIMM
Acme F and B

4900 McKinney Ave
Dallas, TX 75205
214.443.0003
acmefandb.com

SHARON HAGE
Bowl and Barrel

8084 Park Ln #145
Dallas, TX 75231
214.363.2695
bowlandbarrel.com

BRENT HAMMER
Hibiscus

2927 N Henderson Ave
Dallas, TX 75206
214.827.2927
hibiscusdallas.com

JEFF HARRIS
Bolsa

614 W Davis St
Dallas, TX 75208
214.942.0451
bolsadallas.com

JEFFERY HOBBS
The Porch Restaurant

2912 N Henderson Ave
Dallas, TX 75206
214.828.2916
theporchrestaurant.com

DAVID HOLBEN
Del Frisco's

5251 Spring Valley Rd
Dallas, TX 75254
972.490.9000
delfriscos.com

CHAD HOUSER
Parigi

3311 Oak Lawn Ave #102
Dallas, TX 75219
214.521.0295
parigidallas.com

AKILA INOUYE
Tei-An

1722 Routh St #110
Dallas, TX 75201
214.220.2828
tei-an.com

JAMES JOHNSON
Pappas Bros. Steakhouse

10477 Lombardy Ln
Dallas, TX 75220
214.366.2000
pappasbros.com

LUKE KELLER
Dream Café

2800 Routh St #170
Dallas, TX 75201
214.954.0486
thedreamcafe.com

BRIAN LUSCHER
The Grape

2808 Greenville Ave
Dallas, TX 75206
214.828.1981
thegraperestaurant.com

JASON MADDY
Oak

1628 Oak Lawn Ave #110
Dallas, TX 75207
214.712.9700
oakdallas.com

MATT MCCALLISTER
FT33

1617 Hi Line Dr
Dallas, TX 75207
214.741.2629
ft33dallas.com

KATIE NATALE
Le Cordon Bleu

11830 Webb Chapel Rd #1200
Dallas, TX 75234
214.647.8580
chefs.edu/Dallas

ANDRÉ NATERA
Village Marquee Texas Grill & Bar

33 Highland Park Village
Dallas, TX 75205
214.522.6035
marqueegrill.com

PEDRO ORTIZ
Perry's Steakhouse

2000 McKinney Ave
Dallas, TX 75201
214.855.5151
perryssteakhouse.com

MASAYUKI OTAKA
Teppo

2014 Greenville Ave
Dallas, TX 75206
214.826.8989
teppo.com

ELMER PINEDA
Mi Piaci

14854 Montfort Dr
Dallas, TX 75254
972.934.8424
mipiaci-dallas.com

STEPHAN PYLES
Stephan Pyles

1807 Ross Ave #200
Dallas, TX 75201
214.580.7000
stephanpyles.com

MATT RASO
Nobu Dallas

400 Crescent Ct
Dallas, TX 75201
214.252.7000
noburestaurants.com

KENT RATHBUN
Abacus

4511 McKinney Ave
Dallas, TX 75205
214.559.3111
kentrathbun.com

PATTON ROBERTSON
Five Sixty by Wolfgang Puck

300 Reunion Blvd E
Dallas, TX 75207
214.741.5560
wolfgangpuck.com

KATSUTOSHI SAKAMOTO
Tei Tei Robata Bar

2906 N Henderson Ave
Dallas, TX 75206
214.828.2400
teiteirobata.com

TEIICHI SAKURAI
Tei-An

1722 Routh St #110
Dallas, TX 75201
214.220.2828
tei-an.com

ABRAHAM SALUM
Komali

4152 Cole Ave
Dallas, TX 75204
214.252.0200
komalirestaurant.com

AVNER SAMUEL
Nosh Euro Bistro

4216 Oak Lawn Ave
Dallas, TX 75219
214.528.9400
nosheurobistro.com

MARCOS SEGOVIA
The French Room

1321 Commerce St
Dallas, TX 75202
214.742.8200
hoteladolphus.com

JIM SEVERSON
Sevy's Grill

8201 Preston Rd
Dallas, TX 75225
214.265.7389
sevys.com

MICHAEL SINDONI
Charlie Palmer at the Joule

1530 Main St
Dallas, TX 75201
214.261.4600
charliepalmer.com

ALBERTO SOLIS
Maguire's

17552 Dallas Pkwy
Dallas, TX 75287
972.818.0068
maguiresdallas.com

WILLIAM TREVINO
Café Pacific

24 Highland Park Village
Dallas, TX 75205
214.526.1170
cafepacificdallas.com

DAVID UYGUR
Lucia

408 W 8th St
Dallas, TX 75208
214.948.4998
luciadallas.com

CHRIS WARD
The Mercury

11909 Preston Rd
Dallas, TX 75230
972.960.7774
themercurydallas.com

TRE WILCOX
Marquee Grill and Bar

33 Highland Park Village
Dallas, TX 75205
214.522.6035
marqueegrill.com

YUTAKA YAMATO
Yutaka

2633 McKinney Ave #140
Dallas, TX 75204
214.969.5533
yutakasushibistro.com

DENTON

SHEENA CROFT
Hannah's off The Square

111 W Mulberry St
Denton, TX 76201
940.566.1110
hannahsoffthesquare.com

KEIICHI NAGANO
Keiichi

500 N Elm St
Denton, TX 76201
940.230.3410

EL PASO

ROBERTO ESPINOZA
Pot Au Feu

307 E Franklin Ave
El Paso, TX 79901
915.503.8158
potaufeuelpaso.com

MARK HEINS
Crust

5860 N Mesa St #133
El Paso, TX 79912
915.833.6900
gotocrust.com

JASON HUNT
Red Mountain Bistro

631 N Resler Dr
El Paso, TX 79912
915.585.6940
redmountainbistro.com

ADAM LAMPINSTEIN
Ripe Eatery

910 E Redd Rd
El Paso, TX 79912
915.584.7473
ripeeatery.com

JUAN SOLORZANO
501 Bar and Bistro

501 Texas Ave #16
El Paso, TX 79901
915.351.6023
501bistro.com

SIMON TREVINO
Reata

1770 Airway Blvd
El Paso, TX 79925
915.772.3333
reata.net

FORT WORTH

JON BONNELL
BONNELL's, Fine Texas Cuisine

4259 Bryant Irvin Rd
Fort Worth, TX 76109
817.738.5489
bonnellstexas.com

ANTHONY FELLI
Del Frisco's

812 Main St
Fort Worth, TX 76102
817.877.3999
delfriscos.com

DWAYNE GALE
Eddie V's

3100 W 7th St
Fort Worth, TX 76107
817.336.8000
eddiev.com

CHRIS HIGHT
Aventino's

3206 Winthrop Ave
Fort Worth, TX 76107
817.570.7940
aventinos.com

MARK HITIRI
Billy Bob's

2520 Rodeo Plaza
Fort Worth, TX 76164
817.624.7117
billybobstexas.com

ERIC HUNTER
Fire Oak Grill

114 Austin Ave
Weatherford, TX 76086
817.598.0400
fireoakgrill.com

JERRETT JOSLIN
Wild Mushroom

1917 Martin Dr
Weatherford, TX 76086
817.599.4935
thewildmushroomrestaurant.com

LANNY LANCARTE
Lanny's Alta Cocina Mexicana

3405 W 7th St
Fort Worth, TX 76107
817.850.9996
lannyskitchen.com

TIM LOVE
Lonesome Dove

2406 N Main St
Fort Worth, TX 76164
817.740.8810
lonesomedovebistro.com

MOLLY MCCOOK
Ellerbe Fine Foods

1501 W Magnolia Ave
Fort Worth, TX 76104
817.926.3663
ellerbefinefoods.com

DENA PETERSON
Café Modern

3200 Darnell St
Fort Worth, TX 76107
817.840.2157
thecafemodern.com

JUAN RODRIGUEZ
Reata

310 Houston St
Fort Worth, TX 76102
817.336.1009
reata.net

JORGE ROMERO
Michael's

3413 W 7th St
Fort Worth, TX 76107
817.877.3413
michaelscuisine.com

BLAINE STANIFORD
Grace

777 Main St
Fort Worth, TX 76102
817.877.3388
gracefortworth.com

BOB STEPHENSON
FnG Eats

201 Town Center Ln #1101
Keller, TX 76248
817.741.5200
fngeats.com

DANIEL TARASEVICH
Tillman's Roadhouse

2933 Crockett St
Fort Worth, TX 76107
817.850.9255
tillmansroadhouse.com

CHARLES YOUTS
Classic Café

504 N Oak St
Roanoke, TX 76262
817.430.8185
theclassiccafe.com

FREDERICKSBURG

ROSS BURTWELL
Cabernet Grill

2805 S State Hwy 16
Fredericksburg, TX 78624
830.990.5734
cottoninvillage.com

MATTHEW CAVIN
Doss Country Store

14934 Ranch Rd 783 N
Doss, TX 78618
830.669.2160
dosscountrystore.com

BRENDA NICHOLAS
Hill Top Café

10661 U.S. 87
Fredericksburg, TX 78624
830.997.8922
hilltopcafe.com

JOSH RAYMER
Navajo Grill and Bar

803 E Main St
Fredericksburg, TX 78624
830.990.8289
navajogrill.com

LEU SAVANH
August E's

203 E San Antonio St
Fredericksburg, TX 78624
830.997.1585
august-es.com

ASA THORNTON
Tuscan Sun Trattoria

1311 S State Hwy 16
Fredericksburg, TX 78624
830.990.6929
visitfredericksburgtx.com

ROCKWALL

RANDALL COPELAND
Ava

108 S Goliad St
Rockwall, TX 75087
469.698.9920
restaurantava.com

NATHAN TATE
Ava

108 S Goliad St
Rockwall, TX 75087
469.698.9920
restaurantava.com

HOUSTON

GREGG BEEBE
Shade

250 W 19th St
Houston, TX 77008
713.863.7500
shadeandcanopy.com

ARTURO BOADA
Arturo Boada Cuisine

6510 Del Monte Dr
Houston, TX 77057
713.782.3011
boadacuisine.com

CHARLES CARROLL
River Oaks Country Club

1600 River Oaks Blvd
Houston, TX 77019
713.529.4321
chefcharlescarroll.com

ROBERTO CASTRE
Latin Bites Café

5709 Woodway Dr
Houston, TX 77057
713.229.8369
latinbitescafe.com

BRYAN CASWELL
Reef

2600 Travis St
Houston, TX 77006
713.526.8282
reefhouston.com

CHARLES CLARK
Ibiza Food and Wine Bar

2450 Louisiana St #200
Houston, TX 77006
713.524.0004
ibizafoodandwinebar.com

MICHAEL CORDUA
Churrascos

1520 Lake Pointe Pkwy #500
Sugar Land, TX 77478
832.532.5300
cordua.com

DAVID CORDUA
Churrascos

1520 Lake Pointe Pkwy #500
Sugar Land, TX 77478
832.532.5300
cordua.com

MARK COX
Mark's American Cuisine

1658 Westheimer Rd
Houston, TX 77006
713.523.3800
marks1658.com

HORACIO DEGANTE
Sullivan's Steakhouse

4608 Westheimer Rd
Houston, TX 77027
713.961.0333
sullivanssteakhouse.com

ROBERT DEL GRANDE
RDG + Bar Annie

1800 Post Oak Blvd
Houston, TX 77056
713.840.1111
rdgbarannie.com

DAVID DENIS
Le Mistral

1400 Eldridge Pkwy
Houston, TX 77077
832.379.8322
lemistralhouston.com

RENATO DEPIRRO
Ristorante Cavour

1080 Uptown Park Blvd
Houston, TX 77056
713.418.1104
granducahouston.com

VELIO DEPLANO
Antica Osteria

2311 Bissonnet St
Houston, TX 77005
713.521.1155
anticarestaurant.com

TOM ELBASHARY
Smith and Wollensky

4007 Westheimer Rd
Houston, TX 77027
713.621.7555
smithandwollensky.com

RANDY EVANS
Haven

2502 Algerian Way
Houston, TX 77098
713.581.6101
havenhouston.com

MAURIZIO FERRARESE
Quattro

1300 Lamar St
Houston, TX 77010
713.276.4700
quattrorestauranthouston.com

LUIGI FERRE
Luigi's Ristorante Italiano

2328 The Strand
Galveston, TX 77550
409.763.6500
luigisrestaurantgalveston.com

PAUL FRIEDMAN
Peli Peli

110 Vintage Park Blvd
Houston, TX 77070
281.257.9500
pelipeli.com

TERRENCE GALLIVAN
The Pass and Provisions

807 Taft
Houston, TX 77019
713.628.9020
passandprovisions.com

FRITZ GITSCHNER
Houston, TX

LEVI GOODE
Goode Company Seafood

8937 Knight Rd
Houston, TX 77054
713.529.4616
goodecompany.com

EDUARDO GUIZAR
17 at Alden

1117 Prairie St
Houston, TX 77002
832.200.8888
17food.com

CARL HAGAN
Perry's Steakhouse & Grille

487 Bay Area Blvd
Houston, TX 77058
281.286.8800
perryssteakhouse.com

TX

RYAN HILDEBRAND
Triniti

1601 Elm St
Houston, TX 77098
713.527.909
trinitirestaurant.com

MANABU HORIUCHI
Kata Robata

3600 Kirby Dr
Houston, TX 77098
713.526.8858
katarobata.com

JUNNAJET HURAPAN
BLU

2248 Texas Dr
Sugar Land, TX 77479
281.903.7324
blusugarland.com

ANITA JAISINGHANI
Pondicheri

2800 Kirby Dr #B132
Houston, TX 77098
713.522.2022
pondichericafe.com

DOMINIC JUAREZ
Masraff's

1753 Post Oak Blvd
Houston, TX 77056
713.355.1975
masraffs.com

RONNIE KILLEN
Killen's Steakhouse

2804 S Main St
Pearland, TX 77581
281.485.0844
killenssteakhouse.com

TONY MANDOLA
Tony Mandola's

1212 Waugh Dr
Houston, TX 77019
713.528.3474
tonymandolas.com

PATRICK MCCRAY
Divino

1830 W Alabama St
Houston, TX 77098
713.807.1123
divinohouston.com

JULIO MINUTA
Crapitto's Cucina Italiana

2400 Midlane St
Houston, TX 77027
713.961.1161
crapittos.com

HUGO ORTEGA
Hugo's Mexican Restaurant

1600 Westheimer Rd
Houston, TX 77006
713.524.7744
hugosrestaurant.net

NAPOLEON PALACIOS
Damian's Cucina Italiana

3011 Smith St
Houston, TX 77006
713.522.0439
damians.com

SOREN PEDERSEN
Sorrel Urban Bistro

2202 W Alabama St
Houston, TX 77098
713.677.0391
sorrelhouston.com

MICHAEL PELLEGRINO
Max's Wine Dive

4720 Washington Ave
Houston, TX 77007
713.880.8737
maxswinedive.com

MONICA POPE
Sparrow Bar + Cookshop

3701 Travis St
Houston, TX 77002
713.524.6922
sparrowhouston.com

MIKE POTOWSKI
Benjy's Restaurant

2424 Dunstan Rd #125
Houston, TX 77005
713.522.7602
benjys.com

MARTIN RANGEL
43rd Restaurant and Lounge

1415 Louisiana St #43
Houston, TX 77002
713.739.6550
the43rd.com

CARLOS RODRIGUEZ
Vic & Anthony's

1510 Texas St
Houston, TX 77002
713.228.1111
vicandanthonys.com

OZZIE ROGERS
III Forks

1201 San Jacinto St
Houston, TX 77002
713.658.9457
3forks.com

LUIS RUBIO
La Griglia

2002 W Gray St
Houston, TX 77019
713.526.4700
lagrigliarestaurant.com

TODD RUIZ
Hotel ZaZa

5701 Main St
Houston, TX 77005
713.526.1991
hotelzaza.com

PHILIPPE SCHMIT
Philippe Restaurant and Lounge

1800 Post Oak Blvd
Houston, TX 77056
713.439.1000
philippehouston.com

JOHANN SCHUSTER
Charivari

2521 Bagby St
Houston, TX 77006
713.521.7231
charivarirest.com

JOHN SHEELY
Mockingbird Bistro

1985 Welch St
Houston, TX 77019
713.533.0200
mockingbirdbistro.com

CHRIS SHEPHERD
Underbelly

1100 Westheimer Rd
Houston, TX 77006
713.528.9800
underbellyhouston.com

SETH SIEGEL GARDNER
The Pass and Provisions

807 Taft
Houston, TX 77019
713.628.9020
passandprovisions.com

PEDRO SILVA
51Fifteen

5115 Westheimer Rd
Houston, TX 77056
713.963.8067
51fifteen.com

AUSTIN SIMMONS
Hubbell & Hudson Kitchen

4526 Research Forest Dr
The Woodlands, TX 77381
281.203.5650
hubbellandhudson.com

STACY SIMONSON
Chez Nous French Restaurant

217 S Ave G
Humble, TX 77338
281.446.6717
cheznousfrenchrestaurant.com

MARIO VALDEZ
Rainbow Lodge

2011 Ella Blvd
Houston, TX 77008
713.861.8666
rainbow-lodge.com

TONY VALLONE
Tony's

3755 Richmond Ave
Houston, TX 77046
713.622.6778
tonyshouston.com

PACO VARGAS
Rudy & Paco

2028 Post Office St
Galveston, TX 77550
409.762.3696
rudyandpaco.com

KIRAN VERMA
Kiran's

4100 Westheimer Rd
Houston, TX 77027
713.960.8472
kiranshouston.com

CUNNINGHAME WEST
Valentino Vin Bar

2525 W Loop S
Houston, TX 77027
713.850.9200
valentinorestaurants.com

MARCO WILES
Da Marco

1520 Westheimer Rd
Houston, TX 77006
713.807.8857
damarcohouston.com

JUSTIN YU
Oxheart

1302 Nance St
Houston, TX 77002
832.830.8592
oxhearthouston.com

JAMIE ZELKO
Zelko Bistro

705 E 11th St
Houston, TX 77008
713.880.8691
zelkobistro.com

HUNTSVILLE

JOHN ESCHENFELDER
The Homestead on 19th

1215 19th St
Huntsville, TX 77340
936.291.7366
homesteadon19th.com

IRVING

J. JESUS OLIVARES
Via Real

4020 N MacArthur Blvd #100
Irving, TX 75038
972.650.9001
viareal.com

LUBBOCK

DWAYNE CLANTON
Tom and Bingo's Hickory Pit BBQ

3006 34th St
Lubbock, TX 79410
806.799.1514

MIKE MAHER
Lubbok, TX

PAUL RADLOFF
Blue Sky

4416 98th St
Lubbock, TX 79424
806.368.7591
blueskytexas.com

JOHN VENTURA
Stella's

4646 50th St
Lubbock, TX 79414
806.785.9299
stellaslubbock.com

LISA WEST
Double Nickel

5405 Slide Rd
Lubbock, TX 79414
806.792.0055
doublenickelsteakhouse.com

MARFA

ANTHONY CANO
Cochineal

107 W San Antonio St
Marfa, TX 79843
432.729.3300
cochinealmarfa.com

MAIYA KECK
Maiya's

103 N Highland Ave
Marfa, TX 79843
432.729.4410
maiyasrestaurant.com

TOM RAPP
Cochineal

107 W San Antonio St
Marfa, TX 79843
432.729.3300
cochinealmarfa.com

TOSHIFUMI SAKIHARA
Cochineal

107 W San Antonio St
Marfa, TX 79843
432.729.3300
cochinealmarfa.com

MCKINNEY

TIM BEVINS
Rick's Chophouse

107 N Kentucky St
McKinney, TX 75069
214.726.9251
rickschophouse.com

PALESTINE

CHRISTIAN MAILLOUX
Red Fire Grille

400 N Queen St
Palestine, TX 75801
903.723.2404
redfiregrille.com

PLANO

CHRIS YAO
Yao Fuzi Cuisine

4757 W Park Blvd
Plano, TX 75093
214.473.9267
yaofuzi.com

ROUND TOP

BUD ROYER
Royer's Round Top Café

105 Main St
Round Top, TX 78954
979.249.3611
royerscafe.com

SAN ANGELO

JAY LUMMUS
Salt at the Silo House

2503 Martin Luther King Blvd
San Angelo, TX 76903
325.658.3333
saltatthesilo.com

SAN ANTONIO

BRUCE AUDEN
Biga on the Banks

203 S Saint Mary's St
San Antonio, TX 78205
210.225.0722
biga.com

JEFFREY BALFOUR
Citrus

150 E Houston St
San Antonio, TX 78205
210.230.8412
hotelvalencia-riverwalk.com

LIONEL BLACHE
Grey Moss Inn

19010 Scenic Loop Rd
Helotes, TX 78023
210.695.8301
grey-moss-inn.com

MARK BLISS
Bliss

926 S Presa St
San Antonio, TX 78210
210.225.2547
foodisbliss.com

GARY BOATMAN
Silo Elevated Cuisine

1133 Austin Hwy
San Antonio, TX 78209
210.824.8686
siloelevatedcuisine.com

MARK BOHANAN
Bohanan's

219 E Houston St
San Antonio, TX 78205
210.472.2600
bohanans.com

PHILIP BOLLHOEFER
Las Canarias

112 College St
San Antonio, TX 78205
210.518.1063
omnihotels.com

STEFAN BOWERS
Feast

1024 S Alamo St
San Antonio, TX 78210
210.354.1024
feastsa.com

JOHN BRAND
Las Canarias

112 College St
San Antonio, TX 78205
210.518.1063
omnihotels.com

JOSEPH BUONINCONTRI
Luce Ristorante e Enoteca

11255 Huebner Rd
San Antonio, TX 78230
210.561.9700
lucesanantonio.com

THIERRY BURKLE
Grill at Leon Springs

24116 IH-10 W
San Antonio, TX 78257
210.698.8797
leonspringsgrill.com

COLLIN CAMPION
Liberty Bistro

200 N Seguin Ave
New Braunfels, TX 78130
830.624.7876
mylibertybistro.com

CHRIS CARLSON
Sandbar Fish House

200 E Grayson St
San Antonio, TX 78215
210.212.2221
sandbarsa.com

CHRIS COOK
Oro

705 E Houston St
San Antonio, TX 78205
210.244.0146
emilymorganhotel.com

JASON DADY
Tre Trattoria

4003 Broadway
San Antonio, TX 78209
210.805.0333
tretrattoria.com

MANNY ELIZONDO
Zinc Bistro & Wine Bar

207 N Presa St
San Antonio, TX 78205
210.224.2900
zincwine.com

SEAN FLETCHER
Bella on the River

106 E River Walk St
San Antonio, TX 78205
210.404.2355
bellaontheriver.com

COLEMAN FOSTER
The Monterey

1127 S Saint Mary's St
San Antonio, TX 78210
210.745.2581
themontereysa.com

DAVID GILBERT
Sustenio

17103 La Cantera Pkwy
San Antonio, TX 78256
210.598.2900
eilanhotel.com

JOHNNY HERNANDEZ
La Gloria

100 E Grayson St
San Antonio, TX 78215
210.267.9040
lagloriaicehouse.com

DOUG HORN
Dough Pizzeria Napoletana

6989 Blanco Rd
San Antonio, TX 78216
210.979.6565
doughpizzeria.com

GABRIEL IBARRA
Cappy's

5011 Broadway St
San Antonio, TX 78209
210.828.9669
cappysrestaurant.com

DENISE MAZAL
Little Gretel Restaurant

518 River Rd
Boerne, TX 78006
830.331.1368
littlegretel.com

STEVEN MCHUGH
Luke

125 E Houston St
San Antonio, TX 78205
210.227.5853
lukesanantonio.com

TED NAANA
Jerusalem Grill

3259 Wurzbach Rd
San Antonio, TX 78238
210.680.8400
jerusalemgrill.net

FRANCIS PERRIN
Frederick's Bistro

14439 NW Military Hwy
Shavano Park, TX 78230
210.888.1500
fredericksbistro.com

LAURENT REA
Laurent's Modern Cuisine

4230 McCullough Ave
San Antonio, TX 78212
210.822.6644
facebook.com/Laurentsmoderncuisine

JOSE REYES
Paloma Blanca

5800 Broadway St #300
San Antonio, TX 78209
210.822.6151
palomablanca.net

WILL RIVERA
Luke

125 E Houston St
San Antonio, TX 78205
210.227.5853
lukesanantonio.com

ALFRED SANCHEZ
Paesanos Riverwalk

111 W Crockett St #101
San Antonio, TX 78259
210.227.2782
paesanosriverwalk.com

BROOKE SMITH
Esquire Tavern

155 E Commerce St
San Antonio, TX 78205
210.222.2521
esquiretavern-sa.com

MICHAEL SOHOCKI
Gwendolyn

152 E Pecan St #100
San Antonio, TX 78205
210.222.1849
restaurantgwendolyn.com

OSCAR SOTO
Piatti

255 E Basse Rd #500
San Antonio, TX 78209
210.832.0300
piatti.com

CHRIS SPENCER
Fig Tree

515 Villita St
San Antonio, TX 78205
210.224.1976
figtreerestaurant.com

MARTIN STEMBERA
Biga on the Banks

203 S Saint Mary's St
San Antonio, TX 78205
210.225.0722
biga.com

KENZO TRAN
Piranha

260 E Basse Rd #101
San Antonio, TX 78209
210.822.1088
piranhakillersushi.com

SCOTT WARD
Antlers Lodge

9800 Hyatt Resort Dr
San Antonio, TX 78251
210.647.1234
hillcountry.hyatt.com

DAMIEN WATEL
Chez Vatel & Bistro

218 E Olmos Dr
San Antonio, TX 78212
210.828.3141
bistrovatel.com

ANDREW WEISSMAN
Il Sogno Osteria

200 E Grayson St
San Antonio, TX 78215
210.223.3900
pearlbrewery.com

DAVID WIREBAUGH
Q on the Riverwalk

123 Losoya St
San Antonio, TX 78205
210.362.6325
hyatt.com

DAVID YOKUTY
Boardwalk Bistro

4011 Broadway St
San Antonio, TX 78209
210.824.0100
boardwalkbistro.net

SHERMAN

ROBERT MORF
Howe, TX

WACO

BRADLEY BAUCH
Chef Bradley Gourmet Creations

2245 County Road 108
Gatesville, TX 76528
214.683.0019
chefbradley.net

ARIS GALANIS
1424 Bistro

1424 Washington Ave
Waco, TX 76701
254.752.7385
1424bistro.com

 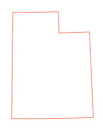

PARK CITY

SETH ADAMS
Riverhorse on Main

540 Main St
Park City, UT 84060
435.649.3536
riverhorseparkcity.com

SHAWN ARMSTRONG
Montage Deer Valley

9100 Marsac Ave
Park City, UT 84060
435.200.0450
montagedeervalley.com

SHANE BAIRD
J & G Grill

2300 Deer Valley Dr E
Park City, UT 84060
435.940.5760
jggrilldeercrest.com

RYAN BURNHAM
Goldener Hirsch Inn

7570 Royal St E
Park City, UT 84060
435.649.7770
goldenerhirschinn.com

JAMES DUMAS
High West Distillery & Saloon

703 Park Ave
Park City, UT 84060
435.649.8300
highwest.com

JERRY GARCIA
Chez Betty

1637 Shortline Rd
Park City, UT 84060
435.649.8181
chezbetty.com

CLEMENT GELAS
Slopes

2100 Frostwood Dr
Park City, UT 84098
435.647.5566
parkcitywaldorfastoria.com

BRIAR HANDLY
Talisker on Main

515 Main St
Park City, UT 84060
435.658.5479
taliskeronmain.com

ZANE HOLMQUIST
Glitretind

7700 Stein Way
Park City, UT 84060
435.645.6455
steinlodge.com

BILL HUFFERD
The Mustang

890 Main St
Park City, UT 84060
435.658.3975
mustangparkcity.com

CHIP MCMULLIN
The St. Regis Deer Valley

2300 Deer Valley Dr E
Park City, UT 84060
435.940.5700
stregisdeervalley.com

CLARK NORRIS
Mariposa

7600 Royal St
Park City, UT 84060
435.645.6715
deervalley.com

ROBERT VALAIKA
Shabu

442 Main St
Park City, UT 84060
435.645.7253
shabuparkcity.com

PROVO

RYKER BROWN
Sundance Resort

8841 Alpine Scenic Hwy
Provo, UT 84604
866.259.7468
sundanceresort.com

SALT LAKE CITY

NACHO BASURTO
Café Madrid

5244 S Highland Dr
Salt Lake City, UT 84117
801.273.0837
cafemadrid.net

LOGEN CREW
Fresco Italian Cafe

1513 S 1500 E
Salt Lake City, UT 84105
801.486.1300
frescoitaliancafe.com

TAKASHI GIBO
Takashi

18 W Market St
Salt Lake City, UT 84101
801.519.9595

BRANDON HOWARD
La Caille

9565 Wasatch Blvd
Sandy, UT 84092
801.942.1751
lacaille.com

DAVID JONES
Log Haven

6451 E Millcreek Canyon Rd
Salt Lake City, UT 84109
801.272.8255
log-haven.com

MATTHEW LAKE
ZY Food Wine and Cheese

268 S State St
Salt Lake City, UT 84111
801.779.4730
zyrestaurant.com

ETHAN LAPPÉ
Caffe Niche

779 E 300 S
Salt Lake City, UT 84102
801.433.3380
caffeniche.com

RYAN LOWDER
The Copper Onion

111 E Broadway #170
Salt Lake City, UT 84111
801.355.3282
thecopperonion.com

GREG NEVILLE
Lugano

3364 S 2300 E
Salt Lake City, UT 84109
801.412.9994
luganorestaurant.com

VIET PHAM
Forage

370 E 9th S
Salt Lake City, UT 84111
801.708.7834
foragerestaurant.com

JAMES PLANT
Spencer's

255 S W Temple
Salt Lake City, UT 84101
801.238.4748
spencersforsteaksandchops.com

NATHAN POWERS
Bambara

202 S Main St
Salt Lake City, UT 84101
801.363.5454
bambara-slc.com

MICHAEL RICHEY
St. Bernard's

12000 Big Cottonwood Canyon Rd
Solitude, UT 84121
435.649.8400
skisolitude.com

ALI SABBATH
Mazza

912 E 9th S
Salt Lake City, UT 84105
801.521.4572
mazzacafe.com

TOSHIO SEKIKAWA
Naked Fish

67 W 100 S
Salt Lake City, UT 84101
801.595.8888
nakedfishbistro.com

JUSTIN SOELBERG
Café Trio

680 S 900 E
Salt Lake City, UT 84102
801.533.8746
triodining.com

ST. GEORGE

RANDALL RICHARDS
The Painted Pony

2 W Saint George Blvd #22
St. George, UT 84770
435.634.1700
painted-pony.com

 VERMONT

BENNINGTON

MICHEL BAUMANN
Chantecleer Restaurant

8 Read Farm Ln
East Dorset, VT 05253
802.362.1616
chantecleerrestaurant.com

AMY CHAMBERLAIN
The Perfect Wife

2594 Depot St
Manchester, VT 05255
802.362.2817
perfectwife.com

BRATTLEBORO

PAUL ESCHBACH
The Hermitage

25 Handle Rd
West Dover, VT 05356
802.464.3511
hermitageinn.com

MICHAEL FULLER
T.J. Buckley's

132 Elliot St
Brattleboro, VT 05301
802.257.4922
tjbuckleys.com

WESLEY GENOVART
SoLo Farm & Table

95 Middletown Rd
South Londonderry, VT 05155
802.824.6327
solofarmandtable.com

BURLINGTON

STEVE ATKINS
Kitchen Table Bistro

1840 W Main St
Richmond, VT 05477
802.434.8686
kitchentablebistro.com

TIM BENZING
Sweetwaters

120 Church St
Burlington, VT 05401
802.864.9800
sweetwatersvt.com

PHOEBE R. BRIGHT
Blue Paddle Bistro

316 U.S. 2
South Hero, VT 05486
802.372.4814
bluepaddlebistro.com

SHAWN CALLEY
Amuse

70 Essex Way #1
Essex Junction, VT 05452
802.764.1489
vtculinaryresort.com

SIMON CHEN
YAMA Sushi House

133 N Main St
St. Albans, VT 05478
802.524.6660

MICHAEL CLAUSS
Bluebird Tavern

86 Saint Paul St
Burlington, VT 05401
802.540.1786
bluebirdvermont.com

PHILLIP CLAYTON
El Cortijo

189 Bank St
Burlington, VT 05401
802.497.1668
cortijovt.com

KEVIN CLEARY
L'Amante

126 College St
Burlington, VT 05401
802.863.5200
lamante.com

DONNELL COLLINS
Leunig's Bistro & Café

115 Church St
Burlington, VT 05455
802.863.3759
leunigsbistro.com

ANDREA COUSINEAU
The Bearded Frog

5247 Shelburne Rd #100
Shelburne, VT 05482
802.985.9877
thebeardedfrog.com

CHIUHO DUVAL
A Single Pebble

133 Bank St
Burlington, VT 05401
802.865.5200
asinglepebble.com

MARCUS HAMBLETT
One Federal
Restaurant & Lounge

1 Federal St
St. Albans, VT 05478
802.524.0330
onefederalrestaurant.com

DAVID HOENE
Pauline's Café

1834 Shelburne Rd
South Burlington, VT 05403
802.862.1081
paulinescafe.com

DAVID HUGO
Inn at Shelburne Farms

1611 Harbor Rd
Shelburne, VT 05482
802.985.8498
shelburnefarms.org

AARON JOSINSKY
Misery Loves Company

46 Main St
Winooski, VT 05404
802.497.3989
miserylovescovt.com

GARY MA
Asiana House

191 Pearl St
Burlington, VT 05401
802.651.0818
asianahouse.com

MAX MACKINNON
Pistou

61 Main St
Burlington, VT 05401
802.540.1783
pistou-vt.com

SAMUEL PALMISANO
Pulcinella's

100 Dorset St
South Burlington, VT 05403
802.863.1000
pulcinellas.us

CHRIS RUSSO
San Sai

112 Lake St
Burlington, VT 05401
802.862.2777
sansaivt.com

BRUCE STEWART
Trattoria Delia

152 Saint Paul St
Burlington, VT 05401
802.864.5253
trattoriadelia.com

JORDAN WARE
The Farmhouse Tap & Grill

160 Bank St
Burlington, VT 05401
802.859.0888
farmhousetg.com

HARDWICK

STEVEN OBRANOVICH
Hardwick, VT

LEBANON

CALEB BARBER
osteria pane e salute

61 Central St
Woodstock, VT 05091
802.457.4882
osteriapaneesalute.com

CRAIG CORNELL
Okemo Mountain Resort

77 Okemo Ridge Rd
Ludlow, VT 05149
802.228.1841
okemo.com

ROGAN LECHTHALER
The Downtown Grocery

41 S Depot St
Ludlow, VT 05149
802.228.7566
thedowntowngrocery.com

NICK MAHOOD
Cloudland Farm

1101 Cloudland Rd
Woodstock, VT 05091
802.457.2599
cloudlandfarm.com

CHRIS THORNTON
Woodstock, VT

JASON TOSTRUP
The Inn at Weathersfield

1342 Vermont 106
Perkinsville, VT 05151
802.263.9217
weathersfieldinn.com

MANCHESTER

HENRY BRONSON
Bistro Henry

1942 Depot St
Manchester Center, VT 05255
802.362.4982
bistrohenry.com

DANA MARKEY
Mistral's at Toll Gate

10 Tollgate Rd
Manchester Center, VT 05255
802.362.1779
mistralsattollgate.com

MONTPELIER

MICHAEL KLOETI
Michael's on the Hill

4182 Waterbury-Stowe Rd
Waterbury Center, VT 05677
802.244.7476
michaelsonthehill.com

ADAM LONGWORTH
The Common Man Restaurant

3209 German Flats Rd
Warren, VT 05674
802.583.2800
commonmanrestaurant.com

SUE SCHICKLER
The Pitcher Inn

275 Main St
Warren, VT 05674
802.496.6350
pitcherinn.com

ERIC WARNSTEDT
Hen of the Wood

92 Stowe St
Waterbury, VT 05676
802.244.7300
henofthewood.com

RUTLAND

ROBERT BARRAL
Café Provence

11 Center St
Brandon, VT 05733
802.247.9997
cafeprovencevt.com

STEPHEN SAWYER
Table 24

24 Wales St
Rutland, VT 05701
802.775.2424
table24.net

STOWE

JACK PICKETT
Frida's Taqueria and Grill

128 Main St
Stowe, VT 05672
802.253.0333
fridastaqueria.com

MATTHEW REEVE
Stowe, VT

JEREMY SOMERSET
Mr. Pickwick's

433 Mountain Rd
Stowe, VT 05672
802.253.7558
mrpickwicks.com

VERGENNES

MICHEL MAHE
Black Sheep Bistro

253 Main St
Vergennes, VT 05491
802.877.9991
blacksheepbistrovt.com

INGREDIENT: MICROGREENS

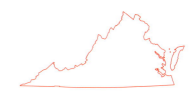

ABINGDON

NATHAN BREEDING
House on Main

231 W Main St
Abingdon, VA 24210
276.619.0039
houseonmain.com

BEN CARROLL
Rain Restaurant & Bar

283 E Main St
Abingdon, VA 24210
276.739.2331
rainabingdon.com

NAOMI FIGAREDO
Figaredo's

309 Falls Dr
Abingdon, VA 24210
276.206.8059
figaredos.com

PHILIP NEWTON
The Harvest Table Restaurant

13180 Meadowview Square
Meadowview, VA 24361
276.944.5142
meadowviewfarmersguild.com

ALEXANDRIA

SERGE ALBERT
Tempo

4231 Duke St
Alexandria, VA 22304
703.370.7900
temporestaurant.com

WENDY ALBERT
Tempo

4231 Duke St
Alexandria, VA 22304
703.370.7900
temporestaurant.com

CATHAL ARMSTRONG
Restaurant Eve

110 S Pitt St
Alexandria, VA 22314
703.706.0450
restauaranteve.com

ANTHONY CHITTUM
Vermilion

1120 King St
Alexandria, VA 22314
703.684.9669
vermilionrestaurant.com

TROY CLAYTON
Geranio

722 King St
Alexandria, VA 22314
703.548.0088
geranio.net

ADRIAN GUTIERREZ
La Bergerie

218 N Lee St
Alexandria, VA 22314
703.519.6114
labergerie.com

JIM JEFFORDS
Evening Star Café

2000 Mount Vernon Ave
Alexandria, VA 22301
703.549.5051
eveningstar.net

FRANCO LANDINI
Landini Brothers

115 King St
Alexandria, VA 22314
703.836.8404
landinibrothers.com

BRIAN MCPHERSON
Grille at Morrison House

116 S Alfred St
Alexandria, VA 22314
703.838.8000
morrisonhouse.com

SHANNON OVERMILLER
The Majestic

911 King St
Alexandria, VA 22314
703.837.9117
majesticcafe.com

CHRISTOPHE POTEAUX
Bastille

1201 N Royal St
Alexandria, VA 22314
703.519.3776
bastillerestaurant.com

MICHELLE POTEAUX
Bastille

1201 N Royal St
Alexandria, VA 22314
703.519.3776
bastillerestaurant.com

CHRIS WATSON
Brabo

1600 King St
Alexandria, VA 22314
703.894.3440
braborestaurant.com

ARLINGTON

ADAM BARNETT
Eventide

3165 Wilson Blvd
Arlington, VA 22201
703.276.3165
eventiderestaurant.com

ANDY BENNETT
Lyon Hall

3100 N Washington Blvd
Arlington, VA 22201
703.741.7636
lyonhallarlington.com

RAYMOND CAMPET
La Cote D'Or Café

6876 Lee Hwy
Arlington, VA 22213
703.538.3033
lacotedorcafe.com

LIU CHAOSHENG
Mala Tang

3434 Washington Blvd
Arlington, VA 22201
703.243.2381
mala-tang.com

LIAM LACIVITA
Liberty Tavern

3195 Wilson Blvd
Arlington, VA 22201
703.465.9360
thelibertytavern.com

MICHAEL LANDRUM
Ray's the Steaks

2300 Wilson Blvd
Arlington, VA 22209
703.841.7297
raysthesteaks.com

ERIC MCKAMEY
Curious Grape

2900 S Quincy St
Arlington, VA 22206
703.671.8700
curiousgrape.com

MOROU OUATTARA
Farrah Olivia

2250 Crystal Dr
Arlington, VA 22202
703.445.6571
farraholiviarestaurant.com

DREW TERP
Jaleo

2250 A Crystal Dr
Arlington, VA 22202
703.413.8181
jaleo.com

NATE WAUGAMAN
Tallula

2761 Washington Blvd
Arlington, VA 22201
703.778.5051
tallularestaurant.com

BLACKSBURG

MICHAEL BEHMOIRAS
The Bank Food and Drink

101 N Main St
Pearisburg, VA 24134
540.921.2981
thebankfoodanddrink.com

SHAENA MULDOON
The Palisades Restaurant

168 Village St
Eggleston, VA 24086
540.626.2828
thepalisadesrestaurant.com

ABDUL SHARAKI
Summit

95 College St
Christiansburg, VA 24073
540.382.7218
summitrestaurant.us

JASON SMITH
Preston's

901 Prices Fork Rd
Blacksburg, VA 24061
540.231.0120
innatvirginiatech.com

CASANOVA

HOWARD FOER
The Manor House Restaurant

9245 Rogues Rd
Casanova, VA 22728
540.788.4600
poplarspringsinn.com

CHANTILLY

NONGKRAN DAKS
Thai Basil

14511 Lee Jackson Memorial Hwy
Chantilly, VA 20151
703.631.8277
thaibasilchantilly.com

CHARLOTTESVILLE

IAN BODEN
Glass Haus Kitchen

313 2nd St SE
Charlottesville , VA 22902
434.244.8439
glasshauskitchen.com

PETER BOWYER
Carr's Hill

1910 Carr's Hill Rd
Charlottesville, VA 22901
434.924.0311
virginia.edu

PEI CHANG
Ten

120 E Main St #B
Charlottesville, VA 22902
434.295.6691
ten-sushi.com

MELISSA CLOSE-HART
Palladio

17655 Winery Rd
Barboursville, VA 22923
540.832.7848
barboursvillewine.net

WILLIAM COOPER
Bella's Restaurant

707 W Main St
Charlottesville, VA 22903
434.327.4833
bellas-restaurant.com

AARON CROSS
Fossett's

701 Club Dr
Keswick, VA 22947
434.979.3440
keswick.com

BRICE CUNNINGHAM
Tempo

117 5th St SE
Charlottesville, VA 22902
434.244.0217
tempocville.com

LUTHER FEDORA
Horse & Hound Gastropub

625 W Main St
Charlottesville, VA 22903
434.293.3365
horseandhoundgastropub.com

MARK GRESGE
L'etoile Restaurant

817 W Main St
Charlottesville, VA 22903
434.979.7957
letoilerestaurant.com

TODD GRIEGER
Maya

633 W Main St
Charlottesville, VA 22903
434.979.6292
maya-restaurant.com

MATTHEW HART
Local

824 Hinton Ave
Charlottesville, VA 22902
434.984.9749
thelocal-cville.com

BRIAN HELLEBERG
Fleurie

108 3rd St NE
Charlottesville, VA 22902
434.971.7800
fleurierestaurant.com

MICHAEL KEAVENY
Tavola

826 Hinton Ave
Charlottesville, VA 22902
434.972.9463
tavolavino.com

HARRISON KEEVIL
Brookville Restaurant

225 Main St
Charlottesville, VA 22902
434.202.2791
brookvillerestaurant.com

CHRISTIAN KELLY
Maya

633 W Main St
Charlottesville, VA 22903
434.979.6292
maya-restaurant.com

DEAN MAUPIN
C & O

515 Water St E
Charlottesville, VA 22902
434.971.7044
candorestaurant.com

ALAN PYLES
Lafayette Inn & Restaurant

146 E Main St
Stanardsville, VA 22973
434.985.6345
thelafayette.com

TOMAS RAHAL
MAS Tapas

904 Monticello Rd
Charlottesville, VA 22902
434.979.0990
mastapas.com

WILL RICHEY
The Whiskey Jar

227 W Main St
Charlottesville , VA 22902
434.202.1549
thewhiskeyjarcville.com

SAM ROCHESTER
Downtowne Grille

201 W Main St
Charlottesville, VA 22902
434.817.7080
downtowngrille.com

BRYAN SZELIGA
Orzo Kitchen & Wine Bar

416 W Main St
Charlottesville, VA 22903
434.975.6796
orzokitchen.com

TYLER TEASS
The Clifton Inn

1296 Clifton Inn Dr
Charlottesville, VA 22911
434.971.1800
cliftoninn.net

ANGELO VANGELOPOULOS
The Ivy Inn restaurant

224 Old Ivy Rd
Charlottesville, VA 22903
434.977.1222
ivyinnrestaurant.com

TUCKER YODER
The Clifton Inn

1296 Clifton Inn Dr
Charlottesville, VA 22911
434.971.1800
cliftoninn.net

CHESAPEAKE

GARRETT BARNER
Passion, The Restaurant

1036 Volvo Pkwy #3
Chesapeake, VA 23320
757.410.3975
passiontherestaurant.com

CULPEPER

FRANK MARAGOS
Foti's Restaurant

219 E Davis St
Culpeper , VA 22701
540.829.8400
fotisrestaurant.com

FAIRFAX

PRAVEEN KUMAR
Curry Mantra

9984 Main St
Fairfax, VA 22031
703.218.8128
dccurrymantra.com

OMAR LAVAYEN
Bellissimo

10403 Main St
Fairfax, VA 22030
703.293.2367
bellissimorestaurant.com

AMIR NASSARI
SABZI

4008 University Dr
Fairfax, VA 22030
703.383.1553
sabzikabobs.com

ANDREA PACE
Villa Mozart

4009 Chain Bridge Rd
Fairfax, VA 22030
703.691.4747
villamozartrestaurant.com

GIUSEPPE RICCARDI
Dolce Vita

10824 Lee Hwy
Fairfax, VA 22030
703.385.1530
dolcevitafairfax.com

WILLIAM WALDEN
Fairfax, VA

FALLS CHURCH

WILL ARTLEY
Pizzeria Orso

400 S Maple Ave
Falls Church, VA 22046
703.226.3460
pizzeriaorso.com

BERTRAND CHEMEL
2941 Restaurant

2941 Fairview Park Dr
Falls Church, VA 22042
703.270.1500
2941.com

GEORGE FON
Peking Gourmet Inn

6029 Leesburg Pike
Falls Church, VA 22041
703.671.8088
pekinggourmet.com

HOA LAI
Four Sisters

8190 Strawberry Ln #1
Falls Church, VA 22042
703.539.8566
foursistersrestaurant.com

SLY LIAO
Sea Pearl

8191 Strawberry Ln #2
Falls Church, VA 22042
703.372.5161
seapearlrestaurant.com

FREDERICK MARK
Mark's Duck House

6184 Arlington Blvd
Falls Church, VA 22044
703.532.2125
marksduckhouse.com

LUONG TRAN
Present

6678 Arlington Blvd
Falls Church, VA 22042
703.531.1881
presentcuisine.com

FLINT HILL

MARVIN SWANER
Flint Hill Public House

675 Zachary Taylor Hwy
Flint Hill, VA 22627
540.675.1700
flinthillva.com

FREDERICKSBURG

BLAKE BETHEM
Bistro Bethem
309 William St
Fredericksburg, VA 22401
540.371.9999
bistrobethem.com

JOY CRUMP
Foode
1006 Caroline St
Fredericksburg, VA 22401
540.479.1370
foodeonline.com

RAYMOND RENAULT
La Petite Auberge

311 William St
Fredericksburg, VA 22401
540.371.2727
lapetiteaubergefred.com

FRONT ROYAL

DAVID GEDNEY
J's Gourmet

206 S Royal Ave
Front Royal, VA 22630
540.636.9293
jsgourmet.com

GALAX

KARL BERZINS
Bogeys

103 Country Club Ln
Galax, VA 24333
276.601.2536
bogeysgalax.com

GLOUCESTER

ERIC GARCIA
Warner Hall

4750 Warner Hall Rd
Gloucester, VA 23061
804.695.9565
warnerhall.com

ROBERT IACCARINO
River's Inn

8109 Yacht Haven Rd
Gloucester, VA 23062
804.642.9942
rivers-inn.com

GORDONSVILLE

GERARD GASPARINI
Restaurant Pomme

115 S Main St
Gordonsville, VA 22942
540.832.0130
restaurant-pomme.com

CRAIG HARTMAN
BBQ Exchange

102 Martinsburg Ave
Gordonsville, VA 22942
540.832.0227
bbqex.com

HANOVER

CHAD SMITH
Hanover Tavern

13181 Hanover Courthouse Rd
Hanover, VA 23069
804.537.5050
hanovertavern.org

HARRISONBURG

MARK NEWSOME
Joshua Wilton House

412 S Main St
Harrisonburg, VA 22801
540.434.4464
joshuawilton.com

RYAN ZALE
Local Chop and Grill House

56 W Gay St
Harrisonburg, VA 22802
540.801.0505
localchops.com

HERNDON

ANTONIO GARCIA
Zeffirelli

728 Pine St
Herndon, VA 20170
703.318.7000
zeffirelliristorante.com

STEVE MANNINO
Thompson Hospitality

505 Huntmar Park Dr
Herndon, VA 20170
202.907.7300
thompsonhospitality.com

MUTTIKA SETAPAYAK
Thai Luang

171 Elden St #171
Herndon, VA 20170
703.478.2233
thailuang.com

HOT SPRINGS

SEAN O'CONNELL
The Homestead

7696 Sam Snead Hwy
Hot Springs, VA 24445
540.839.1766
thehomestead.com

IRVINGTON

T.V. FLYNN
Chesapeake Club Restaurant

480 King Carter Dr
Irvington, VA 22480
804.438.5000
tidesinn.com

LEESBURG

PATRICK DINH
Tuscarora Mill

203 Harrison St SE
Leesburg, VA 20175
703.771.9300
tuskies.com

DAN DUPAY
Vintage 50

50 Catoctin Cir NE #100
Leesburg, VA 20176
703.777.2169
vintage50.com

INGRID GUSTAVSON
Lightfoot

11 N King St
Leesburg, VA 20176
703.771.2233
lightfootrestaurant.com

ANTONIO LAZZETTI
Palio Ristorante

2 W Market St
Leesburg, VA 20176
703.779.0060
paliootleesburg.com

MARK MARROCCO
Magnolia's at the Mill

198 N 21st St
Purcellville, VA 20132
540.338.9800
magnoliasmill.com

LEXINGTON

NATHAN FOUNTAIN
Brix

4 E Washington St
Lexington, VA 24450
540.464.3287
brix-winebar.com

GEORGE HUGER
Southern Inn

37 S Main St
Lexington, VA 24450
540.463.3612
southerninn.com

LOVETTSVILLE

CHRISTOPHER EDWARDS
Restaurant at Patowmack Farm

42461 Lovettsville Rd
Lovettsville, VA 20180
540.822.9017
patowmackfarm.com

LYNCHBURG

BENJAMIN MCGEHEE
Benjamin's Great Cows and Crabs

14900 Forest Rd
Forest , VA 24551
434.534.6077
cowsandcrabs.com

SEAN MEEKS
Isabella's Italian Trattoria

4925 Boonsboro Rd
Lynchburg, VA 24503
434.385.1660
isabellasitalian.com

MANASSAS

WILMER MARQUES
Carmello's

9108 Center St
Manassas, VA 20110
703.368.5522
carmellos.com

MCLEAN

DOMENICO CORNACCHIA
Assaggi Osteria

6641 Old Dominion Dr
McLean, VA 22101
703.918.0080
assaggiosteria.com

MIDDLEBURG

JOHN-GUSTIN BIRKITT
The French Hound

101 S Madison St
Middleburg, VA 20117
540.687.3018
thefrenchhound.com

MONETA

BRUNO SILVA
The Landing

773 Ashmeade Rd
Moneta, VA 24121
540.721.3028
thelandingsml.com

NEWPORT NEWS

IHSAN KORKMAZ
Pearl French Bistro

703 Thimble Shoals Blvd
Newport News, VA 23606
757.223.5370
pearlfrenchbistro.com

CHAD MARTIN
Circa 1918

10367 Warwick Blvd
Newport News, VA 23601
757.599.1918
facebook.com/circa1918

KENNY SLOAN
Fin Seafood

3150 William Styron Square N
Newport News, VA 23606
757.599.5800
finseafood.com

NORFOLK

TODD JURICH
Todd Jurich's Bistro

150 W Main St #100
Norfolk, VA 23510
757.622.3210
toddjurichsbistro.com

TODD LEUTNER
Trilogy Bistro

101 Granby St
Norfolk, VA 23510
757.961.0896
trilogynorfolk.com

JAMES ORNEALAS
Byrd & Baldwin

116 Brooke Ave
Norfolk, VA 23510
757.222.9191
byrdbaldwin.com

KENNY SCOTT
Todd Jurich's Bistro

150 W Main St #100
Norfolk, VA 23510
757.622.3210
toddjurichsbistro.com

PHILLIP CRAIG THOMASON
Vintage Kitchen

999 Waterside Dr
Norfolk, VA 23510
757.625.3370
vintage-kitchen.com

ONANCOCK

SAM YOKUM
Charlotte Hotel and Restaurant

7 N St
Onancock, VA 23417
757.787.7400
thecharlottehotel.com

PARIS

TARVER KING
The Ashby Inn

692 Federal St
Paris, VA 20130
540.592.3900
ashbyinn.com

PORTSMOUTH

SYDNEY MEERS
Stove Restaurant

2622 Detroit St
Portsmouth, VA 23707
757.397.0900
stoverestaurant.com

RESTON

CHRISTOPHER CLIME
PassionFish

11960 Democracy Dr
Reston, VA 20190
703.230.3474
passionfishreston.com

JACQUES HAERINGER
L'Auberge Chez Francois

332 Springvale Rd
Great Falls, VA 22066
703.759.3800
laubergechezfrancois.com

BO PALKER
Vinifera Wine Bar and Bistro

11750 Sunrise Valley Dr
Reston, VA 20191
703.234.3550
viniferabistro.com

RICHMOND

JASON ALLEY
Pasture

416 E Grace St
Richmond, VA 23219
804.780.0416
pastureva.com

CHRISTOPHER BOOTH
The Old Original Bookbinder's

2306 E Cary St
Richmond, VA 23223
804.643.6900
bookbindersrichmond.com

WALTER BUNDY
Lemaire

101 W Franklin St
Richmond, VA 23220
804.649.4629
lemairerestaurant.com

ANTONIO CAPECE
La Grotta

1218 E Cary St
Richmond, VA 23219
804.644.2466
lagrottaristorante.com

PETER CHANG
Peter Chang's China Café

11424 W Broad St
Glen Allen, VA 23230
804.364.1688
peterchangrva.com

FRANCIS DEVILLIERS
Bistro Bobette

1209 E Cary St
Richmond, VA 23219
804.225.9116
bistrobobette.com

RANDALL DOETZER
Julep's New Southern Cuisine

1719 E Franklin St
Richmond, VA 23119
804.377.3968
juleps.net

LEE GREGORY
The Roosevelt

623 N 25th St
Richmond, VA 23223
804.658.1935
rooseveltrva.com

GREG HALEY
Amuse

200 N Blvd
Richmond, VA 23220
804.340.1580
vmsa.state.va.us

MICHAEL HALL
M Bistro & Wine Bar

4821 Old Main St
Richmond, VA 23231
804.652.2300
mbistro-rocketts.com

WILLIAM HARIK
Selba

2416 W Cary St
Richmond, VA 23220
804.358.2229
selbarichmond.com

TAYLOR HASTY
525 at the Berry Burk

525 E Grace St
Richmond, VA 23219
804.382.8390
525rva.com

KEVIN LACIVITA
Blue Goat

5710 Grove Ave
Richmond, VA 23226
804.288.8875
bluegoatva.com

OWEN LANE
The Magpie

1301 W Leigh St
Richmond, VA 23220
804.269.0023
themagpierva.com

MICHAEL LEDESMA
Tarrant's Cafe

1 W Broad St
Richmond, VA 23220
804.225.0035
tarrantscaferva.com

ELIZABETH LEE
The Peacock's Pantry

1731 W Main St
Richmond, VA 23220
804.732.3333
thepeacockspantry.com

ERIC LEWIS
Buckhead's Restaurant
and Chophouse

8510 Patterson Ave
Richmond, VA 23229
804.750.2000, buckheads.com

MANNY MENDEZ
Kuba Kuba

1601 Park Ave
Richmond, VA 23220
804.355.8817
kubakuba.info

CARLOS NAVARRETTE
Azzurro

6221 River Rd
Richmond, VA 23229
804.282.1509
azzurros.com

MEL OZA
Lehja

11800 W Broad St
Richmond, VA 23233
804.364.1111
lehja.com

DALE REITZER
Acacia

2601 W Cary St
Richmond, VA 23220
804.562.0138
acaciarestaurant.com

TED SANTARELLA
Tarrant's Cafe

1 W Broad St
Richmond, VA 23220
804.225.0035
tarrantscaferva.com

JIMMY SNEED
Richmond, VA

RUSSELL STONE
The Ironhorse

100 S Railroad Ave
Ashland, VA 23005
804.752.6410
ironhorserestaurant.com

MATTHEW TLUSTY
Arcadia

1700 E Main St
Richmond, VA 23223
804.417.4005
arcadiarichmond.com

TRUYEN TRAN
Mekong

6004 W Broad St
Richmond, VA 23230
804.288.8929
mekongisforbeerlovers.com

HAI TRUONG
Osaka Sushi and Steak

5023 Huguenot Rd
Richmond, VA 23226
804.288.8801
osakasushiva.com

ED VASAIO
Mamma Zu

501 S Pine St
Richmond, VA 23220
804.788.4205

PAUL WIELT
Hondo's

4024 Cox Rd
Glen Allen, VA 23060
804.968.4323
hondosprime.com

MICHELLE WILLIAMS
Europa

1409 E Cary St
Richmond, VA 23219
804.643.0911
europarichmond.com

JOSH WOOD
Chez Foushee

203 N Foushee St
Richmond, VA 23220
804.648.3225
chezfoushee.com

XIAO-DAN WU
Umi

11645 W Broad St
Richmond, VA 23230
804.360.3336
umisushibistro.com

ROANOKE

BEN GUI CHEN
Ben Gui Sushi

4353 Starkey Rd
Roanoke, VA 24018
540.772.6888
benguisushi.com

LUCIANO D'AVANZO
Chianti Restaurant
International Cuisine

219 Apperson Dr, Salem, VA 24153
540.387.3868
chiantisalem.com

AARON DEAL
River and Rail

2201 Crystal Spring Ave SW
Roanoke, VA 24014
540.400.6830
riverandrailrestaurant.com

JEFF FARMER
Lucky

18 Kirk Ave SW
Roanoke, VA 24011
540.982.1249
eatatlucky.com

MATTHEW LINTZ
Local Roots

1314 Grandin Rd
Roanoke, VA 24015
540.206.2610
localrootsrestaurant.com

JAMES NELSON
Frankie Rowland's Steakhouse

104 S Jefferson St
Roanoke, VA 24011
540.527.2333
frankierowlandssteakhouse.com

ANDY SCHLOSSER
Metro!

14 Campbell Ave SE
Roanoke, VA 24011
540.345.6645
metroroanoke.com

NATHANIEL SLOAN
Local Roots

1314 Grandin Rd
Roanoke, VA 24015
540.206.2610
localrootsrestaurant.com

SCOTT SWITZER
Blue Apron

210 E Main St
Salem, VA 24153
540.375.0055
blueapronredrooster.com

MYLES WALLACE
Roanoke, VA

SOUTH BOSTON

MARGARET MOOREFIELD
Bistro 1888

221 Main St
South Boston, VA 24592
434.572.1888
bistro1888.com

STAUNTON

JAMES HARRIS
Zynodoa

115 E Beverley St
Staunton, VA 24401
540.885.7775
zynodoa.com

STERLING

VIC NGUYEN
Hooked

46240 Potomac Run Plaza
Sterling, VA 20164
703.421.0404
hookedonseafood.com

DANIEL STEVENS
Mokomandy

20789 Great Falls Plaza #176
Sterling, VA 20165
571.313.0505
mokomandy.com

SUFFOLK

HARPER BRADSHAW
Harper's Table

122 N Main St
Suffolk, VA 23434
757.539.2000
harperstable.com

PETE EVANS
River Stone Chophouse

8032 Harbour View Blvd
Suffolk, VA 23435
757.638.7990
riverstonechophouse.com

KENNY REYNOLDS
Vintage Tavern

1900 Governors Pointe Dr
Suffolk, VA 23436
757.238.8808
vintagetavernvirginia.com

JOE STEINERT
Vintage Tavern

1900 Governors Pointe Dr
Suffolk, VA 23436
757.238.8808
vintagetavernvirginia.com

THE PLAINS

TOM KEE
Rail Stop

6478 Main St
The Plains, VA 20198
540.253.5644
railstoprestaurant.com

LOUIS PATIERNO
Girasole

4244 Loudoun Ave
The Plains, VA 20198
540.253.5501
girasole-panino.com

VIENNA

SERGIO DOMESTICI
Ristorante Bonaroti

428 Maple Ave East
Vienna, VA 22180
703.281.7550
bonarotirestaurant.com

EUGENIA HOBSON
Nostos

8100 Boone Blvd
Vienna, VA 22182
703.760.0690
nostosrestaurant.com

BOBBY KIM
Yama

328 Maple Ave W
Vienna, VA 22180
703.242.7703
sushiyamava.com

TIM MA
Maple Avenue

147 Maple Ave W
Vienna, VA 22180
703.319.2177
mapleaverestaurant.com

JOSEPH OCEAN
Café Renaissance

163 Glyndon St SE
Vienna, VA 22180
703.938.3311
caferenaissance.com

VIRGINIA BEACH

CORY BEISEL
Five 01 City Grill

501 N Birdneck Rd
Virginia Beach, VA 23451
757.425.7195
five01citygrill.com

SCOTT BERNHEISEL
Westin Hotel

4535 Commerce St
Virginia Beach, VA 23462
757.275.7834
starwoodhotels.com

JERRY BRYAN
Coastal Grill

1427 N Great Neck Rd
Virginia Beach, VA 23454
757.496.3348
coastalgrill.com

EDDIE LEE BRYANT
Cavalier Hotel

4201 Atlantic Ave
Virginia Beach, VA 23451
757.425.8555
cavalierhotel.com

GIANCARLO CATENESE
Aldo's

1860 Laskin Rd
Virginia Beach, VA 23454
757.491.1111
aldosvb.com

JOHN CHAPMAN
Lynnhaven Fish House

2350 Starfish Rd
Virginia Beach, VA 23451
757.481.0003
lynnhavenfishhouse.net

JASON DUNN
Five 01 City Grill

501 N Birdneck Rd
Virginia Beach, VA 23451
757.425.7195
five01citygrill.com

RODNEY EINHORN
Terrapin

3102 Pinewood Rd #514
Virginia Beach, VA 23451
757.321.6688
terrapinvirginiabeach.com

TONY GARGIULO
IL Giardino

910 Atlantic Ave #200
Virginia Beach, VA 23451
757.422.6464
ilgiardino.com

ERICK HEILIG
Eat. An American Bistro

4005 Atlantic Ave
Virginia Beach, VA 23451
757.965.2472
eatbistro.net

BOBBY HUBER
Steinhilber's

653 Thalia Rd
Virginia Beach, VA 23452
757.340.1156
steinys.com

ROBERT JOHNSON
The Aberdeen Barn

5805 Northampton Blvd
Virginia Beach, VA 23455
757.464.1580
aberdeenbarn.net

BRAD KELLY
Catch 31

3001 Atlantic Ave
Virginia Beach, VA 23451
757.213.3474
catch31.com

TYSON LORD
Burton's Grill

741 First Colonial Rd #107
Virginia Beach, VA 23451
757.422.8970
burtonsgrill.com

JIM MAYER
One Fish Two Fish

2109 W Great Neck Rd #102
Virginia Beach, VA 23451
757.496.4350
onefish-twofish.com

WATARU MIZUNO
Mizuno's

1860 Laskin Rd #115
Virginia Beach, VA 23454
757.422.1200
mizunosushi.com

ERIC NELSON
Thirty 7 North

2105 W Great Neck Rd
Virginia Beach, VA 23451
757.412.0203
thirty7north.com

JODY REDDEN
Mahi Mah's

615 Atlantic Ave
Virginia Beach, VA 23451
757.437.8030
mahimahs.com

ANGELO SERPE
Pasta E Pani

1805 Laskin Rd
Virginia Beach, VA 23454
757.301.7488
pastaepanionline.com

KEVIN SHARKEY
Fusion

3501 Atlantic Ave
Virginia Beach, VA 23451
757.425.9000
sheratonvirginiabeach.com

MARC TAYLOR
Fire & Vine

1556 Laskin Rd
Virginia Beach, VA 23451
757.333.4824
fireandvine.com

JERRY WEIHBRECHT
Zoe's Steak &
Seafood Restaurant

713 19th St
Virginia Beach, VA 23451
757.437.3636
zoesvb.com

ALVIN WILLIAMS
Cobalt Grille

1624 Laskin Rd #762
Virginia Beach, VA 23451
757.333.3334
cobaltgrille.com

JESSE C. WYKLE
Eurasia

960 Laskin Rd
Virginia Beach, VA 23451
757.422.0184
eurasiavb.com

WARRENTON

CLAIRE LAMBORNE
Claire's at the Depot

65 S 3rd St
Warrenton, VA 20186
540.351.1616
clairesrestaurant.com

WASHINGTON

JOHN MOSS
The Blue Rock Inn

12567 Lee Hwy
Washington, VA 22747
540.987.3388
thebluerockinn.com

PATRICK O'CONNELL
The Inn at Little Washington

309 Middle St
Washington, VA 22747
540.675.3800
theinnatlittlewashington.com

WHITE POST

SCOTT MYERS
L'Auberge Provencale

13630 Lord Fairfax Hwy
White Post, VA 22620
540.837.1375
laubergeprovencale.com

WILLIAMSBURG

DANIEL YVES ABID
Le Yaca French Restaurant

1915 Pocahontas Trail
Williamsburg, VA 23185
757.220.3616
leyacawilliamsburg.com

CHUN FELIX
Opus 9

5143 Main St
Williamsburg, VA 23188
757.645.4779
opus9steakhouse.com

BERNHARD KLINGER
Art Café 26

5107-2 Center St
Williamsburg, VA 23188
757.565.7788
artcafe26.com

THOMAS POWERS JR.
Fat Canary

410 W Duke of Gloucester St
Williamsburg, VA 23185
757.229.3333
fatcanarywilliamsburg.com

TIM WESTBY-GIBSON
Café Provencal

5810 Wessex Hundred
Williamsburg, VA 23185
757.941.0310
cafe-provencal.com

WINCHESTER

ED MATTHEWS
One Block West

25 S Indian Alley
Winchester, VA 22601
540.662.1455
oneblockwest.com

WOODBRIDGE

DAWN BURKART
Bistro at L'Hermitage

12724 Occoquan Rd
Woodbridge, VA 22192
703.499.9550
bistrolhermitage.com

ARLINGTON

MARTIN ESTRADA-PEREZ
Bistro San Martin

231 N Olympic Ave
Arlington, WA 98223
360.474.9229
bistrosanmartin.com

BELLINGHAM

JUSTIN GORDON
The Oyster Bar
on Chuckanut Drive

2578 Chuckanut Dr
Bellingham, WA 98229
360.766.6185
theoysterbar.net

BLAINE WETZEL
Willows Inn

2579 W Shore Dr
Lummi Island, WA 98262
360.758.2620
willows-inn.com

DAYTON

BRUCE HIEBERT
Patit Creek Restaurant

725 E Dayton Ave
Dayton , WA 99328
509.382.2625

LANGLEY

MATT COSTELLO
The Inn at Langley

400 1st St
Langley , WA 98260
360.221.3033
innatlangley.com

MOSES LAKE

SAMEH FARAG
Pillar Rock Grill

1373 Rd F. 2 NE
Moses Lake, WA 98837
509.765.8131
pillarrockgrill.com

ADAM JOHNSON
Tendrils Restaurant

344 Silica Rd NW
Quincy, WA 98848
888.785.2283
cavebinn.com

OLYMPIA

JEFF TAYLOR
Waterstreet Café

610 Water St SW
Olympia , WA 98501
360.709.9090
waterstreetcafeandbar.com

PORT TOWNSEND

DOUG SEAVER
Fins Coastal

1019 Water St
Port Townsend, WA 98368
360.379.3474
finscoastal.com

SEATTLE

JEVIC ACAIN
Seattle, WA

ERIC BANH
Monsoon

615 19th Ave E
Seattle, WA 98112
206.325.2111
monsoonrestaurants.com

BILLY BEACH
Japonessa Sushi Cocina

1400 1st Ave
Seattle, WA 98101
206.971.7979
japonessa.com

WILLIAM BELICKIS
Mistral Kitchen

2020 Westlake Ave
Seattle, WA 98121
206.623.1922
mistral-kitchen.com

KENT BETTS
Ristorante Italianissimo

15608 Old Woodinville Duvall Rd
Woodinville, WA 98072
425.485.6888
italianissimoristorante.com

PETER BIRK
BOKA

1010 1st Ave
Seattle, WA 98104
206.357.9000
bokaseattle.com

MARK BODINET
Cedarbrook Lodge
18525 36th Ave S
Seattle, WA 98188
206.901.9268
cedarbrooklodge.com

GARRETT BROWN
Branzino
2429 2nd Ave
Seattle, WA 98121
206.728.5181
branzinoseattle.com

STEVE CAIN
AQUA by El Gaucho
450 108th Ave NE
Bellevue, WA 98004
425.455.2715
elgaucho.com

SCOTT CARSBERG
Seattle, WA

JORGE CASTILLO
Paseo
4225 Fremont Ave N
Seattle, WA 98103
206.545.7440
paseoseattle.com

ZACH CHAMBERS
Anchovies & Olives
1550 15th Ave
Seattle, WA 98122
206.838.8080
ethanstowellrestaurants.com

BRIAN CLEVENGER
Tavolata
2323 2nd Ave
Seattle, WA 98121
206.838.8008
ethanstowellrestaurants.com

SAM CRANNELL
LloydMartin
1525 Queen Anne Ave N
Seattle, WA 98109
206.420.7602
lloydmartinseattle.com

EMILY CRAWFORD
The Corson Building
5609 Corson Ave S
Seattle, WA 98108
206.762.3330
thecorsonbuilding.com

ELI DAHLIN
The Walrus and The Carpenter
4743 Ballard Ave NW
Seattle, WA 98107
206.395.9227
thewalrusbar.com

KEVIN DAVIS
Blueacre Seafood
1700 7th Ave
Seattle, WA 98101
206.659.0737
blueacreseafood.com

JOSHUA DELGADO
Barking Frog
14580 NE 145th St
Woodinville, WA 98072
425.424.2999
willowslodge.com

BRADLEY DICKINSON
Pearl
700 Bellevue Way NE #50
Bellevue, WA 98004
425.455.0181
pearlbellevue.com

MATT DILLON
Sitka & Spruce
1531 Melrose Ave E #6
Seattle, WA 98101
206.324.0662
sitkaandspruce.com

ALEKS DIMITRIJEVIC
La Bete
1802 Bellevue Ave
Seattle, WA 98122
206.329.4047
labeteseattle.com

ERIC DONNELLY
Toulouse Petit
Kitchen and Lounge
601 Queen Anne Ave N
Seattle, WA 98109
206.432.9069
toulousepetit.com

JANINE DORAN
Cafe Flora
2901 E Madison St
Seattle, WA 98112
206.325.9100
cafeflora.com

TOM DOUGLAS
Dahlia Lounge
2001 4th Ave
Seattle, WA 98121
206.682.4142
tomdouglas.com

LISA DUPAR
Pomegranate Bistro

18005 NE 68th St
Redmond, WA 98052
425.556.5972
duparandcompany.com

HAMED ELNAZIR
A La Bonne Franquette

1421 31st Ave S
Seattle, WA 98144
206.568.7715
alabonnefranquetteseattle.com

RENEE ERICKSON
The Walrus and the Carpenter

4743 Ballard Ave NW
Seattle, WA 98107
206.395.9227
thewalrusbar.com

MATT FORTNER
Cuoco

310 Terry Ave N
Seattle, WA 98109
206.971.0710
tomdouglas.com

JASON FRANEY
Canlis

2576 Aurora Ave N
Seattle, WA 98109
206.283.3313
canlis.com

MARK FULLER
Ma'ono Fried Chicken & Whisky

4437 California Ave SW
Seattle, WA 98116
206.935.1075
maonoseattle.com

CHESTER GERL
Matt's in the Market

94 Pike St #32
Seattle, WA 98101
206.467.7909
mattsinthemarket.com

DYLAN GIORDAN
Bin on the Lake
at The Woodmark Hotel

1270 Carillon Pt
Kirkland, WA 98033
425.803.5595
thewoodmark.com

DAISLEY GORDON
Café Campagne

1600 Post Alley
Seattle, WA 98101
206.728.2233
cafecampagne.com

BRENT HARDING
Le Pichet

1933 1st Ave
Seattle, WA 98101
206.256.1499
lepichetseattle.com

MARIA HINES
Tilth

1411 N 45th St
Seattle, WA 98103
206.633.0801
mariahinesrestaurants.com

MARK HIPKISS
John Howie Steak

11111 NE 8th St #125
Bellevue, WA 98004
425.440.0880
johnhowiesteak.com

JEREMY HOLMES
Palomino

610 Bellevue Way NE
Bellevue, WA 98004
425.455.7600
palomino.com

CHRIS HOWELL
Smith

332 15th Ave E
Seattle, WA 98112
206.709.1900
smithseattle.com

JOHN HOWIE
John Howie Steak

11111 NE 8th St #125
Bellevue, WA 98004
425.440.0880
johnhowiesteak.com

MATT JANKE
Lecosho

89 University St
Seattle, WA 98101
206.623.2101
lecosho.com

WAYNE JOHNSON
Ray's

6049 Seaview Ave NW
Seattle, WA 98107
206.789.3770
rays.com

AUDREY JONES
Serious Pie

316 Virginia St
Seattle, WA 98101
206.838.7388
tomdouglas.com

BRANDEN KAROW
Staple & Fancy Mercantile
4739 Ballard Ave NW
Seattle, WA 98107
206.789.1200
ethanstowellrestaurants.com

SHIRO KASHIBA
Shiro's Sushi Restaurant
2401 2nd Ave
Seattle, WA 98121
206.443.9844
shiros.com

RIDGLEY KUANG
Green Leaf
418 8th Ave S
Seattle, WA 98104
206.340.1388
greenleaftaste.com

IAN MACONIE
Melrose Grill
819 Houser Way S
Renton, WA 98057
425.254.0759
melrosegrill.com

HAJIME SATO MASHIKO
Mashiko
4725 California Ave SW
Seattle, WA 98116
206.935.4339
sushiwhore.com

SHAUN MCCRAIN
Book Bindery
198 Nickerson St
Seattle, WA 98109
206.283.2665
bookbinderyrestaurant.com

JUSTIN MEVS
The Lucky Diner
2630 1st Ave
Seattle, WA 98121
206.805.0133
theluckydiner.com

BOBBY MOORE
Barking Frog
14580 NE 145th St
Woodinville, WA 98072
425.424.2999
willowslodge.com

EMILY MOORE
21 Acres
13701 NE 171st St
Woodinville, WA 98072
425.481.1500
21acres.org

TYLER MORITZ
Zig Zag Café
1501 Western Ave #202
Seattle, WA 98101
206.625.1146
zigzagseattle.com

TAMARA MURPHY
Terra Plata
1501 Melrose Ave
Seattle, WA 98122
206.325.1501
terraplata.com

MASA NAKASHIMA
I Love Sushi
1001 Fairview Ave N
Seattle, WA 98109
206.625.9604
ilovesushiseattle.com

TATSU NISHINO
Nishino
3130 E Madison St
Seattle, WA 98112
206.322.5800
nishinorestaurant.com

THIERRY RAUTUREAU
Rover's | LUC
2808 E Madison St
Seattle, WA 98112
206.325.7442
thechefinthehat.com

BRIAN SCHEEHSER
Trellis
220 Kirkland Ave
Kirkland, WA 98033
425.284.5900
trellisrestaurant.net

NATE SIMMONS
Serafina
2043 Eastlake Ave E
Seattle, WA 98102
206.323.0807
serafinaseattle.com

HOLLY SMITH
Cafe Juanita
9702 NE 120th Pl
Kirkland, WA 98034
425.823.1505
cafejuanita.com

LIAM SPENCE
Lola
2000 4th Ave
Seattle, WA 98121
206.441.1430
tomdouglas.com

SCOTT STAPLES
Restaurant Zoe

1318 E Union St
Seattle, WA 98122
206.256.2060
restaurantzoe.com

GAVIN STEPHENSON
Shuckers Oyster Bar

411 University St
Seattle, WA 98101
206.621.7889
fairmont.com

ETHAN STOWELL
How to Cook a Wolf

2208 Queen Anne Ave N
Seattle, WA 98109
206.838.8090
ethanstowellrestaurants.com

JASON STRATTON
Spinasse

1535 14th Ave
Seattle, WA 98122
206.251.7673
spinassebar.com

JOHNATHAN SUNDSTROM
Lark

926 12th Ave
Seattle, WA 98122
206.323.5275
larkseattle.com

JERRY TRAUNFELD
Poppy

622 Broadway E
Seattle, WA 98102
206.324.1108
poppyseattle.com

NATHAN UY
Wild Ginger

1401 3rd Ave
Seattle, WA 98101
206.623.4450
wildginger.net

CHARLES WALPOLE
Blind Pig Bistro

2238 Eastlake Ave E
Seattle, WA 98102
206.329.2744
blindpigbistro.com

CHRIS WEBER
The Herbfarm

14590 NE 145th St
Woodinville, WA 98072
425.485.5300
theherbfarm.com

JASON WILSON
Crush

2319 E Madison St
Seattle, WA 98112
206.302.7874
chefjasonwilson.com

RACHEL YANG
Revel

403 N 36th St
Seattle, WA 98103
206.547.2040
revelseattle.com

LARKIN YOUNG
RN74

1433 4th Ave
Seattle, WA 98101
206.456.7474
michaelmina.net

SHELTON

XINH DWELLEY
Xinh's Clam and Oyster House

221 W Railroad Ave
Shelton, WA 98584
360.427.8709
xinhsrestaurant.com

LUCAS SAUTTER
Restaurant at Alderbrook

7101 E State Hwy 106
Union , WA 98592
360.898.5500
alderbrookresort.com

SNOLQUALMIE

BRUCE DILLON
Snoqualmie Casino

37500 SE North Bend Way
Snoqualmie, WA 98065
425.888.1234
snocasino.com

BRIAN SULLIVAN
The Dining Room
at Salish Lodge & Spa

6501 Railroad Ave
Snoqualmie, WA 98065
425.888.2556, salishlodge.com

SPOKANE

DAVID BLAINE
Latah Bistro

4241 S Cheney Spokane Rd
Spokane, WA 99224
509.838.8338
latahbistro.com

CHARLES CONNOR
Wild Sage American Bistro

916 W 2nd Ave
Spokane, WA 99201
509.456.7575
wildsagebistro.com

JEREMY HANSEN
Sante
404 W Main Ave
Spokane, WA 99201
509.315.4613
santespokane.com

STEVE JENSEN
Luna
5620 S Perry St
Spokane, WA 99223
509.448.2383
lunaspokane.com

BARRY MATTHEWS
Stacks at Steam Plant
159 S Lincoln St
Spokane, WA 99201
509.777.3900
steamplantspokane.com

JASON REX
Scratch
1007 W 1st Ave
Spokane, WA 99201
509.456.5656
scratchspokane.com

SCOTT SCHULTZ
Clover
913 E Sharp Ave
Spokane, WA 99202
509.487.2937
cloverspokane.com

JEREMIAH TIMMONS
Ambrosia Bistro and Wine Bar
9211 E Montgomery Ave
Spokane, WA 99206
509.928.3222
ambrosia-bistro.com

ALEXA WILSON
Wild Sage American Bistro
916 W 2nd Ave
Spokane, WA 99201
509.456.7575
wildsagebistro.com

TACOMA

THAD LYMAN
Brix 25 Restaurant
7707 Pioneer Way
Gig Harbor, WA 98335
253.858.6626
harborbrix.com

JOSH MARTIN
Stanley & Seafort's
115 E 34th St
Tacoma, WA 98404
253.473.7300
stanleyandseaforts.com

MATT STICKLE
BITE
1320 Broadway
Tacoma, WA 98402
253.591.4151
hotelmuranotacoma.com

VANCOUVER

DAVID MORK
Lapellah
2520 Columbia House Blvd #108
Vancouver, WA 98661
360.828.7911
lapellah.com

WALLA WALLA

PENNY ADDISON
The Vine
1072 Oasis Rd
Touchet, WA 99360
509.876.0813
cameoheightsmansion.com

CHRIS AINSWORTH
Saffron Mediterranean Kitchen
125 W Alder St
Walla Walla, WA 99362
509.525.2112
saffronmediterraneankitchen.com

BERKELEY SPRINGS

SCOTT COLLINASH
Panorama at the Peak

3299 Cacapon Rd
Berkeley Springs, WV 25411
304.258.0050
panoramaatthepeak.com

DAMIAN HEATH
Lot 12 Public House

117 Warren St
Berkeley Springs, WV 25411
304.258.6264
lot12.com

BRIDGEPORT

ANNE HART
Provence Market Café

603 S Virginia Ave
Bridgeport, WV 26330
304.848.0911
provencemarketcafe.com

CHARLESTON

NOAH MILLER
Noah's Eclectic Bistro

110 McFarland St
Charleston, WV 25301
304.343.6558
noahseclectic.com

JEREMY STILL
Edgewood Country Club

1600 Edgewood Dr
Charleston, WV 25302
304.343.5557
edgewoodcc.com

HUNTINGTON

JASON OESTERREICHER
Chef Jason's du Soir Bistro

905 3rd Ave
Huntington, WV 25701
304.523.2012
chefjasonsbistro.com

LEWISBURG

REED VANDENBERGHE
Stella's Tea House

111 S Lafayette St
Lewisburg, WV 24901
304.520.4937
stellasteahouse.com

MORGANTOWN

MARION OHLINGER
Richwood Grill

318 Richwood Ave
Morgantown, WV 26505
304.292.1888
richwoodgrill.com

SIMON POULIN
Sargasso

215 Don Knotts Blvd
Morgantown, WV 26501
304.554.0100
dinesargasso.com

ROCK CAVE

DALE HAWKINS
Fish Hawk Acres

1 Fish Hawk Dr
Rock Cave, WV 26234
304.924.9880
wvfishhawkacres.com

SUTTON

TIM URBANIC
Cafe Cimino Country Inn

616 Main St
Sutton, WV 26601
304.765.2913
cafeciminocountryinn.com

WHITE SULPHUR SPRINGS

RICHARD ROSENDALE
The Greenbrier

300 W Main St
White Sulphur Springs, WV 24986
304.536.1110
greenbrier.com

ALL THE FISH IN THE SEA
Chefs are using a wide variety of fish, some that once may have been considered undesirable.

BC|A WISCONSIN

COLLINS

DAVID SALM
al corso restaurant

20931 Main St
Collins, WI 54207
920.772.4056
alcorsorestaurant.com

SUSAN GUTHRIE
Bluefront Café

86 W Maple St
Sturgeon Bay, WI 54235
920.743.9218
thebluefrontcafe.com

DONNY ZELLNER
Donny's Glidden Lodge

4670 Glidden Dr
Sturgeon Bay, WI 54235
920.746.9460
donnysgliddenlodge.com

DOOR COUNTY

BRUCE ALEXANDER
Alexander's

3667 Hwy 42
Fish Creek, WI 54212
920.868.3532
alexandersofdoorcounty.com

JESSE JOHNSON
The Waterfront

10947 Hwy 42
Sister Bay, WI 54234
920.854.5491
jjswaterfront.com

GREEN BAY

ABBEY STEFFEN
Green Bay, WI

MICHAEL CHESLOCK
Wickman House

11976 Mink River Rd
Ellison Bay, WI 54210
920.854.3305
wickmanhouse.com

TERRI MILLIGAN
The Inn at Kristofer's

10716 N Bay Shore Dr
Sister Bay, WI 54235
920.854.9419
innatkristofers.com

MADISON

TIM DAHL
Nostrano

111 S Hamilton St
Madison, WI 53703
608.395.3295
nostranomadison.com

MICHAEL DAL SANTO
Trattoria Dal Santo

147 N 3rd Ave
Sturgeon Bay, WI 54235
920.743.6100
dalsantosrestaurant.com

T.J. SAMONDS
John Martin's

50 S 3rd Ave
Sturgeon Bay, WI 54235
920.746.6666
doorcounty.com

CHRISTOPHER GERSTER
Madison, WI

PETE D'AMICO
Pasta Vino

11934 Hwy 42
Ellison Bay, WI 54210
920.854.7050

ADAM SCHIERL
Whistling Swan

4192 Main St
Fish Creek, WI 54212
920.868.3442
whistlingswan.com

NATE HAMILTON
Harvest

21 N Pinckney St
Madison, WI 53703
608.255.6075
harvest-restaurant.com

MILWAUKEE

BEE KHANG
Sushi Muramoto

546 N Midvale Blvd
Madison, WI 53705
608.441.1090
muramoto.biz

FRANCESCO MANGANO
Osteria Papavero

128 E Wilson St
Madison, WI 53703
608.255.8376
osteriapapavero.com

TORY MILLER
L'Etoile

1 S Pinckney St
Madison, WI 53703
608.251.0500
letoile-restaurant.com

SHINJI MURAMOTO
Restaurant Muramoto

225 King St
Madison, WI 53703
608.259.1040
muramoto.biz

BRETT OLSTADT
Restaurant Muramoto

225 King St
Madison, WI 53703
608.259.1040
muramoto.biz

MICHAEL PRUETT
Steenbock's On Orchard

330 N Orchard St
Madison, WI 53705
608.204.2732
steenbocksonorchard.com

JUSTIN APRAHAMIAN
Sanford Restaurant

1547 N Jackson St
Milwaukee, WI 53202
414.276.9608
sanfordrestaurant.com

ROSS BACHHUBER
Odd Duck

2352 S Kinnickinnic Ave
Milwaukee, WI 53207
414.763.5881
oddduckrestaurant.com

PAUL BARTOLOTTA
The Bartolotta Restaurants

520 W McKinley Ave
Milwaukee, WI 53212
414.258.7885
bartolottas.com

JUSTIN CARLISLE
Umami Moto

718 N Milwaukee St
Milwaukee, WI 53202
414.727.9333
umamimoto.com

JUSTIN CHAN
Milwaukee, WI 53204

MAIKEL CORREA
Smyth

500 W Florida St #102
Milwaukee, WI 53204
414.831.4615
theironhorsehotel.com

SANDY D'AMATO
Sanford Restaurant

1547 N Jackson St
Milwaukee, WI 53202
414.276.9608
sanfordrestaurant.com

MICHAEL FEKER
Il Mito Enoteca

6913 W North Ave
Milwaukee, WI 53213
414.443.1414
ilmito.com

JUSTIN FUHRMAN
Weissgerber's Gasthaus

2720 N Grandview Blvd
Waukesha, WI 53188
262.544.4460
weissgerbers.com

CHRIS HATLELI
Coquette Café

316 N Milwaukee St
Milwaukee, WI 53202
414.291.2655
coquettecafe.com

THOMAS HAUCK
c.1880

1100 S 1st St
Milwaukee, WI 53204
414.431.9271
c1880.com

JAN KELLY
Meritage

5921 W Vliet St
Milwaukee, WI 53208
414.479.0620
meritage.us

DAYN KUMMER
Potawatomi Bingo Casino

1721 W Canal St
Milwaukee, WI 53233
800.729.7244
paysbig.com

ADAM LUCKS
Comet Café

1947 N Farwell Ave
Milwaukee, WI 53202
414.273.7677
thecometcafe.com

PEGGY MAGISTER
Crazy Water

839 S 2nd St
Milwaukee, WI 53204
414.645.2606
crazywaterrestaurant.com

PETER SANDRONI
La Merenda

125 E National Ave
Milwaukee, WI 53204
414.389.0125
lamerenda125.com

ANDREW SCHNEIDER
Le Rêve Patisserie & Café

7610 Harwood Ave
Wauwatosa, WI 53213
414.778.3333
lerevecafe.com

ADAM SIEGEL
Bacchus

925 E Wells St
Milwaukee, WI 53202
414.765.1166
bacchusmke.com

DAVE SWANSON
Braise Restaurant
& Culinary School

1101 S 2nd St
Milwaukee, WI 53204
414.212.8843
braiselocalfood.com

DAN VAN RITE
Hinterland

222 E Erie St #100
Milwaukee, WI 53202
414.727.9300
hinterlandbeer.com

MARK WEBER
Mason Street Grill

425 E Mason St
Milwaukee, WI 53202
414.298.3131
masonstreetgrill.com

JARVIS WILLIAMS
Carnevor

724 N Milwaukee St
Milwaukee, WI 53202
414.223.2200
carnevor.com

MICHAEL WOLF
The Knick

1030 E Juneau Ave
Milwaukee, WI 53202
414.272.0011
theknickrestaurant.com

BRIAN ZARLETTI
Zarletti

741 N Milwaukee St #1
Milwaukee, WI 53202
414.225.0000
zarletti.net

PAUL ZERKEL
Butcher, Baker

Milwaukee, WI
butchercommabaker.com

BEEKEEPING
Keeping bees facilitates community pollination, a nice honey supply and maybe the occasional sting.

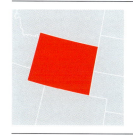

JACKSON

WILL BRADOF
Trio

45 S Glenwood
Jackson, WY 83001
307.734.8038
bistrotrio.com

ARTHUR JEFFRIES
The Wild Sage

175 N Jackson St
Jackson, WY 83001
307.733.2000
rustyparrot.com

JOEL TATE
Rendezvous Bistro

380 S U.S. Hwy 89
Jackson, WY 83001
307.733.5010
rendezvousbistro.net

JEFF DREW
Snake River Grill

84 E Broadway
Jackson, WY 83001
307.733.0557
snakerivergrill.com

JASON KING
Sudachi

3465 N Pines Way
Jackson, WY 83001
307.734.7832
sudachijh.com

JEREMY TOFTE
Thai Me Up

75 E Pearl Ave
Jackson, WY 83001
307.733.0005
thaijh.com

ROGER FREEDMAN
Rendezvous Bistro

380 S U.S. Hwy 89
Jackson, WY 83001
307.733.5010
rendezvousbistro.net

TIM LIBASSI
Blue Lion

160 N Millward St
Jackson, WY 83001
307.733.3912
bluelionrestaurant.com

ERIC WILSON
Jackson, WY

307.690.3615
chefericwilson.com

TETON VILLAGE

JOSHUA GOVERNALE
Café Genevieve

135 E Broadway
Jackson, WY 83001
307.732.1910
genevievejh.com

GREGG LOCKWOOD
The Bird

4125 S Pub Pl
Jackson, WY 83001
307.732.2473
thebirdinjackson.com

WES HAMILTON
Couloir

3395 Cody Ln
Teton Village, WY 83025
307.739.2675
jacksonhole.com

LAURA INUKAI
Nikai Sushi

225 N Cache St
Jackson, WY 83001
307.734.6490
nikaisushi.com

JARRETT SCHWARTZ
Jackson, WY

307.220.2632
chefjarrettschwartz.com

KEVIN HUMPHREYS
Cascade

3385 Cody Ln
Teton Village, WY 83025
307.734.7111
tetonlodge.com

SUCHADA JOHNSON
Teton Thai

7342 Granite Loop Rd
Teton Village, WY 83025
307.733.0022
tetonthai.com

MATT LOVE
Gamefish Restaurant

7710 Granite Loop Rd
Teton Village, WY 83025
307.732.6040
snakeriverlodge.com

PAUL O'CONNOR
Il Villaggio Osteria

3335 Village Dr
Teton Village, WY 83025
307.739.4100
jhosteria.com

WILSON

DUSTIN RASNICK
Sudachi

3465 N Pines Way #103
Wilson, WY 83014
307.734.7832
sudachijh.com

PETER STIEGLER
Stiegler's

3535 Moose Wilson Rd
Wilson, WY 83014
307.733.1071
stieglersrestaurant.com

WASHINGTON, DC

JOSÉ ANDRÉS
Jaleo

480 7th St NW
Washington, DC 20004
202.628.7949
jaleo.com

SEBASTIEN ARCHAMBAULT
Blue Duck Tavern

1201 24th St NE
Washington, DC 20037
202.419.6755
blueducktavern.com

DAVID ASHWELL
Washington, DC

KYLE BAILEY
Birch and Barley

1337 14th St NW
Washington, DC 20005
202.567.2576
birchandbarley.com

DAVID BARIGUALT
Bistrot du Coin

1738 Connecticut Ave NW
Washington, DC 20009
202.234.6969
bistrotducoin.com

JEFF BLACK
Blacksalt Fish Market

4883 MacArthur Blvd NW
Washington, DC 20007
202.342.9101
blacksaltrestaurant.com

HARUN BOLUKBASI
Meze

2437 18th St NW
Washington, DC 20009
202.797.0017
mezedc.com

ERIK BRUNER-YANG
Toki Underground

1234 H St NE
Washington, DC 20002
202.388.3086
tokiunderground.com

JEFFREY BUBEN
Vidalia

1990 M St NW
Washington, DC 20036
202.659.1990
vidaliadc.com

ANN CASHION
Johnny's Half Shell

400 N Capitol St NW
Washington, DC 20001
202.737.0400
johnnyshalfshell.net

SANTIAGO CISNEROS
Prime Rib

2020 K St NW
Washington, DC 20006
202.466.8811
theprimerib.com

TONY CONTE
Oval Room

800 Connecticut Ave NW
Washington, DC 20006
202.234.6969
bistrotducoin.com

R.J. COOPER
Rogue 24

922 N St NW
Washington, DC 20001
202.408.9724
rogue24.com

MATT CORDES
Atlas Room

1015 H St NE
Washington, DC 20002
202.388.4020
theatlasroom.com

MICHAEL COSTA
Zaytinya

701 9th St NW
Washington, DC 20001
202.638.0800
zaytinya.com

LOGAN COX
Ripple

3417 Connecticut Ave NW
Washington , DC 20008
202.244.7995
rippledc.com

DAVID DESHAIES
Michel Richard Restaurants

1001 Pennsylvania Ave NW
Washington , DC 20004
202.626.0015
centralmichelrichard.com

LUIGI DIOTAIUTI
Al Tiramisu

2014 P St NW
Washington , DC 20036
202.467.4466
altiramisu.com

ROBERTO DONNA
Al Dente

3201 New Mexico Ave NW
Washington , DC 20016
202.244.2223
aldentedc.com

SCOTT DREWNO
The Source

575 Pennsylvania Ave NW
Washington , DC 20001
202.637.6100
wolfgangpuck.com

MASSIMO FABBRI
Tosca

1112 F St NW
Washington , DC 20004
202.367.1990
toscadc.com

ENZO FARGIONE
Elisir

427 11th St NW
Washington , DC 20004
202.546.0088
elisirrestaurant.com

MAZIAR FARIVAR
Peacock Café

3251 Prospect St NW
Washington , DC 20007
202.625.2740
peacockcafe.com

HARRIS GANDELMAN
Filomena

1063 Wisconsin Ave NW
Washington , DC 20027
202.337.2782
filomena.com

PAUL GAUTHIER
Café Du Parc

1401 Pennsylvania Ave NW
Washington , DC 20004
202.942.7000
cafeduparc.com

JOE GOETZE
Founding Farmers

1924 Pennsylvania Ave NW
Washington , DC 20006
202.822.8783
wearefoundingfarmers.com

TODD GRAY
Equinox

818 Connecticut Ave NW
Washington , DC 20006
202.331.8118
equinoxrestaurant.com

JOSEPH HARRAN
Woodward Table

1430 H St NW
Washington , DC 20005
202.347.5353
woodwardtable.com

GIOVANNA HUYKE
Mio

1110 Vermont Ave NW
Washington , DC 20005
202.955.0075
miorestaurant.com

MIKE ISABELLA
Graffiato

707 6th St NW
Washington , DC 20001
202.289.3600
graffiatodc.com

GENE ITOH
Makoto

4822 MacArthur Blvd NW
Washington , DC 20007
202.298.6866
makotorestaurantdc.com

CHRIS JAKUBIEC
Plume

1200 16th St NW
Washington , DC 20036
202.448.2300
plumedc.com

HAIDAR KAROUM
Proof

775 G St NW
Washington , DC 20001
202.737.7663
proofdc.com

BOB KINKEAD
Kinkead's

2000 Pennsylvania Ave NW
Washington, DC 20006
202.296.7700
kinkead.com

MARTIN LACKOVIC
Siroc

915 15th St NW
Washington, DC 20005
202.628.2220
sirocrestaurant.com

DORIS LACOSTE
Ris

2275 L St NW
Washington, DC 20037
202.730.2500
risdc.com

ANTHONY LOMBARDO
1789 Restaurant

1226 36th St NW
Washington, DC 20007
202.965.1789
1789restaurant.com

STEVEN LUKIS
Rosa Mexicano

575 7th St NW
Washington, DC 20004
202.783.5522
rosamexicano.com

JOHN MANOLATOS
Cashion's Eat Place

1819 Columbia Rd NW
Washington, DC 20009
202.797.1819
cashionseatplace.com

CEDRIC MAUPILLIER
Mintwood Place

1813 Columbia Rd NW
Washington, DC 20009
202.234.6732
mintwoodplace.com

BRIAN MCBRIDE
Brasserie Beck

1102 K St NW
Washington, DC 20006
202.408.1717
beckdc.com

HARPER MCCLURE
The Federalist

1177 15th St NW
Washington, DC 20005
202.587.2629
thefederalistdc.com

ROBERT MCGOWAN
Old Ebbitt Grill

675 15th St NW
Washington, DC 20005
202.347.4800
ebbitt.com

JANIS MCLEAN
Social Reform Kitchen & Bar

401 9th St
Washington, DC 20004
202.393.5885
thecaucusroom.com

JOHN MELFI
Blue Duck Tavern

1201 24th St NW
Washington, DC 20037
202.419.6755
blueducktavern.com

JOHNNY MONIS
Komi

1509 17th St NW
Washington, DC 20036
202.332.9200
komirestaurant.com

DIMITRI MOSHOVITIS
Cava Mezze

527 8th St SE
Washington, DC 20003
202.543.9090
cavamezze.com

KAREN NICOLAS
Equinox

818 Connecticut Ave NW
Washington, DC 20006
202.331.8118
equinoxrestaurant.com

DARREN NORRIS
Kushi Izakaya and Sushi

465 K St NW
Washington, DC 20001
202.682.3123
eatkushi.tumblr.com

KAZ OKOCHI
KAZ Sushi Bistro

1915 I St NW
Washington, DC 20006
202.530.5500
kazsushibistro.com

PATRICK ORANGE
La Chaumière

2813 M St NW
Washington, DC 20007
202.338.1784
lachaumieredc.com

PETER PASTON
2 Amys

3715 Macomb St NW
Washington , DC 20016
202.885.5700
2amyspizza.com

AVINESH RANAV
SEI

444 7th St NW
Washington , DC 20004
202.783.7007
seirestaurant.com

FRANK RUTA
Palena

3529 Connecticut Ave NW
Washington , DC 20008
202.537.9250
palenarestaurant.com

PAUL PELT
Tabard Inn

1739 N St NW
Washington , DC 20036
202.331.8528
tabardinn.com

MICHEL RICHARD
Central Michel Richard

1001 Pennsylvania Ave NW
Washington , DC 20004
202.626.0015
centralmichelrichard.com

PETER SCHAFFRATH
The Lafayette

800 16th St NW
Washington , DC 20006
202.638.2570
hayadams.com

SCOTT PERRY
Pulpo Restaurant

3407 Connecticut Ave NW
Washington , DC 20008
202.450.6875
pulpodc.com

OMAR RODRIGUEZ
Oyamel

401 7th St NW
Washington , DC 20004
202.628.1005
oyamel.com

DANIEL SINGHOFEN
Eola

2020 P St NW
Washington , DC 20036
202.466.4441
eoladc.com

SEBASTIAN POSADA
Central Michel Richard

1001 Pennsylvania Ave NW
Washington, DC 20004
202.626.0015
centralmichelrichard.com

JAVIER ROMERO
Taberna Del Alabardero

1776 I St NW
Washington , DC 20006
202.429.2200
alabardero.com

NILESH SINGHVI
Bombay Club

815 Connecticut Ave NW
Washington , DC 20006
202.659.3727
bombayclubdc.com

NORA POUILLON
Nora

2132 Florida Ave NW
Washington , DC 20008
202.462.5143
noras.com

SÉBASTIEN RONDIER
Adour

923 16th St NW
Washington, DC 20006
202.509.8002
adour-washingtondc.com

NICHOLAS STEFANELLI
Bibiana

1100 New York Ave NW
Washington , DC 20005
202.216.9550
bibianadc.com

TOM POWER
Corduroy

1122 9th St NW
Washington , DC 20001
202.589.0699
corduroydc.com

JEFF RUSSELL
Charlie Palmer Steak

101 Constitution Ave NW
Washington , DC 20001
202.547.8100
charliepalmer.com

VIKRAM SUNDERAM
Rasika

633 D St NW
Washington , DC 20004
202.637.1222
rasikarestaurant.com

KOJI TERANO
Sushiko

2309 Wisconsin Ave NW
Washington , DC 20007
202.333.4187
sushikorestaurants.com

NOBU YAMAZAKI
Sushi Taro

1503 17th St NW
Washington , DC 20036
202.462.8999
sushitaro.com

FABIO TRABOCCHI
Fiola

601 Pennsylvania Ave NW
Washington , DC 20004
202.628.2888
fioladc.com

NORIAKI YASUTAKE
SEI

444 7th St NW
Washington , DC 20004
202.783.7007
seirestaurant.com

GEOFF TRACY
Chef Geoff's

1301 Pennsylvania Ave NW
Washington , DC 20004
202.464.4461
chefgeoff.com

ERIC ZIEBOLD
CityZen

1330 Maryland Ave SW
Washington , DC 20024
202.787.6148
mandarinoriental.com

DREW TRAUTMANN
District Kitchen

2606 Connecticut Ave NW
Washington , DC 20008
202.238.9408
districtkitchen.com

JEFF TUNKS
DC Coast

1401 K St NW
Washington , DC 20005
202.216.5988
dccoast.com

ROBERT WIEDMAIER
Brasserie Beck

1101 K St NW
Washington , DC 20005
202.408.1717
beckdc.com

HAGATNA

PETER DUENAS
Meskla Chamoru Fusion Bistro

130 E Marine Corps Dr #B103
Hagatna, GU 96910
671.479.2652

TAMUNING

CHRIS AGNON
Table 35 Restaurant and Bar

665 S Marine Dr
Tamuning, GU 96913
671.989.0350
table35guam.com

JO ONG
Al Dente at Hyatt Regency Guam

1155 Pale San Vitores Rd
Tamuning, GU 96913
671.647.1234
guam.regency.hyatt.com

GEOFFREY PEREZ
Proa Restaurant

Ypao Beach Pale San Vitores Rd
Tamuning, GU 96913
671.646.7763

GUÁNICA

ALFREDO AYALA
Copamarina Beach Resort

Rd 333 Km 6.5, Cana Gorda
Guánica, PR 00653
787.821.0505
copamarina.com

SAN JUAN

WILO BENET
Pikayo

999 Ashford Ave
San Juan, PR 00907
787.721.6194
pikayo.com

JOSE ENRIQUE
Jose Enrique

176 Duffaut St
San Juan, PR 00907
787.725.3518

MARTIN LOUZAO
Cocina Abierta

San Patricio Town Center Local #100
Guaynabo, PR 00969
787.708.6960
cocinaabierta.net

MARIO PAGÁN
Laurel

299 De Diego Ave
San Juan, PR 00912
787.522.6444
laurelkitchenartbar.com

RAMESH PILLAI
Tantra

356 Fortaleza St
San Juan, PR 00901
787.977.8141
prtantra.com

ARIEL RODRIGUEZ
Augusto's Cuisine

801 Juan Ponce De León Ave
San Juan, PR 00907
787.725.7700

PETER SCHINTLER
Marmalade

317 Fortaleza St
Old San Juan, PR 00901
787.724.3969
marmaladepr.com

AUGUSTO SCHREINER
Silversea Cruises

San Juan, PR
877.276.6816
silversea.com

ROBERTO TREVINO
Budatai

1056 Ashford Ave
San Juan, PR 00907
787.725.6919
ootwrestaurants.com

ROOFTOP GARDENS
Rooftop gardens are the ultimate local source for fresh herbs, spices and vegetables.

ST. CROIX

KENNETH BIGGS
The Galleon

5000 Estate Southgate
Christiansted, VI 00820
340.718.9948
galleonrestaurant.com

JOSEPH GERACE
Tavern 1844

Company St & Queen Cross St
Christiansted, VI 00820
340.773.1844
tavern1844.net

NEGUST KAZA
Tutto Bene

Boardwalk Building Hospital St
Christiansted, VI 00820
340.773.5229
tuttobenerestaurant.com

DAVID KENDRICK
Kendrick's

2132 Company St
Christiansted, VI 00820
340.773.9199
kendricks.stcroixrestaurant.com

ST. JOHN

ANDERSON ALLEN
La Plancha del Mar

Mongoose Junction & Cruz Bay
Cruz Bay, VI 00830
340.777.7333
laplanchadelmar.com

ALEX EWALD
La Tapa

Cruz Bay, VI 00830
340.693.7755
latapastjohn.com

DUSTIN G. HEISLER
Cafe Collective at AB Cellars

Cruz Bay, VI 00840
340.693.9195
abcellars.com

ST. THOMAS

GREG ENGELHARDT
OffTheGRiD

6501 Red Hook Plaza #201
Red Hook, VI 00802
340.626.0030
offthegrid.vi

KATIE LOMBARDO
Enkai Sushi

3801 Crown Bay
Charlotte Amalie, VI 00802
340.774.6254
enkaisushi.com

TONY MAY
Old Stone Farmhouse

6502 Red Hook Plaza
Red Hook, VI 00803
340.777.6278
oldstonefarmhouse.com

ACKNOWLEDGEMENTS

We gratefully acknowledge the many that helped create this year's inaugural edition. Any serious and significant undertaking such as publishing *Best Chefs America* necessarily involves many dedicated staff and colleagues, and we are quite appreciative of their contributions.

First and foremost we want to thank the true authors of this book: each and every chef who took time out of their busy schedule to interview with us.

Our *Best Chef America* Team working out of 218 King Street (past and present) who assisted with this volume: Amber Posey; Allegra DiNardo; Anna Kate Lister; Baker Powell; Ben Biddle; Bethany Kocak; Brad Norton; Chris Hance; Colin Riddle; Courtney Cowart; Elizabeth Fishburne; Gabe Joseph; Jack Rauch; Jessie Chapman; Justin Johnson; Lindsay Jones; Miles McCormick; Robert McDermott; Sara Rausch; Sarah Bandy; Sarah Jordan; Stefanie Bannister; Sweta Patel; Tyler Osteen; Vas Gnanadoss; Victoria Cairco; Will Freeman

SPECIAL THANKS TO

Andrew Cebulka, our photographer who is without peer.
A more cheerful demeanor cannot be found, and he always gets the shot.

Braxton Crim, our Graphic Designer who designed the book, and whose talent, creativity and efficiency impressed us all.

Carlye Jane Dougherty, our Design Coordinator, whose experience and advice proved invaluable.

Michael Ruhlman, whose clarity of thought and insight into the world of the cook is unparalleled.

Revival Foods' Bradley Taylor and Cat Compton, for welcoming us to their farm, educating us on heritage breeds, and helping us photograph their hogs, goats, and bees.

Ryan Jones, for his indispensable counsel on all things digital.

Warren Johnson of Taste Five Media, for his conceptualization of the *Best Chefs America* brand, and his early enthusiasm for this "important document."

INDEX